THE BEST OF WORLD CAFE®

THE BEST OF WORLD CAFE®

Great Conversations from NPR's
Most Popular Contemporary Music Show

by David Dye

RUNNING PRESS
PHILADELPHIA · LONDON

Printed in U.S.A.

9 8 7 6 5 4 3 2 1
Digit on the right indicates the number of this printing

Library of Congress Control Number: 2007928676

ISBN-10: 0-7624-2768-X
ISBN-13: 978-0-7624-2768-0

Cover and interior designed by Joshua McDonnell
Edited by Greg Jones
Typography: Bembo, Fury, and Minion

This book may be ordered by mail from the publisher.
Please include $2.50 for postage and handling.
But try your bookstore first!

Running Press Book Publishers
2300 Chestnut Street
Philadelphia, Pennsylvania 19103-4371

Visit us on the web!
www.runningpress.com
www.worldcafe.npr.org

CONTENTS

Acknowledgements 7

Introduction 8

Part One: 1991–1998 12
Bruce Cockburn 13
Rickie Lee Jones 15
Tori Amos 21
Townes Van Zandt 24
Jeff Buckley 27
Rodney Crowell 31
U2's The Edge 36
Kate Bush 40
Leonard Cohen 49
Richie Havens 51
World Party (Karl Wallinger) 53
Ben Harper 54
Al Kooper 58
Leo Kottke 63
Joni Mitchell 68
Sarah McLachlan 78
Branford Marsalis 81
Michael Stipe 91
Fiona Apple 97
Billy Bragg 102
Lyle Lovett 110
Elvis Costello 115
David Bowie 120
Phil Walden 127
Patti Smith 132
Ry Cooder 137
Joel Dorn 148
Jac Holzman 156

Part Two: 1999–2006 166

Peter Wolf 167
Beck 175
Rufus Wainwright 179
Bruce Hornsby 188
Joe Strummer 196
Björk 203
Dave Carter & Tracy Grammer 207
Sting 209
David Crosby 216
Ahmet Ertegun 221
John Mayer 225
Jackson Browne 226
Bonnie Raitt 234
Sonic Youth 241
The Clash 246
Merle Haggard 255
The White Stripes 264
Isaac Hayes 274
Joan Armatrading 278
Donovan 284
Joe Sample 289
Mavis Staples 295
Tony Joe White 300
Neil Young 304
Al Green 312
Hall and Oates 318
Gang of Four 326
Hugh Masekela 329
Robert Plant 336
Ray Davies 344
Steve Cropper 351
Rosanne Cash 359
Eric Burdon 364
Soul Asylum 370
John Hiatt and the North Mississippi All-Stars 376
Neko Case 382
Lindsey Buckingham 388
Tom Waits 394
Elton John 401
Paul Simon 410
George Martin 416

world cafe®

ACKNOWLEDGEMENTS

This collection of *World Cafe®* interviews from the last 16 years gives me an opportunity to thank the people who have made the show and this book possible.

Before we thank the individuals, I should thank the Corporation for Public Broadcasting who gave us the seed money to begin the show in 1991. Also thanks to both Public Radio International, who was our original distributor for 13 years, and National Public Radio, our home since 2005.

At WXPN there have been three very different yet very supportive General Managers: Mark Fuerst, Vinnie Curren, and Roger LaMay. Our Executive Producer Bruce Warren, who actually began his work at WXPN as Associate Producer of the *World Cafe* the day we began, has always shared a vision of the show. I thank him.

Bruce Ranes and Tracey Tanenbaum have produced the show over the years; their guidance has been essential.

Thanks to Amy Morrissey, Joe Madden, Mike Morrison, Ali Castellini, Shawn Stewart, and Joe Durrance, along with many other interns and engineers over the years.

Our current staff does an amazing job day in and day out to allow me to remain the tip of the iceberg. Thanks to Chris Williams who has been recording our sessions since the days of two-track audio tape, Dan Reed who books the show and finesses industry relationships, Sarah Mobley who has been as organized as I am not, John Myers who is responsible for the show sounding so good every day, and Beth Warshaw who is always there to pick up the slack. Thanks to our current Producer Kimberly Junod for being equal parts advocate and critic, which is what you need to keep on the right track.

Thanks to my fellow interviewers including Shawn Stewart, Jonny Meister, Helen Leicht, and Jim McGuinn. Two of Michaela Majoun's many interviews for the Cafe are included in this collection. I thank her for years of insightful questions and exceptional work.

Thanks also to the many Special Producers of the *World Cafe* who have been essential in keeping the show afloat financially all these years.

Thanks to my wife Karen Heller and my kids Nick and Cece for putting up with long hours.

Finally this book is the result of a lot of hard work from the people who turned the spoken word into the written. No computer program was involved in the transcription of this book. Instead we thank:

Lauren Bowie, Jack Cotter, Jessica Cross, William M. DeCristofano, David Falcone, Andrew M. Franklin, Lois Fulton, Terri Greenberg, Evan Joblin, Sonya Lott-Harrison, Madeline Morrison, Kim Mortensen, Ellen S. Oplinger, Ann Pagano, Lorraine Porcellini, Susan Rostron, Eric Schuman, Melanie Shellhammer, Laura Sherlock, Paul Sipio, Samantha Stoneburg, Colleen Thornton, Jennifer Tintenfass, Dee Wieczorek, Alexandra Wigglesworth, and John Yeager.

INTRODUCTION

"WELCOME TO THE *WORLD CAFE*. . . ."

For the past 16 years, I've begun our daily two-hour musical adventure with that greeting. It's an invitation to enter our virtual Cafe just as you might a small club, and enjoy a wide variety of music blended together with thought and an ear toward what's new and best in popular music today.

When the show was conceptualized by the initial team in 1991, the daily performance/interview portion was not a given. We weren't sure we were going to talk to people on every show. The audience quickly spoke and disabused us of any notion to not do an interview. This proved to be the most popular segment of each show.

We've gathered our best interviews in this book. As you might imagine, it was a challenge. Which of the seven different Elvis Costello interviews to choose? Where's the tape of that Jackson Browne interview? It was daunting.

Reading over these transcripts, a number of things became apparent. Uh, we've improved! Some early interviews are a little shaky. I admit to being in awe of some musical giants I was assigned to interview in the first years. These transcripts reveal magical moments, some stories never told anywhere else. Almost every conversation lends insight into the creative process. Most artists, when offered encouragement and made comfortable by the environment, proved eager to discuss their work.

The technological improvements in the *World Cafe*'s decade and a half are striking. We began recording live sessions on two-track tape, then edited tape with razor blades. In today's era of digital computerized editing, the technique seems positively Mesolithic. The same can be said for our original *World Cafe* studio, a barely soundproofed room located up three flights of narrow stairs in a funky, turn-of-the-century brick mansion in West Philadelphia. You can watch video of some of these interviews on the accompanying DVD. When I view those images, I shake my head in disbelief that, for 13 years, we were able to capture remarkable sound from such a ramshackle circumstance, bearing witness to the artistry of Chris Williams and the technical staff.

Today, we record in a handsome, large, wood-appointed studio capable of accommodating full rock bands or even a twenty-piece classical ensemble. Sound is captured on a mammoth computerized digital board with so many channels some have yet to be used. We're able to speak with musicians around the globe via digital ISDN phone lines that make it sound as if we're in the same room.

I first started working with *World Cafe* before it even had a name. Mark Fuerst, then WXPN's general manager in Philadelphia, secured a grant from the Corporation for Public Broadcasting to research a program for public radio with popular music. The goal was to attract a younger, more racially diverse audience. I was hired to administer the grant for what we called "The Music Channel." My duties included establishing music surveys of a proposed audience, and securing a host for the show.

Serious thought went into what the *World Cafe* would be. I remember a meeting with a dozen people and at least 50 3x5 cards, each representing a musical subgenre. There was not only blues, both country and urban, but also country, alt-country, and various kinds of "oldies." When it came to "world music," we listed a dozen categories of various forms of African, Brazilian, and Caribbean music, not to mention artists from Mexico, Puerto Rico, and other countries.

Before the music was tested, the assumption was that the *World Cafe* would have strong appeal to public radio listeners if it blended world music with the work of singer-songwriters like Shawn Colvin, whose debut album had been recently released to serious acclaim. We jokingly referred to our "Music Channel" as "From Cheb to Shawn," Cheb being the Algerian rai music singer Cheb Mami.

Our music testing with sizable groups of public radio listeners in Philadelphia and Tucson, Arizona, proved otherwise. Ranked dead last among musical genres was world music. People didn't want to listen to songs in other languages. The most common response was, "It all sounds like salsa." So much for the "*World Cafe*," the name we had selected for our fledgling service.

Topping listeners' preferences were jazz, a genre already well represented on public radio, and oldies, even more so on commercial stations up and down the dial. Before abandoning the research, we dug deeper into the data and located a small but viable genre of singer-songwriters that seemed to have secured a niche among public radio types.

I bring up all the research and the results because our gut reaction all along had been that the emerging singer-songwriter musical world, then populated by artists like Lyle Lovett and Lucinda Williams, was simpatico not only with public radio but the music business and its direction. We labeled the genre AAA: Adult Acoustic Alternative. Pretty soon, radio trade magazines adopted those initials to describe a loosely affiliated set of public and commercial stations across the country which played similar music—but they called it Adult Album Alternative. Whatever the future was to hold, it's good to know we were at least using the right letters.

Now, I'm not sure how to judge my performance as the administrator responsible for finding a program host. We solicited tapes and suggestions nationally, and an array of qualified hosts emerged. Honestly, our team wasn't satisfied with any of them. At some point, I raised my hand, cited 20 years of experience in commercial radio, and asked to give it a try. Lucky me.

So, fully aware that I was the "interim" host, we took to the air in October 1991 with four affiliates: WFUV in New York City; WNCW, a station serving an incredibly diverse area in North and South Carolinas; KUNI in Cedar Rapids, Iowa, serving the entire state; and KUMD in Duluth, Minnesota, covering the upper Midwest, an area with rabid public radio fans. Sixteen years later, I'm happy to report, those affiliates remain part of the almost 190 stations that carry the *World Cafe*.

As we move through the interviews that follow I'll address some of the odder occurrences in our old studio, but here are a few that stand out. To get the proper sound separation, we had to put people in the bathroom and in the hall but, thankfully, never out on the fire escape that was reserved as the "smoking porch." We had very live squirrels that periodically dropped through the ceiling, a band that insisted on being interviewed while fully reclined on the floor, and at least one musician so overweight he couldn't make it up the stairs.

I love to tell the story of the record company who paid a four-figure sum to have a piano its artist endorsed shipped from New York for his session. Because the session preceding the artist's ran long, the baby grand sat out on our lawn on a hot summer day for 45 minutes soaking up the heat. After three sweaty delivery men hauled it up three flights of stairs with much cursing, the piano was dutifully tuned. When the artist arrived and brought his hands down on the keys, there was great discord. The contrasting temperatures had caused the piano to fall out of key in 15 minutes and the tuner had gone home. Luckily the artist promised to record the songs for us in his air-conditioned home studio on his own piano.

We love our new studio, but the old one houses such memories, such as hanging out with Elvis Costello waiting for his instruments to arrive only to borrow a Casio from the frat house across the street. Or the interview with the hard-drinking British band who arrived for an early session still drunk from the night before. The singer performed flawlessly with an empty wastepaper basket at his side, just in case.

I've learned a few truisms about interviewing. If someone is in the Rock and Roll Hall of Fame, chances are the artist will be a great interview with a lot of tales to tell, unless he was inducted on one of the first ballots and then you run the risk that he's forgotten every one of those great stories. Young bands are often among the worst interviews. It's hard to penetrate their gang mentality. Never ask what the producer does. I've learned this from getting too many confusing answers. If the band asks to have lunch first, say no. Otherwise, the guys will be more inclined to nap than talk. Oh, and demand a translator for all Scotsmen!

This book is more about the words than the music. But of the music, I can tell you I have experienced little in life as beautiful as the sound of Yo Yo Ma's cello up close. I've sat within two feet of Richard Thompson's fingers on a guitar and still can't figure out how he does it. Musical bliss can be attained in the midst of listening to Sonic Youth's Thurston Moore and Lee Renaldo's guitars at full throttle.

There have been some exquisite conversations and we've captured some of the best on these pages. Unlike radio, you must imagine the nuance of the voices. Reading over these interviews, I'm honored at how open and sharing most of the musicians have been.

The interviews are arranged chronologically. While we could have selected multiple interviews from individuals who have stopped by many times over the years, we've chosen the best of the lot instead. The choices are weighted slightly toward the most recent guests for a number of reasons. Certainly our memory of more recent guests was sharper. Some of the tapes of early interviews were hard to locate but, most importantly, we've gotten better at asking the harder questions. The newer interviews bear that out.

For the first 14 years, the *World Cafe* was a part of Public Radio International. In 2005, we moved our affiliation to National Public Radio. You can now find us on over 190 of the finest public radio stations throughout the country. Another great resource is our website at www.worldcafe.npr.org where you can listen to many of the interviews from this book, complete with music.

This book is a journey through the last 16 years of music. As I assembled the interviews, it was interesting to take an overview of how musical fashion has changed. There is the rise of the singer-songwriters in the 90s and the coming of indie rock in the new century. Along the way there was electronica, world music, jazz, and so much more. It's all here. Enjoy, and thanks for listening!

PART ONE:

1991-1998

IN THE EARLY YEARS OF THE *WORLD CAFE* WE DID EVERYTHING THE HARD WAY, mostly because we didn't know any better. For instance, we broadcast the show absolutely live nationally at 10 o'clock each morning leaving no margin for error.

In the beginning, we recorded right to two-track magnetic tape. To the layperson, this means we had to get it right the first time or never. If we needed more space, we put singers in the hall or maybe in the bathroom, which had a decent echo. When I joined the band in the studio for the interview, more often than not I would be sitting next to the drummer with a cymbal in my ear. It's possible that our early guests gave us such great interviews because they felt sorry for us.

Our studio was a converted record library in a handsome red-brick building that had once been someone's home. It wasn't very big, it wasn't soundproof, and it was a long way from the front door. We used to jokingly refer to the student interns who helped load bands in up the winding staircase as "Sherpas."

As you read these interviews, try to remember how different the world was in 1991—pre-September 11th, pre-iTunes, and before the bloated blogosphere. If things really weren't simpler back then, at least the music business was. We talked to a lot of guitar-strumming singer-songwriters in the early 1990s. Artists like Sheryl Crow, Sarah McLachlan, and David Wilcox were landing their first major label deals and they were all our guests in the early days. The section begins with Bruce Cockburn, the first interview we aired on the show when it began in October of 1991.

1991

BRUCE COCKBURN

WE ALL BEGIN SOMEPLACE, and this is where we began the *World Cafe* back in October of 1991. Bruce Cockburn was my first guest on our very first show. We had actually done another interview before this with a local Philadelphia band that was getting national recognition called the Low Road, with Mike Brenner, who has recently been on our air with his band Slo-Mo. But that interview was really just a dress rehearsal to check out our equipment, although it later ran on the show.

We recorded Bruce in the old record library on the third floor of the red-brick house on Spruce Street in Philadelphia that housed the *World Cafe* for its first dozen years. Technically, we had no monitors to help musicians hear themselves and we recorded to magnetic tape on a fairly primitive mixing board. And honestly, we were pretty naïve.

For Bruce Cockburn, it was a big moment in his career as he had been signed recently by Columbia Records. It was the beginning of the nineties' singer-songwriter renaissance, and Columbia had high hopes for the veteran Canadian.

It's not just because he got a head start on all our other guests, but more because we love his work, that over the years few performers visited the show more often than Bruce Cockburn. That said, we include this–our first interview–mostly for its historical value!

David Dye: And we're back in the *World Cafe* with the sound of Bruce Cockburn's steel Dobro being tuned up. We know how you spent some of your time off between records—you did a tour that was well documented on a great live album. But what else have you been doing over the last three years?

Bruce Cockburn: Well, that tour ended about mid-December '89, and I'm just starting to work again now.

DD: So you had some fun.

BC: [strums throughout] Well, I had some fun, but I was getting pretty burned out because that culminated a period of five years or so of very intense activity of one kind or another, musical and related to other things, but involving a lot of travel and a lot of intense stuff, and I was really ready for some time off.

DD: Well, one of the things in reading your biography, which I'd never read before, that I was surprised about, was that you started out playing in teenage rock bands. I assumed you were a die-hard folkie from the word go.

BC: Well, the folk music that made me want to play music to begin with was early Elvis and Buddy Holly and Chuck Berry, you know.

DD: American folk music.

BC: What's become folk music was hindsight now in a way.

DD: Do you search out when you travel, I mean, you do travel a lot, do you search out music or is it just part of the environment?

BC: [strumming still] Mostly the music of other cultures that I've absorbed—to whatever degree I've absorbed it—came from a deliberate attempt over a period of a few years in the seventies to seek out that music on record. And in the course of traveling I have been exposed to other kinds of things too, but the travels haven't been really musical in nature, at least the Third World stuff that I've done most of the time. Actually, there was an interesting guy that I met in Nepal, an itinerant musician there, and the roads in Nepal are pathways as some people may know. But we met this guy one day who was from a village in which the men are expected to become musicians, and the music they do is a very traditional, sort of rigidly defined kind of music played on a one-stringed instrument called the "one-string." The songs have religious themes in the Hindu context, and they're expected, when they reach puberty, more or less, they have to leave the village for twelve years and make their living, survive or not, as itinerant musicians doing this particular kind of music, and then they can come back and start a family. This guy had been on the road for twenty years; he did his twelve years and he just didn't want to go back. Very bluesy kind of existence, in a way. Anyway, this is not like that at all, this song.

DD: No, this is not a one-string.

BC: This is called "Great Big Love." This is kind of one of a number of personal manifestos I've come up with.

> Bruce Cockburn performs "Great Big Love"

DD: Our guest is Bruce Cockburn, and that's "Great Big Love" from *Nothing but a Burning Light.* It looks like this is your seventeenth studio album? Something like that?

BC: Umm, yeah, I'd have to check. I think this would be the twentieth album, anyway.

DD: Yeah, there's some live albums and some best-ofs. But you've recorded almost all of them in Toronto?

BC: Yeah, I literally have recorded all of them in Toronto. This is the first time; the new album was produced by T-Bone Burnett, who's used to working in L.A., so that's why we ended up recording in L.A. One of the reasons for doing it there was that most of the musicians that T-Bone wanted to use were mostly there.

DD: Oh man, now you've covered two artists over your career. One of them is Eric Idle, and the other....

BC: [chuckles] The other one is Blind Willie Johnson. An exercise in contrast, in a way. Actually, more than in a way. I worked out a version of "Soul of a Man" years and years ago and have played it occasionally live, but it never fit with the content of any of the albums that I've done previously in such a way that it was right to record it until now, and when T-Bone and I were going through a list of songs, that song came to mind, and I played it for him and he went, "Yeah, we got to do this." We did it as a kind of street-music piece in a way that I hope Blind Willie would have approved of, although my version of it sounds quite radically different.

DD: You want to give it a try?

BC: Yeah! [strums, chuckles] You'll have to imagine [drummer] Jim Keltner. . . .

DD: I won't attempt it.

BC: Or maybe not. You know, the song's pretty good on its own anyway.

Bruce Cockburn performs "Soul of a Man"

1991

RICKIE LEE JONES

THIS IS THE FIRST TIME we had an artist act as guest DJ, and the performance is still the standard for how this works. Rickie Lee Jones had just released *Pop Pop*, her album of covers or what she referred to as "new standards." We decided to listen to it with her and have her go though our library and pick out music to complement her work.

It turns out that listening to music and sitting close in a small recording booth is a very intimate thing, and Rickie and I spent the time reminiscing about times in both of our pasts and I think that intimacy comes through in this conversation. It was the first time we had met.

David Dye: On the *World Cafe*, that's the version of "Bye Bye Blackbird" you'll hear if you get about halfway through Rickie Lee Jones' new album, *Pop Pop*. We're going to be popping our "P's" probably throughout the rest of afternoon. Rickie Lee is here listening to it with me. I got to say, I was previewing the record again last night and I got to that [song] and I had this whole flood of memories, Rickie Lee, about my dad, and that was one of the few songs he sang when he was having a good time.

Rickie Lee Jones: Yeah it was one my dad sang too. . . . It's a dad song.

DD: Was it ones he sang, or were they ones that were played around the house? Or how did that work?

RLJ: No, just that one. I knew "Spring (Can Really Hang You up the Most)" from Carmen McRae; I'd heard that version of it. And "My One and Only Love"—I hadn't ever heard the lyric, I'd learned it from Coleman Hawkins. And I bought some versions from vocalists to learn the lyric. I didn't care for the lyric at all and it took a lot of singing it to extract the sensuality out of it, you know, because it seemed really square, thick. But as I went and really visualized the late afternoon when the person was singing it, and just how sensual it was, then I was able to sing it, but it was touch-and-go for a minute because I didn't know if I was going to be able to do it. But it really is sensual if you sing it, if you visualize it while you do it.

DD: You put out a great list of records here. We have a few of them. So let's get into the bulk of the Rickie Lee Jones Radio Show. You pulled out a Tom Waits album and you said something about, "well these were things that were influential to me as records." I always thought that you knew him when he was making these records.

RLJ: No, I didn't. The thing I was saying was that, I think that as far as jazz is concerned, jazz-influenced pop had much more of an impact on me than just jazz records. I didn't listen to much jazz and I've still only heard really great masters doing their best recordings, for the most part at least. I'm moderately educated in jazz. So I guess I heard Tom Waits about the same year I started hearing Randy Newman. Which seems to me is about '80—how old am I? I mean '72, '73 or so. So I got his record about a year before I met him. That was *The Heart of Saturday Night* record.

DD: Which is almost a perfect record. I don't know if he still feels that way about it, but great from beginning to end.

RLJ: It's good, it's good, yeah.

DD: Anyway this is a real jazzy cut from it. This is "Diamonds on My Windshield."

> Tom Waits recording: "Diamonds on My Windshield"
>
> Taj Mahal recording: "Annie's Lover"

DD: On the *World Cafe*, that was Taj Mahal with "Annie's Lover," and our guest DJ is Rickie Lee Jones. We're listening to some things that you listen to. Great double record. . . .

RLJ: [Tom Waits and Taj Mahal] are two of my favorite men that I have ever seen. [Taj] is a tall man. I didn't meet him [but] I shook his hand in about 1977 or so at this little bar in Topanga Canyon, I went and saw him play. He's so beautiful, and I first heard him when I was about 15. We got this record, my girlfriend and I, "De Old Folks at Home," and we learned to play a lot of the guitar stuff. Learned to sing like him, and he was a big influence on me—I love him very much.

DD: Yeah that's a great song, "Annie's Lover." And "Diamonds on My Windshield" from Tom Waits, one of his initial kind of scatty vocals, and a great song, too—great album.

[Break]

DD: You do one Jefferson Airplane song, and I was really happy that you've kind of revived this one because—I guess I'm a little older than you are—I spent high school time between the speakers on Surrealistic Pillow.

RLJ: Right. I was between the speakers with *Electric Ladyland.* [laughs]

DD: There you go: different bedrooms, same position.

RLJ: That was before headphones.

DD: Mine was KLH. It was the small portable one. But coming back to it, you do a great version of it ["Comin' Back to Me"] and I thought we'd do your version of that from *Pop Pop* . . . and then another Marty Balin slow song.

RLJ: "Today"—yeah, another beautiful one.

DD: Okay, a couple little Jefferson Airplane tunes.

> Ricki Lee Jones recording: "Comin' Back to Me"
>
> Jefferson Airplane recording: "Today"

DD: On the *World Cafe*, our guest DJ is Rickie Lee Jones, and here's one from *Pop Pop*, her new record of standards. . . .

RLJ: But they're not really standards, are they?

DD: No, they're standards from different eras. I mean "Girl at Her Volcano" seemed to be the same kind of concept, wasn't it?

RLJ: Yeah kind of. I wanted to do some of the standards I was doing live. And I also wanted to justify, I think, because I was reading all this stuff in the press that "she was a jazz singer" and I would go, "I don't know how they can derive that from anything I've recorded except that maybe the guy who wrote it knew that about me." But I thought that I ought to record some, you know?

DD: Well, do you consider yourself a jazz singer?

RLJ: I don't put any labels on me, but I think I sing this kind of thing best. So. . . .

DD: Well, I just read another interview where you talk about singing around the melody a lot—how it was good to play with these people [on *Pop Pop*], it was really spare, so I guess that sort of qualifies.

RLJ: I have a kind of time that I cannot sing in time. So I'm always way behind it or right behind it. This was really comfortable for me.

DD: Couple great vocalists coming up. I don't know if they know each other, but I know that Van Morrison has a song about Frank Sinatra. I don't know if Frank knows any Van Morrison songs.

RLJ: And I have sung about both of them [laughs].

DD: Right [laughs]. What were we going to play from Frank?

RLJ: We're going play, "When Somebody Loves You," I think. Yeah.

> Frank Sinatra recording: "When Somebody Loves You"
>
> Van Morrison recording: "The Way Young Lovers Do"

DD: Two great vocalists there, Van Morrison and Frank Sinatra. Sort of the early big-band Van, "(The Way) Young Lovers Do," from *Astral Weeks*. Did you actually pick up *Astral Weeks* when it came out?

RLJ: Let's see. No, I had gone to a rock festival and I met this guy from Eugene, Oregon [laughs], and I ended up going down to his town with him and then like after a day or so we came back downstairs and there's this record on. This record, this was like you entered a new dimension or something. I had never heard anything about it. Now there could have been other influences, but . . .

DD: [laughs]

RLJ: . . . it seems to me that, you know, the poetry of it and the way he sang, and he was "jumping on his merry way over hedges first," and I can still see him jumping over the hedges, you know, off into the distance in Ireland. It was like nothing I had ever heard. It was an upright bass and there weren't any upright basses in the kind of music I listened to.

DD: It's Richard Davis [on bass], I think.

RLJ: Really exciting. I'm still excited talking about it [laughs]!

DD: I can tell. You also pulled out [Van Morrison's] Veedon Fleece, which has a lot of that same kind of jazzy feel to it.

RLJ: Yeah, yeah I think that it has. There's a kind of profound poetry that happens for a moment. It's not maintained as much throughout the album, but when he starts, he starts with this kind of surreal cowboy atmosphere in Veedon Fleece that he talks about. [singing] "and he puts his fiii". . . . And he also sings like a girl. It's like he's possessed for one of the songs. I think it's really incredible. But I wanted to play *Astral Weeks* more because that was the first I heard and it had a truly profound effect on me. They're both incredible records, really.

DD: Let's do something else from *Pop Pop*, because this is something that we get requests for. It's the Oscar Brown Jr. theme ["Dat Dere"]. I remember an Oscar Brown record that I had; it's got a cat on it and an elephant.

RLJ: That your parents had.

DD: Yeah, my parents had actually, I got to confess. The Kingston Trio, *My Fair Lady*, Oscar Brown [Jr.], a Nina Simone record, that's about it.

RLJ: Okay, wait. Now my parents: Harry Belafonte, Nina Simone, Andy Williams and Benny Goodman.

DD: Benny Goodman; yeah, they always had to have the swing records.

RLJ: Right, it's probably like, you know, for our kids, we'll have Crosby, Stills and Nash or something [laughs].

DD: It's true, but now our kids love them!

RLJ: That's just bizarre.

DD: Yeah it is strange, isn't it? Anyway, Oscar Brown Jr. Do you know that much about Oscar Brown Jr.?

RLJ: When I did this I read a little article about him in my local town's paper. What I learned was that he was a lyricist, a songwriter, and that's what I know. What do you know?

DD: That's about it. "Dat Dere" was one of the ones I remember though, so.

RLJ: So this was a Bobby Timmins tune and Oscar Brown Jr. was writing a lyric to another tune that was on the record, and he would finish and it would go partly into "Dat Dere" [laughs], so by the time he was done he wrote lyrics to both of the songs. That was the story about how he wrote music to "Dat Dere."

Oscar Brown Jr. recording: "Dat Dere"

Nina Simone recording: "Black Is the Color"

DD: Interestingly enough, finishing off these records that Rickie Lee Jones has picked here, that the only female vocalist—not the only one you picked out; it's the only one we ended up having—is Nina Simone. And a very acoustic setting for that. Nina at her piano.

RLJ: Oh yeah, I forgot that my dad had that Nina Simone record, too. He used to play her and want me to listen to her and I couldn't stand it. I couldn't bear listening to her sing, but I think that it got under my skin and when I got about twenty or so, and I started to hear her. I guess I could relate to her profound sadness better at twenty than at ten.

DD: Uh, yeah.

RLJ: [laughs] And listen to her, then, when I got older.

DD: It always seemed to me, whatever material she chose—because she chose some material that I didn't always think was well-suited to her—she could really do something with it.

RLJ: She sure can.

DD: I think that made a big difference, as she got older she started writing a lot more of her own stuff.

RLJ: Well, she's a little frightening with the depth of emotion that she puts into everything. And . . . it's kind of unbearable, you know. You have to really, really go with her because every song is filled as much as it can be with her emotion, you know? It's really a quite profound experience listening to Nina Simone.

DD: Let's go from Nina to Jimi Hendrix. You had *Electric Ladyland* on between your speakers. What did you want to play from that? "Still Raining, Still Dreaming," I think.

RLJ: Yeah. It's hard because I'd like to play "Voodoo Chile," but it goes on for fifteen minutes so I think, um, the rainy day thing is—[takes a fake drag] "hey man, let's see what's happening?" [hums]—that's a nice one to play.

> Jimi Hendrix recording: "Still Raining, Still Dreaming"
>
> Rickie Lee Jones recording: "Up from the Skies"

DD: Rickie Lee Jones does Jimi Hendrix; and Jimi himself on *Electric Ladyland.* We've been sampling *Pop Pop* in between listening to some things that Rickie Lee has pulled out of the library. Thanks a lot!

RLJ: You're welcome!

DD: This is fun. Actually it's fun to hear these things, especially Frank Sinatra. We don't play Frank enough.

RLJ: [laughs]

DD: We like *Pop Pop.* We like the songs. We like the versions and the playing on it so, really great. But also I wanted to ask about the. . . .

RLJ: The album cover?

DD: Yeah.

RLJ: David Was [the album's producer], who's like the eternal boy. We were coming back from San Francisco and I was trying, I was talking about the album cover, you know, and he pulled this box out of his pocket and he was holding it, and I said, "Now see now, that has some nice graphics on it, that would, something like that would be nice." And he said, "Yeah that would be a good album cover." And I said, "Yeaaaah." So this is pretty much the box as it was.

DD: It was a firecracker box?

RLJ: Uh-huh. Snappers. I guess they're called. Snappers, a novel trick item—bang, drop it, throw it, step on it, and snap it.

DD: So they just dropped in *Pop Pop* and you. . . .

RLJ: No, that's the name of the snappers.

DD: Ohhh, it is. . . .

RLJ: They just dropped me in. [laughs]

DD: I love talking about graphics on the radio. It's great.

RLJ: Yeah. [laughs]

DD: Thanks a lot for stopping by.

RLJ: You are welcome.

DD: Rickie Lee Jones is our guest on the *World Cafe.*

1992

TORI AMOS

TORI AMOS WAS JUST BEGINNING her ascension to the worldwide cult sensation she has become when she made her *World Cafe* debut in 1992. Her extraordinary debut album, *Little Earthquakes,* had just come out to sizeable acclaim and the cult that continues to follow Ms. Amos had begun to form. We all immediately saw her as someone special and wanted to have her on the show.

Remember, at that time our small studio was on the third floor so a real piano was out of the question and Tori had to play an electronic one. In subsequent interviews, that was an accommodation she wouldn't make again! Here is an excerpt of that first visit.

Tori is the kind of an interview where you ask a couple of questions and off she goes. Nonetheless I felt it necessary to match her provocative nature.

David Dye: My guest is Tori Amos on the *World Cafe.* Whew, that's a great one. That's "Leather" from the album, *Little Earthquakes.* Um, let's talk about sex. [TA laughs.] You have such a great way of being sexual in your music---sex as sacrament or something. It's such a wonderful experience.

Tori Amos: Well, I'll tell you, sex has really taken many forms and steps and changes in my life. I think that growing up in a Christian home . . .

DD: Uh-hum.

TA: . . . and even if you're not a minister's daughter, you can really be influenced by guilt and shame and all those really fun things.

DD: Yeah.

TA: And we have separated love and lust so much in our culture, in the way that we're taught, even if it's subliminally taught. You'd be amazed. . . . Having dinner, I've told people this many times, that if you could be, instead of, you know, fly on the wall's a bit maggoty, but if you could be, say, the pepper on the spaghetti or something, then you would hear ten women at a table talking, from all different backgrounds, about how the good girl and the bad girl are divided. And I'm sure men have their own conversations that I haven't been privy to, but having had many dinners alone with women, it reiterates what I believe, which is so many of us are affected by this division which is lust and love. And we think, to be a mother, to have a loving relationship with a man, that we can't throw them up against the wall or, et cetera, and have this passionate--- We think of "mistress"; we think of the "affair"; that has this illicit experience. It's not the one that you have with your best friend. It's not the--- How can you have both? We're taught that we can't have both, and that really keeps us really weak.

DD: Well what you're describing sounds pretty damn healthy.

TA: It's incredibly healthy, but it's stripping to the fundamental places of childhood where you take on everybody else's beliefs. It's amazing how as a kid, you're told things, and they become your thoughts, because some teacher told you or some adult, or you know, Maria Yon, Linda's sister who's fifteen, who gets all the guys. *This* is the authority.

DD: [chuckles] Right. One of the songs that's going to be newer to a lot of people, I guess, is the lead track on the album, "Crucify."

TA: Yeah.

DD: You want to do that one?

TA: Next single. Yeah.

Tori Amos performs "Crucify"

DD: My guest, Tori Amos, on the *World Cafe.* And that's "Crucify," which you'll find on *Little Earthquakes.* You'll also find [it] on kind of a neat CD single with some unexpected B-sides on it, which is kind of a joy to have you doing Led Zeppelin and the [Rolling] Stones and Nirvana. Are those things you play around the house, or how do you come up with---?

TA: Yeah, I play them around the house, that's what I'm into around the house. I think that being an acoustic piano player, people have real concepts of what that should be. And one of them is "nice," that idea of nice and pleasing, and you don't just pick up Metallica and do it at the piano.

DD: After all, you are a woman, I mean.

TA: Well, yeah [chuckles] after all.

DD: Here you are performing for me, and I guess a couple other people are listening in here, but um, you really, you're such an expressive singer, an expressive player, what's it like for you playing live? How are you, are you playing for small audiences or theaters?

TA: Well it's in the States, because it's the first tour, and nobody's really heard of me.

DD: Right.

TA: I'm doing small venues this go-round, and in the fall, hope to do a college tour.

DD: Well, I was interested in people's reactions to your songs, because you get so close to the bone on so many of your songs, it must touch people.

TA: [snickers] I'll tell you, there's some interesting stories about--- I walk out, and I have, and I won't tell you the places, but where it will be very hostile. They're walking out, they're almost challenging me to not be able to open up to them, because that means if I do, then they might just have to. And, I've had nights like this, where you're going out there saying, "This would be a lot easier if we just all wanted to come to the party." But I haven't always had those nights. The most open people that I've ever played to are the Scottish. [DD laughs]. Because when you go up there, you know they're screaming from the seats, "Tori, I love you lass!" [DD laughs] which is good fun.

DD: That's great. You want to do, I guess, a song which is an introduction for a lot of artists to you, which is, "Silent (All These Years)"?

TA: This is "Silent (All These Years)" and this is---

DD: This is about a lot of things, isn't it?

TA: This is about a lot of things. But I started it with this bumblebee riff, you know, we all grew up playing. You know that bumblebee song everybody grew up playing? And I decided, that song tortured me, so I'm going to pay it back.

> Tori Amos performs "Silent (All These Years)"

1992

TOWNES VAN ZANDT

TOWNES VAN ZANDT MADE HIS ONLY VISIT TO THE *WORLD CAFE* IN FEBRUARY OF 1992. The Texas songwriting legend was then living in Nashville and was between albums. He is best known for a series of albums he released in the late sixties and seventies on Poppy Records. His best-known song is, "Pancho and Lefty," which was recorded many times by various artists, including as a chart-topping hit by Willie Nelson and Merle Haggard.

Townes was not in the best shape the day he came up to the studio. It was within days of his wife giving birth to their daughter, Katie Belle, and he had not had a lot of sleep. Nonetheless we had a more than cordial visit and he played the then-brand-new song about a homeless couple, "Marie," one of the most powerful of his later works. And he also played "Pancho and Lefty."

Townes died nearly five years later, on New Year's Day, 1997.

David Dye: We're back on the *World Cafe.* About, gosh, about a month ago I mentioned how great--- I was playing the late, great Townes Van Zandt album, and I was saying how great it would be to have Townes stop by and give us a visit. Townes Van Zandt is our guest today on the *World Cafe.* Welcome to this part of the country.

Townes Van Zandt: Thanks.

DD: You're living in Nashville mostly now?

TV: Uh yeah, I live a little ways out of Nashville. I've lived there about three or four times over the years.

DD: There are a lot of Texans there nowadays.

TV: Yeah, I mean, in the music business it's really between a half and two-thirds. You're forever surprised at folks from Texas.

DD: Are you there primarily to get your songs recorded by other folks?

TV: Well, that; there's always that. That's kinda the main thing.

DD: It seems that some more mainstream Nashville types are finding your songs. Hal Ketchum, I know, is--- I've heard him do one live. How did he find your songs?

TV: Well I've known Hal for a long time just because he's from Dallas.

DD: Oh, I thought he was from West Virginia; that's interesting.

TV: I think he's from Dallas.

DD: Huh. See, two-thirds, just like you said.

TV: It goes like that. Plus, the opportunity to run into people who might do songs is tenfold if you're in Nashville.

DD: Are you working on some new material?

TV: Oh yeah, always.

DD: Is it harder or easier nowadays?

TV: Well it's kind of uh, I'd say harder, in that they don't just pour out anymore. Because they have to be better, you know? They have to be increasingly better. And I already have so many I've written about a whole bunch of stuff, and just finding a totally new outlook, and then to make sure it's good. Also there's a lot less time it seems like.

DD: How do decide what's good?

TV: Well I just kinda know.

DD: Yeah. You got a good one?

Townes Van Zandt performs "Marie"

DD: On the *World Cafe*, our guest is Townes Van Zandt. That's "Marie," right?

TV: That's "Marie."

DD: Ooh. You really write little short stories. That's a long story actually. Real kind of a [nineteen]thirties feel to that. I mean, it seems like a Dust Bowl song, even though it's a modern story. I was going to ask you about that. A lot of people cite you as an influence, a lot of newer songwriters. What were your models when you were starting to do this?

TV: Well first off it was, had to be, Hank Williams and Lefty Frizzell. When I first started listening to music it was in my dad's car, driving around West Texas. And then, all of a sudden, here came Elvis, and that changed everything. I was about nine or ten and I saw him on the *Ed Sullivan Show*. And we had one of the few TVs on our block, a little teeny TV, and so my older sister had her girlfriends over watching, and I was behind them watching Elvis and watching their reaction to Elvis, and up until then, I never thought of playing anything; I just had listened. And when I saw that, I realized, man, there must be something to this guitar stuff. After that, along came Bob Dylan. And I realized that he was really doin' it. He was really, you know, singing important stuff, with just him and his guitar. And at that point, that's kind of when I started seriously writing songs.

DD: Well, when did you make your first records in relation to that?

TV: Well that would have been, well, it was a ways after. I kind of got turned on to Bob Dylan about "The Times They Are A-Changin'" record, and my first album was, I think it was Christmas of '68. It came about that I was just playing in Houston, and Mickey Newberry saw me, and I was a serious rambling folk singer. In those days you kinda got a little suitcase and a guitar case and went wherever, hitchhiked wherever, you know, or got an old car. You know, "I hear there's a new joint in Oklahoma City, we can maybe pick up twenty bucks. Let's go!" But it was kinda different times.

Nowadays it seems that uh, you kinda go to your basement and work on a tape until it's good enough to get a record deal. So Mickey heard me at this club and said, "You have to come to Nashville." And so I got there and I was just kind of put on a stool, surrounded by these ace players, top-flight Nashville guys. And just show them the song once, and that would be the last you'd hear of my guitar. You know, I like that record now. I had serious doubts about [it] then because it was so different than what I was traveling around doing, you know. And I'd never been to Nashville before, and I hadn't listened to any country music almost since Hank Williams and Lefty Frizzell, because country music took a kind of a vanilla dive there for a long time.

DD: Right. Yeah. You want to do something from those, the early days?

Townes Van Zandt performs "To Live Is to Fly"

DD: "To Live Is to Fly," Townes Van Zandt, our guest today on the *World Cafe*. One you've recorded a number of times. Do you have any favorite versions . . . that other people have done, or is that a tough [question]?

TV: Well, I really seriously like 'em all, you know. Because it's so nice for them to take it and make it their own, no matter what they do. There's a couple way early on where there's some serious word changes. "Pancho's" been recorded and sung by other people innumerable times, and I love Emmy's version. And Willie and Merle, you could kind of tell they were reading it; they didn't quite know it. It arrived in the studio, right as their two bands were packing up. I could just picture--- I'm a friend of Willie's daughter Lana, and she took the tape over there, and I can just picture, you know, "We could do this as a perfect duet! We could even name the album Pancho & Lefty!" "Yeah! We could dress up!" You know, I can just feel every little stage that that went through. [chuckles]

DD: [chuckles] Yeah. I wasn't going to ask you, but if you want to do "Pancho," boy, that's a song that I could hear again.

Townes Van Zandt performs "Pancho & Lefty"

DD: Our guest on the *World Cafe*, the man who wrote that tune, Townes Van Zandt. You must have been happy when you came up with that chord progression.

TV: M-hm. That's one that kind of drifted through the window.

DD: Really? A lot of Texas imagery. Do you get back enough?

TV: Pretty often. That happens about twice a year, at least once a year.

DD: There must be a big set of Townes fans in Texas.

TV: I think they liked me better since I left. [laughs]

DD: [laughs] Remember that, people.

TV: By a long shot! [laughs]

DD: Our guest has been Townes Van Zandt. Thanks a lot for stopping by.

TV: Oh, this has been a genuine pleasure.

DD: Thanks a lot. Townes Van Zandt on the *World Cafe.*

1992

JEFF BUCKLEY

IN THE TIME THAT HAS PASSED SINCE JEFF BUCKLEY DROWNED IN THE MISSISSIPPI RIVER IN MEMPHIS IN MAY OF 1997, HIS LEGEND HAS DONE NOTHING BUT GROW. Looking back on this interview that took place in March of 1992, before his revered album *Grace* had even been released, his legend seems pretty well formed already at least in the advance vanguard of the music business. People who had crammed into the tiny venue, Sine, in New York City, told tales of how the voice and the power and vision of his compositions was already apparent.

What was Jeff Buckley like? In the two times he joined us on the Cafe, this time and a year later with his full band, I found him to be at ease with himself, yet reserved. He was very funny, yet cautious, because it seemed that everybody wanted something from Jeff.

This first time that he joined us, I had been warned that what he didn't want to talk about was his famous father–folk singer Tim Buckley–with whom Jeff shared his multi-octave voice. Looking back, I am surprised that in this short interview with a stranger he was as forthcoming as he was. I think we would all like to have had an opportunity to know him better.

David Dye: I was curious as to how you ended up on the bill at the Tim Buckley benefit concert; because my understanding is that you didn't really know your father that well. Did you know his music well?

Jeff Buckley: I don't know how I ended up--- I think somebody talked to the--- He split before I was born. He didn't really keep contact with me and my mom. Except for one time, and I was asleep at the time. I was probably two. You know, it was like he went off. He decided not to be a father. So it was just me and my mom. And I saw him once for a week, and then it was two months before he crashed on heroin. And in between then there was no contact, and then between the death and the funeral there was no contact, and I guess I missed it, you know; it always bugged me. So I decided--- They asked me to come, the people at St. Anne's, the very beautiful people at St. Anne's. They asked me to come. I said no at first, and then I said okay, but I don't want to be billed and I just want to come on and sing, and come off. This is not a springboard. This is something really personal. And I would never and probably will never ever perform that music, you know, as I've got my own music.

DD: Were you surprised by the reaction?

JB: No.

DD: And were you leery of the reaction?

JB: Leery and not surprised, no. As I didn't think it had anything to do with me at all, in that there's a--- I don't really dig talking about this subject, but my friend Bill Flanagan wrote this really loving article about me. And I came on the stage, and he said he heard Tim Buckley's haunted voice. And if that's the impression I gave to people, it was purely--- It's not, it's not *his* voice; and it's not *my* voice. It's the voice that's been passed down through every man in the family. His father, I found out, sang . . . had a beautiful voice.

DD: Wow.

JB: It's just an Irish thing; you wouldn't understand!

DD: [chuckles] Well that's the thing that hits you first. I mean, actually, all I've ever heard is the Sine tapes, is this incredible voice. Have you always been such a fearless singer? From the beginning? I mean, it's really brave to take your voice out there as much as you do.

JB: . . . I mean, the whole purpose was for me to totally corral all my farthest eccentricities, you know. And also be my conventional self, and my weird self, and my ugly self, and my sexy self, and my stinky self, and . . . everything that art should be.

DD: Well, tell you what, why don't you do . . . a solo version of one of the new songs, maybe? And then we'll talk some more.

JB: Hmmmm. . . .

Jeff Buckley performs "Grace"

DD: Whew! Jeff Buckley is our guest. What is that song?

JB: It's called, "Grace." Me and Gary [Lucas] wrote that.

DD: I'm interested in what vocalists you listened to. I heard you're a Nusrat Fateh Ali Khan [the late Pakistani Qawwali singer] fan.

JB: Nusrat Fateh Ali. He's awesome. We were just listening to him on the way up. He's like my, he's my Elvis. Uh, [sigh] all kinds of people I fell in love with. Fell in love with Billie Holiday. I'm usually totally out of step, like usually it's a crowd of people dig something at one time, and I'm totally--- I'm into it, way into it, way before, or completely after, when it's totally not cool. And I'm always completely out of step. It's really pathetic.

DD: [laughs]

JB: Music has to happen to people in a moment, you know. And then it gets in the bloodstream. It's just you need it, physically.

DD: You need that discovery too, on your own.

JB: Yeah, which is why videos are--- I'm not making a video for this album.

DD: Mmm-hmm.

JB: I'm not making it because it's--- I love visuals, and I will do something visual. I mean, I'm totally in love with them. But they're commercials for the album, and I wouldn't want that to be the object. Actually everybody just stay away from the television. Get a book. [laughs] Turn on the radio.

DD: Now, along those lines, you had all these people coming to see you in New York, kind of waving money at you, I guess, and you kind of resisted until you felt right about it. Was it difficult to pick Sony?

JB: No [he strums softly in the background]. It was a dilemma. It's always a dilemma for everyone, everybody who I know who gets signed. You know the rules that are set up; the way that it's structured for a certain kind of artist to really, really succeed heavily, and some others really not to do anything.

And also I'm really--- Sometimes I have a pretty black soul, sometimes, and I'll stay away from things, like, that will bring out the cynic in me—like the music business, for instance.

DD: Quite easily. Now are you going to re-cut "Mojo Pin" on the new record? Do you want to do a solo version of that?

JB: Okay.

Jeff Buckley performs "Mojo Pin"

DD: Jeff Buckley is our guest. The *World Cafe* version of "Mojo Pin." Is it hard for you to sing like this? Is it physically demanding, or--- I mean you really pour it out!

JB: It's emotionally demanding.

DD: Yeah.

JB: It's everything. Everything's connected. And yeah, it's hard sometimes. But some things are really easy. It just depends on what you feel.

DD: Is it hard to get to a place where you can get inside these songs every time you do them? I mean, here, you know, it's kind of a bland room, and I'm here and nothing else.

JB: Oooohhhmmm, I don't know. I mean, you can tell somebody "I love you," anywhere, really. But it's, it's probably from learning. Just by doing what a real--- The difference between a real distraction and what you don't have to worry about. Real distractions are internal, really. You could drive cattle by my stage and I wouldn't mind.

DD: What was it like doing these songs originally for people who didn't know them in New York, when you were just singing in clubs?

JB: Oh, anything from completely indifferent, to hateful, to liking them.

DD: Well thanks a lot for coming by.

JB: All right, well, thank you.

DD: Appreciate it. Come back with a band, okay?

JB: Yeah! Right in this room. We'll be back.

DD: We will do it, absolutely!

JB: It'll be awesome.

1992

RODNEY CROWELL

RODNEY CROWELL HAS BEEN ONE OF MY FAVORITE SONGWRITERS since I heard Emmylou Harris do his song "Bluebird Wine" on her first album. Originally from Houston, Texas, he traveled to Nashville and ended up hanging out with Guy Clark and a fun bunch of fellow Texans there.

His first album for Warner Brothers is filled with great songs, either ones he wrote or classics he learned playing drums in his father's weekend band. Almost every one became a hit for someone else. Rodney got his taste of country stardom when five songs from his *Diamonds and Dirt* album went to number one on the country charts.

For thirteen years, Rodney was married to Rosanne Cash. The marriage broke up shortly before this interview in 1992.

Rodney has remained a great friend of the *World Cafe*, and he has done numerous interviews with us. About eleven years after this particular interview–in May of 2003–he came to a public radio convention to perform at a showcase we sponsored. We gathered and checked the equipment, and a couple of hours later we did the performance and interview. Rodney was flawless. When it was all over, he told the audience that between the sound check and the show he got the phone call that his former mother-in-law, June Carter Cash, had died. I guess the show had to go on, and it did.

David Dye: On the *World Cafe*, we're very happy that Rodney Crowell has joined us. Ben Vaughn is one of our reporters on the show and said he was down doing some writing with you. Are a lot of people making appointments to write with you nowadays?

Rodney Crowell: Well, I don't make appointments. Now, Ben Vaughn and I got together because I bought one of his records and I loved it, and somebody I knew, knew Ben, and I said, "Hey, I want to meet this guy," so I met him. I said, "What are you doing tomorrow, why don't you come by my place?" So we wound up writing some songs—a couple of songs—and it was fun. Ben's a real bright guy, very talented, a good writer. But for the most part, when somebody calls me—and it's sort of the vogue in Nashville to book songwriting sessions—I say, "Look, you know, let's don't book it, but here's my phone number, and if one morning you get up and the muse is happening and you feel inspired or something, call me."

DD: Do you ever worry about that muse? I mean, do you ever think, "Oh God, I haven't written a song in a certain period of time"?

RC: Well, I trick myself, you know, into different ways of thinking about it. I went through a nice long period where I said, "Oh, you know, if I'm not inspired I'm not going to write anything," and that's great. And then lately I've found myself with a lot of time on my hands, and so I've been going up to the little place where I work in my house and working on it, sort of daily. And I found out that when I work on it daily, I tend to question it, you know, I tend to say, "Oh, maybe I'm just manufacturing these songs." And that's when I find myself yelling down for my twelve-year-old daughter to come up, and I'll say, "Listen to this and tell me if you like it," and I'll play it for her and she'll say, "That's okay, Dad."

DD: Anything you've been working on that you want to try? Anything new?

RC: Oh no, I'm insecure about those! I don't know, we've been doing some new songs. Yeah, I could try something. [strums]

Rodney Crowell performs "Rose of Memphis"

DD: [chuckling] Rodney Crowell's our guest. Is that "Rose of Memphis"?

RC: M-hm, "The Rose of Memphis."

DD: Your latest album is kind of a mix of a lot of swaggery sexy songs, like that one and the other ones.

RC: Yeah, I have a good friend who's a keyboard player in my band, [and] she was saying that some of her friends were taking her to task about working with me because I'd been writing these sort of swaggery male songs. But it's funny. I live in a household of women who don't take that from me at all. I'm kind of amazed sometimes when I'm held accountable for it.

DD: We had Dr. John on the show a while ago picking out music from New Orleans, and he gave a real heartfelt speech about how growing up when he did, where he did, was so important to his music because of the people he learned from. Now, you're from Houston, and your dad had a band and you were the drummer in the band?

RC: M-hm, I was.

DD: Talk a little bit about that experience.

RC: Well, I can see what Dr. John's talking about, because I'm a real fan of his music, and it's very much that New Orleans humid kind of music. And Houston is equally as humid. I have this feeling about humidity and music; I remember with a lot of humidity in the air the sound carried very well. So I was used to hearing music from four houses down drifting on a humid night through the window. . .

DD: This is cinematic, that's great.

RC: . . . and for the most part, that music was really hillbilly music. So, all this is a long-winded way of saying that it seems as though New Orleans, the humidity, held up a kind of R&B, a gumbo of black music. And go the distance over to Houston, it was more like George Jones and Hank Williams and the humidity kind of carried those sounds. And those were the first sounds I remember.

DD: What kind of joints would you end up playing in with your dad?

RC: Well, they were called icehouses then. But what they were, they were these structures with like two garage door things, and in the summer time or during the open hours they would just raise these garage doors up. And they had these ice chests out front, you know, the length of the building. And inside was a jukebox, and over in the corner—it wasn't even a stage, just in the corner they'd set the band up, and we played over in the corner. And my father had a cigar box, and people paid by, you know, if they wanted to hear, "From a Jack to a King" or some song, they would put a dollar in the cigar box. My father took a lot of pride, you know. His thing was—he had a certain amount of arrogance about him—he said, "I can keep a dance floor full." But it was true; he could keep a dance floor full, because he knew so many songs.

DD: Sounds like a human jukebox.

RC: He was a human jukebox, my dad was.

DD: Rodney Crowell's our guest here on the *World Cafe*. You want to do something from that era?

RC: Well, let me see. Let me think about what would be a good song to kind of--- I always liked--- [strumming] I don't remember what key---

Rodney Crowell performs "Wedding Bells"

DD: Rodney Crowell, our guest here on the *World Cafe*. That is a pretty one, that's a great verse. The other thing that's really been interesting about you throughout your career is what you brought up [when] you started talking about Hank Williams, you started talking about Bob Dylan. You've been at that cusp, in the way your albums were always done, up until *Diamonds and Dirt*, kind of going down that middle of the road. I've been thinking about this for a long time—does that middle place exist? Because there are so many artists—Mary Chapin Carpenter sort of rides that, and then she has a big country success—and so many people who are sort of riding that line are having more success now with songwriting than in country.

RC: Well, I've noticed that, and I've noticed it with myself. I'll listen to Miles Davis and the Chieftains back to back, and I want to reserve my right to be eclectic about music. But I've found in the real world that we deal with, that people need definition. And especially record stores and radio stations, for the most part, they need definition. And it seems as though to have that kind of success that I've flirted with, say at the *Diamonds and Dirt* time, it required that

I focus in on one particular aspect, which was more the country root.

DD: The big success for you with *Diamonds and Dirt* came later in your career, and the cliché is, "Oh, it probably didn't affect him, he was used to everything at that point."

RC: Yeah. The good lesson for me was that, you know, having five number one records in a row and selling all those albums and going around and playing everyplace where there was a stage—it just wasn't fulfilling, and I can't say I particularly enjoyed it. But I'm really committed to the fact that I'm here to entertain, I'm in the entertainment business, but there's different choices to be made. So I didn't have a lot of fun, no.

DD: Well, listen. You did a new one, you did an old Hank Williams tune; you want to do another new one?

RC: I was thinking about, you know, the old Luke the Drifter slash Hank Williams song "Lost Highway." I wrote this song for a movie that I've been working on, and the character's a songwriter, and I was thinking about the old idea of the old lost highway. The original was like, you know, "If you go down the lost highway, you know, your life is over, you're in for sin and pain and sorrow." I was thinking, in this day and age, maybe we ought to look at this from, "If you go down the old lost highway, you'll actually do a little Jungian twist on it and say you'll actually, by going into the dark, find yourself."

> Rodney Crowell performs "Lost Highway"

DD: Another new one from our guest, Rodney Crowell, "Lost Highway." That's a good one. One could see that coming out of your experience. I wanted to talk just a little bit about [your album] *Life Is Messy*. It was kind of promoted as, and you can really see it as, a chronicle of your marriage breaking up. But there's a song on it that's been a centerpiece to it for me, and it's in the center; it's the one you and Rosanne [Cash] wrote together, which has so much to do with a relationship, too—learning how to be myself. Were you happy with how that came out? I mean, you sort of wrote it half and half, or---?

RC: Well, that song is (it being, "I Hardly Know How to Be Myself") it was right at a time when--- you know in relationships---We were married for thirteen years, and the marriage was dissolving. But it was dissolving because the relationship was evolving, and we had to become something else to each other because the man-and-wife aspect of it didn't fit for who the people were anymore. And the power struggles—I was on the road a lot, and Rosanne's history was that the life on the road holds no romance for her, and she thinks that it's a vanity pursuit for the most part. And maybe I shouldn't go that far, you know—that's me interpreting how I think she feels about it.

DD: Well, we could just say she doesn't do it much.

RC: She doesn't like to go on the road, and her idea of a relationship with a man who was on the road a lot was not very fulfilling for her, and I understand that and I don't blame her. Your needs are what they are. But I came home from being on a long road trip and went up in my writing place there and I saw the first two verses to the song lying on my desk, and I thought, wow, she left this here on purpose. It was really powerful, very powerful to me, and immediately I said, "God, I know what this is about, I hope she doesn't have a melody." So she was making tea downstairs and was going to bring it up and we were going to have a cup of tea together, and I grabbed my guitar and wrote the choruses and some more verses and a melody, and when she came up, I said, "Wow, I found this on my desk, I sure hope you don't have a melody for this. Listen to what I got here." So I played it for her, and she goes, "I don't even remember writing that." But it was truly her handwriting. So the end thing that really intrigues me about the song is that it's two people in a relationship with opposing--- It's a power struggle sometimes in a relationship, and with two people so far apart on an issue--- When I wrote my side of it and she wrote her side of it, it really was the same side. I've scratched my head, going, "How could we be feeling the same thing so clearly and simply, yet interpreting it in two entirely different ways?" That's what I like about the song, and that's how I relate to it when I perform it.

DD: I'd love to have you play it.

RC: Let's do it. Let's do it like this.

Rodney Crowell performs "I Hardly Know How to Be Myself"

DD: "I Hardly Know How to Be Myself," that's one that's on *Life Is Messy*. Our guest, Rodney Crowell. Kenny Vaughn on guitar. Boy, that's a--- You know, it's funny who wrote what, because when I listened to it, I said, I can tell Rodney wrote that first line. [chuckles]

RC: Yeah, no. Rosanne wrote that first line.

DD: Great song. Are there old songs of yours that you've grown tired of over the years, that are sort of coming back into the repertoire now, that you're beginning to like again?

RC: Yeah, yeah. They come and they go, they kind of have an ebb and a flow to them. Some of them, I rediscover them. This is a nice way to rediscover them in a real intimate acoustic setting. I certainly get tired of them with a band. You know, you get an arrangement of a song with a band and you play it for a while; sometimes you get past the passion of the song or the real connection to the song and you start pretending the song, you know, and when you get to a place where you're pretending the song, I hate that. I hate that feeling, I feel like I'm phony, and I usually have to get rid of 'em. But sometimes they come back, you know, and if they go away and they don't come back, good riddance, you know?

DD: Well, thanks a lot for coming by.

RC: Thank you, David.

1992

U2'S THE EDGE

THE FIRST PRODUCER ON THE *WORLD CAFE* WAS BRUCE RANES, who came to us with experience working on the *King Biscuit Flower Hour* syndicated radio show. He not only knew a lot about crafting a radio show, but also had a full Rolodex (remember "Rolodexes," another technological artifact of an earlier era?). After a year of the *World Cafe*, we had all been frustrated that our fledgling show with fewer than fifty stations hadn't been able to attract any internationally major names. Bruce felt, as we all did, that once we got one it would give us the credibility to attract others.

Bruce pulled in all his favors and used all his contacts to get the *World Cafe* an interview with U2–the biggest rock band of them all–in the summer of 1992. It wasn't Bono, but it was guitarist The Edge and bassist Adam Clayton.

Adam was my first experience with the major rock star interview–the good, the bad, and the absurd. I interviewed him at the band's posh hotel, and for the first time had to wade through the layers of security that finally left me sitting in Adam's suite with the freshly arisen bassist attired in only a big fluffy bathrobe. The fact that that was the only garment he was wearing became alarmingly evident as he slid down in his chair. . . .

Getting to The Edge, who interviewed in the depths of Veterans Stadium in Philadelphia, involved a similar level of security but produced a bit more interesting interview. I talked with the stellar guitarist for U2 in a "living room" area assembled for the band in one of the locker rooms. The band was in the midst of their "Zoo TV" Tour in support of the *Zooropa* album, and we talked about guitar techniques and other subjects close to The Edge.

DD: On the *World Cafe*, The Edge in his snakeskin shirt here backstage. Welcome.

TE: How you doin'?

DD: Very good. Very good. Caught my second show last night—the first outdoor one. You'd think with the whole spectacle it wouldn't be an intimate experience, and I found it to be even more intimate than the arenas. Is that a conscious thing on your part?

TE: Well, it's a comment that I've heard from a few different people. You know, intimacy is something you can only hope for, and a stadium, it's such a vast space. How can you possibly plan for it? You know, I think the music is the thing that communicates, and when we go out into the middle of the stadium on the small B stage, that's our opportunity to play the songs in a real stripped-down manner. And I think that's probably the key to this show, is the contrast between that and the big production on the main stage.

DD: Let's speak for just a second about the whole Zoo TV concept. Is it a concept that came out of TV, or was there any other media that was in mind when you were putting it together?

TE: Well the name came first, and the idea of using visuals live. And we just started talking about—if we did use images live, what would it be or what wouldn't it be. And we started looking around at what other people were doing. And we'd already done some stuff with John Klein, who's a New York editor who worked on Buzz TV with Mike Pellington, and John co-directed the "Fly" video. And that was the first use of text in the context of one of our pieces of work, and that kind of gave us a kind of feel for the way this could go, you know? So, I mean, the idea started to just grow and it started to take on its own personality, bringing in the influences of other electronic media like CNN, MTV, and just the stuff that's going on out there at the moment. I mean, it seems in the nineties that technologies are converging and I suppose we've just taken some of those new technologies and brought them into a rock and roll concert.

DD: What's feeling the best for you to play right now? Does that change?

TE: You know, we constantly have to look at certain parts of the show, certain songs that are, that we're playing, and make sure that they're up to scratch, you know, because you just get, you can get a bit tired, you know. Not tired of the song, but . . . the performance idea just gets a bit old and you'll have to kind of find a new angle on it. So right now I'm really enjoying things like "Bullet the Blue Sky" and "Where the Streets Have No Name" and "Desire" and songs like that which, they've got like a new angle to them on this tour which always, you know, it keeps the band interested as well as the audience.

DD: We're talking with The Edge on the

World Cafe. Explain the "Infinite Guitar" a little bit. You do use it, clearly.

TE: Yeah.

DD: What does it do for you; what can you do with it?

TE: Michael Brook is the inventor. It's--- the Infinite Guitar is not a unique concept, you know; there are other devices that do the same thing, which gives the guitar player the ability to sustain a note for as long as he wants to. Uh, there's a device called an "Ebow" which is, uh, a small little silver device you place over the string, over the pickup, and that creates kind of an oscillation of the string. The difference between, for instance, Ebow and some of the other manufactured guitars, the difference between those and the Infinite is that the Infinite has a much more controllable kind of sustain because of the way Michael designed it. You can have any one of a number of degrees of sustain and you can bring in the note very slowly, let it trail off very slowly. It's just a more musical kind of a device.

DD: Give a good example of something you think it sounds good on---

TE: On *Joshua Tree*, "With or Without You."

DD: Is "Van Demon's Land" the only song you've written lyrics to?

TE: That's a good question. No, I've, I wrote some lyrics to a song on the *War* album called "Seconds." It's the only song I think I've written all the lyrics to that's made a U2 album. You know, I actually wrote the lyrics in that outline for the song as kind of a demo, and I always thought the melody was really strong while I, in my own mind, I thought, "Well we'll, you know, we'll get to rewrite this one at some stage and it will probably go on the album." But Phil recorded me or filmed me playing the song one day, and just towards the end of the making of *Rattle & Hum*, he just came to me and said, "Look, I'd really like to use this as the title sequence and, you know, would you have any objection?" So I went, "No, sure, it's fine with me if, you know, you like it." So that's kind of how it ended up on the album. I mean, as I wrote the lyrics I knew it was an exercise in a particular style, you know? Most people think it's, you know, a couple of hundred years old.

DD: Right, right, right. Traditional, with lyrics by The Edge.

[Break]

DD: U2 on the *World Cafe*. So many people in the audience last night who, the more obscure a song you would play, the older a song you would play, the more they would react. Your fans go way back to the beginning. I was surprised at such a large show. So many people to me seemed to really be so intense. Is there anybody out there now you feel a fan relationship with; bands?

TE: Oh yeah, a lot of bands. I love the Heroes; I like what they're doing a lot. I like Arrested Development, Nine Inch Nails. Ministry I think are doing some good stuff. Some of the more extreme techno things I like, Front 242, and some of the grunge things are kind of cool, as well. I mean, you know, I'm just into music so my tastes are pretty broad, as well, you know?

DD: How do you think that U2 has become so big and yet no one is ever uncomfortable calling them an alternative band?

TE: There is this assumption that big means out of touch, that big means bloated, that big means sell-out, you know, and it's a cliché that I really, completely contest—I don't buy it. And most bands that become successful unfortunately just seem to nod off and they become parodies of themselves, but it doesn't necessarily have to be. . . . I don't know whether it's because of our musical upbringing being, coming out of punk, where you have to survive on spirit rather than on technique. We don't know any other way of doing it, you know, and so the struggle is part of the thing for us, therefore I don't think we could ever become that complacent; I just don't think it would work. So I think it must be that, you know, we're just destined to be constantly struggling against the limitations of our own ability and our ambition, you know?

DD: Good place to be.

TE: [laughs]

DD: Very good place to be. Our guest on the *World Cafe*, The Edge, thank you very much.

TE: Great, it's been a good interview. Thank you.

DD: Thank you.

1993

KATE BUSH

IN THE SPACE OF THE 16 YEARS the *World Cafe* has been in existence, Kate Bush has only released two albums. There was a four-year gap before *The Red Shoes,* as well. You can imagine we were very excited to talk with Kate considering it was a bit of an event to even have her in the U.S. due to the fact that her fear of flying had kept her grounded for years. The interview took place in the only quiet spot we could find in the East-Side hotel–the closed bar. She curled up in a wing-back chair with a cup of tea, and we talked.

David Dye: It's another *World Cafe* road trip; this time we're on the East side of Manhattan, and we're talking to Kate Bush. Now welcome, first of all, I should say.

Kate Bush: Thank you very much. It's very nice to be here.

DD: Now there's at least one song, I think a couple songs, that refer to New York on this record. Are you here more often than we think you are?

KB: Well I haven't been here for about four years, but when I was last here I got the opportunity to meet some friends, who are very dear to me, and their presence was quite strongly felt on the album, which is one of the reasons why New York keeps appearing.

DD: It's been another four-year gap between Kate Bush albums. For your fans, that sometimes seems like a long time. Does it seem like a long time to you?

KB: Yes it seems like forever.

DD: What brings those gaps about?

KB: Well I spend a long time in the studio making albums, and it's become a bit of a joke, really, that it takes me so long.

DD: Was there some confusion of the timing of release? Now I understand there's a film you've done, which is a string of videos from the album, or is it a narrative film?

KB: Yes it was an idea really to try and make a short film that included tracks from the album, and the idea was that it wouldn't be so much like promotional videos put together, but that hopefully it would come across as a short story.

DD: Well I want to play the title track, "The Red Shoes," to start off with. Now you've always been a dancer. And was it the film *The Red Shoes* that inspired this? Or inspired you to dance?

KB: Well I think really the influence on this song was very much the film *The Red Shoes* by Michael Powell, and I'm a very big fan of his work. I think his films are just extraordinary and I was very lucky to be able to get to meet him a few years ago when I came to New York. And I was writing this song some months later, and there was kind of a musical idea for the track, and I hadn't got an idea for lyrics at all. And it sort of had, rhythmically, had the feel of something running away with itself. And the story *The Red Shoes* came into my head. And I'm sure had I not met Michael, I wouldn't have thought of that story, but it sort of took on this whole fairy-tale-like quality. And I think it's got quite a strong sense of humor as well—the idea that the shoes actually take over the person that puts them on and they can't get the shoes off.

Kate Bush recording: "The Red Shoes"

DD: That's "The Red Shoes," the title track to Kate Bush's new album. Now are those your red toe shoes on the cover?

KB: Yes they are.

DD: I thought so. Large parts of this record kind of sound to me sort of like Kate Bush's R&B album. There's a lot of kick drum in it, a lot of songs based on some very funky feels; I'm thinking of "Rubberband Girl" or "Eat the Music." "Red Shoes" to some extent. Was that feel your intent?

KB: Yes it was, really. I think initially, what I wanted to do was make an album of songs; that there wouldn't be any kind of theme or concept to the album. And I was hoping to try and make the whole approach much more direct, from a sound point of view, that it would sound like a band. And to have less emphasis on the kind of layered production. And when I set out to start the album, I hoped very much that it wouldn't take very long. I thought it would be quick and that we'd have it done in hopefully about six months, but I should really know better by now.

DD: Well it seems like there's a band, a core band on a lot of the tracks. Was it important to you to play with the same players a lot?

KB: Yeah, again that was the idea to try and get a good feel, a good band feel. But mainly the tracks were: the drummer and the bass player would work together, and then musicians would be layered on top of that. But the actual sort of basic rhythm sections were what we were doing with the two players all the time.

Kate Bush recording: "Rubberband Girl"

DD: We're talking with Kate Bush, here on the *World Cafe.* I wanted to play another track from the record, "Big Stripey Lie," which is one of the ones I think that Nigel Kennedy is on. I know he was on the last album too. How did you meet him?

KB: Well I met Nigel years ago as a sort of strange coincidence. I'd just turned on the television and I saw this fantastic violinist playing. And I said to my friend, who I was with, I've got to work with this guy, you know, I just feel that we could really work well together. And the next day, my mother actually told me she's seen the whole program, and it must have been five minutes before I turned on, he had just said on the television program how he would like to work with me. And I thought it was so coincidental, it was just a matter of us making contact.

DD: This is "Big Stripey Lie." Listen for Nigel towards the end of this piece.

Kate Bush recording: "Big Stripey Lie"

DD: Nigel Kennedy on violin, viola, violin I believe, on "Big Stripey Lie." We're talking with Kate Bush. That's another track from *The Red Shoes*. And we're talking about strings. I know you've used string quartets in the past, and always have wonderful string arrangements, and Michael Kamen's are very nice on this record too. I was thinking about "Moments of Pleasure." You talked about how songs got more and more complicated. This is actually one of the simpler songs on the record, in terms of melody line and layers.

KB: Yes. It's a very simple song in that it's a straightforward production, but I think in some ways it's actually quite an intricate song from a structural and lyrical point of view. And it was one of the few songs that I wrote in the old way where I just sat at the piano, and I just wrote the song on the piano as opposed to being in the studio, surrounded by technology and working onto tape. And it was actually very pleasurable to me to get back to this old way of writing where it's basically you confronting yourself.

Kate Bush recording: "Moments of Pleasure"

DD: A few of the moments of pleasure, from the many that's on *The Red Shoes*, Kate Bush's new album. "And So Is Love"—it's one of my favorites on this record. It's kind of a sad song, kind of a resigned song in a way. And Eric Clapton plays so achingly on this record. Did you specifically go get Eric to play that solo, or was he just another friend, or how did that work out?

KB: No, he was very specifically in mind for the track, and I was so excited when he said that he would come and play. And when I actually heard what he was playing, I was very moved. I think it's beautiful, his performance on this song, and he was so sensitive to the track. It was just great working with him. I'd always hoped that I would have the chance to work with him some day, and I'm just so pleased with what he did.

Kate Bush recording: "And So Is Love"

DD: That's "And So Is Love," another beautiful track from *The Red Shoes*. One couldn't confuse you with sort of the string of confessional singer-songwriters which are rampant here in America, but can we find out things about you emotionally, personally, from your songs?

KB: I think it's impossible for any writer to not put themselves into their work. That is part of the process; its self-exploration, and a lot of ways I find that my work is a lot to do with me finding out about myself. And even if the subject matter isn't about one's own life, it still very much reflects how you feel at that point in time. I think albums—and books, paintings—they're almost like extracts from a person's diary, where they're talking about what they were influenced [by] at that time, how they felt. And hopefully, a writer is just trying to communicate to that part in their listeners.

DD: The Prince collaboration, the song "Why Should I Love You," it's a great song. And it sounds like a collaboration, it sounds like you could say, "Oh that's the Prince part, that's the Kate part." Did it work that way?

KB: No, no. I think it was probably one of the most unusual collaborations. I'd written this song, and I thought how wonderful it would be if Prince would get involved to play some guitar, and we worked by sending tapes to him, and then he sent them back. So it was almost like pen-pal recording. And he put a lot of stuff on the tracks that I then had to sort out. So it was really fun for me and very interesting to feel how someone else had played with the track, and then it came home to me.

DD: This is "Why Should I Love You."

Kate Bush recording: "Why Should I Love You"

DD: "Why Should I Love You," from *The Red Shoes*, Kate Bush's new album, recently out here on Columbia. Now your success in England and Europe has been, it's no surprise to say, much broader than it has been here in this country. Do you have any feel for why that is? Does that bother you?

KB: No it doesn't bother me at all. Like I said, I think very early on I made the decision that what I really want is to make the best music that I can, and if that's received warmly by anyone, I'm very happy. It's not my intention to sort of conquer the world. I'm not terribly ambitious to be famous, but I am ambitious for my work to be as good as I can make it. I haven't been here much, and I think early on in my career I had a few handicaps—the records weren't released. But I've been very pleased how well the albums have done here. Particularly the last couple.

DD: The last couple have done well.

KB: And I'm very happy with the record company that I'm with now, so, you know, if people want to buy it, I'm thrilled. But like I say, it's not, you know, it's not everything.

DD: Clear this up about your not traveling and touring. Is it really about control of your time, or is it, do you not like to travel?

KB: Well for a few years I had a lot of trouble flying.

DD: M-hm.

KB: So I didn't fly places, and so it made it very difficult for me to get anywhere, you know, by train and stuff like this is just a joke. So that grounded me for a few years. But touring—I think a lot of people got the impression that it's something that I don't want to do or didn't like doing. But we did a tour years ago in England and Europe and I had a wonderful time. But from that point onwards, I think I felt I really wanted to spend more time in the studio, and learn about recording, and to just concentrate on trying to make the best records that I could.

DD: Now I went back and I rented your video compilation last night, and there were some live clips on there. The live production was quite elaborate, as one would expect it would be. That seems like a lot of work in and of itself, just putting that all together.

KB: Well I think again at the time it was something very unusual, what we were doing. We were kind of putting dance and theater together with rock music that hadn't really quite been done on the scale it is now. And I'm not sure that it's something I feel that I need to do anymore; in some ways I kind of like the idea of doing something very simple. But, you know, there are no plans to do anything yet, so who knows—it might turn out to be all laser, all dancing.

DD: Well if it grows like the records grow, from a simple beginning [laughs].

KB: It could be trouble, couldn't it, yeah.

DD: I wanted to play something, an earlier piece, before *The Sensual World.* Is there something back there that you're really proud of, that maybe wasn't as big a hit as some of the others?

KB: I don't know if I could say that I'm really proud of anything; you have a bit of a love/hate relationship with your own stuff.

DD: You hear the mistakes, you hear the....

KB: Yeah. And also you tend not to listen to stuff that you've done. Obviously, when you're making an album, you're hearing it all the time, and once it's actually finished there comes a saturation point where you don't want to hear it anymore. So I very rarely hear any of my old music. Why don't you choose? [laughs]

DD: I had an idea you'd do that. Well I'll go back on part of my statement because it was kind of a hit. Let's play "Cloudbusting."

Kate Bush recording: "Cloudbusting"

DD: Talk about great string arrangements, there's one from *Hounds of Love*—"Cloudbusting." We're talking with Kate Bush here on the *World Cafe*. Are you aware that you are one of the kind of touch-points of comparison in music criticism? I mean, when a new record comes out, very often people say, "Oh it sounds like Kate Bush."

KB: [laughs] No I don't think I'm aware of this.

DD: Well are you aware of any of the artists who that has been applied to?

KB: No, but I have great sympathy for them. [laughs]

DD: [laughs] Who were you compared to early on?

KB: Early on I'm not sure. I'm not sure they really knew who to compare me to, really. But there were points where people would compare my approach to that of Peter Gabriel, which, you know, I'm very happy to be compared to him.

DD: Did you choose "Rocket Man" as your part of the Elton John tribute?

KB: Yes I did. I was so knocked out to be asked to be involved, and it was like a big kind of completion of the circle. When I was about 14 or 15 I was such a big Elton John fan, and my favorite track of his was "Rocket Man." I played it to death; I thought it was absolutely wonderful. And if I'd have even thought at that point that I'd reach a stage where they would come and ask me if I'd like to sing an Elton John song, and which one, I could never have dreamt of that. So it was a complete honor for me to be involved. And to actually be able to do that song was great fun.

Kate Bush recording: "Rocket Man"

DD: "Rocket Man" from the Elton John tribute album. Our guest, Kate Bush with a great rendition of that one. Who were some of the other songwriters that you were fans of as a teenager?

KB: Well Elton John was by far my biggest hero. I think what was really great about him for me was he was a songwriter who played the piano, and most of the songwriters at that time were very guitar orientated. And I thought he was such a brilliant pianist as well as having a great voice. The way he played was so dance-y, and he was a very big inspiration to me, as someone who could sing and play the piano, and I really wanted to be able to play the piano like him.

DD: What did he think of your "Rocket Man"?

KB: He said he really liked it. It was a lovely moment for me when, you know, he came up and said that he liked it. It was really nice.

DD: Well thank you so much for spending time with us.

KB: My pleasure, thank you.

DD: Thank you for getting back to this side of the Atlantic. We look forward to if you ever come back touring. It will be wonderful to see you.

KB: Well thank you, I've got my wings back now.

DD: [laughs] Yeah.

KB: So I should be able to come over more often.

DD: Thank you a lot, Kate Bush, our guest, here on the *World Cafe.*

1993

LEONARD COHEN

TALKING WITH LEONARD COHEN WAS ALL THAT I HAD IMAGINED IT WOULD BE. EXCEPT THAT HE WAS FAR MORE POLITE AND ACCEPTING THAN I HAD EXPECTED. He walked off of his tour bus wearing a "Field Commander Cohen" embroidered jacket, and we repaired to a reverberant dressing room at the Keswick Theater outside of Philadelphia and talked. His album *The Future* had recently been released and our discussion centered on it. It was a joy.

David Dye: On the *World Cafe,* we're not in our usual music studio as you can tell from the acoustics; we are backstage at the Keswick Theater in Philadelphia talking to Leonard Cohen between his sound check and the show this evening. You spent four years essentially, I guess, going through a lot emotionally and time-wise putting out the new record. Is it a relief to you, is it a reward to you, to go on the road and perform these songs?

Leonard Cohen: As they say in rock and roll, they don't pay you to sing, they pay you to travel. The concerts are a reward often, especially if they go well and especially if the people like it. That is the reward, you know. You spend most of the night on the bus, most of the day in the airport, and you just get here for sound check and you get back on the bus after the gig, so if the music itself doesn't deliver then you really feel you're cheating yourself. That's why we take it seriously.

DD: I want to talk some about *The Future*, which is a wonderful record. I want to talk about "Democracy." I understand that song has many more verses than are on the record?

LC: Yeah, there are about five or eight notebooks filled with verses for "Democracy." I took a long time to write this song. I started around '89 when the Berlin Wall came down. That's what really occasioned it. Because I asked myself, "Is the democracy really coming to the East? To the Soviet Union, to Hungary, to Romania," and I was very doubtful that democracy--- And I think it is the religion of the West. It is the real thing that we have going. And it's the American experiment. That version of it is the most vibrant. As screwed up as things are, this is the place where they're confronting the problems that they're just beginning to look at in Europe now: racism, real confrontations.

DD: So, its relevance to the U.S. election is just an historical perspective.

LC: Incidental.

DD: Let's listen to it. Here's "Democracy" from *The Future.*

LC: Okay, sure thing.

Leonard Cohen recording: "Democracy"

DD: That's "Democracy" from *The Future*, Leonard Cohen's latest album which is his second one. His first one in the 90s--- You had two in the 80s, that's. . . .

LC: What did I have in the 80s? *New Skin [for the Old Ceremony]*. No, no, um, *Various Positions* and *Recent Songs*, I guess.

DD: Well, and *I'm Your Man.*

LC: *I'm Your Man.*

DD: Another song that I hear as an AIDS metaphor is "Closing Time," and I was wondering if that had anything---

LC: AIDS?

DD: Yeah.

LC: I thought my song that talked about AIDS was "Ain't No Cure for Love," which I had a kind of reference to and, you know, there's a condom company that's about to put out an ad in Canada and I let them use that hook, "Ain't No Cure for Love." I think "Closing Time" is just the sense that things as we know it are coming to an end and that the flood is already here. The apocalypse is already occurred, there's no need to wait for it. You know, on the inner level all the landmarks are down and all the lights have been extinguished and all the signs have been swept away, so we are in this period of closing time. But all these songs, these sinister songs are married to hot little tracks.

DD: Yes! Absolutely. I guess that's what's really important about this band that you have traveling with you, being able to do all these.

LC: So the words melt into the music and the music melts into the words and you're left with a kind of refreshment, a hope.

DD: Well, there's certain Johnny Walker wisdom in this song; this is "Closing Time."

Leonard Cohen recording: "Closing Time"

DD: Kind of very much of a C&W—kinda warped C&W—feel to that. Country music was your first love, musically?

LC: The first band I was in was a little trio called the Buckskin Boys in Montreal. I've always been interested in country music and there are a lot of good bars around Montreal when I was growing up, where French versions of the Nashville standards were being sung.

DD: That must have been wonderful. Is that still going on?

LC: Yeah it's still going on. There used to be tour buses that used to go down from Montreal to Nashville.

DD: Oh boy.

LC: So there was always a country audience in Canada.

DD: I want to talk more about cover songs in a bit, and we'll get back to those days, *The Future,* in many ways--- The song "The Future," on *The Future,* is kind of a look at the present in a way.

LC: Yeah, you're the first interviewer who's said that; I appreciate that. Of course it's about the present.

DD: Did you write that at your home in L.A.? I could see some Los Angeles imagery.

LC: I started that song the same time I started "Democracy." All those songs were occasioned by the collapse of the Berlin Wall—which you had to affirm the rejoicing of people—but I did have a clear sense that this was going to produce a lot of suffering. And unfortunately that was borne out.

DD: "I've seen the future, and it's murder"; a bleak picture, but you always--- The redemptive properties of love seem to fit themselves in there somehow.

LC: This is all they're giving us, murder. I mean this is what we're fed, you know? "I've seen the future, baby, it is murder." Well of course that's a colloquial expression. "How hot is it? It's murder!" "What was the traffic like, it was murder!" But, I mean, it *is* murder. And that is the great unspoken secret that politicians hardly even address, that you can't go outside anymore.

DD: That perspective, what I was mentioning, you always seem to hold out love as the redemptive possibility in all this. Do you still feel that way as strongly as you always have?

LC: I always know it on a personal level, it's true. In that song, I say, "when they said repent, I wonder what they meant." The sad thing is those redemptive possibilities, those redemptive mechanisms, have become obscured and lost. All the religions have them. The whole notion of the resurrection is an idea of a return, of a renewal. Unless people understand and can grasp the idea that they can renew their lives, then we're in a very sorry situation. But those mechanisms exist; they're available, and everywhere from the Catholic Church to AA.

DD: This is "The Future" from *The Future.* Leonard Cohen.

Leonard Cohen recording: "The Future"

Rufus Wainwright recording: "Hallelujah

DD: That's just one example of so many other people's success with your songs. Are you still flattered when other people do your songs?

LC: Flattered is one thing, definitely, but "knocked out" is a better expression. When somebody does one of my tunes I go into immediate critical suspension. People ask me, "What do you think?" He's doing the song! That's good enough for me.

DD: I was talking to a member of your crew that said in Europe a lot of the bands, younger bands, Faith No More, I heard, would come to see your show.

LC: Yeah, yeah. I've always had a good rep for--- You know, my daughter's 18, she's in the crew here, and four-five years ago she began to tell me like, "Dad, a lot of the kids I know are playing your stuff. A lot of garage bands are doing this stuff." So I knew that something was cooking down there. But it's been very nice to see that what you have to say has some relevance.

DD: Well, I was just thinking about the film *Pump up the Volume* where "Everybody Knows" is used so effectively. It's kind of the anti-anthem for a generation.

LC: That was a guy from Montreal that made that film, Alan Moyle, my hometown.

DD: I'll tell ya what, let's listen to "Everybody Knows."

LC: Okay!

Leonard Cohen recording: "Everybody Knows"

DD: "Everybody Knows," from one album back, from our guest Leonard Cohen. You've done some video work. How comfortable are you with the visual interpretation of your songs?

LC: I don't care too much about it. You know, I recognize that it's a convention of the industry now that you gotta have one. Not that they ever play them. I've made some pretty good ones that they don't play. They play them in Canada where the culture is not dissimilar and nobody seems to revolt or rebel or anything. I made some pretty good ones, but they're not my work. They're the work of Dominique Isserman, who's a French photographer. She made a couple of them. And then we made "Closing Time" in Canada. It's real good.

DD: Oh I've never seen it; I'd love to see it.

LC: It won the Canadian, our Canadian Emmy, or Grammy, video award. It's a good little video. We made it in Toronto.

DD: We were talking about covers earlier. Do you have a favorite of Jennifer Warnes' interpretations?

LC: Oh, Jennifer Warnes has the best pipes in the business, I think, the most underrated singer in America. Her album of my songs is a little masterpiece. Almost everything she does is superb. I love her "Bird on a Wire."

> Jennifer Warnes recording: "Bird on a Wire"

DD: That's Jennifer Warnes' "Bird on a Wire" version of Leonard Cohen's song, who is here with us. Especially in this room where it's resonating so well, your voice has been described as the Barry White of folk. There are a couple of covers---

LC: [laughs] The Barry White of folk!

DD: There are a couple of covers on *The Future.* Have you ever thought of doing a reverse of *I'm Your Fan* and doing an album of other people's songs? Are there ones that you love?

LC: There are a lot of songs you really get into that you think you might do. You got a million plans but finally it comes down to the urgency of that moment, I mean, what are you going to spend it on? And usually I want to find out what I'm thinking about.

DD: I think I read somewhere, writing, you have to be in a place to write, it's your job to write, you can't write when you're doing this?

LC: No, I can't write on the road, I can hardly read. Television looks good to me.

DD: That's quite understandable. You have a volume of poetry coming out this fall?

LC: I got this compilation, this anthology, a very thick anthology of, you know, four or five hundred pages of selections from my very first book to the very last record. So it's quite a comprehensive, although not entirely complete, but comprehensive selection.

DD: Have you been editing that or has someone else?

LC: I helped with the editing. I finally gave it to an old friend of mine, a girl I grew up with in Montreal, Sam Street. She kind of made the selection with Rebecca De Mornay, and I kinda looked in.

DD: It's hard to be objective, I suppose.

LC: It's hard to be objective, and you just can't face the stuff after a while.

DD: Well, good luck on the rest of your tour. We appreciate you talking with us.

LC: It's very kind of you to come down, you know, I appreciate all the help I can get in this country; I don't get played that often and I really want to thank you.

DD: Great, it's a wonderful new record. If you haven't had a chance to spend time with *The Future* do it soon. We'll be back in a moment here on the *World Cafe*.

1993

RICHIE HAVENS

ONE OF THE MOST CHARMING GUESTS EVER ON THE SHOW was Richie Havens, who has been by a number of times. This time his visit coincided with the 25th anniversary of Woodstock. There was a big modern-day Woodstock in 1993, and then there was an impromptu free event at the original Bethel site. Richie Havens was there along with Arlo Guthrie, Melanie, and others like Soul Asylum. It has much of the spirit of the original Woodstock, which made Richie happy. I asked him about the original event and his famous performance of "Freedom."

David Dye: A lot of people know about you, at least visually, from your appearance at the first Woodstock. You know you've talked about wanting to play percussion; you and congas.

Richie Havens: Mmm-hmm.

DD: Is--- "Freedom" was essentially an improvisation.

RH: Oh yes, yes it was.

DD: [laughs]

RH: Because I had been on stage two hours and forty-five minutes and I just didn't know what else I was going to sing. By the time I went back the eighth time, they sent me back on the stage.

DD: They were trying to get other things together.

RH: Well no, there wasn't anybody else there to go on.

DD: Ohhh.

RH: I was the only person there besides Tim Hardin because they didn't have a helicopter big enough to fly the bands and their equipment. The roads were all blocked. That was--- There wasn't going to be a Woodstock. I might have been on there for two days. . . .

DD: [laughs]

RH: . . . if they, if the army didn't show up. And I always tell everybody that a lot in the movie doesn't really tell the real story. In fact it doesn't tell the story of what actually happened there. It shows a lot of the sense of time that we were living in, and it referred to through the music much more the lay of the land we were living in, you know, but if you were there and you took the camera all around the place you would have seen that a third of the people were over fifty years old. About forty thousand kids under ten were there as well. And it was not just sex, drugs, and rock and roll, as they portray it in the movie.

DD: Yeah, that's interesting.

RH: One and a half years post the event, three hours of which there for five days, [laughs] seven to eight days. So it's wonderful to be able to talk about it because I end up, you know, setting the record straight for twenty-five years, every single day of my life [laughs]. And that's wonderful to do, because a lot of kids want to know.

1993

WORLD PARTY (KARL WALLINGER)

KARL WALLINGER IS ONE OF ROCK'S GREAT CHARACTERS. He is the leader and, for all intents and purposes, the sole member of World Party. World Party began releasing their twist on classic rock conventions in the 1980s with the album *Private Revolution* and their masterpiece *Goodbye Jumbo*. Karl came into our lives with the release of his *Bang!* album. I wanted to include a bit of his wit and wisdom here, including the story of blowing up Mick Jagger's keyboards.

David Dye: You're kind of taking less time in making these records, it seems like. It was about a year and a half in the making, this last one?

Karl Wallinger: Oh yeah, I suppose so. I mean, it could have been a lot sooner, but there was a lot of, I guess it was--- Most of the songs that are on the record were sort of finished about a year before it sort of was finished. And then there was, like, a year of more recording and more sort of working things out that went on.

DD: So you like being in the studio.

KW: Yeah, I do. Yeah, I like having a life as well, you know. And I'm not too keen on actually coming out every three months and going around and doing tours and releasing a record three times a year. It would just be impossible, and also, the system today just can't really handle it, you know. To get sort of attention and to get what you call prioritized, it takes months of setting things up. It's not spontaneous at all, although the business likes to give the impression that it is. It's well thought out.

DD: What's your studio like? What's the environment in there like?

KW: It's just a funky space, really. It used to be an electronics company in England, and they invented really good things, but unfortunately seemed to stuff all the profits up their nose. And it's good because it looks out over London, and it was used as a fire watch. It's in an old biscuit factory and it was used as a fire watch in the war to look out and see which particular building was on fire when the Germans had gone over in their planes.

DD: A studio with a window, that's---

KW: Yeah, I mean, it's really good, you know. I sit behind the desk and look out at St. Paul's and I can see what the IRA have blown up today, you know.

DD: Now, I read a story about some other people trying to use your studio. At some point Mick Jagger wanted to use it, and you kept blowing up his equipment or something? [laughs]

KW: Oh, yeah, I blew Mick Jagger's keyboard up. I was just trying to do the world a service. No, I just got in there sort of early to set things up and was being very efficient and plugged his American voltage keyboard straight into the English voltage [outlet], and there was a lot of nice white smoke around, and he hadn't arrived yet, so I was a bit nervous about that. I seem to have this effect whenever I get together with people who I sort of like or have respect for or enjoy the company of, kind of thing. I sort of deal with that, put them on the right course. [laughs] Stay away from this Welshman.

DD: Well, [when you were playing] I had to stand on my head to figure out it was in the key of G, because Karl is left-handed and plays his---

KW: No, I'm actually not left-handed, but I made the foolish mistake many years ago when I was sitting opposite someone who played guitar that I'd put the neck out the same way, you know, like a mirror.

DD: [laughs]

KW: And I also thought, because I'm right-handed, why make all the difficult shapes with my useless hand? And I thought all you had to do with the other hand was go scrub-a-dub-a-dub as I do now, sort of, years later. There's some things I can't do, quite a lot. But there are some things I can do that other people can't.

DD: Have you thought through everything this thoroughly in life?

KW: No, obviously not. Or I wouldn't be doing this lark; I'd be a politician or something sitting in a big house somewhere being corrupt.

1994

BEN HARPER

HERE'S ANOTHER ARTIST MAKING THEIR DEBUT ON THE *WORLD CAFE*.

With Ben Harper we had a bit more of an idea of how his career was unfolding; he was already drawing crowds to live shows. The native of the Inland Empire area of California grew up around his grandfather's music store crammed with instruments. Folk, blues, soul, and later the music of Bob Marley and Jimi Hendrix were all big influences. His career has steadily grown and he has returned to visit us at the Cafe many times. I think this look at his initial visit gives great insight to who he was and who he has become.

David Dye: We're welcoming Ben Harper into the *World Cafe* today. His debut album, *Welcome to the Cruel World*, is a wonderful blend of some great slide playing. A great funky band you have with you, and some good songwriting, so I'm glad you stopped by.

Ben Harper: Glad to be here, David.

DD: Well you've got this instrument here, this is the first time I've seen it, and I understand it's a Weissenborn?

BH: Weissenborn, yeah.

DD: Weissenborn. Explain this instrument to people. It's not a Dobro; it's not any kind of a resonator guitar, but it's a slide guitar.

BH: It's hollow all the way up the neck. And it's got a square neck on it so it's only a slide guitar. You can't fret it.

DD: Right.

BH: And that's one of the qualities; it gives such a unique resonance, the hollow neck. Also, it's from the 19-teens/1920s. And it's made of koa wood. The whole guitar, back, sides and top, are koa. And I believe that koa has the best resonance of any wood for guitar making and---

DD: Why would that be?

BH: Just the koa guitars that I've heard have just all been incredible.

DD: Well, tell ya what; why don't you do something on the Weissenborn while you have it out?

Ben Harper performs "Like a King"

DD: "Like a King" [a song about Rodney King and the L.A. riots]. That's Ben Harper, our guest here on the *World Cafe*. How long after the verdict did you write that song?

BH: I suppose the next day.

DD: When you were doing that, I was thinking about folk music and what folk music is. You know, that's a folk song, written about you in reaction to an event. And you look at music being made in the cities today—rap—that's folk music, too.

BH: Exactly. Exactly. I say hip-hop and rap is the blues. They're direct. It's not the blues, it's hip-hop and it's rap, but they're directly connected for the fact that they both come out of slavery. The blues is a direct descendant of slavery, as is rap and hip-hop. It's just rap and hip-hop come out of legalized slavery, which is inequality and oppression. See what I'm saying? So often, people point their fingers and wave their hands, "Rap is so violent. Hip-hop is so violent." And there *are* offenders who go overboard, but at the same time, what about heavy metal, man? What about *Terminator*? What about the Eleven O'clock News? See, that's pure social irresponsibility. That's pure social irresponsibility. Heavy metal has some of the most violent lyrics I have ever read. I won't even go into the ones I've read and I don't even want to talk about them, but they're as bad as or worse than rap. But it's okay, right? No one says a thing. No, it's like if you watch the news the only drugs you think that are in existence are in the lower-income areas where, give me a break, there's far more drugs in the higher upper echelons of society and, you know, so on and so forth, but no attention to that, right? None. So, and my point is so many people are busy just pointing their finger at what they consider to be "the cause," when it's the effect. It's the effect. Hip-hop and rap are the effects of slavery. That's what you get when you hold someone down.

DD: Now you have a song called "Mama's Got a Girlfriend Now" that we've been playing the band version of. I was wondering if you could do a solo version of that.

BH: Definitely, definitely.

Ben Harper performs "Mama's Got a Girlfriend Now"

DD: Now there must be a story behind that one.

BH: Yeah there is, and I usually tell it before I play the song, too, just because they go hand in hand. I was at home watching the *Geraldo* show, you know, "Today on the *Geraldo* show, you will have women who have left their husbands for another woman." You know, it's just ridiculous man, it's ridiculous how--- It's really dangerous and it's the marketing, it's the continual marketing, of human degradation. This has led us to where we are and I refuse to let it take us where it wants to. I refuse to go with it. You know, go where that continual downward spiral is going. That's not how I live. See, I don't live that existence. I can't, man. You can't live like that. But it's, it's just dangerous. It's truly dangerous when a culture can consider other people's sexual preference their own business. I mean, is this country, is this culture so bored with their own sexual lives that they feel that they can consider other, that they can involve themselves in other people's relationships? I hope not man, because that's dangerous! You know what I'm saying? It's unhealthy.

DD: Oh, okay. People often think [that] when people's debut album comes out their career begins. But you've been doing a lot of touring since you recorded this. I was looking at your cases here with the Air France stickers on it; you went to Europe.

BH: Yeah, I've done quite a bit of traveling, even before the record has been out. I've been over to France and did the Rennes Festival there. Been up north before the record came out—Seattle, Portland, San Francisco, you know, playing around the L.A. area.

DD: Have you got a chance to play with anybody that you've been looking forward to?

BH: Yeah, John Lee Hooker, man.

DD: Ohh ho ho. Tell me about that.

BH: Yeah, great. He, he's the kindest man I think I've met. He's a wonderful individual. He's a wonderful human being just, you know, he's one of the last founding individuals of what I consider American classical music. So to illustrate what I mean by that, is that you say we listen to Bach and Beethoven now, you know, composers, the great composers from the sixteen, seventeenth centuries. As you listen to them now we will be listening to the blues in four hundred, five hundred years from now. He is one of the founders of what has established all of American music. John Lee Hooker. So it's an honor to play with him.

DD: It's interesting to see where samples are coming from on hip-hop records. You know there a lot of samples from jazz records now, but there are some people, I'm thinking of Arrested Development, took samples from a Buddy Guy and Junior Wells record.

BH: Yeah, exactly.

1994

AL KOOPER

AL KOOPER IS NOT YET IN THE ROCK AND ROLL HALL OF FAME, DESPITE THE FACT THAT HIS CONTRIBUTIONS HAVE BEEN EXTRAORDINARY. From essentially sneaking in to play organ on Dylan's "Like a Rolling Stone," to forming the original Blood, Sweat & Tears, and then discovering Lynyrd Skynyrd, his contributions have been extraordinary. He is a talented keyboard player and just as adept at telling a story. I sat down with him for this Blindfold Test to get his take on his work over the years.

David Dye: Our guest today has done it all, and usually in the right place at the right time. Keyboard man for Bob Dylan, for some of the most influential albums of all time; member of arguably the first progressive rock band of its era, the Blues Project; producer of some great records; songwriter; and he's sitting in front of me in sunglasses, and he's got a keyboard, so I guess he's going to play some for us today. Al Kooper has joined us. Welcome. A lot of people, at least I didn't know this--- I didn't realize you didn't start out as a keyboard player. You were a guitar player, right?

Al Kooper: Yeah, yeah.

DD: Why did you become known as such a--- I mean, you're a fine keyboard player, but why did you give up on the guitar?

AK: Because I heard Mike Bloomfield play.

DD: [laughing] Yeah.

AK: He was like light-years, we were the same age and he was like light-years ahead of me. I mean up until that moment I thought I was okay, you know. And then I heard him play and I said, "Well, yeah."

DD: And that was at a Dylan session?

AK: That was at the "Like a Rolling Stone" session.

DD: Right. I want to play some more things from here and talk, have you do some more things, but we have prepared combination of *This Is Your Life* and Blindfold Test because you don't know what we're going to play. But you were just telling me you were recognizing all these pop records in one-second bites, so I don't think you're going to have any trouble with what we're going to play for you today.

AK: Okay.

DD: So. We'll start at the first thing I knew about your career, which would be this.

> Gary Lewis and the Playboys recording: "This Diamond Ring"

AK: Yeah.

DD: Now is that you on glockenspiel or---

AK: No. I had nothing to do with that record. That record horrified me the first time I heard it. Turn it off! [laughs] Thank you.

DD: But you co-wrote the song, right?

AK: Yeah. I mean I like the song, but the record was so different than the way we wrote it.

DD: How was it when you wrote it?

AK: It was--- Let me see if I can do this. [playing keyboard and singing a slowed-down soulful version of "This Diamond Ring"] "Who wants to buy this diamond ring. . . ." Like that.

DD: Wow.

AK: So when I heard that, I was like, "Get out of here. It's a milkshake."

DD: [laughing] Yeah it is.

AK: My publisher, you know, called me in the office and said, "Hey we've got a record out this time." And he played it and I went, "Aw man." It just depressed me the whole day. Of course later on, I was very glad when it was number one.

DD: [laughing] Now did you get any money for that?

AK: Oh yeah, yeah. As a matter of fact, of my whole catalog--- That song's in the BMI, what they call the Million Airs Club, which means it's been played over a million times. So that's nice.

DD: Yeah that's incredible. Okay, number two on our test here.

> Bob Dylan recording: "Just Like a Woman"

DD: Wanted to get that little organ entrance in there. This record sounds so, you know, as time has passed, sounds arranged.

AK: It is, yeah.

DD: Is it, was it?

AK: The *Blonde on Blonde* sessions were very different from the *Highway 61* ones, in that we would record at night. We used to record during the day on the *Highway 61* ones. During the day, in the *Blonde on Blonde* sessions, I would go to Bob's room, and he had a piano in his hotel room, and he would teach me a song, and I would act as his cassette player or sequencer because they didn't have cassette players or sequencers in 1966, when we did this. And I would, you know [plays chord], play the song over and over, and he would sit there and write it, so that in the nighttime, I would know the song. So I would say, "Well let me go down there, why don't you stay here for an hour." You know, if the session's at eight o'clock, I say, "Why don't you come at nine o'clock and I'll rehearse the band, so you don't have to sit around while they learn the song, and then you walk in, bam, we can do it in one take," which I knew would appeal to him. And this particular one was done really late in the morning, like at two or three in the morning, and it's beautiful because it embodies that. You know, it sounds like it was done at two or three in the morning. It's really nice.

DD: Now the other difference is that it was cut in Nashville, as opposed to New York.

AK: Right.

DD: Was that your first time working with those musicians?

AK: The first time I'd ever been in Nashville, I mean, it was, you know, the whole thing was like a very amazing experience for me.

DD: Did you think you were creating a great record while you were doing it?

AK: I was much happier with it than I was with *Highway 61*, in that *Highway 61* is like a punk record, and this is like a real studio record, this *Blonde on Blonde*, and I guess I prefer that in some ways.

DD: Okay, next on our Blindfold Test.

Blood, Sweat & Tears recording: "I Love You More than You'll Ever Know"

DD: Our guest is Al Kooper, and using all the elements of your voice on that one—all octaves.

AK: [laughs] This is a period where I was writing some good material, but I hadn't learned how to write these things down to my own voice. So this song is like three keys too high on this record, and most of them are because I hadn't gotten that far yet. I was only 23.

DD: Hmm.

AK: That, to me, is "Child Is Father to the Man."

DD: Right.

AK: And the rest of it is Blood, Sweat & Tears.

DD: Gotcha.

AK: And so it's sort of embarrassing to me when, if somebody like hasn't heard that record and they say, "Oh this is Al Kooper, he started Blood, Sweat & Tears." Because I don't, you know, I don't want to take the rap for "Spinning Wheel," or any of that stuff, because you know that wasn't what I wanted to do. So it's my least favorite thing on my resumé.

DD: I want to play something else from the same period, because the whole feel of the record is so completely different. Were you looking to add more horns? Was that your idea with Blood, Sweat & Tears, to do an Al Kooper big band thing?

AK: No, no, not at all. What I wanted to do with Blood, Sweat & Tears was play rock and roll, with horns. Matter of fact, what Chicago did, especially on their first two albums. They were doing exactly what I heard in my head, except probably better than I could have done it. So it really worked out well for me. Because they went and carried the ball after I left, and did that thing that I wanted to do. And Blood, Sweat & Tears went and did something else entirely that wasn't what I wanted to do. But the fact that someone did do what I wanted to do is the important thing to me.

DD: Well, let's play this next track.

> Blues Project recording: "I Can't Keep from Crying"

DD: Much grittier-sounding band.

AK: Well yeah, this is--- We're out of chronology.

DD: Right. Yeah, I realize that.

AK: But yeah, Blues Project was a punk band comparatively. Again, same analogy; Blood, Sweat & Tears was, you know, the polished studio thing, Blues Project were punks. And I love the Blues Project, in retrospect.

DD: Now you've recently had your 50th birthday show at the Bottom Line. Who came to that show?

AK: The Blues Project played, and really was amazing. "Child Is Father to the Man." It was only the second time we'd gotten together in 25 years.

DD: Boy.

AK: So that was exciting. And then playing with the people from Rekooperation.

DD: Oh okay, you did three sets in one night. Wow, that's incredible.

AK: Yeah.

DD: Al Kooper is our guest. We're playing him some bits and pieces from various points in his career, and we move into Al Kooper, the producer.

> Clip of recording by Lynyrd Skynyrd: "Gimme Three Steps"

AK: You hate to fade it out. [laughs]

DD: I know; it's a great intro. Of course that's Lynyrd Skynyrd. Now this grew out of--- You formed the record company and found them? Or how did that work?

AK: It was sort of concurrent. I was in Atlanta, producing a record, and some guy I knew from my past was running a club there, and this band was playing there. And in those days you played for a week, so they were there every night. And by the second and third night I'm going, "Hey this is good," you know, "This is catchy."

DD: How were the sessions for you. I mean, it's pretty--- There's very little keyboards on the record, some, but I guess it's just making a record to you.

AK: The thing we had in common was we both worshipped the band called Free. That's my favorite band of all time, and I think it was theirs too. And that was really the thing we had in common. And we would do at least one Free song on every album; that was just an out-and-out tribute to Free.

DD: That's really interesting. And then, we have got some more, another production piece here, completely different.

> Clip from the Tubes recording: "What Do You Want from Life"

AK: You didn't play that one too long, did you? [laughs]

DD: Completely different-sounding band.

AK: The Tubes.

DD: The Tubes. Now how did you approach them, when you started working with them, your production?

AK: This was a—not this particular track, but this album in its entirety—was, the demos were like way over my head musically. It was like, "Whoa, what's this?" And so when I got the demos, I stalled them, I told them I had another project and I couldn't start their album for another month. And then I went home and learned that stuff. It took me a month to like learn it, because I had a lot of arrangement changes I wanted to make. And I couldn't do it in all good conscience without understanding the music first.

DD: I want to play one more piece because, I've heard, you know the piano part here pretty well.

> Clip of Muddy Waters recording: "Long Distance Call"

AK: Got to be Otis Spann.

DD: Otis Spann on piano in the Muddy Waters Blues Band. I guess Luther Johnson doing the vocal on that version of "Long Distance Call." You were an Otis Spann fan, I've heard.

AK: Big, big Otis Spann fan. He used to give me lessons at the Cafe A Go-Go. It was great; couldn't have a better teacher.

DD: Now he always--- He was such an embellisher of things, he's got such a great right hand sort of. What did you learn from him?

AK: That right hand [laughs].

DD: Yeah?

AK: Oh yeah. [plays on keyboard] Stuff like that.

DD: Now he made a number of great

solo recordings, which we get a chance to hear what he really does on those. Did you know him when you were playing at the Cafe A Go-Go? You were with the Blues---

AK: That's where I met him.

DD: Yeah, did you know his recordings before that?

AK: Yeah. Not very much before then, because when I joined the Blues Project was when I learned about the blues, because growing up in New York, they didn't play much blues on the radio, believe it or not.

DD: I believe it. I definitely believe it. We haven't really talked much about keyboard players. Have you developed affinities for different people at different points in your career? When you were really young, who did you admire? And who do you really get into now?

AK: When I was really young I admired Jerry Lee Lewis and Otis Spann. Then my middle period was Horace Silver, and Bobby Timmons, and Thelonious Monk, Dave Brubeck. And now it's Johnnie Johnson, and Dick Hyman, and Reese Wynans is really good too.

DD: Thanks a lot for coming by and playing our semi-piano here.

AK: No problem.

1994

LEO KOTTKE

SOMETIMES LEO KOTTKE SINGS, ALTHOUGH HE DOESN'T LIKE HIS VOICE. He has been known to liken it to "goose farts." But his acoustic guitar playing on both 6- and 12-string has always been intricate and graceful. Kottke's heyday was in the 70s and his recordings for Capitol Records befuddled many a bedroom guitarist as they tried to duplicate his dexterity.

I've always found his recordings satisfying and his manner charming. His visit to the *World Cafe* was much anticipated, partially because it was delayed, as you will read in the interview. He joined me to promote an album, recorded with Rickie Lee Jones as producer, called *Peculiaroso*. She is the "Rickie" referred to in the interview. Also mentioned in the interview is another giant of American acoustic folk guitar, John Fahey, who passed away subsequent to this interview in 2001. This interview is a personal favorite because I am reminded of the ease of conversation with the master at his instrument.

David Dye: We are very happy that Leo Kottke has joined us. I say that we are very happy because he was supposed to join us once before and he was a casualty of one of the great ice storms of '93 and '94. Do you remember what happened that time?

Leo Kottke: Yeah, I was a casualty but I lucked out; I made good use of it. I hung out with a saxophone player in Washington. A tenor I think it is. Bill Clinton. I went down to see a friend of mine, Shawn Colvin, who was playing in the place where I played the night before. And George Stephanopoulos listens to her and there were a bunch of people there. It was nice. It was really nice; it's the second president that I've been in close proximity to.

DD: First one being?

LK: Being Kennedy. The only thing he ever played was a cigar, I think.

DD: [laughs]

LK: He had one at the time. I was holding a trombone when that happened; I was playing it on the White House lawn.

DD: School band.

LK: School band.

DD: Well, I was trying to add up how many records you have had out and my calculator broke, but I know this is your sixth for Private Music. Is it hard to make the recording process interesting each time you approach it again?

LK: It's not hard to make it interesting because it has an element of terror that never goes away. The only thing that it resembles is embalming. I can't imagine anything to compare it to except that. It's not like taking a picture of a performance. You can do it that way, but it's not really the way records are made anymore.

DD: Preservation of a piece?

LK: Yeah, of a performance, a snapshot of something.

DD: Well you've got the six-string up now. Do you want to do one on that?

LK: Sure, let me play something off of a record; what is it now? Two before this one, called "Odd Ball."

Leo Kottke performs "Odd Ball"

DD: "Odd Ball" from our guest, Leo Kottke, a perfect example of something that I wanted to ask. I mean, as difficult as it must be to compose that, I would think that the real challenge would be in naming all of these songs.

LK: Oh, it's tough. This one was originally called "Jane's Nut Bread." I decided that was too granola-y. Jane was the wife of a guy who used to send me pieces of his fingernails in the mail and I didn't want to commemorate that, so I decided to pick on the nut bread. Ah, so I changed it to "Odd Ball" and I really wish I would have left it as "Jane's Nut Bread."

DD: You do a great diverse set of covers on your records, but this one is particularly good in that it really strikes a chord in me because I think the only slow record that AV crew had in my high school was Bert Kaempfert's "Wonderland by Night."

LK: [laughs] The AV crew.

DD: They were always in charge of the dances, of course.

LK: Yeah, yeah. That tune is, I shouldn't interrupt you, but it seems to hit that spot with a lot of people for a lot of, with a lot of different tastes, you know? Some of them don't want to admit it, but once you're playing it, they will.

DD: It's a slight guilty pleasure, I must admit.

LK: That's right.

DD: Reminds me of Mr. Acker Bilk, things along the same time era.

LK: Sure, yeah.

DD: What made you think of that? Just the melody?

LK: Well, what I found out was, at least to my ears, a lot of those tunes, which in their original setting can sound pretty corny, fall into the guitar perfectly as if they were written on a guitar. There's just something about them that makes them stand up and walk. And they lose, they lose for me, any association they might have with that, you know, kind of commerce that they were a part of then. And so out pops this melody that has a benefit of being familiar, and they're frequently really inventive, very hooky melodies, and at the same time brand new.

DD: Now that has a really nice string quartet on it that Van Dyke Parks did.

LK: Right.

DD: Have you worked with him before?

LK: No, we have threatened to do that. I made two records with my musical idol Buell Neidlinger as producer, and they're old friends, and it almost happened then but it didn't, and I finally got the chance to do it with Rickie.

DD: Could you do a string quartet-less version of that?

LK: Sure.

LK: [playing a few chords] You know, Bert Kaempfert invented the click bass. You know, that sound that we really don't want to hear again [strikes a chord]; it was more muted than that, [plays a few more chords] with a guitar actually playing another octave up in unison with it, but just a clink. I think that's how he got his first million.

> Leo Kottke performs "Wonderland by Night"

DD: The immortal "Wonderland by Night." Leo Kottke is our guest. Now, did the arrangement of that change up from what you recorded?

LK: Well, let's see. This stuff where it jumps a half step [plays an example on his guitar], I just make something up every time that comes around. Otherwise it's pretty close. Oh no, the most Bavarian part of the tune is now more Bavarian than it was on the record. As a matter of fact, he used the same Austrian trumpet player. He also invented the lonely trumpet, you know, that guy-in-the-other-room sound, and on all of his hits except this one; and on this one he imported a Bavarian.

DD: [chuckles] I wonder why.

LK: I do too, and I'm sure the Austrian is being told every day of his life, "You know the one that I really like, your best job was. . . ."

DD: How do you decide what's a six-string piece and what's a twelve-string piece?

LK: It usually happens on the instrument that I'm playing at the time. I mean, an idea pops up because it's generated by the guitar. I don't really--- They don't precede themselves in my head. My head, as we had been discussing earlier, doesn't work that way, or that well. So it depends on where my affections lie, I think, in general. And I'm hot and cold on the twelve-string sometimes, very much in either direction, rarely neutral about it.

DD: You mean you wouldn't ever do a whole show and not play one or the other?

LK: Oh I did. For quite a while I played nothing but twelve-string, and then recoiled in disgust one day and did nothing but six-string for a while, and that really didn't work. I could get away with, excuse me, with all twelve-string though, and that told me something. It's really when I took off as a guitar player, I mean in terms of developing some technique, was when I found my first twelve-string, and I think that's what got my audience in the beginning.

DD: Yeah, I was thinking about that too. I want to talk—if you want to play a piece on twelve-string, that would be great—I want to talk a little bit about John Fahey.

LK: Great.

DD: I know he was a big influence on you and I'm not sure everybody knows that much about him. But why don't you do a twelve-string piece?

LK: Okay, this is on the new record, and it's called "Peg Leg." And I named this for Rickie, but I'll tell you about that later.

Leo Kottke performs "Peg Leg"

DD: That's the one that starts off *Peculiaroso*, called "Peg Leg."

LK: "Peg Leg," yeah, for Rickie's grandfather who was a dancer in vaudeville with one leg. Peg Leg Jones.

DD: [chuckles] Sort of a tap and a thunk.

LK: Yes, that's right. [chuckles] Or maybe just a thunk thunk thunk. That'd be pretty impressive.

DD: Well, it's funny, your fame at this point has far exceeded John Fahey's fame, who was the first person I knew who spent a lot of time playing his own music on acoustic guitar in sort of the genre that so many people do nowadays. Were you playing guitar before you heard his playing?

LK: Yeah, as a matter of fact I had been playing for quite a while and I was playing--- What I'm getting at was there was a Canadian guitar player and I wish I could think of his name now.

DD: Robbie Basho?

LK: No, I can't think of it, but who told me one year, he said, "You know the first time I heard Fahey I thought he was doing you." I usually get the reverse of that. That was a--- John is the guy, John's, I think, a real cultural hero. We don't have many of those, and he's the genuine article. And you're right; I don't think this kind of guitar would be around if it weren't for him. Maybe it would have found its way in some other fashion, but he kind of made it what it was; he got the point of view, he synthesized all the sorts of elements, he found the laugh in it for one thing, and for sure. I see him now and then, and he's still playing, still working, still records. He's living in Salem, Oregon, now.

DD: If you have an encyclopedic memory of his, pick a Fahey piece that you might want to play here.

LK: Oh, let's see, well [strums his guitar] one of the first ones that caught my ear was an arrangement that he did of a tune, of an Episcopalian hymn.

Leo Kottke performs.

DD: That's a John Fahey arrangement and Leo Kottke is the guitar player. Now, he always played well slowly; that's one of the things that was so beautiful, *is* so beautiful about his playing. I hate to talk about him in the past tense.

LK: It's true though, you don't hear much of him and part of that is due to John. You know, for a long time he didn't want to go out and perform. But on the other hand, he created a record label, Tacoma Records, and recorded people like Charlie Nothing and the Psychedelic Saxophone. He was the first guy to record Charles Bukowski.

DD: I didn't know that.

LK: Whose only requirement on his [Bukowski's] rider was that there be a refrigerator full of beer on the stage with him when he did his reading. I think it was the Golden Bear where he did that.

DD: You've mentioned a non-affinity with singing, but I was wondering, I was thinking about one of your songs that was more like talking, which would be

"Jack Gets Up." Would that be something that you would be able to do?

LK: Sure, yeah, give me a minute again here to tune this thing [tunes his guitar]. So this is called, "Jack Gets Up." I wrote this after smoking a cigar that Joe Pass had given me. I was flat on my back when I started, and even worse about halfway through the cigar.

Leo Kottke performs "Jack Gets Up"

DD: Leo Kottke is our guest. I don't know what's better: the kid with a face like a walnut, or the snort fort [chuckles].

LK: [chuckles] You know, I get letters about the snort fort from kids whose faces probably screw up like walnuts. They like that but they're not sure of it. I have another one about a dog that bursts into flame called "Husbandry," and the kids--- Lately I get more mail than I used to from little kids, I mean little kids, you know, sometimes their parents have to write these for them. They love "Husbandry," but they want to know why the dog had to burst into flames. They don't like that.

DD: [sighs] Well, thanks a lot for coming and playing for us.

LK: Thank you.

DD: Leo Kottke, our guest. We'll be back in a moment here on *World Cafe.*

1994

JONI MITCHELL

WE TRAVELED TO NEW YORK CITY TO RECORD JONI MITCHELL IN A SUMPTUOUS HOTEL SUITE. Just to meet Joni, let alone interview her, was a thrill. To add to my nervousness, my boss at the time, Mark Fuerst, who I didn't know very well, asked to come along. We are ushered in and Joni is on a couch, introductions are made and we set up our gear. Joni is a chain smoker. It's not so much, "Is it all right if I smoke," as, "Got a light?" So she smoked, we talked, and I took her matchbook as a souvenir. As you can tell, she was thrilled that we actually wanted to talk about music.

David Dye: Joni Mitchell is our guest on the show today. She has released her 17th album back on the record label where she started, Reprise. She is a poet, a painter, a pinball player, and . . .

Joni Mitchell: [laughs] Anything that begins with P.

DD: . . . one of the most influential musicians of our time. I'm glad you could be on the show.

JM: Thank you, it's nice to be here.

DD: We're going to be introducing people to *Turbulent Indigo* and talking about that, and hopefully some other work; have you pick some other music that's been influential to you over the years.

JM: All right.

DD: There's some new musical textures, and there's this buoyant music with these harsh reality songs. Is it a challenge to you to talk about serious subjects in these songs and keep them non-ponderous for people?

JM: I've always felt that usually the music comes first, and so, you know, you're in search of the right text, and the music dictates plateaus which will hold a long, narrative, descriptive passage. And certain chordal movement shows you, the chord dictates a short and clear statement you made here. Like Noël Coward—I've been listening to him over the weekend—made some very heavy statements to some very light music.

DD: For instance?

JM: From Noël? Oh God, I mean, a lot of it. There's a song that I had never heard before—[sings] "What, what, what's going to happen to the tots? What's going to happen to the children, when there are no more adults?!" And this was written in '55, I think, about, and we have everything now, appliances and so on, and Mummy's going for her facelift and, you know, like, Mummy and Daddy are as high as kites, Benzedrine, you know, it's about the drug/facelifts culture. But it was written in the 50s, so this was a very, very, very visionary song for the times.

DD: I want to talk about certain songs on this record. It seems to me, listening to this record the few times that I've been able to so far, "Sex Kills" and "Job's Sad Song" kind of seem like centerpieces for the record. "Sex Kills," really powerful song, the irony that sex is used as the lure that keeps our society, economy, everything, kind of going, and yet, sex kills.

JM: Well, the strange thing if you look at it like in terms of a hundred years, or the turn of the last century, we were also in the midst of a sexual plague which had no cure, and the reaction at that time under the guidance of Queen Victoria was to pretend that sex didn't exist. So it was very extreme in the opposite direction; even the legs of things were considered suggestive, and Victorian furniture was frequently skirted to cover the legs—anything, "Ooh, a leg," you know, like it might imply a glimpse of stocking. So here we have another sexual plague at the turn of the next century and yet the fashion designers, like, have you running around in your underwear.

DD: Let's listen to it. This is "Sex Kills."

Joni Mitchell recording: "Sex Kills"

DD: From *Turbulent Indigo* that's "Sex Kills." There seems to be more acoustic guitar texture on this record; maybe it's just the way it's mixed in. Did you set out to do that?

JM: I set out pretty much the same way nearly every time, with the exception perhaps of two projects, and that being the

Mingus project, where I wasn't an instrumental player but the writer and the singer, and *Dog Eat Dog*, which was more collaboration than usual sonically. You know, I played a lot of that stuff, but those colors were set up for me either by Thomas Dolby or Larry Klein. But ordinarily it begins with the song, with the voice and the guitar or the voice and the piano, and then I orchestrate. If I want to put strings on I go straight to a string sound or a stringy sound. Like all the strings on this album, for instance, are distilled from remnants of fabric left by a guitar player named Bill Dillon. We make them into—my husband, Larry Klein, it's hard to title him, Larry Klein, my ex, it's hard to--- You know, we're still in each other's lives. He distills these pieces of fabric that Bill leaves for him into orchestral sounds that we used on this project in lieu of the usual string section, so the music is really kind of like a guitar orchestra. "Job" has a lot of Billitron on it in the background string passages that you hear that sound like strings.

DD: Yeah.

JM: It's a collaboration of sound between Bill Dillon and Larry Klein, Billitron—synthetic strings.

DD: Going back to the beginning of the record, it begins with this very visual short stark song, "Sunny Sunday."

JM: It's the shortest song I ever wrote.

DD: Where did that come from?

JM: Oh, just a bit here and a bit there, the way songs do, you know. I had a friend, a painter, who had a roommate who was a painter, and from time to time she took pot shots at the streetlights, you know, so, you know, an image here and an image there.

Joni Mitchell recording: "Sunny Sunday"

DD: You're a painter. And songwriters, a lot of them, actually, have referred to the creative process as resembling sculpture in that you chip away at words to refine them. Does being a painter influence how you work or think about music?

JM: Yeah, I would say so. To me, music has a visual--- I see it kind of like fluid architecture; it has gables. I know that--- Okay, within the limited range of my guitar, which is broader than normal guitar playing because of the tuning so that it's orchestral range, so that where there would be an E on the bottom there may be a C or a B-flat. It definitely has more bass than normal guitar playing, and I tend to think of the upper three strings as a horn section, and the sixth string, the thumb string, as the bass, and the mid-range is like celli-viola. So when I add other players I usually give them minimal instruction in a lot of tracks and I let them play and discover the music without much guidance, and then I edit them after they're gone, so that too is compositional. And since a lot of the songs are modular in form, even if they play a figure I like on the third verse and

I want to put it on the first, with the aid of Fairlight and tools like this I can move what they played around and compose them in that manner. So it's more like collage for the ears, or tone poems. I kind of see the notes in terms of, you know, especially linear players like horn players, the line is breaking too soon, or, you know, when it comes to the editing, why do I reject this line and thrill to this particular piece in twelve takes, say. Okay, it's the way that little silver line adheres to the rest of the drawing, either because it's loose and lovely there or because it's just beautifully tight and parquet, or because it's playing—in "Yvette in English," for instance—off the lyrics so well. In the last verse of "Yvette in English," you hear Wayne playing the high heels of the girl walking away. He's a pictorial thinker and plays more than notes, you know, he really does play like a tone poem.

DD: Let's listen to that. This is "Yvette in English."

> Joni Mitchell recording: "Yvette in English"

DD: "Yvette in English," another track from *Turbulent Indigo*, one written a few years ago with David Crosby.

JM: It was the first of this collection of songs.

DD: It was part of this to begin with?

JM: It was really David's project, you know, that triggered it. David called me up and he wanted me to produce him. The way his album was, he had different people produce him, and David's never been a prolific writer, so he asked me if I had--- First he asked me to produce him and I said, "Oh, I don't believe in producers, really, you know, I don't think I could do that." I don't like being produced myself, you know, like, I'm unproducible, frankly, so how could I produce anyone else, you know?

DD: Right.

JM: So anyway, he came back again and said, "Well, do you have any songs?" And I said, "No, I don't have any at this point, you know, I'm just beginning to write." "Well, would you look at some lyrics of mine?" he said. So he faxed me basically just some jottings; there was no rhyme, no structure. There was a premise—girl meets boy in Paris; there were some images that needed paraphrasing; and there were some good lines. So I phoned him back and said, "Well, what do you want me to do with this? You want me to mark on it, you want me to mark your paper, or what?" And he said yeah, so I said, "Okay, I'm going to mark you as hard as my seventh-grade teacher did," who made a poet out of me, you know? So I circled a lot of it, "cliché, cliché," [laughs] and sent it back, but in the process I took some of the clichés and paraphrased them and next thing I knew I had a few rhymes going and it came together fairly quickly. So out of this premise that he had, and a few good lines like, "So quick to question her own worth," or the chorus line, which is, "She offered him a little bit of instant bliss," "Un-insulated wires laid bare," these were some of the good lines. There were some strange ones like, "You look like Picasso drew you." [laughs] I said, you know, you could just see a breast where the eye should be, you know, and an ear in the navel. So the thing I thought of was a quote from Picasso. He was standing in some beautifully scenic place and he said to the people with him, "Ahh, if I was a painter I'd paint this," and so that line evolved to, "'If I was a painter,' Picasso said, 'I'd paint this girl from toe to head.'" There was another line, "The moonlight spilt like wine," we wrote that to, "Burgundy nocturne tips and spills, they trod along nicely in the spreading stain."

DD: Really beautiful, I like that line.

JM: To get the rhymes too, you know.

DD: I want to get back to talk more about *Turbulent Indigo*, but I wanted to talk about some other records. I wanted to talk about Jaco Pastorius because, of all your collaborators, he and Wayne Shorter are playing on a lot of your records. It's so beautiful, it breaks my heart in a lot of ways.

JM: Thank you, I appreciate you appreciating Wayne, especially. A lot of people appreciate Jaco, but I don't think a lot of people really hear how splendid Wayne is.

DD: Not a man of many notes, but he weaves them so well. You tell him to?

JM: No, no, I wipe holes in it, [laughs] a lot of it, you know, but he is economical. But he has the freedom in that climate to just explore without any concern. There's no worry as to whether he plays--- He can just stretch out knowing that the best of what he lays down will be chosen, and also that, you know, he can play through areas where I don't want him to play, but I can always put silence in there.

DD: Yeah. I know you're a Miles Davis fan.

JM: Yes.

DD: Was that where you first heard Wayne, on those records?

JM: Yep. *Nefertiti* and *In a Silent Way*.

DD: Well, pick something--- It's hard to pick something from *In a Silent Way*, but pick something from *Nefertiti*.

JM: *Nefertiti*?

DD: Yeah.

JM: Because that's an amazing piece of music. Now, to jazzers it's a very strange form. It's really Wayne's composition. The melody is haunting and strange, you know, wonderful intervals. Even the starting note is an unusual starting note. And the fact that it's kind of almost like a folk structure, it's not a standard structure like jazz is normally played—around a longer melodic form—but this is like a verse-verse-verse-verse structure. And Wayne and Miles begin playing in unison fairly tightly, but they begin to pull apart and phrase their own way. It's almost like a 50s silkscreen, you know, where one color is laid a little offset over the next color of the printing. In the meantime, the free instrument on it is the drums, so you have Tony Williams just purring. He's like, it reminds me of living in Soho as I did for a long time, like you hear drunks at four o'clock in the morning, really pissed off at God-knows-what, screaming at the sky and knocking over everything as they walk along, kicking garbage cans and, you know, it's just got that long-walk-from-downtown-to-uptown-in-an-angry-state to it. [laughs]

DD: Miles Davis, Wayne Shorter on saxophone.

Miles Davis recording: "Nefertiti"

DD: We're talking with Joni Mitchell about--- Actually, I mentioned Jaco and then I mentioned Wayne Shorter too, so we ended up playing something from Miles Davis from *Nefertiti.* I was curious about working with Jaco because--- Was recording *Hejira* as free-flowing as it ends up sounding on the record? Did you all play together?

JM: No, I had my vocal and my guitar part down for the most part as I usually do before I bring in players, with a few exceptions. But in that case Jaco was added after my performances were laid down, I think, for the most part, though I'd have to listen—I haven't listened to the record for years—to be absolutely sure that that's true.

DD: Right. How did he come to mind to record that with you? You'd been playing with him?

JM: No. What happened was, I was hearing the bass as I learned, as I was adding colors to my own music. I had opinions about them, and one of the things that disappointed me when bassists came in to play on the music was, why did they always root the chord? I mean, when they would play, it seemed so predictable to me, everything that they played, and I would be disappointed. I'd think, "Well, it's not thrilling me, it's so predictable," you know, and I didn't really know why. So I would encourage them to lift off the bottom and go up into the midrange, and travel around and throw in something and come back down, and they'd say--- There'd be rebellion. Also, the sound of the bass at that time was--- Bass players didn't change their strings; dead strings were in vogue, and I craved a more resonant, round, ringing bass sound, and you couldn't get them to go against the hip. You know, everybody was hip together, and this was the way it was. They were all hip, and this was hip and that wasn't, and they wouldn't do it. So when the first keyboard/synthesizer that had some presets on it, the first one

I ever saw, it was called a Farfisa, and it was sitting out in the hall at A&M, and I said to my engineer, "Henry, what is that?" And he said, "That's a Farfisa." "And what's it doing there?" "Oh, it was on a session and they're coming to pick it up." "When?" And he said, "In half an hour." I said, "Drag it in here." So we dragged it in and I worked out a bass part for—on *Hissing of Summer Lawns*—for "The Jungle Line," and I tried to get Max Bennett to play it, and he wouldn't play it! I said, "Why not?" And he said, "It's not playing the root of the chord." "Why does it have to play the root of the chord? Why can't it lift up into the midrange?" "Well, it just can't." You know, I said, "Well gee, harmony seems to have so much more freedom on the upper end; why is it so locked in on the bottom?" Well, I tried a lot of bass players and I guess they all heard this lament: "Well, why, why, why?" Finally somebody said, "You know, there's this kid that plays in Florida; he plays with Bob Hope and Phyllis Diller in some of those showplaces. He's a really weird bass player," they said, "you might like him." [laughs] So I sent for Jaco and when he showed up with that sound, you know? He had a terribly bushy ego, I mean, I loved it. He offended everyone in town in a very short space by saying things like, "I'm the baddest bass player in the world. I'm not bragging, I'm just telling the truth!" But to me, you know, he was telling the truth because he wasn't playing the root of the chord! He was zipping up and playing little Stravinsky countermelodies and, you know, it was just thrilling. But, I mean, he did mix himself up really hot in the mix on that album, like, you know, I had more of a blend between him and the guitar, but he kept going, "No!" and he'd push himself. I'm almost his background singer on *Hejira*. But, you know, that too was a new idea; the bottom end of music was changing. Stevie Wonder was one of the pioneers, and I took people over to Stevie's because he was using Moog bass, and saying, "Look, you know, the rhythm is not ptt ptt, you know, all these little ditzy sounds and these dead sounds, you know, the kick with the pillow in it and, listen to what Stevie's doing!" You know, Stevie's one of the great composers of this century. People don't like to admit that because he's working in the pop arena; it upsets people. And he's black, you know; it upsets white people, you know: "We don't have black geniuses," you know? [laughs] But he was a real musical innovator. But all of that--- It was just hard to buck the hip, you know; the hip was a very communal concept.

DD: Well, let's play something from *Hejira* after talking about it. Let's play "Coyote."

Joni Mitchell recording: "Coyote"

DD: "Coyote" from Joni Mitchell. We were talking about the bass player on most of that album, *Hejira*, Jaco Pastorius. Probably one of your biggest influences on a lot of people has been your guitar sound and your tunings. I was wondering, on your first record, you were using your tunings. When did you first discover what you could do?

JM: Almost immediately when I began to write my own music. I had polio and my left hand is a bit impaired. I was never going to develop the facility to get at the chords that I heard in my head. There were tunings floating around that came out of the black blues tradition, mostly open major chords, and there was D modal which was, you know, the dropped D, and—or the dropped D's—and people knew of those. And of course there was a Hawaiian slack key tradition, but that hadn't really leaked into folk music much at that point. So it was Eric Anderson who showed me open G, I think, Tom Rush played in open C. I collected a few of them, I think Buffy St. Marie had a couple of her own. I just started tuning the guitar to the chords that I liked.

DD: Are you still developing different tunings?

JM: Oh yeah, I have fifty. Fifty tunings, and those are the ones that I've written songs in. So for every one of them, I probably lost--- I've probably come across maybe seventy-five tunings at this point and lost them just because I didn't write anything in them.

DD: I'm curious, and I was trying to figure out a way to get to this, the voicings that you develop with these guitar tunings, do they have any bearing on the wonderful intervals when you stack your vocals on records?

JM: I just think that's my innate sense of harmony, because it goes over to the piano too. Wayne said to me---"Ethiopia," for instance, he came in to play on that, and he said, "Well, these are not guitar chords and these are not piano chords. What are these chords?" So idiomatically, to him, the harmony was different. I don't know why, I mean, I know the vocals have parallel seconds. Somebody told me that, you know, the dissonance was necessary. When you think of these women, you know, with these babies with flies in their eyes and their ribs sticking out and homeless and foodless, walking somewhere with some kind of vague optimism, the harmony is not going to be in a major key. [laughs] In that particular situation, it would be unsuitable.

DD: Right. So we'll play "Ethiopia."

Joni Mitchell recording: "Ethiopia"

DD: We're back on the *World Cafe*; we're talking with Joni Mitchell. I saw you performed a lot of this material at Edmonton at the folk festival over the summer?

JM: A little of the new and some of the very new, which is not on this record yet, and some of the old.

DD: How did that go?

JM: It was lovely.

DD: Are you comfortable performing? I know you haven't performed in a while; would you consider doing that? Or is it mostly--- I heard it was a physical problem, holding instruments.

JM: Yeah. I am a polio survivor, and we now have kind of another gauntlet to run, it turns out. It's kind of like, post-polio syndrome is a little bit like multiple sclerosis, you know, your wiring is kind of burning out. And also you don't metabolize correctly, so you can't--- extremes in heat and cold, same with MS, you can't--- air conditioning, fluorescent lights, all these things weaken you, you know. So, the muscles in my back, a lot of them are gone, you know, and the ones that are left are being driven by wires that are--- One wire that should be driving one muscle is maybe driving three or four, and they're weakening, and so the contortion that you put yourself in guitar can lead to pain, and I don't want to---[laughs]

DD: Yeah, right, right.

JM: I don't like to think about it too much, but that's part of the reason. The other reason is not a pretty topic either, but I'm not an arena artist, and my music doesn't suit big halls, and the cost of renting little halls is amazing, and we are surrounded--- The artist pays all the expenses, everybody's hotel rooms, and last time I was out I was out nine months, you know, I made less than the roadie. You know, people don't realize, the artist is the last to get paid, so to go out for a period of time and break even is not attractive in my condition.

DD: We talked to Rickie Lee Jones a while back, and she talked about a wonderful peace offering you sent her and. . . .

JM: Yeah.

DD: But she wrote her own bio when she made her last record, and this is a little funny story I wanted to read here. She said she was born in Chicago on November 8, 1954. "Bonnie Raitt and I are born on the same day. We learned this many years ago in Seattle riding in an elevator together. We were talking about---" She was talking about having met Bette Midler at a big party. She came up to Bette and Bette was wearing a dress in which her breasts were prominently displayed in a friendly way . . .

JM: [chuckles]

DD: . . . and Rickie Lee says that before she realized it she just reached out and cupped one of them in her hand, "Like one might appreciate a fine sculpture," she says. And Bette was kind of taken aback. She was laughing at this when Bonnie reached out and said, "Oh, you mean like this," and of course she reached out and held Rickie Lee's breast. And then she goes on to say, "I like to think that Joni Mitchell, who was born on the 7th of November, would actually stop just before the moment of contact, to smile, light a cigarette, something like that. . . ."

JM: [laughs]

DD: But then she goes on, and this is the part I would really love to get your comment on: "The point of this is nil," she says, "except that lately I have begun to feel a certain affinity with women where I once had a vague vacant disdain. Women were invited guests in a private club, and in order to gain membership the old boys who ran the place would always liken you to that other woman they had let join," which is something, sort of, what you're talking about, about the people who ended up being compared to you.

JM: God, my mind ticker-taped over a lot of territory in there.

DD: Yeah, right.

JM: I don't really have anything too focused to say about it. Well, what people call "the new Joni Mitchell, the new Joni Mitchell"--- I don't see--- They're girls with guitars. To me, they all have their own identity; I hear very little of myself. But do you hear much Edith Piaf in me, or Billie Holiday? Maybe a little? You know, but it seems strange to me, for instance, like, to hear myself referred to in one place as a jazzer and in another place as that folk singer from the 60s, you know? [laughs] And a lot of my roots are in rock and roll and swing era and classical and, you know, black southern blues, and it's like, I like a lot of different kinds of music.

DD: In honor of the fall, I was playing a couple days ago Tom Rush's "Urge for Going," and I was just playing it as, you know, "Here's another record," and four people just kind of wandered in with this glazed look in their eye talking about what a big effect that song, and actually in many ways that album, had on people. Besides Fairport Convention, was he the first person to record your songs?

JM: First the playing, and when the recording came out I'm not sure, but it opened up certain clubs for me. Club 400 for instance, which was very cliquey and hard to play, like, and Tom's playing my song kind of heralded and opened the doors to some club work. Buffy St. Marie also took a couple of songs and traveled around with them. Dave Van Ronk took a couple, and George Hamilton IV recorded "Urge for Going" too, and it was a country hit at that time. And then later Judy Collins. So yeah, all those people. . . .

DD: Pretty much at the same time, I guess.

1994

SARAH MCLACHLAN

THE 1990S WAS THE DECADE OF THE SINGER-SONGWRITER, and nowhere was that more apparent than in the Lillith Fair, the all-female concert tour organized by the Canadian singer-songwriter Sarah McLachlan. The sense of purpose and the idealistic concept that the Lillith Fair encompassed was already a part of Sarah's vision when she joined us to talk about what became her breakthrough album *Fumbling Towards Ecstasy.*

Once again we had little or no forethought that she would become the cultural figure she did as the 90s progressed.

David Dye: On the *World Cafe* that's "Possession," the lead track from *Fumbling Towards Ecstasy*, a wonderful title, we'll find out where that one came from. Sarah joins us in the studio, welcome!

Sarah McLachlan: Hi.

DD: "Wait" is a track we've been playing. What's that song about? If it's easy to answer.

SM: It's not, really. I mean, it's sort of about loss of innocence and that sort of feeling that--- With every generation there's a group of individuals who will go outside of the norm and outside of society and will be the outcasts and will try to make a difference, but it seems eventually that they all get sucked back in, or they lose their minds completely. So it's kind of a sad thing for me, but I still have that sort of idealism.

DD: Thank God.

SM: [laughs] Yeah, I've got to have it.

DD: Hard to believe that when you were signed your record company knew you could sing and knew you could play, but had no idea that you could write.

SM: Blind faith, I call it, yes. They--- I am amazed, the longer I'm in the industry and the more horror stories I hear about how artists get sort of eaten up, especially whether they know what they're doing or not. I was so lucky for Nettwerk to find me and give me that opportunity.

DD: A lot of your songs are not real specific as to, they're not very visual, necessarily, or certain places, but there's one song on this new one, "Good Enough," that seems to have a few specific touchpoints, things that happened.

SM: Yeah, in the past my songs have been pretty ambiguous and vague. Yeah. I've gone through a lot of emotions and different types of things within every song, because usually they span four to six months in writing, and then I sing about the songs in this record, like I said before, they came out really cohesively. "Good Enough" is one of those songs that came out in almost a day, and I don't really know where it came from. I know now, but when it happened it just sort of came out. But it's sort of a song--- it's sort of about my mother, in one sense, and it also was inspired by another singer-songwriter in Canada called Jane Siberry. And she is going around doing these [performances]—this is not a concert-concert kind of thing—where she shows her videos and she does spoken story and stuff, and one of her stories was aimed at her mother and their relationship. And I don't know quite what grasp I had on it, except that it affected me tremendously, of the relationship she had with her mother, and the women of my mother's and her mother's generation of being so completely out of touch with their bodies and not really having any friends to talk to about everything. Like, I have amazing female friends—and this is another thing it came from—that I can say absolutely anything to, and I trust them to be able to say these things to and to talk about and work things out. And my mother's generation is just, "Oh, let's not talk about it." And so I sort of wrote that for her, on the perspective of, "I'm not just the daughter anymore, I want to be your friend now."

DD: Well, if you could do that one, it's one of my favorites on the record.

SM: Yeah, thanks. [strums]

Sarah McLachlan performs "Good Enough"

DD: Sarah McLachlan's our guest. That's "Good Enough." It's helpful to hear you talk about that song before you hear it, because you could see a lot of different things in it.

SM: Well, and I write that way for a reason, too, because I want people to relate it to their own lives. And I want also to--- As much as I do write from a very personal and emotional point of view, I need to save a bit of it for myself, for my privacy. I can only give out so much, and thus the ambiguity.

DD: That makes sense. Now, you've mentioned this; you're originally from Halifax. And I learned something today I didn't realize—that if you're from Halifax, you are indeed a Haligonian?

SM: Haligonian, Blue-Noser, there's a number of them. [laughs]

DD: Oh, okay. But now you've moved to the other side of Canada. You're in Vancouver, which seems like a great city. What's Vancouver like? Is there a music scene?

SM: Yeah, there's a pretty diverse musical culture happening. I mean, there's a lot of blues, a lot of R&B, a lot of jazz, a lot of industrial-type alternative bands that have been there for a number of years. And then of course there's Nettwerk, which is this sort of in-house thing that they've got, all sorts of different kinds of acts. It's really nice, I mean, especially within Nettwerk, all the bands know each other and we tend to use each other from time to time musically and stuff, so it's really kind of a big family out there. And of course it's beautiful. There's mountains and ocean and still relatively—I said relatively—unpolluted. It's getting bad, but it's a big city and it's getting incredibly bigger. Every year there's a huge influx of people coming from all over the place. Everywhere in Canada—everywhere else in Canada—is depressed, so they're all coming to Vancouver because there's work, so it's filling up really quickly.

DD: Sarah McLachlan, our guest. Another one from *Fumbling Towards Ecstasy*. Whose title--- Who came up with that? That's a wonderful phrase.

SM: I've been trying to use those words. Actually, they came to me at first in a different configuration from a Wilfred Owen poem called "Dulce et Decorum Est Pro Patria Mori." And he was talking (he's a war poet), he was describing the soldiers in the field; they were getting gassed. And for some reason I just fell in love with his poems. I guess because they were so beautiful. But they were talking about something so horrible, and the way he melded the two things together, two complete opposites, and made it sound so beautiful. He was a total romantic too, this guy. He was talking about an ecstasy of fumbling, gas, gas, quick boys, and an ecstasy of fumbling as they tried to fit on the masks so they wouldn't die, and he was watching people not make it and fall and stuff. And that little phrase stayed with me for all these years. I think I heard that first in grade nine or something like that, and I've always wanted to use it. But "an ecstasy of fumbling," or "fumbling towards ecstasy," how to fit that into a song? It's quite a--- pointed, pointed words. And I thought, wow, what a simple, beautiful metaphor for my life, for what I'm trying to do! I mean, you can put in the place of "ecstasy" any adjective or whatever, anything, whether it's inner peace or nirvana, or whatever. I think I'm definitely trying to reach that. And being human and making mistakes, I think, for me, is one of the greatest learning things that I have. And there are mistakes all over the record. And another interesting thing for me is that there were mistakes, and we tried to take them out, and I realized that the mistakes were what made it wonderful, because they were what made it unpolished and human. So it seemed like just a perfect title, and I said, I've always wanted to use those words, so there it was. And it also--- Another great thing is that it made people laugh. When I told Arista, they laughed. They said, "Yeah sure." And I was like, "No, really!" And I think they didn't believe it. And it's nice, because people would laugh and go, "Oh, right on!" And before, my two past records, *Touch* and *Solace*, have been very melancholy and dark, and I really wanted to get away from that because, myself as a human being, I'm so much--- I've always strived for happiness. But I really feel like this album, there's places and moments on it that you can really see that. So I wanted to dispel that depressed myth, you know?

DD: Thanks a lot for coming by.

SM: My pleasure, thanks for having me again.

1995

BRANFORD MARSALIS

I'VE ALWAYS BEEN A FAN of Branford Marsalis's playing. The saxophone-playing brother of Wynton in the great New Orleans musical Marsalis family is a solid tenor player. It was a no-brainer to have him live on WXPN, the station that produces the Cafe, for a guest DJ session. This happened when his *Buckshot LeFonque* project came out–a funky, jazzy pop record. At the time, he was on leave from his position leading the *Tonight Show* band, a position that he gave up shortly thereafter.

When people ask me about my favorite interviews over the years, I often mention this relaxed afternoon hanging in the old on-air studio with Branford. We really had a great time playing and talking music. I think he enjoyed himself as well. At the end I asked him to sign a copy of one of his older albums, *The Royal Garden Blues.* He wrote, "I had a really great time," underlining really. So did I.

David Dye: On the *World Cafe*, our guest this afternoon, Mr. LeFonque.

Branford Marsalis: Mr. Branford.

DD: Mr. Branford Marsalis.

BM: LeFonque's the group, it's not me.

DD: Oh, okay, there you go. But it was Cannonball's name for himself?

BM: Well, in a way.

DD: Yeah.

BM: It was--- I've actually read it. I don't know, I guess it's wrong in my bio, because I didn't write that thing.

DD: Oh, yeah, yeah.

BM: They said that he would use that name whenever he played on pop projects, and it's totally untrue. What it was, was that a lot of jazz musicians or a lot of musicians at the time was subject to those—it's actually going on even today—these ego wars between record companies. So if like Cannonball Adderley was called by a great musician like Wes Montgomery, and he says I want to play on this record, he says, "Oh you can't; we don't like Blue Note today."

DD: [laughs]

BM: So you just do the session anyway and you use a name that's so absurd, that they say, "Wait a minute, there's no way a guy's name is Buckshot LeFonque," so then you really listen to it and say, "Oh, it's Cannonball." You know, and Charlie Parker . . .

DD: Charlie Parker. Charlie Chan.

BM: . . . used to be Charlie Chan.

DD: Yeah, right, I remember that.

BM: There are a lot of instances. Kenny

Washington, the drummer out of New York, he knows all of the aliases.

DD: Cool.

BM: He has a list of all of them.

DD: Well we're going to play "Some Cow Fonique" to get things underway.

BM: Cool.

DD: And you've got some records picked? We'll play some music?

BM: I guess so, yeah.

DD: All right, this is "Some Cow Fonique" with Branford Marsalis.

> Branford Marsalis, aka Buckshot LeFonque, recording: "Some Cow Fonique"

DD: He's probably still playing.

BM: Yeah, right. [laughs]

DD: "Some Cow Fonique." Branford Marsalis is our guest. That's one of the tracks on Buckshot LeFonque. Now tell me about this whole project because you must have approached it completely different than you would making, you know, a straight-ahead jazz record, definitely.

BM: Actually no, I approached it the same way. It's just, the thing that's great about music, to me, is that if you really think about it in the right way, good music transcends all of the limitations we spend so much of our lives trying to place on it. Because there's a line of logic and all the good music is above it, and all the mediocre stuff's at it, or below it, you know? And when you go above that certain line of logic, which is impossible to explain, it's just like everybody has this general understanding of what it is—you have this transcendency that doesn't matter whether you're listening to Wagner, or Hendrix, or Led Zeppelin, or Earth ,Wind & Fire, or James Brown. It's just this thing, and just you're there and you hear it and it's euphoric. It's orgasmic even, to a degree, it's pretty--- So when I was making the record, I thought about it the same way that I would think about doing a jazz record, except I realized that the style and the sounds would be completely different.

DD: Right. Well I was listening to the Maya Angelou tune "Caged Bird" on the way in, and one thing—I don't know if it worked out this way—but it sounds like you've picked up the rhythm of her speech and wrote the thing around that. And I don't know if it's just a happy happenstance, but is that---

BM: No. Well what it is, is everything in the world to me is an instrument. And the voice is an instrument. And I think that that's one reason this record is so interesting, is that we don't use turntables as though they are turntables. The turntable is an actual instrument; the sampler is an instrument. I didn't actually meet Maya until eight months after we'd recorded the song. She sent me a tape of her saying it. And we cut up what she said and used it like in a sampler; we just put certain parts of it. So I laid it in as though she was playing a trumpet solo.

DD: That does float, I love that. That's great.

BM: Oh thanks.

DD: Great piece of music. So tell me about this live group that is going out playing this stuff. You've got some great players on the record. Roy Hargrove's on the record; we were just talking about him. Nils Lofgren . . .

BM: Nils Lofgren, yeah.

DD: . . . does a little piece on that track. Who's playing, and how hard was it to get it all together?

BM: It was easy. It was relatively easy because you hire musicians based on their ability and not their name. And some of it, it hinges upon whether the name players want to do it. For instance in percussion; when I think percussion I think Mino Cinelu and, end of conversation. But for the most part there are a lot of good musicians around; it's just a matter of finding them, and hearing them.

DD: I wanted to talk a little bit about your family and coming up, and I wanted to play a little bit of a piano player here who plays on one of your early records here.

BM: I wonder who that guy might be. [laughs]

DD: I want to talk a little bit about him.

BM: Yeah.

DD: Play a little bit of this.

BM: Okay.

Branford Marsalis recording: "Swinging at the Haven"

DD: That actually goes back to the first record of yours I bought, *The Royal Garden Blues*, and that's your father on that version of "Swinging at the Haven."

BM: Right.

DD: Ellis Marsalis.

BM: That's his song, actually.

DD: Yeah, and it's a beautiful song. I really, I love the version of it. Now how old is that song?

BM: Oh man, '57, something like.

DD: Really?

BM: My grandfather owned a motel during the days of segregation. He owned one of the two colored motels, as they called them, that were around during the time, and his was more popular.

DD: The Haven.

BM: Yeah. No, it was actually called, "Marsalis's Mansion," but my father somehow, and you don't understand how, I would be diplomatic and use the word "frugal," my grandfather is.

DD: [laughs]

BM: So I don't know how he talked my grandfather into allowing him to open this club, called The Music Haven. And of course my father would be the owner, the proprietor, and the band every night. It was his band, and basically it was a way for him to practice. [laughs] He'd get paid to do it.

DD: Oh, okay.

BM: You know, and every now and then some musicians would come and he'd book musicians in The Music Haven. I think Coltrane played there once. But basically he had this band called the A.F.O. Jazz Ensemble—All for One Jazz Ensemble—and he wrote this song for them called "Swinging at the Haven." And I heard it on an old record that Harold Batiste, who's like the cousin of---

DD: The New Orleans---

BM: Yeah he's a big New Orleans guy, and he's basically dedicated his life to researching and re-releasing old New Orleans recordings. And he re-released this record that my dad made in the 50s, and I heard the song and said that's a pretty cool song. And Delfeayo [Branford's brother] said, "Well let's play it." And I said, "Well I have to rearrange it a little bit, Delph, you know, I don't want to play it like that." So, and he said, "Well you should get dad to play on it," because Delfeayo's like, the one--- he's constantly Mr. Family Guy, you know, "Get everybody in the family on the record." I'm like, "Shut up, we're not doing that."

DD: But tell me about this, I mean, you know, there are lots of families who have a lawyer for a dad, and not everybody in the family grows up to be a lawyer. Was it---

BM: It was an accident.

DD: Yeah?

BM: It was just complete coincidence that we became musicians because we didn't really have one of those musical families that you keep hearing about, "You grew up in a musical family." No, we didn't really talk about music a lot in our household, but there was an extensive amount of dialogue in the household, and a tremendous amount of philosophy flying all over the place, constantly. And most of the arguments we had in the house were philosophically based, and not, you know, regular like, when they talk about sibling rivalries. Wynton and I are very different in a lot of ways, and those arguments were based on our differences, not on, you know, "Why do you always sleep on the top bunk?" You know, "I wanted that girl you go out with." We didn't really have that kind of--- but we did have these, you know, and still do have these marvelous philosophical, you know, diatribes about the existence of God, and humanity, and why we behave the way we do, and you know. [laughs]

DD: How did he react to the Buckshot record?

BM: Oh we stopped talking about music a long time ago.

DD: Oh yeah?

BM: Because music is an extension of everything else that you live in your life anyway, so we know how we feel about that and it's just asking for an argument, you know. He didn't even--- I've seen him two or three times, whenever he's come to California since the Buckshot record came out, because I was in television land and couldn't leave.

DD: Right.

BM: So he never brought it up, and I never mentioned it.

DD: Hmm, interesting. Well you've got a bunch of CDs there, why don't you hand me that Elton John record.

BM: Okay.

DD: Because I am interested as to how you ended up doing an Elton John tune on the Buckshot record.

BM: Well I was ten years old when I bought my first album. I was very proud of myself. I saved up money that I had earned doing chores around the house, and I bought Elton John's *Honky Chateau* and Cheech and Chong's *Big Bambu.*

DD: [laughs]

BM: Which is essentially my philosophy on life [laughs]. So I was like every other kid in the universe; you buy an album and you play one song on it, the single, over and over again. And my father would always lambaste me, "Man, it was ridiculous to spend $3.99"—which is what they cost then—"$3.99 on an album and only play one song. This is absolutely absurd. You should play the whole record." And finally I started playing the whole record, and I fell into that song, "Mona Lisas and Mad Hatters."

DD: Mmm.

BM: Which is--- I fell in love with. And at that time I was not even considering being a jazz musician. So I said if I ever make a record, one of the first songs I'm going to record on the record is "Mona Lisas and Mad Hatters." So it took me, what, 25 years from the time I made that promise to myself, 24 years, but I kept my promise to myself by working on this song. And even though ours is dramatically different from his—his is a ballad, ours is a little more up-tempo—it's just I'm a huge Elton John fan.

Elton John recording: "Mona Lisas and Mad Hatters"

BM: Oh man [laughs].

DD: Elton John, a pick of our guest. Branford Marsalis is with us here on the *World Cafe.* [laughs] We said pick five records, and that is cruel.

BM: That is really cruel.

DD: But I wanted to talk about--- You picked out *Nefertiti*, Miles Davis, and I was mentioning to you that we did an interview with Joni Mitchell, and she picked something from *Nefertiti* too. It's interesting because there's just a lot of records in that same period, with Miles in the same group, and I'm kind of wondering---

BM: Well that was the first one for me.

DD: Yeah.

BM: That was the first one I heard, that's why I picked it. It's not that--- Well it's a favorite of mine because it was the first one I'd heard in that style. I was a big Wayne Shorter fan because I was introduced to Wayne Shorter from Weather Report, like in '74, '75. I think *Black Market* was the first Weather Report record I heard. And then picked up all the other records after that: *Tale Spinning*, and *I Sing the Body Electric*, and on and on and on. And I was a fan of Herbie Hancock from the Headhunters Band. And my father's band actually opened for Herbie one day, and Wynton and I went to the show and we talked to Herbie for like 35, 40 minutes before the show, just talking. He was really skinny then, with a huge Afro and a dashiki, but he still had those freckles, you know.

DD: [laughs] Right.

BM: And I had never heard any of the Miles Davis material with Wayne Shorter and Herbie Hancock; I had no idea who Tony Williams or Ron Carter was. That same year I picked up a Tony Williams record that he did called *The Joy of Flying* on Columbia. It was like a really eclectic commercial record type of record, and before they unceremoniously dropped him from the label. But I didn't hear this record until I was a freshman at the Berkelee College of Music, and my roommate at the time, Mr. Marvin "Smitty" Smith, said, "Man, you know, you ever heard this record?" I went, "What? *Nefertiti*, Miles Davis." And I started reading the back. I said, "Wayne Shorter? Is that the same guy that played on Weather Report?" He says, "Man, where have you been?" He said, "Yeah, and it's the same Herbie Hancock too." You know, and he put on the record and then absolutely blew my mind because that record opened an avenue to me for playing jazz that I didn't think was possible before, which is why I didn't pursue it.

DD: Such a group concept on this record.

BM: Well it's such a group concept and the harmony is so advanced. I just had this idea that if I was going to play jazz I would just be regurgitating bebop licks, like a lot of other guys that I hear, even now, are guys that I'd heard in the late 70s, in the early 70s, mid 70s, late 70s, 80s, and the guys that were playing around Berkelee. I'm like, "Man, I don't want to do this for the rest of my life," you know? "There has to be an avenue to approach this music in a way that you can play the music of Charlie Parker, without trying to sound exactly like Charlie Parker." And then when I heard this record, I said, "Uh oh. Bam."

Miles Davis recording: "Hand Jive"

DD: Wayne Shorter, Miles Davis, Herbie Hancock---

BM: Ron Carter, Tony Williams, "Hand Jive," off the album *Nefertiti* on CBS.

DD: Your DJ, Branford Marsalis, joining us on the *World Cafe* today. Grammys; you're nominated for "The Star-Spangled Banner."

BM: Yeah, right. It's a pop song once again.

DD: Yeah, yeah, interesting. Well I wanted to bring that up because it's with---

BM: Bruce.

DD: Bruce Hornsby. Well I wanted to play something from the *Trios* record that Rob Wasserman made, which you and he and Rob did a cut of together. Now was this done together, in one room?

BM: Yeah, well, what it was, was, we were doing some Levi's commercials, with me, Bruce, Rob Wasserman, and Jerry Garcia. We were doing a Levi's commercial---Spike [Lee] wanted us to play. He was doing, Spike was doing, his series of Levi's---

DD: Right.

BM: This was for one of the things; he wanted some really ethereal music. So we were planning on getting Rob, and in his wonderful voice was like, "You know, Bran, I'm working on this trio of records." Sounds like Jack, you know what I mean.

DD: [laughs] Right.

BM: "And I was wondering if you and Bruce could do a song?" I said, "Well we don't have a song." And Bruce says, "Well I have one." I said, "Well here we go, let's just do it right here while we're here." And we knocked it out in about, you know, 45 minutes.

Bruce Hornsby, Branford Marsalis, and Rob Wasserman recording: "White Wheeled Limousine"

Earth, Wind & Fire recording: "Serpentine Fire"

DD: Earth, Wind & Fire from *All 'N All*, a wonderful, wonderful record and influential to our guest today. Branford Marsalis is being the guest DJ. We're talking about Buckshot LeFonque and all kinds of things. That, I know, that's a wonderful record. You know, sold a whole lot of copies. How did you come to that?

BM: Well this friend of mine, actually, Kermit Campbell—the piano player who's in the Buckshot band—Kermit Campbell and I would talk daily about music. And the day it came out, he called me up and said, "Hey man, Earth, Wind & Fire, new one's in the store, right now." So Wynton and I jumped on our bikes and we drove down to the record store to pick it up. And it was in the box; they hadn't even opened up the box yet. And we like convinced them that even, you know, we knew how much the records cost, so they just gave us one without the stamp on it; we bought it and took it home. And usually, it was my job in the band to learn all the arrangements, because all the other guys in the band were like getting women and just being trifling and lazy. So I would learn all of their parts, which like, you know, pissed my mom completely off---

DD: [laughs]

BM: ---because she felt I was being used. And I was trying to explain to her that by learning all these parts it was helping me because I was learning the function of each instrument, you know, the limitations of each instrument, so if it came-- if I ever had the opportunity to produce or write an arrangement, I would understand the function of every instrument in the band just from doing these arrangements. And for the average pop tune, I mean, it'd take you 45 minutes to write out an entire arrangement because it's like the same stuff over and over again; it's really simple. When this record came out, man, it took like two weeks for one title. "Serpentine Fire" was impossible, because there were so many things going on. And it was one of the things that, as I look back on it, it was great to be a teenager and actually be frustrated listening to a pop record, trying to learn it, whereas today you really don't have a situation like that, where you have really accomplished musicians playing commercial music. It's just funny when you think back as a kid, when we were listening to this stuff, it's like, "We will never get this." Whereas now, if I had to do an arrangement like this, like writing for *The Tonight Show*, man, you know, 25 minutes tops. It's just amazing how your mind can adjust, you know, as you grow older, you know. Things that seem really advanced are really quite simple.

DD: Indeed. Somebody wanted to find out some more about the Buckshot LeFonque record, and one of the things is there's a track where I know you use some material that's already been recorded by Béla Fleck and the Flecktones. But Victor Wooten, their bass player, is listed on this. Does he play or is it just the sample?

BM: Yeah well, what it was, was this. We had— I was listening to their record, I can't remember, I think it was *UFO Tofu.*

DD: Right.

BM: And they have a song called "Sex in a Pan." And with my warped mind I'm listening to that section where it breaks down. [scatting] I said, "Man that would make a great rock tune." So I just took the sample, got the clearance, and got David Berry—who's the guitar player with Janet Jackson, who's an amazing guitarist—to come in and just play eight tracks of Marshall distorted rock and roll stuff on it and change the entire nature of the sound. And Victor was playing on the show, and I said, "We're working on this song with your sample." He says, "I want to hear it." So he comes down and we're listening to it and it is cool. And what we wanted to do is do the first machine-driven breakdown that I'd ever heard where you don't have live drums, and it just breaks down and the whole song pops down and you just have this little beat. And I says, "Man it would be great if you just come in and play something on it." And he says, "Well I have my bass in the car." So towards the end of the song when Albert Collins is playing that killin' solo, you can hear Victor very clearly playing in addition to the sample. And he just has such an amazing ear, like he would--- It's little things, he would play along with it exactly like he did on the record and then just throw little [singing bass]. Just like amazing stuff.

DD: He's a great player. We're just going to pick this up in the middle of---

BM: Towards the end, yeah.

DD: Yeah.

Buckshot Lefonque recording: "No Pain, No Gain"

BM: Victor Wooten.

DD: Not to mention the guitar player.

BM: Oh pretty good, huh?

DD: Yeah.

BM: Albert Collins. I miss him a lot.

DD: And this was one of the last things he cut?

BM: This was *the* last thing he cut.

DD: Wow.

BM: We had actually--- When we were doing the *I Heard You Twice the First Time* tour, Albert was the guitar player. So we had actually been on tour for about six months, and then when I, you know, got him on *The Tonight Show*, and he came in the studio, I just found out he had cancer, but I don't think any of us realized how severe it was.

DD: Hmm.

BM: So he came in, you know, I said,

"Do you want to play on this song?" He said, "What kind of song?" I said, "A hip-hop song." And he just couldn't stop, "A hip-hop song? Damn." And he starts laughing. The whole time he's in there saying, "You crazy man, got me playing on a hip-hop song." And he just kept playing.

DD: You sound great.

BM: Yeah, we actually, we want to release another version though because I actually have like eight minutes left of him just playing. I just want to do a version where, like, just the Albert Collins version, where the groove comes up and he just starts playing.

DD: Branford Marsalis is our guest. We're talking about *Buckshot LeFonque*, which is his latest project, latest band, which is out on tour across the country, and for a while.

BM: Yeah.

DD: So is this what you're going to do with your entire time off, is do this? Or---

BM: This is what I took the time off for. This is what I'm doing.

DD: Yeah. How hard is it for you to play otherwise when you're doing *The Tonight Show* thing? It must be frustrating to you.

BM: Well it would have been easy if that's the only thing that I were doing. If I was just doing the show, then I'd go and play a gig here, or a gig there. But my son lives with me, he's in school, I have to take care of him, help him with his homework, do this, cook the meals, uhh, the whole thing.

DD: Yeah, yeah. Life.

BM: Life, yeah. The rest of my life really makes it difficult, and projects come up—a soundtrack here or there, or a recording project—and I would always, the performance would always get sidetracked. And I just really wanted to be in a situation again where the people that came to the show came to hear us; where we were the primary reason for them to go.

DD: Makes sense. I want to thank you for coming by.

BM: My pleasure.

DD: Really appreciate it. We've got one more of your picks, which is the Marvin Gaye record.

BM: Marvin Gaye.

DD: And pick something from that.

BM: This is such a seminal record for me, because they say that a couple of Marvin's other records have been concept albums. And they were concept albums to a degree, but I feel they were, in terms of lyrically, they were concept albums. Musically the songs didn't really seem to come together. Or they were like, you know, just . . . recapitulations of the original. This one is amazing because the music and the lyrics actually go together. I think that this is an album called *Here, My Dear*, that part of his divorce agreement is that he would make a song and the proceeds would go to his ex-wife. But I don't really think that they thought he'd make a record like this. And it was very heavy for me to hear it; it was an amazing--- I couldn't believe it. I was eighteen years old, I was in college, and I just couldn't get over this album at all, you know, because I'd never really heard a person with that much pain just put it out there for the world to experience. And it taught me a valuable lesson, when this record came out and the public didn't buy it. It taught me a valuable lesson on what you're dealing with when you deal with commercial music, and it's a lesson that I've never really forgotten [laughs].

1995

MICHAEL STIPE

I'VE BEEN A BIG REM FAN SINCE *MURMUR*, and was very excited when we heard that Michael Stipe was going to stop by for an interview. We love to have performances on the *World Cafe*, but I figured Michael was going to be a pretty interesting guy to talk music with.

At that time we usually set things up in our threadbare third-floor studio, but this time we figured for rock royalty we'd use the station's conference room with the incredible hand-carved woodwork. We set things up and Michael arrived with a posse. We are used to managers and record company reps, but Michael Stipe had about 10 people along including someone videotaping the whole thing. So I did this interview with an audience, yet Michael was totally engaged.

It was right after their album *Monster* was released. It was also shortly after Mike Mills had his appendix out and Bill Berry had an aneurysm on tour. In fact, Michael himself was recovering from surgery for a hernia.

David Dye: On the *World Cafe* today, Michael Stipe is our guest. Welcome. Thank you so much for joining us.

Michael Stipe: Thanks, happy to be here.

DD: We know that you're a supporter of public radio. Doesn't the band like sponsor Mountain Stage in Athens or something?

MS: Yeah, we do.

DD: And you did that show---

MS: And *All Things Considered* we sponsored as well.

DD: Well thanks a lot for supporting this show; it's great to have you here. We saw the show last night and I want to talk a little bit about it.

MS: Okay. It was kind of a wild night. Sometimes Thursdays are like little weekend, you know, and last night was kind of of like that.

DD: I wasn't sure if it was a good one or if it was---

MS: It was okay. It was okay for me.

DD: One of the things that I thought was really interesting now that you're, you know, an arena band--- You defy this arena, you work very hard at it, defying it from the lighting to everything.

MS: Yeah.

DD: I mean, it was very club-like last night.

MS: Good, that's good. Yeah, I mean, I feel really comfortable with a--- We're not really that new to arenas; we've been doing them since 1987 on our own. But I never liked going to a show and having all the stadium gestures kind of thrown at me, and feeling like I was getting the same rap between songs that whoever is talking was doing the night before, and the next night and the next night and the next night. And so, you know, we mix up the set list a lot and play new songs, we play some old songs, and I try to communicate between songs without coming off like a puppet.

DD: I like that, because you were making fun of the conventions as you were doing the parts of the conventions that you sort of had to do. You've got to say hello to everybody.

MS: Yeah.

DD: You know, you got to go, "Hey Philly!" you know?

MS: We started the tour with me not doing that. I mean, I kind of consciously set out not to talk between songs, or not to talk at all, because I think on the last tour I really talked too much and it's uncomfortable for the band—they don't know what to do—but at the same time you don't want to come off as smug and sanctimonious. You don't want to come off like you're offering the audience the privilege of having come to their town to perform for them. You want to let them know that you're really excited to be there, but it's hard to do that without saying, "Hello Philadelphia! Let us rock!" So, I mean it's all too easy to mock and make fun of the whole, the way that the whole thing is set up; that's a little too easy. To communicate something more powerful than that, not only through the music but with what you're doing and saying and how you're composed on stage, to me is a little bit of a broader stroke. And that's not a bad thing.

DD: You are very kind to people in the audience, particularly younger, more alienated people. You said a lot of things and dedicated a lot of songs to them. You know the people in---

MS: Yeah, well I always want to be in the last row because that's where it's really happening, you know? [laughs] Because you can't really see what's going on onstage, it's more of a vibe of being there and, you know, really every night what I'm--- It's my job because I'm the front person or I'm the vocalist, so it's my job to basically communicate with the audience. And what's going on there is an exchange of energy, and that's the wild card every night. We could get up and perform the same set and kind of march through it—clock in, clock out. But every single audience is completely different, and sometimes it's a real struggle to get that energy flowing and to make--- without sounding very, very hippie-ish, and sometimes it's really, really easy. Sometimes they throw a curveball at us. We played in Richmond, Virginia, last week, and you know even though we haven't toured in five years I can look out and there's kind of a standard for the audience. There's, you know, I kind of know who's going to be out there. And Richmond, Virginia, there was all these rave kids that were like fifteen years old, and they were doing the rave dances to "Crush with Eyeliner" and to "Losing My Religion," and that was kind of a shocker for me.

DD: What songs are constant? What songs do you end up having to do every set?

MS: The songs that we like that we do--- We always do "Losing My Religion," and we always do "End of the World" and we always do "Country Feedback."

DD: Yeah, you said that was your favorite song.

MS: It is.

DD: Of this week or of a---?

MS: No, I guess of the year. I mean, we started--- When we made that, when we recorded that song for whatever record it's on, I can't remember, we performed it once and that's the version that went on tape. It was actually a demo tape. It's on *Out of Time.* And then we didn't play for three years, and so it's kind of a new song for us in a way, but it's one that we all really like a lot.

DD: That's interesting, that not being one of the big hits is one that you all want to do every night, and that's great. I mean that's such a touchstone place for you all in the set. There were some amazing visuals that go along with this show, but not in—I'm not putting them down, but not a U2 bombast thing—but very subtle things, and I wanted to find out about the clips that were shown. Were you involved in putting those together?

MS: Yeah. What we did was, having decided that we wanted to have films behind us, we had to decide between film and video. We chose film and went to a lot of independent filmmakers who we really respect a lot, and basically said, "What would you like to see at an REM concert?" Some of them are with us today, actually—Lance Banks. And they put forth some ideas and we checked off a whole lot of them and they went off and filmed this stuff and put it together for us.

DD: You would take a song and say, "These are the images that this conjures up for us?"

MS: Actually the films change from night to night, from song to song, so there's really a lot of--- Nothing is really that---

DD: Really? There are a lot of water images. I mean, it is one thing you did last night.

MS: Water, yeah.

DD: Which was wonderful, with the naked people and things. It was just beautiful, beautiful stuff.

MS: Yeah that's Jem Cohen, a filmmaker from Brooklyn who did a video for us to the song "Nice," and he had a lot of--- I was actually kind of his still cameraperson in that shoot. It was really fun. We got a bunch of people together and we all went night swimming and he filmed it. And there was a lot of leftover footage from that that couldn't go on MTV because, you know, it has some---

DD: It has some genitalia.

MS: ---genitalia and nipples and butts, and people don't want to see that on TV, so we thought, well, we can probably do it here and get away with it.

DD: How do you keep from being compartmentalized when you're on the road? I mean, being so isolated, in a way it's a real strange lifestyle.

MS: Yeah it is. I guess we're kind of used to it. I mean it's really hard to travel to all the places that we've traveled to and not--- and kind of remain as isolated as you probably should be to get enough sleep and to eat right and to be able to do what you do. But it helps everything if you can get away from it even for a half a day or a few hours, go to a museum, go for a walk, you know.

DD: Just for, on the record, is the HIV-AIDS rumor [a rumor at the time that Michael was HIV-positive]--- Where did those come from?

MS: I don't really know, I don't really have much of an idea about that. Um, but they were out there and I didn't really feel like it was, you know, I just really didn't want to respond to them. It seemed very kind of kibbles and bits journalism, and mean-spirited and nasty and unfounded. So I didn't respond to it for a long time, and then when I did, you know, I think people were shocked and probably relieved that I was happy and healthy and doing fine.

DD: Speaking of health, you were singing pretty strongly last night. I guess your hernia is healed; you wouldn't actually be testing it on the road.

MS: I'm actually testing it on the road.

DD: What does your doctor say?

MS: Actually, my doctor, my doctor has been really--- I've got two doctors; they've been really great through the whole thing. In retrospect I can't believe that I went on tour three and a half weeks after having a hernia operation. And the hernia was caused from singing. The pressure of singing for fifteen years is what brought it on, but everything's fine. There are certain songs that we can't perform yet because I can't hit the notes.

DD: So it's high notes that cause you to strain, or is it---?

MS: No, there--- I think if you speak to any singer, there's like a middle area between, probably, if you're looking at a graph, it'd be between like 65 and 80. There's a place in there that I think every singer has trouble with, and those are the ones, the songs that are in that range, for me, are the ones that are really difficult.

DD: Huh. Can we talk a little bit about lyrics?

MS: Yeah, sure.

DD: There are some things that--- Your lyrics have [changed], and your approach to them seems to have changed over the years, as we've been able to understand the lyrics better. You seem more direct now in what you're trying to communicate. I want to talk about a couple of different things. Rock songs always, to me, seem to be fragments. Whenever you listen to the radio or something, you hear the hook, you hear the lyric that goes with the hook. Was that--- did that affect how you wrote in terms of a fragmentary, you know, notion of rock songs, anyway?

MS: Yeah, I mean, really if you look at it from a writer's point of view, you have three minutes in a pop song to get across an idea. And you're not going to get even a good short story in that amount of time, so you have to take, you have to kind of try to--- If you're actually trying to get something across more than just, you know, rock out or whatever, you have to kind of reduce and get to the essence of what you're trying to say, and then within that make it seem not forced. I mean, keep in mind; I was 19 when we started the band and had never written a song before. Speaking as a lyricist and--- You know, our first two albums, our first three records, and our first two albums are really the four of us learning how to write songs, and some really great stuff came out of that. I mean I really like those records a lot and I'm proud of them but, you know, it's a cliché to say but you've really seen us grow up [laughs] in front of your eyes.

DD: One of the things that you're talking about [with your early songs] is kind of a layering thing that's like film, it's like video now, with so many images coming at you. And you do that lyrically in a song, but now there is more of a linear nature it seems in a way.

MS: Yeah. I mean a lot of REM for me has always been really filmic and visual, and my favorite visual things, my favorite films, are layers upon layers of things. And what you're presented with is not just a veneer, but it's a veneer that's covering something else and that's covering something else. That's important in music, I think. That's what lends interpretation to each individual listener, to take from a song or to take from music what they need or what they want from it. And that's why I think music has such a powerful, emotional impact on so many people. To be able to provide that as a musician and as a lyricist is sometimes difficult and sometimes easier than you would think.

DD: Easy as in?

MS: Well a lot of songs, a lot of songs, we've got a new song that doesn't have a name yet, but--- The new song "Departure," the song "Let Me In," all these songs are what I refer to as vomit songs where I just kind of like ralphed onto paper and I threw up on paper and I looked at it at some point and realized that it was a complete song and basically read off the paper and that's what went on tape. God, I'm looking at this record and I'm realizing like how many, we're looking at *Automatic for the People* here. "Drive" was a vomit song, "Sidewinder Sleeps Tonight" was a vomit song, "Ignore Land," "Star Me Kitten"---

DD: Really?

MS: "Nightswimming" were--- All of those just kind of came out of me and I didn't even really--- I mean, obviously, by the time a song makes it onto record I have a pretty good idea of what I'm trying to say and what's being said with it then, but.

DD: That's a frightening amount of creativity that just comes from---

MS: That's kind of cool, huh? [laughs]

DD: Yeah, from out of nowhere. What is one that went the other way? One that took a long time to construct.

MS: Where is the record? Okay here's the record. "Everybody Hurts" was a difficult song to write because it just seems so maudlin and sappy and I didn't know if it was the right thing to do, for whatever reason. It transcended that, I think, for most people and--- but that was kind of--- that was a little bit of a stretch for all of us to do a song that was that direct and was that simple.

DD: You did "Man on the Moon" last

night, and a real poignant intro about a journey that we're all going to take. That song is so goofy, you know, and poignant at the same time.

MS: I think death can be goofy [laughs]. I don't see why it can't.

DD: Well I guess Andy could be goofy.

MS: What--- Do you want me to describe that somehow?

DD: Yeah.

MS: I don't--- I'm not even sure where that came from, Andy Kaufman was a real figure for me when I was a teenager. On television, I remember the first time I saw him and I just thought, "This is the strangest thing I've ever seen in my life." I didn't even fully understand it, but it made me laugh and I connected to it because I was a big Mighty Mouse fan and, you know, blah blah blah. I'm implicating Andy Kaufman into the Elvis Presley conspiracy theory that he's still alive and doing well, and taking that and making it into a song that's basically questioning organized religion's idea of the great beyond—[it] is maybe a little bit of a leap. But I think for the most part, people kind of get what the song goes on about.

DD: Well thanks a lot for coming by.

MS: Yeah, thank you for having me.

DD: We really appreciate it.

1996

FIONA APPLE

AT LEAST A COUPLE OF TIMES A WEEK I WALK INTO THE STUDIO TO MEET A BRAND NEW ARTIST. Obviously, to get booked on the *World Cafe* we have to like their music to begin with. But we have no idea what's going to happen with their careers.

Over the years I can only think of a handful of artists that I was sure were going to make it on a bigger scale. I'd like to say that I knew that John Mayer was destined for stardom, but honestly I just thought he was another decent singer-songwriter.

I wanted to include this debut performance by Fiona Apple from 1996, when her debut album *Tidal* was released, because I did have a feeling that good things were in store for her.

It's also remarkable because it was recorded on her 19th birthday. The straightforward answers, the "ums" and "likes," are pure teenager. Having interviewed Apple again ten years later in 2006, I'll say her honesty and self-awareness really haven't changed that much.

David Dye: So it's kind of a gray day here in Philadelphia. And Fiona Apple is our guest. Welcome, thanks for coming.

Fiona Apple: Thank you. Thanks for having me.

DD: I drove in this morning and it was misty, and "Slow like Honey" was--- I was playing it in the car. And it was one of those perfect moments, melding of music and environment. It was really great. *Tidal* is Fiona's debut album, and it's just such a cohesive, wonderful work. And we're really happy you could come by here today.

FA: Thank you.

DD: It's interesting, now you're playing live, and I understand that's a completely new thing for you.

FA: Yeah, I've--- so far in all I've done like ten shows.

DD: And? How's it going?

FA: It's going well. The weird thing about it is that, I think that like for a while I [was] thinking, "Yeah, you know, I'm so lucky that I didn't have to go through playing like a bunch of gigs, like years and years and years of gigs before I got signed." But now I think that, you know, it's a mixed blessing just because, one, you know, I didn't have to go through all that. But then on the other hand, I didn't have the practice, so I've kind of had to like develop my own, you know, stage presence through my performances, which are being watched by everybody, so it's kind of like I'm under a lot of pressure to, you know---

DD: You didn't have that first album that failed completely, you know, to go through that. Well, you couldn't pick better people to play with, a couple of folks who were on the record, and some other folks. I'm curious. I heard that a lot of the record was cut pretty live?

FA: Right. Well a lot of it was like demos that we had first done, that we did overdubs on. And some of them were first takes. And a lot of it, the instrumentation and everything, was just like of musicians going and just doing what they wanted to do. A lot of it was just like the improvisation of all the musicians.

DD: So not totally different from what's going on here today?

FA: Right.

DD: Yeah. Why don't you do a tune, and we'll talk some more.

FA: Okay.

Fiona Apple performs "Shadowboxer"

DD: Fiona Apple on the *World Cafe*, along with Keith Lowe on bass, Matt Chamberlain on the drums, and the string-like and organ-like sounds are coming from the instrument . . . that Patrick Warren is playing with us today. You sound like you have been playing together for a while. It sounds great. Do you sculpt the words a lot? Do you move them in and out?

FA: Yeah, well it's different on different songs. Sometimes it's just all about trying to say what I want to say in the simplest way possible, but also in a way that really properly expresses the way that I feel, the way I want it to feel when you hear the words, you know.

DD: Well, you have mentioned Maya Angelou in other interviews. And I'm wondering what it is about her writing you appreciate.

FA: Well it's a number of different things. I think that mainly, the main thing about Maya Angelou's writing that has been such an inspiration to me, is the fact that she writes. And I think this has ended up to be like the theme of my album. She writes a lot about her strength, but based on what struggles that her strength has come from, you know. A lot of people try to avoid revealing any kind of weaknesses that they have, or any kind of pain that they have been through. Everyone wants to seem like the total, content, stable, perfect human being. And she seems to be able to write about her weaknesses and her vulnerabilities, her sensitivities, and her painful moments, even her embarrassing moments, and even sound proud of them, and be able to--- And it showed me that, you know, you can be proud of everything you feel, even the things that make you hurt. And she just also is--- she crafts her words so incredibly, you know. And she is very direct, and very simple.

DD: Now you started writing at a really early age, I understand. Like 11 or something?

FA: Yeah, well that was when I started writing songs with words. I mean I was writing like piano stuff before then, I think.

DD: A lot of people find it really hard to be creative. They find it really, as you say, kind of frightening, and they don't want to reveal themselves. Now both of your parents are in the arts in some form or another. Do you think that had anything to do with you having the confidence to create?

FA: I think that my parents being in show business, I think, it didn't influence me to be in show business, or it didn't give me confidence to do it. What it did was, I think a lot of people grow up and they want to be artists and their parents don't think that that's a legitimate career and I, fortunately, got to avoid that kind of obstacle because my parents did consider the arts very, very legitimate and, you know, a very important part of the world. And so that was one thing. I think that having to do with confidence, I don't think that's even a question of that kind of stuff when you're young and you're writing. I think that I was writing when I was younger not because I was confident; if anything because I wasn't confident and because it was what I had to do. Because if I were really confident when I were younger, I think I would have been going and telling actual people what I felt instead of writing it down on paper, you know. But it's just what I had to do.

DD: Interesting. You don't use a guitar very much.

FA: No, there's just something about me—my voice and the guitar—that our voices just don't really mix that well.

DD: And I love the vibes all over the record. You used some vibraphones, which create really great textures. Did you spend a lot of time figuring out what the sound was going to be of the record? Or did you go right in and do this?

FA: With me, I can't really take any kind of credit for the sound of the record. I can say that I wanted--- I told basically like all the musicians here and everything and Andy Slater, manager and producer, I told him the mood of the songs that I wanted to hear. But the thing was, when I went into this, I was very, very—as I still am—musically illiterate. Like I don't know, you know, all the names of the drums, and different instruments, and everything. When I first saw the vibes, I was like, "Oh look, a xylophone," you know, I don't know all this stuff. So I would say what I wanted something to feel like. And then you know, Andy would say, "Well, you got to get this musician and this instrument," and we'd just play.

DD: Well that's--- the combination of the two of you is just great. I mean the sound of this record just seems almost perfect for you. And it is interesting because using the chamberlain makes not having--- You get strings without strings, and that's a really wonderful way to do it. Oh, and happy birthday. Today's your birthday, right?

FA: I totally forgot.

DD: No one can ask you questions about being 18 anymore.

FA: I know, I know. It's kind of sad, because I can't be special anymore because I'm 18.

DD: Yeah, right. It's funny, you wanted to do "The Child Is Gone," which really isn't about that. But tell me about that song. Did that happen from a specific incident?

FA: Actually it started--- I think I started writing that like just before we started tracking the album. And I was on the phone with Andy. And I was in New York and he was in California. He was telling me like a bunch of stuff that would be going on, just months from now, basically what would be happening, what we're doing right now. And I started thinking, man, that's a lot of stuff to be doing. And I had just been kind of writing something, and anyway it just kind of motivated me and gave me the inspiration to finish it off. And then I only wrote part of it then, but then later on I finished it.

DD: Good song. Fiona Apple, here today on the *World Cafe*. Now I know being on the *World Cafe* is probably the high point of your career so far, but I also saw you on Jay Leno.

FA: Oh yeah.

DD: Was that real nerve wracking?

FA: It wasn't nerve wracking, but it was really frustrating, because we had to cut the song and we only had one day of rehearsal with the full band beforehand. And it was frustrating, and it was hard to concentrate and everything, and try to be presentable on camera, and try to remember that the cuts in the song came here, and also try to be into the song, and also try not to be nervous, and have my voice [laughs]. I guess it was a little nerve wracking.

DD: So what's number one? Trying to be into the song, I guess, is the hardest thing to keep together.

FA: Yeah, yeah. Actually it's not the hardest thing to keep together, it's the easiest thing because once I start playing usually my mind wanders and I'm just in the song. It's when I have to keep other things in mind that make it hard. Like, you know, don't sing the verse you normally sing; keep your face up so they can see you on the camera. That's what distracts me from the song, and it makes it harder.

DD: We should tell you, she's not playing--- You usually play like a grand, or baby grand piano. You've got a really cool-sounding electronic keyboard, but it's not quite the same.

FA: No, it's cool the way it sounds, it's cool the way it feels. It's actually, the actual physicality of this thing that's making me feel a little awkward.

DD: You're not kidding.

FA: I feel like, unprotected. I feel naked because I usually have this big solid thing in front of me. Now everyone can see me.

DD: Girl at her piano. You should make a deal that you tour exclusively at, like, you know, wood-paneled, small jazz clubs or something. It's like the perfect context for this music.

FA: Yeah.

DD: I understand your parents are, one on each coast.

FA: Actually I have three parents, because I consider my stepfather, who is now my ex-stepfather, one of my dads too. So I have a parent in Queens, a parent in Manhattan, and a parent in Los Angeles.

DD: So were they surprised at how quickly this all came together?

FA: Oh yeah, I don't think there was anyone who isn't surprised. I mean this is not the kind of thing that usually happens this fast.

DD: No, but it's a good thing. Thanks a lot for coming by.

FA: Thanks.

1996

BILLY BRAGG

BILLY BRAGG HAS BEEN A GUEST ON THE SHOW MANY TIMES. Some of his *World Cafe* recordings with his band the Blokes have made their way onto his box sets. I picked out this interview because it was an intimate session in our old studio right after Billy's first child, Jack, had been born. It's great to get his reaction to that life change, and as you can read, it was quite significant. As always with Billy Bragg, politics is discussed with maybe a bit of a softening of his stance brought on by parenthood. You'll find out the difference between a "lad" and a "bloke" and what football means to Billy.

David Dye: One of our favorite guests ever on the *World Cafe* is back with us today. Billy Bragg has joined us again.

Billy Bragg: Hi folks.

DD: It's been a while!

BB: It's been a while. It has been a while. I took some, some parental leave. I was pleased to see your, your government pushing through a standardized parental leave if you're, if one of your members of your family's sick or if you become a parent. And I became a parent, so it was rather extended leave, but that's--- Instead of making an album in '93 as, probably, I should've done, logically I got together with my "Mrs." and we made a baby instead.

DD: Worthwhile work.

BB: I think so, yeah. I think so. Although it didn't go into the charts as high as the last album, but I don't look down at that as a drop in the career.

DD: [chuckles] Ba-doom. It's interesting. If you listen to this new album, *William Bloke*—great title, I must say . . .

BB: Thank you, thank you.

DD: . . . you, you can see changes in you.

BB: Yep.

DD: And I suppose they are to be expected. Were you surprised by them?

BB: No, not really. I suppose when I started writing the songs after, after Jack was born, and he started turning up in one or two of 'em, I was quite pleased about that because, obviously, when you've been leading a kind of bachelor lifestyle for all of your life—and that's been what inspired you to write songs; that and the vagaries of politics—you do, you do worry when that changes. So when I began to write the songs, I realized actually that there was just as much heartbreak to be found in family relationships as there are in purely personal relationships. Which I know is a surprise; I should've known that from when I was, you know, in my family. It was that light and dark.

DD: That passes you by at a younger age,

it definitely does. Now, one other thing we have in common is our sons were born pretty near to each other—mine in October and yours in December of the same year. So I sort of understand a lot of the things you're going through, and I'm kind of surprised that Jack doesn't make more appearances in these songs.

BB: Yeah.

DD: He does appear in the song, "Space Race Is Over."

BB: He does, yeah. He does appear in the song and--- I think the problem is when you've been away for--- The urge to come back and kind of make a "Dad's record" is very strong. And I, I genuinely attempted to make some small concession to all those people who aren't interested in politics. Who aren't interested in parenthood, I mean; I'm sorry. I was just thinking, as I said, of something I read in the paper the other day, which was purported to be a guide to fathers, which was interesting. And one of the things was, you realize that you, after a while, that you don't have any friends anymore who don't have children. And all your people who you used to think of as friends, who now don't have kids--- Or actually, you realize now that they are very selfish people who only think about going out to parties and worrying about wars that are happening a long, long way away, which I thought was [laughs]--- Someone like myself, who's always been into that kind of thing--- It's actually in some ways what "Red to Blue" is about, the song that opens the album, which talks about a friend who goes--- "Red to Blue," for your listeners, is the political colors in Britain—red being the Labor party and blue being the Conservative party. I suppose in America it should be from donkey to elephant, or the other way around, which isn't quite the same metaphorical ring.

DD: No.

BB: But, and you know, I mean, I think when you do become a parent, a lot of your priorities do change. And, but sometimes you don't even have as much time as you did before to engage in the political process, so it becomes, it becomes necessary to sort of, like, to back pedal a bit. And I'm just trying, in that song, not to say, "I'm more political than you are," but just to say that there are some differences, and that you don't have to become a reactionary as you grow older.

DD: And I mentioned that song, "The Space Race Is Over," because it's such, it's such a sweet, longing song---

BB: Mmm.

DD: ---for, for something that one could see as being politically incorrect, or politically unimportant. But as a metaphor for a lot of things, it's very important.

BB: Yeah. I don't--- See, I was eleven at the time that Neil Armstrong and Buzz

Aldrin walked on the moon, and . . . political incorrectness hadn't been invented then. As far as I was concerned it was a wonderful, wonderful event. And looking back, they were both Americans and you were rightly proud of what your country achieved in the 1960s and 70s with the manned space program. Because you couldn't see that when they took their helmets off, they, had a very short haircut, and big dark glasses, and smoked cigars, and all those other American things, you didn't--- You know, they just looked like everybody else! They had two arms, two legs, and they just looked like, you know, it was humans. And that's what it was. And I think I took it in that way. I, I--- We all felt very much part of it when I was a kid. And we, I did believe, that—as obviously Stanley Kubrick did believe—that the world of *2001*, the movie [*2001: A Space Odyssey*], would come to pass, and that you would be able to go on some kind of shuttle craft and go back and forth to the moon. And the fact that that hasn't happened has not--- It has saddened me, but it just makes me realize that we shouldn't really rely on technology to solve all our problems; that we really should make—when we're young—we should make some provision for ourselves in the future. What is going to happen? It's not, you know, someone isn't going to come along and save and replant all these trees. Someone isn't going to come along and rejuvenate this part of the city. If we--- When we leave the forest, and when we leave the city, and we just leave it to run down, it takes a mess of help to get those things back. And you can't just rely on some guys at NASA, or whatever, to come along and solve all the problems. Or some guys to come from Mars and solve all the problems! I read recently that the majority of Americans now believe that people from Mars, or wherever, are going to come along; probably with Elvis. And I think that kind of longing for, for technology—whether it's terrestrial or extraterrestrial—to solve all our problems, I think, blinds us and stops us from actually putting our own personal house in order, in a personal way. It's kind of like, don't have local responsibility and just think, "Well, you know, somebody's going to come along and save you." And I think the lesson of the last thirty years is actually—actually, that's not true.

DD: [chuckles] Yes, indeed. Can you do that one?

BB: I can, indeed, yeah. "The Space Race Is Over," yeah.

Billy Bragg performs "The Space Race Is Over"

DD: "Space Race Is Over." Billy Bragg's with us here today on the *World Cafe.* Well, it's interesting, other changes have happened between the eighties and the nineties, too. Political changes that--- There were clear-cut people to focus on in the eighties, and now lines—just like everything else—get a little blurry.

BB: Exactly. In my country, as well as in

your country, obviously, the end of the Cold War is something that everybody welcomes. But it does make things rather difficult for people who want to talk about politics and arms manufacturers.

DD: Yeah.

BB: Because it's hard to work out where your audience is anymore. And most--- I hope the arms manufacturers never do find another audience. Those of us who have a political undercurrent to what we do, we have to feed off the politics that are happening at the time. The changes in Eastern Europe have led us all to think that there must be other ways of expressing our left-wing views other than just in terms of socialist ideology. And then the right--- The years of the Thatcher experiment have actually delivered very, very high social cost to us in Britain, that we are now thinking, actually, maybe it wasn't such a good idea after all.

DD: One of the songs on here brings up a wonderful thought. It's not an ideology, but it's "Socialism of the Heart"---

BB: Yeah.

DD: ---which is---

BB: "Socialism of the heart," yeah.

DD: ---which is a song, "Upfield."

BB: Yeah.

DD: Talk a little about that.

BB: Well, I mean, as I was saying, in Europe we have had strongly socialist parties. We have a very long socialist tradition that's in the forefront of our politics, rather than in the United States where socialism is perhaps a political backwater here. The idea that we don't need an ideology based on compassion and on equality; obviously that's wrong. We do still need those ideas. So, what I'm talking about in "Socialism of the Heart" is looking—not in an ideological way, but in a much deeper way—at what we have in common with those people who aren't in political parties, but are on our side, so to speak. And I would argue that at its very core, socialism is based on, on the human spirit, on the idea of the human spirit. I think the alternative ideology is based on greed, but ours is based on compassion and understanding, and we need to get back to those ideas. Get back to people who are inspired to do things by their heart rather than by some intellectual idea that they picked up at college, or down the library, or from their friends, or something like that. I mean, I think that makes a lot more sense to me now than just going back to the ideology that's written in tablets of stone, and realizing that was written a hundred years ago, and it doesn't take into account all the changes that have happened.

DD: Well, this song is called, "Upfield," which is a football metaphor. Now, to me, that means "going on the attack."

BB: It does mean "going on the attack,"

as well, but it also means going forward. And I'd like to think whatever we do on the left—whatever it is—it's a progressive, forward-looking idea. And it's, it's something that I'm not--- I don't wish to suggest to your listeners that I am pointing here and saying this is how we're going to go forward. I mean, I'm as much concerned of where this new socialism is going to come from as ever. I mean, it's becoming more easy in Britain to define yourself as a socialist because the Labor Party is moving towards the center. All I have to say now—instead of explaining myself ideologically—all I have to say in Britain to prove that I'm a radical socialist is that I believe that rich people should pay more tax than poor people. And this sort of song is a radical idea; you see where the political debate is going in my country.

DD: [chuckles]

BB: And, and so that's all I need; that's my socialist credential. I don't need to really go any deeper than that now for you. This is called "Upfield."

Billy Bragg performs "Upfield"

BB: Thank you.

DD: "Upfield." Billy Bragg's playing that on his telecaster today. It's got the great horns on the---

BB: That's right. Yeah, you have to hum your own brass harmonies today, I'm afraid, David. [This was] one of the tracks on the album that I felt would take more production. The good thing about this album—because of the break that I had—I was playing the songs before I recorded the album. Often I've got three or four songs when we go in the studio, or half a dozen; I write the rest in the studio. And you--- The temptation when you've got a new song is to see how far you can push it, and then you go out and play it live and you realize, actually, you know, you might have over-egged it a bit.

DD: Who--- I'm a little confused as to who this guy is that you're talking to, or talking about, in "King James Version."

BB: Well, in "King James Version," is something that I, I kind of like started to write a few years ago, probably before I packed up. And its underlying scenario really is the rise of the conservative Christian right and their attempts to change the world by sending money to this post-box number in, in Chattanooga, wherever. I mean, that in itself is, I find, strange enough just as a way of salvation. But when they become organized politically and their main message is a message of commercial fundamentalism and control, it worries me. Since I've become a parent, I've a bit more of a handle on family values, and I realized all these years that [what] politicians have actually been talking about is actually not family values, but one single point of what it means to be in a family, and that's the discipline. They're talking about family discipline, because the basic, fundamental family value, it seems to me, is compassion. A family that does not have forgiveness in it, seems to me, it must be dysfunctional. You know, if someone in your family's unemployed, you don't cast them out and don't send them a Christmas card. And you don't forget their kids. And you don't leave 'em to whatever society sends to them. You know, if someone in your family becomes pregnant, you don't scapegoat them. If someone in your family becomes ill, you don't sort of put them out and not worry about them. If someone in your family has something wrong with them, you gather round as a family, and you make--- You know, your sister might do something, your mom--- Everybody puts in and everybody helps out, and whoever's the richest in the family generally helps out at Christmas and does those kind of things. So I'm all in favor of family values, and I have to tell you this now, not particularly as a political idea, but just generally as a means to, to--- If you want to talk about family values in this society . . . there's a lot worse, there's a lot dafter ideologies that you can come up with, of the left and of the right. So I think that's what I was trying to get about, because I believe very much in the Bible as a compass to help you through your life. Any book that can offer you--- My mother, when my father died, found a lot of, got a lot of benefit from going back to her faith. She was a Roman Catholic, but she kind of, when she married my dad, she stopped going and everything. So I'm all for people having faith in that. But it's when they start using that—what they've found or what they've read there—to control other people's lives, I think then, then it becomes a bit of a problem. So I think the--- What I was trying to write about, the guy in the song, is just one of your soldiers of the moral right. It's one of those oxymorons that you hear from time to time. Because the morality of the right, as far as politics is concerned, is the morality of the Wall Street Stock Exchange, which makes the jungle look like a friendly place, really.

Billy Bragg performs "King James Version"

BB: That's for all those people who can find more in the Bible about homosexuality than they can find about compassion and loving people.

DD: And that's a hymn.

BB: It's a kind of a hymn, yeah.

DD: It, it's phrased that way.

BB: Yeah, it's kind of. . . . It does borrow that kind of hymn imagery in it. . . .

DD: And the way the choruses have the great last line that everybody can sing together.

BB: Yeah, yeah.

DD: Add then, "A-men." [chuckles]

BB: I saw that that wonderful phrase in the article that I read on the way down here—"It's morning in America"—is around again. And I love when I hear that phrase because, if it's morning in America, that means it's teatime in England, which is nice.

DD: [laughs] That is good. There's a couple of really vitriolic songs on here. I mean, you tell people off really nicely. "Everybody Loves You Babe," I was thinking. And the guy, "The Goalhanger."

BB: "The Goalhanger," yeah.

DD: I love that song!

BB: Yeah, well, I think everybody knows a guy like that. And I just happened to be honing my songwriting. You know how it is when you've been away for a while; you get your songwriting and you sharpen it up. And the metaphors started coming! And they, in England--- I did find out, actually, when I was trying this song out earlier, earlier in the season here in the United States of America, somebody told me the metaphor, the equivalent in ice hockey, which, apparently, is a goal-sock! Which is a horrible image, isn't it—a goal-sock? I don't know if there's--- Can you be offside in American football?

DD: No, not in the way you can in football/soccer.

BB: No, you can't, can you? See, it's a game to us that we just don't understand, American football. We don't, and to differentiate---

DD: You can be offside, but not during the play.

BB: No, no, there's no kind of goalhanging in that sense, is there?

DD: Yeah. Right, right, right.

BB: To differentiate between "world" football, which the rest of us play--- And we call it "football," if you're just wondering, those of you American football fans. We call our football, "football," on account of you play it with your feet. And your game, to differentiate, we call it, "Kicky-Runny." And or---

DD: And their game, we call soccer.

BB: That's right. That's the one—soccer, yeah. So this is a, kind of like a metaphorical person who, basically, it's that kind of person who does absolutely nothing, but gets all the glory. I mean, that's what we're--- That's the ballpark. Can I use that baseball metaphor?

DD: Absolutely.

BB: Thanks very much.

> Billy Bragg performs "The Goalhanger"

DD: "Goalhanger" is another one from *William Bloke*. Billy Bragg's with us here today. Did you ever have any other title for this record, besides *William Bloke*?

BB: Yeah, I did. Me and the producer, Grant Showbiz, and also the engineer, for some reason, during the making of it, we had a hell of a lot of dentistry work. And we kept coming in with swollen faces [talking as if with a swollen face], and sometimes I couldn't do the vocals because the anesthetic hadn't worn off in time, and stuff like that. And we got a bit ditzy with one another during this, so we were going to call it, *It's Just the Toothache Talking*, was one of the titles and--- But in the end, *William Bloke* seemed to me to sum up the album inasmuch as it was trying to make a resonance that it's perhaps--- Being, becoming a parent, it's made me learn this, that it is acceptable to have a spiritual side. Not in a religious sense, but in the sense that you under--- you use the human spirit as your main point of reference. And it's not at all in a new-agey or, you know, anything other than the--- What it means—the spark of the human spirit. And I think it's hard to sum that up in an album title. So *William Bloke* [laughing] seemed to--- I don't know if the word "bloke" has as much resonance here in the U.S., perhaps, as it does. We have a---

DD: But part of your whole image here in the--- is the, you know, guy from Great Britain telling us these things, so it fits well.

BB: Mmm. Yeah, I suppose so, yeah. We have a "lad" culture at home at the moment where there's a couple of magazines. One's called *Loaded*, which just is all about being a "lad." And being a "lad" is all about drinking loads of lager, and driving a big, big motor, and, and being pretty, you know, pretty much up for it—for loads of it, in fact. And being a bloke, it seems to me, is having passed all those things, and being a little bit more comfortable. You still have a beard, you still like to drive your motor and everything, and you still go to football, but you're a bit more comfortable with who you are and don't need to define yourself by those things. And also, if it comes to a pinch, you could probably lend someone a ladder or something like that from a bloke, which I don't think you could from a lad.

DD: Has anybody ever offered you a radio show?

BB: No, not really! I mean, I have done a bit at home on radio shows and stuff like that.

DD: Right.

BB: But I'm just kind of one of those--- I suppose I'm never in the same place three or four weeks. I am a bit more now that Jack has come along.

DD: Right.

BB: And stuff like that. And I'm always, but I'm always liable to say something odd on the station. They always worry that I'll, you know.

DD: Right, right—take it in a different direction.

BB: Yeah, I always have to think to myself, imagine my mom's here.

DD: [laughs]

BB: Sitting here. So I don't say anything too over-the-top.

DD: Well, you're welcome here anytime.

BB: [laughs] Thank you very much for having me. I do appreciate it.

DD: Billy Bragg, our guest on the *World Cafe.*

1996

LYLE LOVETT

THIS INTERVIEW ISN'T PACKED WITH INFORMATION, ALTHOUGH WE DO GET TO HEAR A LOT ABOUT LYLE LOVETT'S HAT! I wanted to include it because you just get a feel for what a tremendous guy Lyle is. I remember this session specifically from our old building. Lyle was running late and his entourage was pushing him to get moving. But Lyle's attitude was: I'm here, I'm going to make the most of what's in front of me. And he did with some fabulous performances and some fine stories.

Some background is in order. During this interview we refer to "Fiona." Fiona was Lyle's nickname for his ex-wife Julia Roberts. In an earlier *World Cafe* session within days of their getting married, Lyle came to the *World Cafe* with his full large band and, unbeknownst to us, Julia, on the bus outside. Had we only known, we could have had a *World Cafe* scoop.

Lyle Lovett performs "Private Conversation"

David Dye: "Private Conversation" from *The Road to Estenada.* Lyle Lovett is our guest today here on the *World Cafe.* It's funny, I was thinking, we didn't get a chance to talk to you when *I Love Everybody* came out. But you did a song—you seem to be including all your friends in your songs, yet—that old song with Robert Earle [Keene] . . .

Lyle Lovett: Oh that's right. Yeah, that's right.

DD: . . . shopping at the record store. And it's ironic that you did a tribute to Uncle Walt's Band on this new album and then you ended up dedicating this song to the late Walter Hyatt.

LL: I've always enjoyed picking on my friends and putting them in my songs. And the whole thing with Walter, it's a real tragedy.

DD: Um, one of the neat things about that record—I guess it's you and Billy working together on it—you suggest the whole era of western swing bands with that one fiddle and steel run, sort of at the beginning of it. It's kind of cool how that arrangement came about.

LL: Thank you very much. Yeah, that's a song I wrote with Willis Alan Ramsey and his wife Allison Rogers. We wrote it a couple of years ago and started playing it live right away. So we've been playing it on the road and just got around to recording it.

DD: What's the vintage of most of these new songs?

LL: . . .The last record, the *I Love Everybody* record, was all old songs. So all these songs were written since the *Joshua Judges Ruth* album. Some of them are really new and, you know, some of them are two or three years old.

DD: Um . . . can we talk about your hat?

LL: Sure.

DD: You didn't bring it with you.

LL: No, I don't always carry it because people always try to mess with it. So.

DD: If you fold out Lyle's album, there is a little foldout [with] a beautiful picture of the inside of your hat . . .

LL: Thank you very much.

DD: . . . that says, "Like hell it's yours—This hat belongs to Lyle Lovett, Kline, Texas."

LL: There's a great hat store down in Houston called "The Hat Store"—it's what's left of the old American Hat Company, which is a hat-manufacturing company. And I have one of my grandfather's old American hats that has that same sign in it. You know, from like the 30s.

DD: Wow, that's great. So you can still get 'em made, though?

LL: Yeah you still can. They've always put those little signs in them; that's a very common thing. You know, it's--- If you go somewhere and you hang your hat up like people used to do; because used to [be] that people didn't wear their hats indoors, you know.

DD: People used to wear hats, which is the first difference.

LL: And now people who wear hats, it's more of a, you know—ornamental. And people go in someplace and leave their hat on, you know. But used to [be that] the reason for a sign like that, like putting your name in your hat, was that somebody would know when they had your hat.

DD: Well how about [playing] that one about hats on here? Can you do that one?

Lyle Lovett performs "Don't Touch My Hat"

DD: Lyle Lovett, a man with his priorities slightly askew. [laughs] Who knows? Maybe they're right. I was trying to think of all these times I've seen you recently and--- Didn't--- You played with Randy Newman on the Oscars, didn't you? Doing that song?

LL: Yes I did. Randy Newman, who I'm a great fan of, invited me to sing with him on his soundtrack for the movie, *Toy Story*, and he was, of course, nominated for Best Sound Track and Best Song. And he asked me if I'd sing with him on the Oscars and, you know, it was a lot of fun.

DD: It worked out really well.

LL: You know, Randy Newman has been one of my songwriting heroes, and to get to work with him--- I met him through one of our engineers on my album project, Bill Kinsley was his name. He worked on Randy's *Faust* album. And we had just cut "Long Tall Texan" for my album and just sort of standing around, you know, with my mind kind of wandering. I, thinking out loud, said, "Wow, Randy Newman would sure sound great on this." And Bill, who I didn't know knew him at all, spoke up and said, "You want me to call him?" And it was as simple as that. He called him up and Randy came down and he sang on my record. And then we got to do the *Toy Story* thing.

DD: Yeah, it's great to hear. Is "Long Tall Texan" possible without Mr. Newman?

LL: We could. You know, you wouldn't hear him.

DD: That's true, but we can all imagine, can't we?

LL: You could sing it. Sure, we could do that.

DD: How come you decided to do that one?

LL: You know, that's a song I've always liked. It's the first song I ever performed in public when I was like eight years old. And uh---

DD: What was the occasion?

LL: It was like the end of school year, sort of show-off deal for the parents. And my friend Rodney Fisher and I sang "A Long Tall Texan," and the rest of the class sang Randy's part, sang the background part. And it was a hit in '63 by Murry Kellum and I knew it from the radio, so I've always played it. And finally this record, with songs like "That's Right (You're Not from Texas)" and "Don't Touch My Hat," it seemed like the appropriate place to put it.

DD: Yeah, it fit really well, an acoustic version. Lyle Lovett, our guest today on *World Cafe.*

> Lyle Lovett performs "A Long Tall Texan"

DD: I don't know if I should come in. [laughter] Lyle Lovett is our guest today on the Cafe. It has been a while since you've been here. A couple of other things have happened that I wanted to talk about which, number one, is what it was like to sing with Mr. Al Green [on their duet "Funny How Time Slips Away"].

LL: Oh, singing with Al Green; meeting Al Green; being in the same room with Al Green; being, you know, in the same city, you can feel---

DD: [chuckle] Memphis does sort of have the vibe, yeah. Now I mean it must have been--- He's one of the greatest singers on the planet. And Lyle, I love your stuff, you're a great songwriter, a great singer, but---

LL: What are you saying, David?

DD: I'm saying, it's tough to keep up with Mr. Green, I would think.

LL: That whole record, record of duets---

DD: Right.

LL: I kept thinking to myself as we were running the song down--- We took it, maybe twice, and that was it.

DD: Wow.

LL: I kept thinkin', "He's Al Green and I'm not." I really just tried to stay out of the way, just tried to watch him and listen to him and, you know, find a little spot to sneak in.

DD: Well one of the neat things on the record is to sort of let it go after it's done. So you can tell he had a ball.

LL: He always--- We performed the songs a few times, you know, after we recorded it and, yeah, he always has a ball. Yeah he's a great singer, like you said.

DD: Um, Lyle Lovett is here today. Boy, I'm just sort of going through, because there's so many things I wanted to--- Oh, it's funny, you were here last time and you dedicated a number of songs to a "Fiona," and then this mythical Fiona appears in another song here, although she seems to have changed shape and form on this one.

LL: You know, that's the way she is. [laughter] Yeah, we can play that.

DD: Could you? That would be great.

LL: You, you're great with these segues.

DD: [laughs] That's all I do.

LL: [laughs]

DD: I sit here and worry about the segues.

LL: [chuckle] This is--- you know, Louisiana is a land of mystery if you grew up in Southeast Texas.

> Lyle Lovett performs "Fiona"
>
> Lyle Lovett performs "The Road to Ensenada"

DD: Title track to *The Road to Ensenada.* James Kilmer on the percussion; John Hagen on the cello. What a great idea it was--- You started using cello back on the second album or the first, all the way back.

LL: It was--- I met John. John was playing in a band around Austin and occasionally he'd come over to College Station where I was going to school and play shows, and I'd get to open for him. And I met John really because I was starting to copyright some of my songs, and John would write up my lead sheets for me and that's how we started working together. And we started playing together and, uh, the three of us, when our first record came out in 1986, the three of us--- The first record was, you know, came out of the Nashville part of the record company. And we were out on the road with country acts and we were out opening, the three of us. We did several shows with Reba McEntire and the Judds and Rickie Skaggs, Merle Haggard, and it was quite an education.

DD: I'll bet, I'll bet. You know what I'd really love [to hear] is the rodeo song, whatever it is. I mean, if I'm given this opportunity to request songs.

LL: "Farther Down the Line"?

DD: "Farther Down the Line."

LL: Yeah, that was my very first single in 1986.

DD: I always loved this song.

> Lyle Lovett performs "Farther Down the Line"

DD: Always great when you get to make a request. Lyle Lovett doing "Farther Down the Line," finishing up our session here on the *World Cafe.*

ELVIS COSTELLO

ELVIS COSTELLO has been a guest on the *World Cafe* many a time, often with classical accompaniment! Elvis has made albums with the Brodsky String Quartet, with the opera singer Anne Sofie von Otter, and with numerous other guests. He's always been a delight to talk to, and is one of the most erudite guests to make their way into our studios. Of all those visits, I chose this interview from a beautiful May weekend day in 1996 because it's so light-hearted.

Elvis had a fine new album called *All This Useless Beauty*, and he and his keyboard player from the Attractions were touring. When they came to the *World Cafe*, their instruments failed to follow and we had a lovely hour hanging out with Elvis and Steve hearing stories while waiting for delivery. With patience waning we went to the frat house next door where a band had been practicing and borrowed a half-size Yamaha keyboard that Steve Nieve made his own with impossibly strange sounds. A very fun, loose session ensued beginning with a version of the song "You Bowed Down."

Elvis Costello performs "You Bowed Down"

David Dye: "You Bowed Down," the duo version. Elvis Costello with Steve Nieve on--- Explain this keyboard, Elvis.

Elvis Costello: Well, we were on our way from the airport and we left happily to come to the *World Cafe*, only to find that somebody has kidnapped all of our guitars and taken them off to an unknown destination. So, a very kind gentleman across the street, Mr. Tim Allen, from the group Chelsea, has lent us his DX7 here which is heavily customized. Any sort of strange sounds that come out here are due to Steve's technical expertise at extricating these wonderful electronic noises from it.

DD: There's some buttons that have XXX written on them.

EC: Definitely these are triple-X sounds and forbidden! [laughs] This is the Ishtar version of *All This Useless Beauty*. We're going to take this on the road. Afterwards we're going to Tunisia with this sound.

DD: I can't wait actually. [laughs]

EC: In the Society Lounge.

DD: So that song he began with is one that Roger McGuinn added his jangly guitar to. Did he ask you for that?

EC: Yeah, he did. I ran into him in New Orleans—the Storyville Club in New Orleans—one night in the very late 1980s, very late in the evening, and I was rather drunk and I made kind of a fool of myself talking complete rubbish to him. And he was very understanding. I'd admired him for a long time. I'd seen him play several times with the Byrds and kept my eye on his solo records. He was doing lots of great songs and I thought it would be great if he was recording. Next thing, I made the record, *Spike,* and I invited him to come in and play on one of the tracks on that record. And around that time he got another record deal and he asked me for a song. So I wrote this one for him, and it has this little signature in it which you heard sort of somewhat on this guitar that I normally play [plays riff], which is really a twelve-string guitar riff. He did it up fine. As you heard there's the little tribute to "MacArthur Park" in the middle of it where it goes all kind of psychedelic.

DD: Right, right!

EC: His producer prevailed that that was not what radio would play. Which I think is a lot of nonsense because some of the Byrds' best records changed time signature, and in our own records like "Veronica" has a bridge in a different rhythm than the rest of the record. If you allow everything to become very straight ahead then it's a boring world. There we are.

DD: That's interesting. This someone-covering-your-song phenomena; I mean, it happened with "Shipbuilding" a long time ago I guess.

EC: Yes, that's one other occasion. I've had a bit of luck writing songs for people, with people in mind, and then later recording them without me having anything to do with it. So presumably I did a pretty good job in imagining them singing it because they could see themselves in it. On other occasions, as in the case of this record, I have an idealized idea of somebody singing the song. It doesn't necessarily follow that they will agree with you. Nevertheless, I mean this record isn't truly about songs that are written for other people. Really there's only four songs that have been issued before. And quite a lot of the songs were written for myself. The connections with other people are tenuous to say the least. I tend to think that the record's definitely about where the songs are headed next rather than where they've been.

DD: Right. It's interesting. Left to your own devices in the studio, would it take you a long time to figure out how a song is going to end up on the record? Do you try it a number of ways?

EC: What we wanted to do on this record, apart from the fact that there's a lot of ballads--- The heart and soul of the record is really in the ballads and everything they're singing about, and we didn't want the record to become, therefore, very still—too still and too repetitive of mood. So from time to time there's an outburst of the kind of music that we've done a lot of in the past. But hopefully we've approached it from a different way. So we've got songs like "Complicated Shadows" and "You Bowed Down," and its full band arrangement is a pretty forceful-sounding record. But we found new ways to propel the songs by--- Steve and Pete got together and we made some loops up using sometimes found sounds, and sometimes things we created ourselves. And there's things to be learned just about propelling a song so it isn't all slow and predictable. We didn't imagine where we'd have this lovely electronic keyboard with all the magical sounds that we're drawing from it...

DD: There are many.

EC: . . . with our magic wand.

DD: You talked a little bit about [how], even on this tour with Steve, the songs are changing from night to night.

EC: Well, you hear them in a different way. Each new circumstance changes it. Even where you place a song in the show can change it. Because if you play when you first go on the stage, you're nervous the audience is wondering what's going to happen tonight, what is it going to be about. They know that we're coming to play, to present the new songs. One of the reasons we've done this tour is that when we first came [to] Philadelphia, we played in the hot club or something like that . . .

DD: Exactly.

EC: . . . and we were right up close on people. Of course we had the benefit of surprise. We were a new group and, like any new group that's got good stuff, people are anxious to see you. When you come back as you get more successful, you inevitably have to satisfy the demand of the people that want to see you. And the venues get bigger and somebody's sitting further and further away from you. And it's no accident that the songs that people still have the most affection for are the ones that we all heard together develop when we were all sitting a lot closer to one another.

DD: Ahh. Interesting.

EC: Now it's easier; you could say the songs in the meantime maybe aren't as good. Well maybe that's true. I don't think that is true. Part of the consequence of people only falling in love with them through records is that, to introduce a lot of new material in a concert is quite difficult, as any musician will tell you.

DD: You want to stick one of those older ones in here that you've been working up?

EC: [laughs] I don't know what will sound good on this.

DD: Yeah, I don't know if Steve's got the right stops there.

Steve Nieve: No, but it's okay. Whatever you want to do.

Elvis Costello performs "Man Called Uncle"

EC: I mean that was the odd man out. A couple of odd men out on the album *Get Happy* which was a record where we did all--- we had one kind of style or arrangement for a whole bunch of songs written kind of similar to this record, *All*

This Useless Beauty. These songs are written over seven years and, as you said before, some of them were previously recorded by other people, but a lot of them were ones that didn't fit with the set of songs that might have been written currently with. And the songs on *Get Happy* were songs that we'd had out on the road during the tail end of the very furious period of touring that we did when we first started out—two and a half years straight, from '77 to mid-'79. The arrangements that we came back home with at the end of that were very nervy, very much a product of the times and everything that we did and everywhere we went. But they didn't necessarily make a good record, and we started out to try and find a rhythmic way of getting them down, and we started to use R&B grooves to try to space out all these millions of chords and words that I was writing. This song was one of the ones that survived kind of the original intention, which was to make it like a Beat group song. As you heard, it ends with the famous 6-chord like "She Loves You" does. And the funny thing about it when it was written it was, it was sort of an of-the-time song in my frame of mind. Now I want to sing this second verse, "If you say I'm the one do you think I'm serious"—you get that kind of talk from older men. Well I am an older man [laughs], so it has a different kind of humor to it.

DD: That's why I was laughing when you were singing it!

EC: Yeah, there's a few of the lines in a few of the songs that have taken on a different meaning. Steve's got a beautiful arrangement which we would love to play for you if we had a piano—the piano which is probably circling, actually it's probably halfway on its way to Sicily by now, I think.

DD: I wanted to ask you a question, vis-à-vis that record and Sam Moore. Did you meet him when you covered the Sam and Dave tune?

EC: No, we didn't meet Sam. We met Sam like in, I think it was 1984. Actually, Sam Moore, we came to meet him when Demon Records released some Sam and Dave B-sides. We did a record called "Can't Stand Up for Falling Down," which was the Sam and Dave which we covered in 1980.

DD: Which you completely changed.

EC: We made it an up-tempo song, and it was a ballad. And Demon Records, which I'm involved with in England, licenses a lot of stuff from major companies who can't be bothered to do a decent job reissuing some of the beautiful stuff they've got in their vaults. Occasionally we get some real gems and we put stuff out. And it came to Sam and his manager's attention that this company was one that I was involved in, and we were introduced. And he came and sang it with us one night in Los Angeles, and it was terrifying because I started singing and I couldn't hear anything. I mean, he's so loud. And as you can tell from being in this room, I'm not exactly a quiet singer. But it was really amazing. And actually, he had something to do with Steve and me getting back playing together because he came to London and he was going to make a record and he was looking for material. And I had just written "Why Can't a Man Stand Alone," and I just thought he was the perfect guy for it because he'd bring this authority to it. I came down to the session, and I hadn't seen Steve in a couple of years, and he was down there playing piano. And he did sound great. I don't think the record ever got finished, though. They started a few sessions and then something else happened. And you know these things often happen.

DD: You talk about not being able to tell whose record was whose. I didn't know which was the Sam Moore tune, and I just assumed it was that.

EC: Well, it does have this R&B root to it. And I was concerned when we were making the record that I wouldn't really have the voice for it. I mean, I can't sing like Sam Moore, I can't sing like Curtis Mayfield or any of the people I can imagine doing this song in a perfect, ideal world. But some of the ideas in the song are mine. I don't know if everybody would agree with them, but I'm of the mind that the things that men are taught to feel that are a necessary part of their identity are not just an encumbrance and a burden to them; it distorts them to the point of their inability to treat their fellow human beings properly, whether they be women or children. The least worst of it is the way they treat women, and the worst of it is the way they use their power against defenseless children. I mean, I'm not on a soapbox about this, but the song is just what I wanted to say [and] I wanted to say it clearly because I was planning on giving the words to somebody else to sing. I would love to hear somebody with a really powerful, gospel-singer voice do this song someday.

EC: So this is a song I wrote in Italy. And it's about a woman who is looking at the pictures on the wall of a picture gallery there of all this classical antiquity. And she looks at her late-20th century lover and says, "How the hell did we go so wrong?"

> Elvis Costello performs "All This Useless Beauty"

DD: Elvis Costello performs "All This Useless Beauty" to wrap up our conversation.

1997

DAVID BOWIE

THIS WAS ACTUALLY THE SECOND TIME I TALKED WITH DAVID BOWIE, CERTAINLY ONE OF THE MOST REMARKABLE MUSICIANS OF OUR TIME. Few people have kept in the game and so attuned to not only what was happening, but what was next!

First time we talked with David was at the legendary Sigma Sound Studios in Philadelphia where he recorded the *Young Americans* album in marathon sessions. It was essentially a performance in front of an invited audience who were as charmed as I was.

This time it was a transcontinental hookup as a very energetic Bowie talked about his drum- and bass-inspired album *Earthling*. We managed to roam off topic a lot as we discussed the new "Bowie Bonds" he had used to raise money from future sales of his back catalog. As you hear, he's a charming man.

David Dye: "Little Wonder" from the wonderful new *Earthling* album from David Bowie. As we hook up with David Bowie via some kind of technological miracle I'm not really sure about. Hi David; where are you?

David Bowie: I'm in Hollywood, of the great "H."

DD: Of course you are. Good to see you. Good to hear you, at least!

DB: [laughs]

DD: I'll tell you, this album is being described as David Bowie's "Jungle" album. And Jungle in this country is still very underground, and yet in Europe and England it's omnipresent. Is it fair to call it your Jungle album?

DB: It might be a bit misleading. I think there's probably only three tracks that are actually Jungle on the album.

DD: Right.

DB: I think that probably people notice that a lot because it is such an unusual sound in America. It really hasn't been heard very much over here. So it really takes your ear when you first hear it.

DD: When did you start hearing it in England?

DB: About '93. I got it from a girl who's a great clubber. [She has] a huge stack of vinyl. And she said, "You've got to get behind this stuff. You got to do this." And I put it on; it just overwhelmed me. I thought, "This is such exciting music." Really, really cool. And the two elements of it that I think I'm working with more than anything else are the sub-bass and the actual percussive elements. Not so much the top lines, the top lines that I'm keeping very much in my own area. It's very melody driven, I guess, and some quite strange takes on what you can do with Jungle. Because most of the Jungle that's coming out of England is fairly minimalistic and it's a cumulative music; it has more of a chant-like quality. And

I'm just sort of going against that tide in a way, I guess, with what I'm doing. I don't think it's really been, it's not really been amalgamated with quite such a hard rock sound as I'm using. I think that's, it's sort of, it's really--- for me I think it's a pretty new direction for it.

DD: It seems that way to us. You have--- The melodies on these seems like you (even though you're co-writer on a lot of this), seems so much like your melodies. And the way that they're juxtaposed is just beautiful; the way it works out.

DB: Yeah it is. The way that Reaves [Gabrel] and I work, we combine chord structures together. We sort of almost play alternates. So I'll do a little bit, he'll do a little bit, then I'll go back again and work out some interesting structures. And then I'll go into the booth and kind of ad-lib vocal lines and whatever. And then we'll kind of cut them up when I come out, and make things kind of work. It's good spontaneous stuff. We spend about—with the band, recording and writing—the actual muscle work I guess took about two and a half weeks. So it was a very, very fast make, this album.

DD: Now had Reaves and Mark been putting together some of the loops already when you came off the road, or did you know what you wanted to do?

DB: In fact, I started off early on in the year with Mark. We did a piece called, "Telling Lies," which was really, that was the direction I wished the album to go in. And so I used that as almost a blueprint for how the album should sound. And then during the course of the tour, that underwent several different variations as we sort of finessed and honed into what we really wanted to do. And I put three of the mixes out on the internet halfway through the year, and then we kept the one that I really felt was pretty much the tonality of how I wanted the album to be for the album itself. So it's been--- I get--- The first time we really fooled around with the idea of those kinds of percussions, rhythms were, was--- Outside, there are a couple of tracks on there that sort of give a nod to that particular currency, and one was "We Prick You," and another one was called "I'm Deranged." And I kind of felt--- When I did things with Brian, I thought this is definitely, this is an area I really want to get more immersed in.

DD: This seems a little more direct than, in some ways, than that record.

DB: Yeah.

DD: It kind of hits you over the head, much more so. And I wanted to play this, the version of "Telling Lies" that finally made it on the CD.

DB: Yes, please do.

DD: And this is "Telling Lies." This is the non-internet version, or one of the internet versions, from David Bowie.

David Bowie recording: "Telling Lies"

DD: "Telling Lies" from *Earthling*. David Bowie is our guest today. I wanted to talk about another track because I love it. It's a dance track about aging. Which is, "Dead Man Walking."

DB: [laughs] There's nothing like old men dancing.

DD: [laughs]

DB: Better than "Dead Man Walking," I suppose. Well if you're that particular old man, yeah. [laughs] Yes it is about aging.

DD: Aging comfortably I would say.

DB: Aging and knowing what to wear.

DD: Exactly.

DB: Yes I think so. Yes, you know it's a strange question. I'm often asked these days how it feels to be fifty, and don't--- I really don't know how to answer. It's like, sort of like being asked, "What's it like to have legs?" It's almost unanswerable. You know, it's sort of, well, "I don't know, I've got them." It's like the same with being fifty. It's like, "I don't know; I'm just fifty," you know? I think, I think one of the things that keeps you buoyant is that, when you turn around, how much you've gotten through and are still surviving. And secondly, how much you're enjoying life right now. And I think having those two things makes it a really exhilarating thing to be, and it--- I never really thought that being fifty would be anywhere as enterprising and enthusiastic and full of life as twenty-five is supposed to be, but actually, I'm a lot, I'm probably a lot more aggressively life-conscious now than I was at twenty-five. And I was probably a pretty depressed little recluse if I think about it too much, which I don't like to.

DD: [laughs] Well let's spin that. This is "Dead Man Walking," another one from *Earthling*.

David Bowie recording: "Dead Man Walking"

DD: "Dead Man Walking" from Earthling. David Bowie is our guest today. A very open David Bowie. You've been doing a lot of interviews, a lot of talking.

DB: And I can't stop! I thought, well, this mouth of mine just won't shut so I thought I better put it to work.

DD: Do you like explaining what songs are about? You haven't done a whole lot of that in the past.

DB: I'm not sure really, it's a little bit, yeah. I mean, I don't know. As a fan, I'm not sure that I actually like to hear how or why they were actually written in the first place. Sometimes it's a real insight, but other times it's a bit of a letdown. I remember not quite being--- having a song explained to me, but reading a lyric copy of a Fats Domino song. I think it was probably "Walking to New Orleans" or something like that, and the words were completely different to ones I thought he was singing, and my version was much better, I thought, in my head anyway. So I'm not sure. It has its up and down sides, I think.

DD: Well one song on here that almost needs you to say something about it is—or I'm not sure I would understand it is—"Seven Years in Tibet." What was the inspiration for that?

DB: Well the genesis of that song--- I had, I've had sort of an off-and-on long-standing thing about Tibet and its accompanying philosophy, Buddhism. And I studied off and on for three years in the sixties when I was younger and it really meant a lot to me, especially what I gleaned from the philosophy of Buddhism. And I guess over the last couple of years, my memories of that period, and also pangs of guilt for not having paid more attention to the plight of Tibet and to the Chinese, was sort of brought into focus with the lectures and speeches that the Dalai Lama is giving particularly, over the last couple of years. And I just kind of wanted to maybe have it emerge again in my writings. So that's why I wrote it.

DD: And it begins kind of like you're in Memphis in the Hi Studios, and it goes somewhere else.

DB: Yes, yes. I guess that's because it's me writing it and not some little kid out of Tibet. It's almost--- there's almost a parody of a blues in there, in a way.

DD: This is "Seven Years in Tibet."

David Bowie recording: "Seven Years in Tibet"

DD: "Seven Years in Tibet." We are talking with David Bowie who is, we'll guess, a month or so off of your fiftieth birthday celebration which I understand we're going to be able to attend in a way?

DB: Yup, it's a Pay-Per-View special on March the 8th. And I would like to add that all proceeds go to Save the Children fund. So even if you miss it, please buy it.

DD: Okay, okay. There was a really interesting interview you did in *Pulse* a while ago that--- Talk about how comfortable you are being with people nowadays, and how before you really felt that you sometimes would go and have a relationship with a city that was easy for you because it could be one-way.

DB: Yeah, I don't think--- I wasn't at all a social animal. I think that I was, at heart, quite awkward and shy, and that sort of devolved into being an absolute recluse at one point. But over the last ten years or so I've just widened my social abilities. [laughs] Now I'm just like, I'm just like a party animal!

DD: Well I was curious as to what cities you'd had relationships with; I was thinking Berlin.

DB: Yes, Berlin very much, and off and on over the years the recurring cities back to my own country—London, of course. Philadelphia, I suppose, and New York keep becoming touchstones for me. So much during my life has happened or originated in those cities, and for some reason or other they still keep cropping up prominently in the way I live and what happens with me.

DD: Well it's interesting. Philadelphia, of course, you recorded the *Live* album here.

DB: Yeah.

DD: And then recorded *Young Americans* here, and that was a different kind of immersion in a different kind of R&B dance culture kind of way.

DB: Yes, exactly. Once again, as you said, it was dance once again. And I think that's been a recurring thing in my work. The underpinning of most of my—creatively—most of my successful stuff has always had some acknowledgment of the dance form in the fabric at the time.

DD: And I thought we would play something from that. Well we have to play "Young Americans" because it's so perfect.

DB: [laughs] All right.

David Bowie recording: "Young Americans"

DD: Recorded in one of those cities that David Bowie has had a relationship with, "Young Americans." He's our guest today on the *World Cafe* and we're talking about *Earthlings*, the new album, and so many projects. I'm interested--- I have a question with these Bowie Bonds being issued. What label can we look for---

DB: Me too; I can't buy any! I've tried; I've been on the street. No scalpers in sight.

DD: Now these were all based on, I guess, future royalties. Does that mean we will look for a change on where your albums are available, what label they're available on?

DB: Not at all. That's probably--- The innovative part of this whole structure is that I keep very close creative tabs on everything that happens to my work. That's what makes it far more interesting than a lot of those ventures. So creatively . . . or artistically, nothing changes from the way I wish it to be.

DD: And they will remain on Rykodisc? Or what will happen here in the States?

DB: Yes, until our agreement comes up for reconsideration.

DD: Gotcha. One of the other interesting things I saw in this *Pulse* article was a desert-island disc list, and one of the . . .

DB: Oh really?!

DD: . . . one of the people on there was Prodigy, which I guess had to have something to do with what you've been doing lately.

DB: Yes, I think they're probably the face of what has been for quite a few years an almost anonymous musical form. I really think--- I've been sort of quite big on them for a year or two. I think they're the most exciting of the British bands. And I do hope that they get more recognition outside of Europe.

DD: They have a new release here in the States, *Fire Starter*, and I thought we'd . . .

DB: They're really excellent; they really are.

DD: . . . throw that on. Here's something that David Bowie might take to a desert island, or at least that's what I read here. And you have a couple of your discs, and *Outside* is on there and it seems to me that *Outside* did not get its due here in the States as an in-depth layered album, as it is. And it seems to me that--- I just read somewhere that a couple songs are making their way into films now.

DB: Yeah, I've just been so happy that directors generally really seem to like that album an awful lot. We got one song away pretty early actually, in *Seven*. It became the end credits music for that. David Lynch has picked out one of my favorite tracks on the album, "I'm Deranged," which as a matter of fact is one of the tracks that we were sort of tapping into drum and bass for the first time on that particular song, and that's in his next film, *Lost Highway*. It's both--- It opens the movie and it closes the movie. It really gets--- He really went crazy about that song. I was very happy with that. And generally it's been an extraordinary year of--- I think something like fifteen, fourteen or fifteen, films are either in the process of coming out with my songs in or have been out over the last eighteen months. It's been just incredible. *Breaking the Waves* is another film that's out there with some of my stuff, and *Trainspotting* of course. And the interesting thing is--- Ang Lee, who is one of my favorite directors—he did *Sense and Sensibility*—really great director, and his next film is called *Ice Storm* which is the cinematic version of a wonderful book by Rick Moody, who I've had the pleasure of meeting a couple of years ago. And he's taken a Tin Machine song, believe it or not, for that [film] called *I Can't Read*. So those songs are really kind of almost finding a new life in cinema. It's really, that's really great.

DD: Well there's always been obviously a visual element to what you do, but you usually control the visual aspect of it and it's interesting to see what someone else will do with your song.

DB: Yes. I think, yes [laughs], absolutely, definitely, it's going to be quite an interesting year to see what comes out.

DD: Couple other things I wanted to ask you about. Well I have my vinyl copy of *Man Who Sold the World*, but unfortunately we're a continent apart so you can't sign it. Did Nirvana's "Unplugged" version of that take you by surprise, when they did that?

DB: It did, and it was very poignant because I didn't actually get to see the performance until after Kurt left us. So it was very strange to see. My immediate reaction was that I really wanted to talk to him, you know? And ask him how he discovered the song and stuff like that. It was very touching and I'm very proud that they did it and it's been really nice, you know, because over this last year we've worked with Foo Fighters a couple of times on the festival tour last year and we really got on very well and they came, as you probably know, and did the Garden Show. And just a couple of nights ago we were in the studio, as well, just fooling around with Frank Black from the Pixies, and that was pretty exciting. It really was great energy.

DD: What was your baptism by fire with Nine Inch Nails like on that tour? I've heard it said that you were--- It was kind of surprising to find the audience so leaning towards Nine Inch Nails on that tour.

DB: Well frankly it didn't surprise me. I thought it was going to be like that and I thought I was a real--- the sense of--- It was a kind of challenge that makes me work really hard, and I think that by the end of the tour it was probably one of the best things we could have done. Apart from really sort of giving me a real respect for Trent [Reznor] as a writer and a musician, I discovered that the guy really has great abilities in that area and I would expect to see a lot more really interesting work coming out of him over the next few years, and I would imagine he'll broaden in quite an unsuspected way. He's a great talent. I like the way that they focused. I liked his energy level. And it really sort of made me focus back in on what it is that I'm really good at, and it really set me up for working on the festival tour over in Europe for that next year. Also I think probably a major thing was it helped me bring down the size of the band in a way, because I just realized that we were too complex a sound. It was not the easiest thing in the world to mix; [a] nine-piece band is pretty hard to mix in those big-sized places. And so when I brought us down to—we are now a four-piece with me—I think everything kind of gelled for me, and now I would say that we're a pretty formidable unit.

1997

PHIL WALDEN

OVER THE YEARS, the *World Cafe* has continued to find new music and interview new artists. But being able to find out about the history of music, particularly as it pertains to certain scenes that developed over the years, has definitely been of interest to me.

Phil Walden looms large in the history of southern soul music and rock music. He was Otis Redding's manager, and he went on to found Capricorn Records, home to the Allman Brothers, the Marshall Tucker Band, and Wet Willie, as well as people like folk singer Jonathan Edwards and Martin Mull.

I talked with Walden in 1997 when a compilation of Capricorn Records had just come out accompanying a reissue project. He died of cancer in 2006 at the age of 66.

David Dye: Kind of unusual show on the *World Cafe* Live today. We often have musicians; certainly we've done producer profiles; but it's not often that we have a record company president. And not many are as visionary as our guest today, Phil Walden from Capricorn Records, who is as vital here in the 90s to young bands like Cake and 311 as he was in the 60s when he was managing the career of folks like Otis Redding and Clarence Carter and uh, Mr. Walden, welcome.

Phil Walden: Thank you. It's good to be here.

DD: I thought we would take a little chance today to do a couple things because I think a lot of people are very interested in the past of Capricorn, and certainly your past. And one of the reasons I want to really talk with you was the release of the Capricorn Classics, which is not just all of the hit records from the period, but a lot of the records you had out that were just great records that may not have even, at that time, gotten air play that they deserved.

PW: Thank you. We felt there were a number of particularly important albums that we recorded in the 70s that weren't commercial successes that the current audience at least should have an opportunity to hear. And therefore there were several albums selected that we weren't known for in terms of spectacular sales.

DD: Now, was it just the fact that you were in Macon that you ended up becoming such good friends with Otis Redding, or did you know him before you moved to Macon, Georgia?

PW: No, no, no. I met him--- I had heard of him--- I had sort of secretly planned in my own mind some way to get into the music business, or more specifically, to get into rock and roll. I was just overwhelmed with this business and I desperately wanted to get into it some way or other. And due to the fact that I was not a player or performer, the next best thing seemed to be: why not get involved in, try to be either an agent or a manager or something along those lines. And it was a local talent contest in Macon, Georgia, and week after week there was this one performer, "Rock House Redding," as they called him in those days, that won the talent contest. And my group, generally, came in second or third. And it was several weeks later that I actually had the opportunity to meet Otis Redding when he had become the vocalist with a former client of mine, or early client of mine, Johnny Jenkins and the Pinetoppers. We sort of formed a relationship after that first meeting, and it was a long and fabulous friendship and business relationship.

DD: Now one of the things that was unusual about Otis Redding was how he broke through with rock audiences, more so than a lot of other--- I mean, obviously there was much more crossover then, actually, than there is now, but--- Did you urge him to go in that direction? Did you say, "Hey, go to Monterey. Get on that bill. Do that."? Or was this just stuff he wanted to do?

PW: The Monterey Pop Festival performance developed out of a meeting that I had had in London with the Rolling Stones' management, only two or some few months prior to the Monterey Festival. And [I] received a call and asked if Otis would like to participate on this and that. And I consulted with Jerry Wexler, who at that time was executive vice-president of Atlantic Records, and the end result proved to be--- It was one of the real sensational performances of his career. It proved to be a dramatic turning point in his crossover into a--- It really solidified his rock following that he had very carefully developed.

DD: Let's do a classic from Otis: "I've Been Loving You Too Long."

Otis Redding recording: "I've Been Loving You Too Long"

DD: "I've Been Loving You Too Long," a classic from Otis Redding. And we're talking with Phil Walden, whose earliest days of the music business were as personal manager of Otis Redding. And how did Otis's death affect your career path? It must have been devastating for you.

PW: It was devastating. I mean, it was impossible to accept. It just--- I could not have imagined this happening to him, and at that point, to us, I mean. But out of that tragedy, Capricorn was formed. Otis and I had spoken about it and had planned to organize a record company, and if Otis Redding had survived to this time, there is no doubt in my mind that Otis Redding would have been one of the principals in Capricorn. It was at the suggestion of Jerry Wexler that Capricorn Records--- He founded it. And thank goodness he prevailed and Capricorn became a reality. I've certainly never regretted that decision.

DD: Now, what was your first act? Because my understanding was, at that point--- Everyone associates Capricorn with the Allman Brothers, but at that point wasn't Duane [Allman] working mostly as a studio musician?

PW: That's correct. Duane was not the first signing to Capricorn. Initially, Capricorn was put together to sort of, not take the place, but to . . . fall into that slot that Stax had previously occupied. Stax had been purchased by Gulf and Western and had left the Atlantic fold. So Jerry Wexler suggested that I assemble a studio group very similar to Booker T and the MG's rhythm-section concept, and basically cut R&B and soul singles.

DD: I'm curious, because one of the first things that you have out on the Capricorn Classics series is a record that I remember when it came out absolutely loving, and it didn't really go anywhere, is the Johnny Jenkins record. You already mentioned him. Was he one of the first people signed?

PW: Johnny Jenkins was probably, in reality, my first real client. Johnny Jenkins came out of a band--- The first band that I ever booked was called Pat-T Cake and the Mighty Panthers, and Johnny Jenkins was the guitar player in that band. He left that band and formed Johnny Jenkins and the Pinetoppers. So, Johnny Jenkins--- When we organized Capricorn and we decided to go forward in rock, Jimi Hendrix was enjoying the early sensational days of his career. So, we decided to see if Johnny Jenkins could make a more progressive or more modern type of album. And Johnny Sandlin, the producer, worked with him as well as Duane and various other members of the Allman Brothers. It is true, it did not sell very well, but it has been a highly collectible, very well known album from our early days at Capricorn.

DD: You bet. And that's the only reason I'm upset that it's on CD, is that my vinyl is less valuable now. [laughter] I thought we'd play "A Walk on Gilded Splinters," because it is just a perfect realization of this track. And I guess Dr. John was on this session, also?

PW: Dr. John had moved to Macon shortly thereafter. I don't think he was on that particular session. And I would point out that the sample was the basis for Beck's first big album.

DD: *Loser.* Yeah, and it's interesting because people sometimes assume it was the Dr. John version, but it was this one, which is where the sample came from. Ferocious rhythm section. Let's do this one from *Ton-Ton Macoute!* This is Johnny Jenkins.

> Johnny Jenkins recording: "I Walk on Gilded Splinters"

DD: That's "I Walk on Gilded Splinters" from Johnny Jenkins' *Ton-Ton Macoute!*, if I'm pronouncing it properly. And I'm talking with Phil Walden from Capricorn Records. And that was, that's one of the Capricorn Classics that have been reissued, and it was one of the original records out on Capricorn. Let's talk a little about the beginning of the Allman Brothers. Whose idea was it to actually form that band? Were Duane and Greg looking for other people to play with, or how did that work out?

PW: The first time I heard Duane Allman, and consequently heard of Duane Allman, I was in New York for a series of meetings and one of which was to take place at Atlantic Records. And I had gone by Rick Hall's hotel room to speak briefly with him before we went to Atlantic, and he said, "Let me play you something. We just finished the Wilson Pickett session and I think I got some pretty sensational stuff here." So he put on "Hey, Jude." And just a few minutes into it I asked him to stop, and I said, "Rick, who in the hell is this guitar player?" And I said, "Is he available to form a group?" And Rick says, "I would think so. Why?" I said, "I'm very interested in trying to put together a rock group," to try to prove that I could do something other than the rhythm and blues management agency thing that we had been so involved with. And so I flew to Muscle Shoals, Alabama. Dwayne was scheduled for a session on Arthur Conley, another artist that we managed and was also under production contract to the company that Otis Redding and I had. [I] walked in the studio and Duane Allman was sort of off to the side fiddling around with his guitar. And I walked over, introduced myself. He stood up and asked me about my agenda there. And I said, "Well, I'd be delighted if we could have lunch today, and I got some things I would like to talk to you about." He says, "Great. What do you want to talk to me about?" I said, "I'd like to talk, to discuss with you the possibility of becoming your manager." And he said, "Well, you got it." And it was probably about ten months or so later that the Allman Brothers ventured out on the road to Boston to play their first gig.

DD: I thought we would do something going back to that very first Allman Brothers band record. Thought maybe "Not My Cross to Bear," which is such a great piece of music. The Allman Brothers here on the *World Cafe.*

Allman Brothers recording: "Not My Cross to Bear" and "Don't Want You No More"

DD: The two things that flow together at the very beginning of the first Allman Brothers album, "Don't Want You No More" and "Not My Cross to Bear," and we're talking with Phil Walden, who's been the guiding light behind Capricorn Records over the years. And as he puts it, he sits there and the music comes to him. And that's a great place to be. Mr. Walden, definitely! I just want to talk a little bit about the southern-rock label that Capricorn, I'm sure, embraced in some ways. But when you look at a lot of the acts that came out at that point, even somebody like Elvin Bishop, who certainly got all tied up in that--- He's from the Bay area, or at least he was at that time, I guess. Did you have an A&R strategy as such? I mean, you look at somebody like the Marshall Tucker Band coming out of the box next; you think, uh!—brothers and multiple guitars and all that. Was there any kind of a strategy?

PW: No. I wish I could lay claim to some sort of strategy. But, quite honestly, it really sort of happened in such a nice organic natural way. And to be very, very frank, when I signed Marshall Tucker Band, I was accused by many of just taking complete leave of my senses. Everybody said this band is not a rock band and it's not a country band. We don't know what this band is. I said, "That may be true, but I think they're a very good band. That's the one element that you're missing, that there is something going on here. These guys have got something that they are developing that I think we should be involved in." That's pretty much the way we have signed bands over the years. I hope we are able to continue like this because I think the music will continue to be very interesting if we abide by these same principles and keep music at the forefront of this company.

DD: Well, we'd be remiss if we didn't do one from Marshall Tucker. We'll do "This Old Cowboy." Stick it in here on the *World Cafe.*

Marshall Tucker Band recording: "This Old Cowboy"

DD: So great to hear that—the Marshall Tucker Band with "This Old Cowboy." I'm curious about some things, because obviously southern rock was what everybody was talking about, but you had, I remember, a whole lot of records that Martin Mull had out---

PW: But "southern rock" thing, that was a term I never really smiled upon. To me, I don't know, in this country, in this business, we seem to have to put everything on a shelf, and I just--- I have a hard time putting music on a shelf. It seems to me we are sort of confining or restricting the people that should listen to it when we say, "This is alternative, this is triple-A, this is rock." And maybe we have to do that, but I don't know. So, the southern rock thing just sort of developed. I think that was more of a--- It was developed more by the press than it was Capricorn, because, as you mentioned, certainly Martin Mull was not southern nor was he a southern rocker. So I just never really sort of understood that term but, hopefully, it will be remembered for just a lot of good music that came out of the South.

DD: Absolutely, absolutely. I want to talk about the rebirth of the company because, you know, when people--- I'm sure some people . . . thought, "Well, Phil Walden's bringing Capricorn back. Who's he going to sign? What's he going to do?" And I'm just curious as to some of the bands you were initially just intrigued by that you wanted to start putting out records again.

PW: We made a very conscious decision not to try and resurrect the past in the initial days of its reforming. And we talked. There were some possibilities of some of the acts that formerly recorded for us returning. But we decided that it was time to launch a new era for this company, and since it had been inactive for some eleven years, that we should start with music [that] was being birthed in the 90s as opposed to trying to reconstruct something from the 70s. And our first signing was Widespread Panic from Athens, Georgia, a very progressive modern group which incorporates any number of the ingredients from what, I think, what was good about the 70s, from Capricorn's music standpoint. And shortly thereafter we signed 311. And once again, this is a group that developed a fan base, fan by fan. I can recall the early days; they would have as few as 25 to 30 in an audience. And yet they would do a full and complete show, and then next time they would come back to this city there would be 150; and the next time there'd be 500; time after that it would be 2,000. It just developed like that. This band really built the fan base via their making great little albums and then by performing day after day after day on the road.

DD: Well, tell you what, let's do something from the first 311 album after this one from the latest Widespread Panic, "Hope in a Hopeless World"—just a great song and a great version of this one, too. So we'll go out with that and, Mr. Walden, thank you very much.

PW: Thank you very much for having me.

1997

PATTI SMITH

I'VE TALKED WITH PATTI SMITH A NUMBER OF TIMES OVER THE YEARS. SHE IS ONE OF OUR TRUE ARTISTS AND IS VERY PRESENT WHEN YOU TALK WITH HER. In 2007 she was inducted into the Rock and Roll Hall of Fame.

Funny story. Patti grew up in Deptford Township, New Jersey, outside of Philadelphia. In the early 90s, the station that produces the *World Cafe* in Philadelphia, WXPN, decided to salute Patti's work over the years and declare a day of programming: Patti Smith Day. Turns out her mom, who still lives in New Jersey, heard the programming and called Patti and said, "You have to become a member of this station!" Well, she did. This was during the time that Patti was living with her husband, Fred "Sonic" Smith, in Detroit and raising her kids. When we met her, she said she had two cards in her wallet: her Detroit public library card and her WXPN member card!

This time she was particularly outgoing about her early days and about her creative process. She had just released her album *Peace and Noise*. We began by talking about "1959," her song about Tibet.

Patti Smith recording: "1959"

David Dye: That's "1959" from *Peace and Noise*. Patti, welcome, first of all. It's good to see you again.

Patti Smith: Oh, thank you.

DD: Good to have a new record. That song seems to have a double meaning—a lot about Tibet in 1959 and the Chinese, and the other meaning seemed to be contrasted with what was going on in the States. And I was just wondering personally what 1959 meant to you.

PS: Well when I was, I don't know, about 11 years old, I was doing a report for school on Tibet. And about a month or two after I had started my report—it was a year-type thing—the Chinese invaded. And I had become at that point extremely attached to the country and the Dalai Lama. I was extremely shocked that something like this could happen in our world, because I was taught by my parents that my father had fought in World War II and war was over—you know, that we had fought the wars and the world was free now. At the same time I was also quite aware of the freedom surrounding our country. America was enjoying a certain amount of prosperity and also creative exploration. We had experienced Jackson Pollock and jazz and the Beat generation, cars were big and there was a lot of optimism and a real sense of self and a sense of artistic and physical freedom. And so the song addresses these two things happening—our freedom here, and the taking away of the Tibetan people's rights, human rights.

DD: And I'm wondering how many people in America were aware at that time of that going on.

PS: Many people might have been aware but I think more important: how many people cared? I just don't think they were very interested.

DD: Now, let's jump ahead a few years. Before you moved to New York, I understand you made a start in Philadelphia, or at least in Camden, in this area. Because you were originally from Woodbury, which is not very far from here.

PS: I'm from the Deptford Township area.

DD: Okay.

PS: It's right, crossing over into Woodbury. So I used to come to Camden and Philadelphia. When I was a teenager I used to get the bus and hang out, go to White Tower, White Castles, and look at the Walt Whitman Hotel, and there was a lot of Goodwill stores and . . . down in South Jersey you really couldn't get the new records when they came out. So when *Blonde on Blonde* or *12 by 5* or something like that came out, you had to go to Camden or Philadelphia. I usually crossed the line into Philly to go to Sam Goody's to get my records, so---

DD: So you didn't move out and come to Philadelphia?

PS: I never moved to Philly. I got a job in Philly in '67 and thought I would move to Philly. I was working some high-tech camera at some technical place where they made technical manuals, but um, one day I got laid off and I had, you know, $37 or something and I really--- I just didn't want to start over, so I just got a train to New York City and stayed there.

Patti Smith recording: "Gloria"

DD: There's been a lot written about the first times you've performed. Recently, I guess I'm thinking about *Please Kill Me*, the oral history of punk that just came out. And a lot of people . . . everybody says that the first time they saw you perform, at the church at St. Mark's, that you seemed very confident as a performer at that time. Was that because of the acting that you did before that?

PS: I don't know, I just--- When I was a kid, I really, I thought of being in a missionary for a while. And I was also a Jehovah's Witness, so I was used to going door to door and confronting strangers and having to improvise or be able to discuss ideas. And then I . . . started watching the Johnny Carson show and I sort of admired his situation, and the way he communicated and improvised with people, making them laugh but also making them think. And I was in some plays and I've just always been very comfortable talking in front of people or talking with people or interacting with people in that particular way.

DD: Now when you started writing, did you see your poetry being performed at that time, or did you---

PS: When I was younger I wanted to be a writer in the sort of like Louisa May Alcott vein, because Jo in *Little Women* was the first actual description of a writer. And as I was writing poetry, I used to write a lot to Coltrane records when I was in high school. So I, at a early age, was writing with music behind me.

DD: With meter, with uh---

PS: And I just sort of evolved; it just seemed like a natural progression for me to speak my poetry, or to perform it.

DD: We talked last when *Gone Again* came out, and I actually saw you in a number of situations surrounding that record, and every time I saw you, you were surrounded by sort of total love and admiration from a group of people, and they all seem to have been affected by your work at one time or another. Was that a comfort to you at the time?

PS: Oh, certainly. I mean, doing *Gone Again*, I had a lot of--- Right from the very seed of that album I had a lot of support. First of all, I had--- You know, in his last months of his life, Fred [Patti's late husband, Fred "Sonic" Smith] had taught me chords, and I am a slow learner but I did work very hard to, you know, get a basic rhythm pattern, pretty much a waltz or, you know, that--- I guess it's waltz-time pattern that I like.

DD: Right.

PS: And I learned enough chords to

write my own songs. And I had certain ideas. I was very inspired by Bob Dylan at that time, he put out *World Gone Wrong*, so that greatly inspired some of the songs on *Gone Again* or that gave me the sort of the freedom to write songs that simply, you know, just on acoustic guitar. And I started working with Oliver Ray then, and we spent long, long hours practicing or working on songs. He was very patient, and we spent hours and hours and hours working on songs like "About a Boy" and "Fireflies" and--- So that was very encouraging for me. And then, entering the recording process with old friends, it greatly helped me get through that process honorably, I think.

Patti Smith performs "Beneath the Southern Cross"

DD: The Patti Smith Group, doing that one live: "Beneath the Southern Cross." I want you to talk for just a little bit about the difference in the focus of *Gone Again* and *Peace and Noise*, because on the surface there's a lot of death and loss in both of them. I mean, in this album beginning with "Waiting Underground" and finishing with "Last Call," about the Heaven's Gate [cult]—how is the focus different on the two records for you?

PS: The only difference with *Gone Again* to me, of any of the records, is just that *Gone Again* does specifically address Fred as a human being . . . and gave me a format to tell people just a little about him. But all of the records I've done address that kind of scope, from *Horses* which we had "Birdland" and "Elegy"--- I guess I'm just the kind of person that honors the dead or honors the departed or honors, actually, the human chain. In this record we saw the passing of Allen Ginsberg. The last day that we finished the last mix William Burroughs passed away, who was greatly admired by all of us, and our friend--- I think it's important to salute these people because they saluted us in life. They shared their ideas, their energies, and, you know it's--- I happily salute them.

DD: This is "Whirl Away."

Patti Smith performs "Whirl Away"

DD: We're talking with Patti Smith. That's "Whirl Away" from *Peace and Noise*. And what is that song about?

PS: Well, "Whirl Away" addresses--- In one hand it's addressing a lot of the urban violence that's happening and taking down a lot of our young people, and often for material things. I mean, there's always, it seems there's always something in the paper about, you know, a young boy being killed because somebody wanted his sneakers or his, you know, his new leather coat. It's just addressing the fact that we've become a very materialistic society and we're gauging our value by our material things instead of our intellectual or spiritual enlightenment.

DD: There's a lot of a focus on America on this disc, too, it seems, but not focused in any kind of jingoistic way, but focused on us.

PS: Yeah, it just seems, it's just like that. That's unlike me, too, because I've always been, you know, as an artist I've always had such an affinity with like French literature or German poetry or---

DD: Right.

PS: I don't really know why the record turned out like that; it just did. My mother actually said to me--- My mom's great; she listened to the record and she called me up and she said, "Patricia, I figured out what the record is." And I said, "What?" And she said, "It's an American quilt." I thought that was really beautiful.

DD: You've written a lot of things on this with Oliver Ray, and I've always assumed there was a lot of band writing that went on in the past.

PS: Well, there's always--- I mean, things are constant, you know? There are--- We did a lot of band writing. Tony Shanahan brought in some chords and we literally wrote "1959," we improvised our way through his chords and created "1959." Lenny Kaye and Oliver and I sat in our living room and wrote. It's been a very exciting process. I've--- And I just am so grateful to Fred for having the patience to teach me the chords that he did, because I've been able to write my own songs and it's been a really great experience.

DD: It gives you more power in a way.

PS: Well, it's also--- It's just there's something very, very comforting to be able to express yourself, however simply. You know, I'm pretty much like--- Michael Stipe calls what I write "porch music," you know. I'm sort of like, you know, have that Appalachian kind of approach to songs, you know. I like to be able to sit and, two or three chords and I'm really happy. But you can express quite a bit over two or three chords, as we did with "Gloria," "Land of a Thousand Dances," and many of our songs. Look at Hank Williams; he's done a lot of great, great songs with three chords.

DD: And what are the plans for live performance?

PS: Well, we just, we'll be performing. I mean, we'll go where we can. You know, I have to--- I have a lot of different responsibilities, and we all do, as people within the band, we all have work that we're doing, and family--- And we'll find our way. I think really what we'll do is visit the towns that have appreciated us. You know, I don't really have the time nor the desire to go all over trying to break ground. I feel like, you know, I've done as much as--- You know, I continually try to break ground in my work and, so not having a lot of time, we'll just stop by certain towns and say hello to people that have said hello to me.

DD: Amen. Patti, thank you.

PS: Thank you.

RY COODER

I HAVE DISCOVERED SO MUCH MUSIC THANKS TO RY COODER. He first became known as a hot slide guitarist, teaching Keith Richards a thing or two and adding slide and mandolin to Rolling Stones recordings. His early albums for Warner Brothers are primers in American roots music. I had a chance to interview Ry in 1974 when he released *Paradise and Lunch*, about as perfect an album as he has made. That interview lasted three hours, sitting around playing music on the radio. Twenty-three years later, I made a train trip to New York to interview him again. It was a wide-ranging conversation centering on the then new Buena Vista Social Club recordings.

The Buena Vista Social Club album was one of the cultural highpoints of the late 1990s. These octogenarian Cuban musicians touched something romantic in people around the globe. Ry Cooder went to Cuba and produced it all. He found the musicians and helped create the music. When we had this conversation they hadn't even been released yet. No one knew what they were to become. It was all about the music.

David Dye Introduction: This *World Cafe* features a two-hour conversation with Ry Cooder, recorded recently in New York City. Roots and World Music fans have certainly been familiar with Ry's playing since the early 70s, and albums like *Paradise and Lunch* and his early collaborations with Flaco Jimenez. More recently there have been award-winning CDs, like the collaboration with Malawian guitarist Ali Farka Toure and Indian composer V. M. Bhatt, along with Ry's growing stature as a composer for film. Ry Cooder's latest musical journey took him to Havana, Cuba, in 1996 for a couple of weeks of recordings that gave us three extraordinary discs: The Buena Vista Social Club, The Afro-Cuban All-Stars, and a solo CD by pianist Rubén González.

David Dye: We're on a road trip for the *World Cafe*, and we're in New York City, and we're talking with Ry Cooder. And I just told you that this is our, our second interview in twenty-three years, and the last . . .

Ry Cooder: Man!

DD: . . . time we did it, we took three hours to cover a lot of the music you've been involved in.

RC: Three hours? We did?! [laughs]

DD: Unbelievable. And that was twenty-three years ago, and I don't think you'd, well, you certainly hadn't been to Mali, Okinawa . . .

RC: No.

DD: . . . Havana. So we have a little bit of ground to cover today. The reason for our visit is the recording a couple years ago now, and the release just this year, of three recordings that Nick Gold and World Circuit did in Havana in what must have been a magical couple of weeks and, particularly, Buena Vista Social Club . . .

RC: Yeah.

DD: . . . the record that you were involved in. So, did you know what to expect when you arrived in Havana?

RC: Oh, no. All I knew was that Nick's original idea of getting West Africans and Cubans together wasn't going to go because the Africans couldn't make it. I mean they, he had, he had figured all this out, and he's pretty connected over there, so I think these, this was, this could've been a great thing, and it may happen sometime.

DD: Uh-huh.

RC: But it didn't happen because they didn't come, and so you're sort of saying, "Well, we're here, you know, we better do something." So we, we kind of took a look around and invited these people in, you know, sort of from one day to the next. And within three days the room was pretty complete, pretty packed up, you know. We had everybody, somehow or other. It just was some kind of a--- For instance, they said "Rubén [piano player Rubén González], I think, I mean, is, is dead," and the next thing they said was, "No, he's got arthritis and can't play, but," you know.

DD: Rubén González?

RC: Yeah. Incredible, really.

DD: Well, I want to talk about a few of the people that you record with and maybe play some of their contributions to this record. One thing I think people ought to realize when they get a hold of *Buena Vista Social Club*, it's not a lot of, of Ry Cooder soloing with other people; you are a part of a band.

RC: Yeah, yeah. I'm trying to simply help out, you know, and see that we get the best out of everybody that we can. I mean these are the guys who play this music for real; these are the creators. Some of them, you know, well, Compay Segundo's 90 years old already. But it's not for me to sit there and twang too frontally, you know? Besides, they do it, you know? They do it real well and I just was kind of--- I go in there as a student more than anything else.

DD: Talk about people who aren't familiar with—which probably is a lot of people—with Compay Segundo. What is his contribution to song and Cuban music?

RC: Yeah. Well, let's see. It's, it's, it's probable that he's the last—there might be a couple others, but I mean, ninety years old—he's the last practicing, you know, the oldest from the golden era of this music. This is, this is, this Cuban classic, root, core music from which came salsa and all of the popular forms that we know about today, you know, and all this. But this is music that was kind of put together somewhere around, let's say, from 1890 to about 1940. By 1940 there was--- something new was added. Up until that time you had these songs with the Afro rhythms and the Spanish and French melodies and things, and, and the beautiful poetry. They're very poetic down there in Cuba; they have a lot of--- They, they set a lot of store by poetry.

DD: Mm-hmm.

RC: And originally, I guess in the 1800s, these, these troubadours, these traveling musicians, were as much poets as they were musicians. And so gradually, from almost nothing, these songs began to--- these little story songs began to sort of take shape. And they're--- they put a lot of time into this. It's very well worked-out, very well-wrought, you know, very crafted. And Compay, he's--- Most of them have died, you know, over the years, of course. But he's one of the main ones. He's written hundreds of songs, and for some--- in some incredible way, he survived, you know. And, and he's, of course, up-and-at-'em all the time.

DD: I thought we'd do the one where you got to do a little bit of a guitar duet with him on, uh, "Y Tú Qué Has Hecho?"?

RC: "Has Hecho," yeah.

DD: "Has Hecho."

RC: Yeah.

> Buena Vista Social Club recording: "Y Tú Qué Has Hecho?"

DD: Compay Segundo, singing on a recording with our guest today, Ry Cooder, here on the *World Cafe.* From *Buena Vista Social Club.* "What have you done?" I guess, that was how you would translate---

RC: Yeah, it's a great song, great idea for a song.

DD: Now, explain a little bit about what music means in Cuba today. I've heard from people who've come back who say the music is everywhere.

RC: Yeah, it's, it's--- I think it's at the center of the national identity. You might even say the culture comes through the music. They express everything about these people in these songs, really. They are always sort of letting you know who they are; that's kind of where the resonance is. There's this greasy kind of funky, elegant, juicy thing that is just happening in Cuba all the time. It's like everywhere, everybody walks in this rumba gait, and the old people aren't stooped over; they're riding their bike and they're, you know, greeting one another, and it's like a village. Havana's a little, a little city, you know? It's, it's got two million people in it, but it's very compact, and everybody seems to know everybody else, and they play instruments! You hear trumpet coming out of somebody's apartment, and somebody's on the street playing bongo, and everybody's getting a group together up. It's just like heaven for music, really.

DD: Another person I want to talk about who was a whole--- My discovery for 1997 is Rubén González.

RC: Yeah.

DD: Whoa! [laughs]

RC: Yeah.

DD: I, I--- Actually, the first recording I heard was the one with the Afro-Cuban All-Stars . . .

RC: Right.

DD: . . . which he plays a whole lot on. And he's all over your record. He is, what? 78?

RC: Just, just right around in there, yeah.

DD: Right. And he is just an incredible soloist. Did you--- You didn't know he was alive when you---

RC: Well, I had, yeah, I had tapes of him. I had records from the 50s, 60s, but you heard nothing about this guy. And you don't hear about musicians in Cuba like this. These people are sort of hidden from view and, and I've, I asked, you know, "If Rubén is around, bring him down." And they say he's dead; the next guy says he's arthritic. He actually hadn't played any piano for ten years, it seemed; he didn't have one. He didn't have a piano. But he came down. He's fine. I mean, he's, of course he's fine; he's great. He was Arsenio Rodriguez's first piano player back before the war and, among other things, has to be considered one of the creators of the modern Cuban piano style. And, and, I just, I've never heard anything quite like it, really.

DD: There's a piece he plays from, from your disc, the Buena Vista Social Club, called "Pueblo Nuevo". . .

RC: Yeah.

DD: . . . which is just beautiful. And I thought we'd do that one.

Buena Vista Social Club recording: "Pueblo Nuevo"

DD: Rubén González on piano at the center of that piece, called "Pueblo Nuevo."

RC: Pueblo; "New Town."

DD: He is also featured on his own record, which is *Introducing . . . Rubén González*, which is also part of this whole series that World Circuit has out here in the States on Nonesuch, which is just an incredible series. There's one track on here—and I forget which one it is—which is kind of an American jazz track. It has a whole different---

RC: Well it's a Cuban song but, unusually, it's written by a friend of Compay's who was obsessed with—as he told me in the '30s—American music in film. So he would go to the movies every day, and then he'd go home and try to write music like that. It's very unusual because they don't do swing tunes in Cuba; they don't play that.

DD: Right.

RC: No backbeat down there.

DD: And it just totally surprised me.

RC: Yeah, me too. Very unique.

DD: Uh-huh. Which piece is it again?

RC: "Orgullecida."

DD: Right. Now I, I must say, sometime, you lay back on most all of these.

RC: Mm-hmm.

DD: Is this a more comfortable tune for you to play on? Or, or, or were you just feeling your way with all of them?

RC: Well, he saw me with my bottlenecks, Compay, and he goes, "Oh, si, hawaiano," you know, "I, I know about that stuff." I said, "Oh, do you," you know, "What have you heard?" "Oh, I had a friend." And then he tells this story. So I said, "Great, let's hear this song." I mean, paydirt, right? This is, like discovery here. Who would've--- Nobody else knew this tune; he knew it. He knows all the songs. Compay knows all the music, so. And then he says, "Now you"—he speaks, of course, only in his archaic Spanish—he says, "You can play your, uh, that thing you do in this tune. It's--- there's, there's, you know, take your solo," he's telling me. So, of course, it's set up for it. It's, it's obviously derived, it's like Hawaiian music coming through, Tin Pan Alley coming down to Havana, I guess, is the root of a, of a musical expression like that. So, that's why I take that solo, because there's obviously a reason to; there's room for it.

Buena Vista Social Club recording: "Orgullecida"

DD: "Orgullecida," a wonderful piece from the Buena Vista Social Club. I wanted to do another one from the Afro-Cuban All-Stars, as long as we're basking in this great richness of music that's come from these sessions. It's the one that--- It's a very funny song if you follow the lyrics on "Alto Songo."

RC: "Alto Songo" is a funny song.

DD: With everybody kind of trying to up one, up oneself about their singing.

RC: Right. Exactly.

DD: And then at the end it's, "Como Ry Cooder!"

RC: [laughs] Yeah, yeah, yeah!

DD: It's so funny when you come in on your solo! [laughing]

RC: I know.

DD: Did, did--- Were you expecting to

take a solo on that? Or was that---

RC: Uh, he asked me to do it—Marcos, the bandleader who runs that group and, and, and sort of a head guy when they do that stuff. These guys are good. I mean, you know, they're the greatest musicians I've, I have to say, I've been around. So you have to, you have to step lively, you know, you have to get with it, you know!

DD: "Alto Songo."

RC: Yeah.

Afro-Cuban All-Stars recording: "Alto Songo"

DD: That is one that Ry Cooder, our guest today, plays on with the Afro-Cuban All-Stars. One more player I was taken with is the laoud player?

RC: Laoud, yeah. Mm-hmm.

DD: Barbarito Torres?

RC: Torres, yeah.

DD: Who tears it up!

RC: Tears it up, just totally tears it up.

DD: [laughs] What's his story? He's fairly young!

RC: He's pretty young; I guess he's in his early forties. The laoud—being a kind of weird, Spanish, Moorish, hybridized, evolved instrument—is, even today in Cuba, considered kind of archaic. It's, it's not really part of anybody's musical scene anymore.

DD: Mm-hmm.

RC: But it was traditionally there to accompany singing. There was a kind of a flamenco style that's now quite gone from music down there. But this sort of flamenco style that this laoud was a kind of a counterpoint to. And you would've heard this regional music. I mean, it's not city music; it's not a city instrument.

DD: Well, in fact, the singer on this---Eliades Ochoa?

RC: Ochoa.

DD: Ochoa, umm, calls himself a country man?

RC: He, he is; he's a cowboy; he's "Guajiro." He's from Oriente Province, which is the countryside. It's in the eastern part of the island where the tobacco and the sugar cane and all that stuff is from, you know. It's where the Africans were brought. And it's like the Mississippi of Cuba, so people from there are considered country and, in fact, all these musicians—most all of them—are originally from there; the music is originally emanating from there. But Eliades is really country. But he's like your, your preeminent country musician in Cuba today.

DD: "El Cuarto de Tula."

RC: Yeah.

Recording: "El Cuarto de Tula"

DD: I guess that's "Tula's Room," and that also has some funny lyrics.

RC: It has some very funny lyrics. If you can pick up on the, all the stuff. These tunes have two--- they have a second layer, and then they have a third layer. And the third layer's the one that, if you know your Spanish and you know your idiom, it's hysterically funny. Some of the stuff that goes on, if you, you know, as I understand, it's mostly sex references and very funny.

DD: We're back talking with Ry Cooder on the *World Cafe*, on our road trip to New York. And, as I said, we talked [chuckles], we talked some twenty, twenty-three years ago, and I want to talk about a few things we talked about then. But it's been so many wonderful things that you've been involved in since then. A lot of duets involved here! A lot of you playing with someone else, and it's, it's . . .

RC: Yeah.

DD: . . . it's always interesting to see how you interact and, as in that, how they react . . .

RC: Right.

DD: . . . I guess, to you. Umm, and I guess we're sort of moving towards the recording you did with Ali Farka Toure. And, and I wanted to play the one that Gatemouth [Brown] is on, too.

RC: Yeah, with the fiddle.

DD: I recently talked to him, and he is extremely proud of this recording.

RC: He is?

DD: Yeah.

RC: Well, good, because at the time he wasn't so sure.

DD: Right.

RC: I mean, you know, he didn't know from Ali Farka and wasn't going for the act, except that it was awful good when it got done. I thought it was pretty hot stuff.

DD: Indeed.

RC: Yeah, his, Gatemouth's thing on the fiddle is, is like, it comes in there like, an attack! It's fabulous, you know. It's like, "Let's get going here. Let's jive it up a little bit." Fabulous band, too.

DD: Now, I heard there was at one point a cancelled tour, when you and Ali Farka---

RC: Yeah, he had a war he had to go stop back home; a skirmish he had to go take care of, you know. Kind of like *High Noon*, you know.

DD: I've heard the story told that he, he is a farmer, and people were overrunning his farm and he---

RC: Well, the nomads don't like the fact that he's growing rice in a mass. He's trying to feed the region; he's the chief there. And the nomads come by, they've been coming by for about 2,000 years or so to graze their herds, and they see all this rice where the grass used to be, and they get mad, and they start shooting. They come into town; you can picture this, right?

DD: Oh, yeah, yeah! [laughs]

RC: And it's like one riot, one ranger. You know, someone's got to go put a stop to it, so he went back and put a stop to it because he's a tough guy. And I don't think anybody's going to go upside Ali Farka. I wouldn't. Very rough character.

Ry Cooder, Ali Farka Toure, and Clarence Gatemouth Brown recording: "Ai Du"

DD: That's our guest today, Ry Cooder, along with Ali Farka Toure and Gatemouth Brown on that recording, "Ai Du," from *Talking Timbuktu*. I want to talk some about your film work and in the--- sort of in the liner notes to the collection on some of your film music. You use a couple words that have, really, we've been talking about all the--- throughout what we're talking about today: "intuitive" and "exploratory"---

RC: Yeah.

DD: ---in, in how you approach things. And I'm curious: I guess, Walter Hill was the first director---

RC: Yeah.

DD: ---you worked for?

RC: Yeah.

DD: How, how do you work? Does he show you a film? Do you work towards it, or---

RC: Right. I mean, he--- The only way I know— Because I'm not trained to do this work, and I didn't study it, I don't know composition, and I don't know theory at all. In other words, all of the basic tools that you're supposed to have—it's a foregone conclusion that you have—I don't have. So how come? So he comes in, you know, you--- It's sort of the same process; you look at a film and you talk. And hopefully the director has some idea that he can steer you, he or she can steer you on the right path, you know, or give you an indication, give you some pointers, what they're thinking of. Even conceptually, something is better than nothing.

DD: I had a conversation with Tim and David Robbins about *Dead Man Walking*.

RC: Yep. Right.

DD: Which they did a whole companion album, and I guess they were thinking of using a lot of those songs in the film, but it--- Not very many of them actually appear in the film.

RC: Well, yeah. They don't have room for 'em.

DD: One of the things they talked about—particularly in a film that was set in Louisiana—is that they did not want a Louisiana feel to it.

RC: Yeah.

DD: Was that operative in what you were doing with that?

RC: Well, my take on all that was--- I was brought in kind of . . . on the side to wrangle this Eddie Vedder and Nusrat Ali Khan session here in New York, and so I had a little piece of the thing . . .

DD: Right.

RC: . . . that I was supposed to wrangle. But my opinion of it all was that he had a story which could've had very specific Christian, religious overtones, and he seemed to want to avoid that. And he seemed to want to make more of a . . . universal statement, keep it from becoming such a Christian story. And one way to do that—that's my opinion of this anyways—and one way to do that is to just bring in, you might say, spiritual qualities from other references. And the way to do that is, of course, through music.

DD: Well, let's, let's do that. Something from that session that you wrangled [chuckles] with uh, with Eddie Vedder and the late Nusrat Fateh Ali Khan.

Recording: "The Long Road"

DD: That's "The Long Road" with Nusrat Fateh Ali Khan and Eddie Vedder—a piece that our guest today, Ry Cooder, helped put together for the soundtrack to the film, *Dead Man Walking*. Well, we're talking about movie music that Ry's been involved in. One of the most beloved pieces he's done is the music for Wim Wenders' film, *Paris, Texas*, and I ask him how he felt about it when he got started working on that.

RC: Well, you could see it was working. I mean, you know, there was a good idea there; there was beautiful film. I mean, obviously perfect for this kind of work that, that, whatever it is I'm doing, you need to have. You need to have a film that's shot, and conceived, and is operating in a certain realm. I mean, in other words, it's an interior kind of quality that it has, rather than events, event-oriented, or, or episodic, you know, and action-oriented. I don't know . . . how they refer to this in movies, but I mean, Wenders' is the kind of guy who makes films like that.

DD: Right.

RC: Or some of the time, anyway. And so, he says, "Well, play that Blind Willie Johnson tune." And I'm saying, "Oh, okay. We can make that work. Just shape it a little bit here, and---" You know? It's like building a little wall, you know? We put it over here, and we mortar it down a little bit over there. Had three days to do it. You know, simple, easy thing as long as--- Because, you know, if you overdo it, you'll ruin that film. It's a very delicate situation, you know?

DD: Still, the fact that it holds up on its own, outside of the film context, is kind of beside the point.

RC: Well, I guess it's beside the point as far as the film's concerned. I'm always trying to--- You hope that you're making music that is worth listening to, though.

DD: Right.

RC: It's not--- They say, you know, there's some kind of an idea movie music's supposed to disappear, and I don't really know about that. I'm not so sure that's true. Everybody loves Georges Delarue in Truffaut's films, classic films, and that music didn't disappear.

DD: Nino Rota, yeah.

RC: Right! I mean, you know, and so on. The guys that--- That guy that used to score Kurosawa's pictures; what's his name? Masaru Sato? I'm telling you, anything but disappear! But it enhances the picture. And I'm not going to argue with people who know about film theory because, what do I know? But it sure is interesting to listen to some classic film scores and realize that there's some, you know, fantastic thing going on some of the time.

Ry Cooder recording: "Dark Was the Night"

DD: "Dark Was the Night," from the film, *Paris, Texas.* Our guest, Ry Cooder. We're talking film music with Ry Cooder, and I also asked him about the soundtrack to the film, *Performance*, in which Mick Jagger jumps on top of a table and does a song called "Memo from Turner," and exactly how that recording took place.

RC: They sent his vocal, Jagger's vocal was sent with a click-track, and then all the group in L.A.—the studio band that was scoring the film that we were all doing together—we just laid the rhythm, the entire music track, underneath the voice.

DD: As opposed to the other way around, which is how things often happen.

RC: Yeah, well, it just so happened that, naturally, he was over there and he said, I mean, you know, however it got done.

DD: Right.

RC: The magic of modern recording, right?

DD: [laughs] And who was in the band? I always heard it was the Meters, but that wasn't true?

RC: In, in *Performance*?

DD: Yeah.

RC: It was me, Russ Titelman on rhythm guitar, umm, Gene Parsons—I'm so sorry, pardon me; I'm old and in the way here—on drums, Randy Newman on piano, or organ, or something. Who was on bass? Jesus; Chris Ethridge, maybe? You know, it's a lot of years, alright?

DD: Yeah.

RC: So I can't be responsible! [laughs]

DD: [laughs]

RC: But that's kind of the band as it was. It was a great band, of course, interesting band. And a few other people here and there; Milt Holland on percussion.

Recording: "Memo from Turner"

DD: "Memo from Turner." That's Ry Cooder on the slide guitar on that, and Mick Jagger on the vocals, from the soundtrack to the film, *Performance.* More conversation with Ry Cooder coming up here on this very special *World Cafe.*

DD: So, as we wind up our visit with Ry Cooder, our trip in New York, let's go full-circle and go back to my--- Ry, I got to tell you, my favorite record in 1997 is . . .

RC: No doubt about it.

DD: . . . *Introducing . . . Rubén González.* And there's a piece, well, there--- Throughout this there's such a combination of things.

RC: Mm-hmm.

DD: You were pointing to a piece called, "Danzon" . . .

RC: Yeah.

DD: . . . which is almost--- I mean, it seems like classical influences.

RC: It's the nineteenth, it's the sound of nineteenth century music in Cuba, and that means to me the root. The starting point for all this other stuff comes from this danzon music, which this is one such piece. I'm not saying this was written in the nineteenth century, but it is certainly in the style. It's number seven here.

DD: Right.

RC: You know, it's where it all came from. This is what they did in the 19th century. And this, this is Rubén like nobody else playing this stuff, and it's just, to me, it's just incredible sound to hear in the nineties. It's quite a thing. Quite, quite amazing, really.

DD: Ry, thank you very much.

RC: Thank you.

Rubén González recording: "Almendra"

DD: "Almendra" from the great Cuban piano player, Rubén González, from the wonderful album called *Introducing . . . Rubén González.* Big thanks to Ry Cooder for being our guest today. It was great to be able to play all this music he's been involved with over the years, here on the *World Cafe.*

1998

JOEL DORN

JOEL DORN IS ONE OF A NUMBER OF RECORD BUSINESS FIGURES WE HAVE HAD ON THE *WORLD CAFE* OVER THE YEARS. He is a producer with hits by Roberta Flack and Leon Redbone, and seminal albums by the Neville Brothers and many others, particularly in the jazz field when he worked for Atlantic records in the 1960s and '70s.

Two things about Joel made this particularly fun for me: He is a former jazz DJ, and he's originally from Philadelphia, home of the *World Cafe.*

One of the people we refer to in this interview is Hal Willner, now a well-known producer of avant-garde concerts and albums, but at one time Joel Dorn's humble assistant.

My only regret is that we just touched on a fraction of the work Dorn has been involved in over the years.

David Dye: Our guest today is Joel Dorn, who started his career here in Philadelphia as a DJ at a legendary jazz station—which has a lot in common with what happened in radio in the late 60s, with people who loved music taking over the radio—and [in] his career went on to be one of the premier staff producers at Atlantic [Records], then on his own. In fact, his production company is called The Masked Announcer. So, I think it all begins with being a DJ.

Joel Dorn: Well it does for me.

DD: Yeah.

JD: I mean, that was--- I went on the air in 1961 when I was 19, at WHAT-FM, which was one of the pioneer 24-hour 7-day-a-week jazz stations, FM jazz stations, in the country, and I was on from '61 to '67. I always wanted to be a disc jockey, but I always really wanted to be a record producer, so I knew it was a stepping stone to that.

DD: Obviously, I want to talk about your transitioning into becoming a producer, but what did you learn from being a DJ that helped you be a producer?

JD: Well, one of the peculiar things about the radio station I worked at was that there was a telephone in the studio. So, the listeners could actually call in and talk to you while you were on the air. So, in the seven years that I was on the air, I spoke to thousands and thousands of people who listened to that station, my show, you know, and you start to get a sense of what real people like. You know, there is a rarified atmosphere when you're doing anything, exclusive of being one of the people you're doing it for, if you know what I mean. So, I would play a record and the phone would light up in three seconds, people either say I love it, I hate it. It doesn't mean--- You know, any one of a thousand different responses, so you had a sense from that audience of what worked, what didn't work, what was good, what was bad, how it affected them, whether it made them happy, whether it made them angry. There was so much you learned from each phone call, and a lot of that was kind of like college for me when I went on to make records.

DD: Well I'll tell you what I want to play. I want to start off with the Oscar Brown Jr. tune. There's a lot of Oscar Brown Jr. tunes that people know. To me, this is a less familiar one: "Forty Acres and a Mule."

JD: This used to, this used to really get people crazy.

> Oscar Brown Jr. recording: "Forty Acres and a Mule"

DD: "Forty Acres and a Mule," one of the songs that lit up the phones when our guest today, Joel Dorn, was being a DJ back between 1961 and 1967. He's gathered the things together on a, I'm sure, what was a labor of love, called *Songs That Made the Phone Light up*, a collection of material from, I guess, the early 60s mostly.

JD: Well---

DD: A couple things go back---

JD: I was on the air from '61 to '67, so not all the records were made in that timeframe. For instance, the Jimmy Rushing wasn't; the Lambert Hendricks & Ross cut wasn't; the Austin Cromer Dizzy Gillespie wasn't. But, they were all still being played on the radio at that time, or at least I was playing them.

DD: So, there you are. Being a DJ--- And you had a relationship with the folks at Atlantic Records already.

JD: Oh yeah.

DD: From when, how did that---

JD: Well I, when I was 14, I was sitting in my grandmother's kitchen on St. Bernard Street, in West Philadelphia, a few blocks from here. And I was listening to Georgie Woods on WDAS. It was 9:15 on a Friday night in the winter of 1956, and I heard a Ray Charles record called "Ain't That Love." And I lost it. I went nuts. I couldn't--- I never heard anything like that in my life. It was the beginning of a ten-, twelve-year obsession with Ray Charles that I won't even bore you with but, he recorded for Atlantic Records. And, if it was good enough for Ray Charles, my newfound friend, it was good enough for me. So, I started a correspondence with one of the three principals at Atlantic Records, Neshui Ertegun; he was a vice president. He was in charge of the jazz, and the packaging, the covers, the liner notes—all that stuff. And we started to write back and forth to each other. I should say I wrote to him and he was kind enough to write back to me, and he sent me free records. I told him I wanted to be a producer, and he kind of encouraged me, but Atlantic was a small- to medium-size company at that time and they had all the producers they needed, and I figured if I went on the air and I became important to Atlantic and other record companies as a record seller in this market—Philly was always a good record town—maybe I could, you know, increase the value of my stock a little bit. And it never occurred to me [that] I wasn't going to do what I wanted to do, and it was a 24-hour a day obsession.

DD: So, the first record, first artist you produced was Hubert Laws?

JD: Hubert Laws. Once again, Neshui Ertegun said to me, "You want to produce records?" "Yeah." "Okay, go find somebody." So, in those years when I was here in Philly, there used to be two clubs in the city—Pep's and the Showboat. And I was there every night after I went off the air at one in the morning; I'd catch the last set at Pep's. I guess, you know, I drove everybody nuts. I wanted to meet the musicians, and I was too young to go in the clubs. But Jack Goldenberg from Pep's, and Herbie Spivak from the Showboat, used to let me come in as long as I didn't drink and as long as I didn't make any noise. You know, so I had a chance to hang. And I get a call from Jack Goldenberg one night, he said, "I know about your offer from Atlantic Records." You know, I told him I was looking for an artist. And he said, "Just get down to the club." Mongo Santamaria was appearing that week and he had this flute player. [Goldberg] said, "There's a flute player in Mongo's band that will blow your mind," he says, "just get down there." So I went down to the club and I caught the last set. And I walked in and Hubert Laws was playing "Manha de Carnaval" with Mongo, and

I never heard a flute player like that in my life and I just, you know, lunged at him. I said, "I can get you on Atlantic Records," because Neshui--- Neshui said, "I'll sign anybody you want, but you got fifteen hundred bucks. That's for the artist, that's for you, that's for the musicians, that's for the studio, that's for everything," he said, "so you better make a good record." You know? And I was lucky: I picked the right, like I told you before, I picked the right piece of talent. And I remember the group—in Hubert's group, for the session—was Richard Davis on bass, Joe Chambers on drums (who's from Chester, Pennsylvania), and Chick Corea, a young piano player from Boston, on piano. And the record was good. Hubert's good, and that led to more things, and then I got my full-time job at Atlantic because I recorded a Philadelphia artist, a bagpipe player from Philly, a jazz bagpipe player named Rufus Harley, and the record broke in Detroit. It sold 5,000 copies of that record in Detroit. So I got a call from Neshui, after Hubert and I had financed it. I financed it; I borrowed the money from a guy to pay for the Rufus Harley record. And he said, "Come up to New York." So I went up to New York, and after begging him for a job for ten years, he said, "You're going to work at Atlantic now."

DD: Let's play something from that Hubert Laws disc.

Hubert Laws recording

DD: From the first album that our guest today, Joel Dorn, produced, that's Hubert Laws.

You know, I was going through my collection, all my free records from Atlantic back in the day, and I pulled out one of my records, one of my favorite records, which was the one you did with Yusef Lateef. And you told me it was one of your favorites, but it didn't sell.

JD: Oh, it didn't sell at all.

DD: Yeah.

JD: What happened was, I told them, I said, suppose you were sitting in the middle of space, you know? And, it was just you and a radio. And the radio had no beginning and no end; like when you turned the dial, it could be any time. You could turn the dial and it could be the 15th century, you could turn the dial and it could be the 38th century. Or it could be from 1923 to 1968. I said, just make all different kinds of music starting in the 20s and going up to today, and I want to do a space radio thing. He didn't even blink, you know? He really gets it. So he says, "I got it." So, each one of the selections here is based on either a different genre or a different timeframe. And then we went in and we made the montage, the radio montages. And that's the part that fascinates me because, have you ever listened to those with headsets?

DD: Oh yeah. They're great.

JD: Some interesting stuff in them [laughs].

DD: Now where--- You spent a lot of time on that.

JD: Whew!

DD: That was your artistry.

JD: Or lunacy.

DD: We were talking about Ray Charles, so I thought we'd do "Rock House."

Yusef Lateef recording: "Rock House"

DD: I wanted to play something from Gary Burton because you did a number of albums with Gary Burton. Which one?

JD: An album called *Throb*. That was a hell of a record, the Gary Burton/Keith Jarrett thing. I was Gary's producer, so when he said he wanted to do an album with Keith--- I knew Keith and Charles Lloyd, you know, from that little explosion from the Chico Hamilton thing, you know.

DD: Right.

JD: And that's a real example of a record where I sat in the control room, ate dinner, made sure the lights were the level that they wanted them to be and the mikes were plugged in, and sat back while it happened. Because there was nothing to do. You had two guys that were excellent musicians that had a clear view of what they wanted to do. And I was lucky enough to be in the room and kind of supervise it, you know.

DD: Well, let's do one of Keith's tunes from that.

JD: "Grow Your Own," that was the song.

Recording: "Grow Your Own"

DD: Gary Burton and Keith Jarrett. From your first Grammy award-winning album?

JD: I don't know. There was a period there where, you know, you hit a stride, right? Where everything you do is good, regardless of what you do. So there was a run there where I won a bunch of Grammys and they just were like coming in the door and I was happy to accept them. But, you know, it's weird when you think about those things because they kind of happen. You can't plan for that.

DD: I want to talk about Roberta Flack. Tell me about your relationship with her. How did it begin?

JD: I had a call from Roland Kirk. He wasn't Rahsaan [a name Kirk added in 1970] yet; he called me. He was playing in D.C. and the bass player in his group, Steve Novosel, was married to a schoolteacher who played piano and sang at nights and on the weekends in a club called Mr. Henry's in D.C., up by the

Capitol. And, Rahsaan calls me up like 7:30 in the morning, or 9 in the morning, and he said, uh, I said, "Hello?" He said, "I heard a singer you should sign." I said, "What's her name?" He said, "Roberta Flack." I said, "What's she sing like?" And he said, "She sings like a colored lady" and he slammed the phone down because he was insulted that I didn't--- because . . . I didn't say, "Good, I'll sign her over the phone right now," you know, before sunrise or something.

DD: Right.

JD: And he never talked about her again. And then about a year later, I had made a record with Les McCann, "With These Hands," and it was kind of like a jazz/R&B hit. And Les was hot, and it was the first record for the label and the first one we had done together. So Atlantic always had a policy—be nice to the artists, they're our friends. So Les calls me like six in the morning one morning from D.C., and he said, "Just do what I'm telling you." And I said, "What are you telling me?" He said, "There's a chick down here named Roberta Flack. Sign her and record her; she's going to be the biggest thing in the country." So I remembered what Rahsaan said, and now Les is saying the same thing. I'm saying, okay. So I went to Neshui and I said, "Les McCann told me there's a singer," blah, blah, blah. He said, "What do you want to do?" I said, "You know, how can we get hurt, you know?" He said, "Alright, you got $10,000. Make a record with her." So I made a record with her. We sent her a contract before I heard her. And when I heard her, it was like unbelievable, you know. I went down to the club and caught her live. The resulting album, *First Take*, terrific album, and it's her really at the height of her innocence. I mean, she'd been doing these songs for years. I didn't have to give her a song; I just had to record what she did. And, we sold, we did well, we sold about 100-150,000 albums in the first year, year and a half. But we didn't have a single. Now the jazz guys were calling us and saying, every time we play "First Time Ever I Saw Your Face" by Roberta Flack we get dozens of calls. I went to Atlantic, I said I'd like to put a single out on this. They said no, it's too long. Blah, blah, blah. Alright, good, but the album was selling and I was already into this record, *Chapter Two*, so the second record I knew was going to be a step up and we'd sell more and she'd be bigger and all that stuff. Anyway, I got a call one morning at the office from Clint Eastwood, who was directing his first film, *Play Misty for Me.* And he called Atlantic and he asked for me because he had--- On the way to work he was listening to KBCA-FM, which was the jazz station in LA, and they played "First Time Ever I Saw Your Face"--- And the key moment in that movie is a sequence in the forest, and he didn't have any music for that, and he said, "This would be perfect for that scene but I'm out of money, and it's my first movie. It's the first movie I'm directing and I don't have any more budget. I got a thousand bucks." I think he actually paid it out of his pocket. He said I have a thousand dollars, that's all I can pay you. And you know, that's well below what you get for making music for the movies, but Clint Eastwood, first--- cool. So I went to Neshui and I said, "You got a chance to be in a Clint Eastwood movie." He was a little reluctant at first, surprisingly; it wasn't his style. But he said, "A thousand dollars isn't a lot of money." I said, "Yeah but I think it's a--- " Anyway, so he said okay, do it. So I called Eastwood back, I said you got it. He said send me a clean tape. He said I got to chop it up a little bit and put it in the film. So he did, right. I don't hear from him for six months. All the sudden, the movie comes out and we start getting calls from all over the country from radio stations who are saying people are calling the station looking for this Roberta Flack record—"First Time Ever I Saw Your Face"—you got to put a single out. Now it's not the jazz stations, it's the pop stations. So I said, cool, we'll put a single out. Especially in New Orleans, a guy named Bobby Mitchell down there who was the program director at the pop station. So he said it's too long for us to play, edit it. So I went to the studio and I edited down what I thought was a good single. Sent it down to Bobby Mitchell. "Special delivery" in those days; you know there was no FedEx, right?

DD: Right, right.

JD: Sent it down to him. Calls me back, he said my secretary wants to talk to you. So, the secretary gets on and she said, listen, you edited the single wrong, it's no good. I said really. You know, I was going to say do I tell you how to type letters, you know, but I thought better of it. She said, I'll tell you how to edit it. I said okay. She said, I'm going to go into the studio here and edit it and I'll send you my version of how you should do it. She sent me her version and it was perfect. So we used her version. Put it out, within six-eight weeks we sold four million records and she was off and running.

DD: This is the unedited version.

Roberta Flack recording: "First Time Ever I Saw Your Face"

DD: "First Time Ever I Saw Your Face." Roberta Flack, one of the early successes of our guest today. Joel Dorn is with us. He is many things. He was producer at Atlantic Records for years. As the Masked Announcer, he's been going on and producing records for lots of companies since then. And, one of your assistants has gone on to do some really wonderful things too—Hal Willner.

JD: The lovely Hal Willner.

DD: Yeah.

JD: Who's also from Merion, this neighborhood.

DD: See, Philadelphia folks.

JD: His father owned Hymie's, the delicatessen on Montgomery.

DD: I wanted to move on to a couple more vocal things, more pop things. Leon Redbone seems like a great artist for you.

JD: Perfect dream artist. You know, one of a kind. Oddball. Strange.

DD: Did he search you out or, how---

JD: [laughs] Everything that ever happened to me, happened to me by mistake. I'm really a lucky guy. Everybody hated him but me. Nobody could see what it was like, and I knew this guy was a star. So I signed him. Then we signed him to--- I signed him to me, then we signed him to Warner Brothers. We made the first record and Warner Brothers hated it. But anyway— *Saturday Night Live*, that was their first year on the air. So I went there, you know, it was a new show and I knew some of the people who ran it, you know. It was a place to hang out. It was pretty wild in those days, so it was a place to go hang out at three in the morning when everyone was wide awake. And I just kept begging the talent coordinator who I knew from either the *Cavett Show* or the *Tonight Show* or something. I said, I got a guy, put him on, he's perfect for your show. If you put him on, people are going to--- "No, no, no." Then one Wednesday I get a call. Whoever the act was they had booked for that Saturday night couldn't make it, or got sick, or got busted or something. And they needed to fill in real quickly and they were going to take a shot on Leon Redbone. So we had sold about 2,000 records, 3,000 records on Redbone in the first seven or eight months. But, like I thought, when people saw him on *Saturday Night Live* they went crazy, and when the Warner Brothers people came in on Monday morning, there were orders for 25,000 albums. And then in the next few months it became a million seller and they brought him back on *Saturday Night Live*, he started touring, the whole thing took off. So I caught another break.

DD: Well let's do something from--- Actually, this goes a couple albums down the line. *The Champagne Charlie* album; I wanted to do "Big Bad Bill Is Sweet William Now." Joel Dorn, thanks so much for . . .

JD: Oh thanks for having me. I really appreciate it.

DD: . . . coming by. Joel Dorn is our guest today on the *World Cafe*.

1998

JAC HOLZMAN

HERE'S ANOTHER FASCINATING INTERVIEW with a record company president, Jac Holzman of Elektra Records. He started the label himself, and while he was with it Elektra always had his imprint. Elektra was initially successful in the folk music area vying with another independent, Vanguard, for supremacy. But then came the Doors and later Queen and other enormously successful rock acts.

It's interesting to revisit this interview from 1998, because after Jac's book, *Follow the Music*, he curated a five-disc box set of Elektra's music for Rhino called *Forever Changing*, named after the song by the group Love that was released last year.

There is too much music to talk about, but we do our best in this interview.

David Dye: Our guest today on the *World Cafe* is Jac Holzman, who really in many ways started the progressive music movement in our country with Elektra Records. Elektra was certainly never the largest record company, but it was possibly the most influential in the 60s and 70s. And I know from my beginnings, coming into music through folk music, that it was Elektra that was responsible for a lot of my education. And Jac, I think I have you to thank for that, so---

Jac Holzman: Well thank you. Wonderful to participate in your life.

DD: [laughs] As you did for a number of other people. Now, I've been reading a wonderful book that you've just put together called *Follow the Music* which is kind of a printed version of an oral history of the time that you spent with Elektra Records, starting in October of 1950 and moving on to when you left the company in 1973. And, I'm just fascinated by how much time it must have taken you to put this book together, to get all of the living people who were involved and, actually, you've gotten interviews with a number of the people who are no longer with us.

JH: Well we didn't do that through the use of a medium. First of all, every word that I write as providing the narrative and spine of the book was written. The interviews were shaped to fit the narrative. So that if Jackson Browne or Ray Manzarek are being interviewed, we would cut from that interview exactly what we needed to fit exactly where we were in the book because very often the interviews would wander. The reason some people who are dead are now in the book is that we did those interviews about eight years ago when they were still alive, and so we were able to get them into the book. I started the book in 1991; I was stuck and I couldn't figure a way out. My friend, Gavin Daws, who is a very experienced writer with ten books to his credit, he said he thought the oral history concept would work. I was somewhat leery of oral histories because they never really moved the book along. They seemed to be a bit staccato. But he assured me as custodian of everybody else's words, he would be able to shape it, to give it real movement.

DD: And he did. There's a real chapter-to-chapter feel to it in how the different subjects are dealt with. But I think we have to set it all up right at the beginning as to what an unusual thing it was that you did in 1950, from your college dorm room, to start a record company. And how you were able to do that in a way that's much more difficult than today, and have the impact you had. What made you do it, Jac?

JD: Well, I really wasn't fit for anything else. Something very interesting had happened in the period of 1948 to 1950. The unbreakable LP was invented. The result of that invention meant that the pressing plants who used to have to press five of these big discs in order to make one album, suddenly had tremendous excess capacity because now they only had to press one long-playing disc to encompass an entire album. That excess capacity was made available to independent record companies to go ahead and produce their own albums. That, combined with the emerging interest in high-fidelity FM radio, and most importantly perhaps the availability of high-quality, low-cost tape recorders, made it possible for me and about 500 others who felt that the music that they loved, in my case it was folk music, was being under-served to be able to start their own record companies.

DD: Well, let's talk about some of the artists that were in that area and some of the people may not know about. I wanted to talk a little about Judy Henske because, to tell you the truth, I learned more about her through your book than I had known in the past. And I wanted to know more about this banjo-playing folk singer that everybody thought was going to be the biggest star that you had on your label. Tell me about how you came in contact with her music.

JH: Well I had heard about Judy Henske through Art Cohen, her manager, and I went out to see her in California. And she was this very, very tall—almost, about the same size I was, I'm six three—rangy, stringy-haired lady sitting up on a stage stomping her foot right through the floor who had this most incredibly aggressive and funny persona. A lot of the Cass Elliot and Bette Midler in-your-face kind of confrontational humor, they both admit, came directly from Judy Henske. Judy played an adequate banjo and she sang these outrageous songs and had a wonderful blues voice. And we did two albums with her and both of the albums did moderately well, but she never really attained the kind of fame that I thought she deserved.

DD: Well let's listen to "Wade in the Water" from Judy Henske, from her first disc or second disc?

JH: Uh, it's her first disc, her first album.

> Judy Henske recording: "Wade in the Water"

DD: That's "Wade in the Water" from

Judy Henske, one of the early artists recorded by our guest today. Jac Holzman was the president, the guy who packed the records and everything for Elektra Records from 1950 to 1973, which was a great era for that record company. And we're moving into the era here where I kind of came into Elektra's world. And one of the ways I came in was through the Nonesuch label, which was at the time an incredible innovation in the record business—to sell low-priced, classical recordings. And it's funny, Jac, to this day, I'm not sure that people see, remember, Nonesuch so much as a classical label as for the other explorations it did into world music and a lot of recordings, field recordings, that were done later. But, originally, it was a classical label?

JH: The idea came to me one evening when I was waiting for a friend: Wouldn't it be nice if young people—mostly college students, probably whose tastes were similar to mine, say fifteen years ago when I was in school—could buy a record at the price of a quality trade paperback, which was in 1963 two dollars and fifty cents? And that was the whole idea behind the label. Give them a first-rate, quality album; excellent recordings, well selected; superior notes which discussed not only the music but the social ambience in which that music was created; and put on whimsical covers. Well, we put this series out starting with ten albums. Not much was happening, and then I kept issuing ten albums a month for about three months, and then suddenly the orders started flooding in. We had tapped into a rich vein of interest in baroque music, and the success was so great that I was able to branch out from just recording classical music to doing original things, like commissioning works for recording, especially synthesizer works. We did Morton Subotnick's "Silver Apples of the Moon," which won numerous awards. And of course, I'm a folkie, so I began to do all kinds of serious ethnic music, what we would call today "world music explorations." The label was such a success--- It started in 1964, it was throwing off so much profitability. In 1964 dollars it was throwing off between five hundred and six hundred thousand dollars a year in profitability. We plowed that money back into a more aggressive recording program, recording singer-songwriters and then eventually artists like Love and the Doors.

DD: Well, tell you what. We're going to play just a smidgen from one of my favorite recordings on the Elektra Explorer/Nonesuch Explorer series, which is the "Ramayana Monkey Chant."

JH: Oh yes. Absolutely.

DD: And this is just--- We're obviously not going to be able to play the whole thing, but I thought we'd just play a snatch of this. And David Lewiston recorded these?

JH: Yes, David Lewiston was one of these guys that called me up one day, and he was an ethno-musicologist and he had these tapes and we listened to them and they were absolutely fantastic stuff. And we made a deal on the spot, all of which is described in *Follow the Music.* And we sent him out again and he kept making field recordings for Nonesuch and I believe, until this day, he is still doing the occasional record. Some of his more famous records are *Music from the Morning of the World*, the *Gamalan* album, the *Monkey Chants* album, just really extraordinary material.

Recording: "Ketjak: Ramayana Monkey Chant"

DD: An early recording on the Nonesuch label, which was part of Jac Holzman's realm with Elektra Records in the 1950s, 60s, and early 70s. We're talking with Jac primarily on the occasion of a wonderful history of Elektra Records, and really, a history of the times called *Follow the Music.* And we are following the music throughout the days of Elektra. Now the company was centered on the East Coast at this point, and a lot of the music you were recording came up in the Village or came from Boston. But one of the earliest successes for the record company, in terms of affecting other artists to this day, was a recording that came out of Minneapolis by Koerner, Ray and Glover. And I am curious as to how that came to be an Elektra record?

JH: It was issued on the Audiophile label, a local label up in Minneapolis. And one of the people who was involved with Koerner, Ray and Glover, a wonderful guy named Paul Nelson, was also the editor of *The Little Sandy Review.* Now *The Little Sandy Review* was a small, definitely in-your-face folk magazine which would take me to task for not being sufficiently ethnic. So they decided to send me this record and it went to the bottom of the "to listen" stack and it surfaced a couple of days later. And it opened with "Linin' Track," three white boys, absolutely incredible voices, guitar chops, probably the earliest examples of whites being able to do blues with that incredible, interpretive ability. Just a superb record. I heard the record, I called Paul Nelson right away and flew out to Minneapolis to pick up the band and pick up the masters.

DD: Here's the "Linin' Track" from Koerner, Ray and Glover.

Recording: "Linin' Track"

DD: "Linin' Track" from Koerner, Ray and Glover. We're talking to Jac Holzman about the history of Elektra Records. And we're not moving very fast, Jac; we're still in the early to mid-60s and there's so much to cover here, but we should get to some more things here. During this period of time there was a number of records that were incredibly influential in singer-songwriter circles, and I would say that the Judy Collins recordings, "In My Life," "Who Knows Where the Time Goes," all in that period of time, plus Tom Rush's records, are really so seminal to the singer-songwriter world primarily because these people were interpreters in a lot of ways and they used such a wide variety of songwriters. Now, you've been working with Judy Collins, and you've been assigning her producers who would bring her material--- Or was she involved in getting this? Or how did that relationship work?

JH: Well, let me tell you how it works. First of all, at Elektra, I would--- My most important decision always was to find the right producer to work with the artist in the studio. We never assigned tunes to an artist. We would sit down with Judy and her producer, Mark Abramson, and I would just sift through all kinds of material until we found things that she felt comfortable singing. But it was always done with great mutuality. In the case of *In My Life* album, we had finished the album and none of us were really quite that happy with it. It just really--- It didn't leap up at us. And then Judy found Leonard Cohen and "Suzanne," and the whole album changed in character because suddenly there was another singer-songwriter available whose material could be brought more into the mainstream in terms of other people hearing it. One of the interesting things about the folk music movement, and one of the reasons I think it probably came to a natural conclusion, was that as long as you were relying on traditional songs, sooner or later you were going to run out of material. And so that when people starting writing material in the style or milieu of direct one-to-one folk-type songs, they became, as far as I was concerned, folk songs. Pete Seeger once said that, "If folks sing 'em, it's folk songs." And I think it was Muddy Waters who once said, "Well I never heard a horse sing one."

DD: [laughs] Well, from this era that album and the ones that came right after it were just absolutely great records, so I thought we'd just sneak in the title track of Judy Collins' *In My Life.*

Judy Collins recording: "In My Life"

DD: We're talking with Jac Holzman about the history of Elektra Records, something you can read about in wonderful form, the book called *Follow the Music,* which has many different voices telling the history of these times. And I just want to quote a little bit from what Arthur Gorson—who was the producer of that last record—had to say when you started spending a little bit more time on the West Coast, and a small band called the Doors started to happen. Arthur says in this book, "The game shifted, suddenly the attention went elsewhere from singer-songwriters and rock was what they meant. Now suddenly Elektra is moving into a different game which of course changed the history of Elektra." And he says, "We were pissed because as folk managers and artists we were no longer the most important thing to the label. But obviously, you were following the music to the West Coast." Now, I would never say that Elektra left behind the singer-songwriters but certainly there was something else calling on the West Coast. And we're talking about a couple of bands, really: Love and the Doors. Love was your introduction to the West Coast?

JH: Well, I had been combing the West Coast for a long time. In fact I had moved out there in 1962 and as a result had totally missed Dylan when he was in New York, so that wasn't too bright a move of mine. But by 1964 or 1965 I could smell that the West Coast was going to emerge as a major center for artists, and I felt that Elektra should have a presence there. It was during one of my many visits to the West Coast that I went to a club called Bito Lito's, which was in Hollywood, and I walked into this amazing scene of the most gorgeous blond young ladies with their hair ironed, dancing with great intensity to fantastic rhythms that were certainly musical and sexual at the same time. And there was a band on the stage, Arthur Lee, with his feet in his boots with the tongues hanging out and Arthur peering over a pair of granny glasses with prismatic lenses, one red and one blue. And he was doing "My Little Red Book," and I just was knocked over. This was something I had been looking for. I had been looking for an electric band ever since I heard Dylan go electric at Newport in 1965. And after a few near misses, I almost had been able to sign the Lovin' Spoonful but could not sign the Lovin' Spoonful because I had no track record in singles. And singles were the name of the game back in the mid-60s if you were having a rock band. And I had never had a single. But, Love had not been offered a record contract by anybody else and they didn't know to ask about singles. So, we went ahead and we made the record and I produced it with Marc Adamson from my office, and we did it in about a week. This was before bands got into their bad habits of rehearsing in the studio. And the record was an enormous success. It sold about 150,000 right away. And it was when I was coming back to see Arthur Lee one evening in 1966, I had just gotten off the plane, it was very late at night, I was very tired, I really wanted to go to bed. But I went to see Arthur playing at the Whiskey A-Go-Go. And he said, stick around there's an interesting band on the bill. And I stuck around, and the band was the Doors, but I didn't really hear it that night. Yet, something kept drawing me back. And on the fourth night, I got it. And the fourth night I spoke to the band, who had just been signed to Columbia but had been released from Columbia because nobody at Columbia saw any future in the group. And another record company was a tough sell for them. However, the fact that I had recorded Koerner, Ray and Glover made them think that we were really pretty terrific. And then I assigned them Paul Rothschild as a producer, and he had done the Paul Butterfield Band album and they liked that as well. Eventually we got the Doors to record, and that of course totally changed the history and direction of Elektra.

DD: Well let's put a little Los Angeles set together. Let's do the Bacharach/David tune "My Little Red Book" and "Break on Through." Love and the Doors.

Love recording: "Little Red Book"

The Doors recording: "Break on Through"

DD: Love and the Doors. Two records recorded a couple years apart in Los Angeles by our guest today, the CEO and, as I've said earlier, the guy who ended up taking the records to the post office for Elektra Records in the early years. And then later on, we're talking into the 70s, when it was part of the WEA [Warner-Elektra-Atlantic] conglomerate, Jac stayed on to work with the record company. Let's move on a little bit further into that period. Actually, before we move too much further, there's a Detroit connection here that I'd love to hear about; how that came about. I'm talking about two bands—the two most influential bands from Detroit at the time—the MC5s and the Stooges. What was your connection to Detroit, and how did those bands come to be part of Elektra?

JH: Those bands came to us as a result of Danny Fields who was the company freak. Now, "company freak" sounds like a pejorative term, but it really wasn't. They were people hired generally by record companies who'd spend their nights, their days and nights, out on the street hearing what was going on and giving people back in the office feedback. And they would travel a great deal. Danny was really a public-relations person and an artist-relations person. He would travel with the artist and he would be hearing things out in the field, and he came to see me one day and told me about the MC5 and brought me a little snippet of the music (which is very hard to hear because it was like a wall of noise). But I was intrigued by the MC5 and the way they used their music to propel their political agenda. There was a very much confrontational in-your-face type of band, "Kick Out the Jams MFs," as an example.

DD: Uh huh.

JH: And I went out to Detroit to take a look at them, and while we were talking about signing the MC5s they say, "Well we have this little kind of baby fraternal band that we play with a lot, why don't you sign them." And that was Iggy [Pop] and the Stooges. I didn't realize at the time that the MC5 would end up becoming a footnote in history, whereas Iggy and the Stooges and the whole punk movement that he really kind of generated would end up being the real value of that excursion into Detroit music. But it was like, I really didn't want to sign the Stooges, but Danny insisted and it took him a long time to put any records together at all because they had personal problems within the group. And it was like one of those things—a painting that somebody strong-arms you into buying, and then later you do do it, and then later it has inestimable value. That's exactly what happened. We went to sign the MC5 and we got the Stooges, and the Stooges' music is the music that has lasted.

DD: Now, it's interesting, neither of those records really sold well. Was that more of

Elektra's naiveté in the singles market, or why do you think that?

JH: Well, by the time that we recorded those bands, FM radio was coming along strong so that you no longer needed singles. They were basically local bands. First of all, I think the Stooges were way way ahead of their time, and when people are too far ahead of their time it's very difficult. But the MC5 was a local phenomenon. And when they did play in New York, they did well in New York, but there wasn't enough music there. It was really more of a concept; it was an idea. It didn't have the kind of song structure I think that most people were used to.

DD: Which makes a lot of sense. Let's talk a little bit about some of the bigger artists towards the early 70s, during your WEA period. Carly Simon has to be mentioned as someone who I guess had recorded earlier as the Simon Sisters. Were you aware of those recordings?

JH: Yes. I was very much aware of them. In fact they had recorded a little lullaby called "Winkin, Blinkin and Nod" that I liked a lot. So I knew who Carly Simon was, as being a derivative of the Simon Sisters. I was given an audition tape to listen to. I took it to Japan with me, listened to it in Japan and absolutely fell in love with it. And the minute I got back, arranged to meet with Carly and sign the artist, and it was one of those incredibly good collaborations. With Carly, I pushed her about her songwriting and I got her always the right producers. And I think that was why Carly has such affection for the label, is that it was an extraordinarily good working association. She loved the company. Everybody at the company loved her. We knocked ourselves out for her. What I did not know at the time was that she had an absolute phobia about performing live. And we needed to get her seen live. And we kind of talked her into it and put a lot of Valium in her and put her up on a stage. And she did just great.

DD: This is "That's the Way I've Always Heard It Should Be."

> Carly Simon recording: "That's the Way I've Always Heard It Should Be"

DD: That's Carly Simon. There's some wonderful things in the Jac Holzman book that we're talking about today, called *Follow the Music.* Some wonderful scenes of early performances of Carly Simon and the early promotional efforts that Elektra did on her behalf, with roses on the tables and a lot of very appropriate promotion which was really very well done. Of course, really very well received. Carly Simon, one of the biggest-selling artists for the label.

JH: Carly said something in the book that I thought was rather important. She said that when you're releasing a single, the first song that anyone hears of an artist—what may become the calling card of an artist—you must pick a song that captures the essence of the artist themselves. Not just a good performance, but captures their persona fully.

DD: And to that end, did you work with her to pick the singles that did that? Or did she pick the singles?

JH: No; I picked. When I listened to all the material going into the album before we actually recorded, it was our practice to tape every song once so that I began to get the feel of the album and know whether we had enough material or not. Because I generally reserved the programming of the album to myself, I programmed most of the records that were released on Elektra. There were only about twenty-five of them a year, so I was able to do that readily. But for me, how an album was put together was essential. And so I was deeply involved in all of the tracks. One of the failings, I think, of the current way in which records are made is that the people who run the record companies are not involved with the music anymore, and that's a shame. But when I went through all the material with Carly, I said I think I know what the single is. It's an odd choice, but I think it's so odd that I think it will capture attention. And she agreed to go with the song that you just played.

DD: I want to talk to you about something you just said. Why has it become necessary now that the people at the top of the record companies don't know all the music that's on their label, and don't know it intimately?

JH: Because the music business has changed from the MUSIC being all caps to the word BUSINESS being all caps. It's become highly concentrated. Far, far too many records are being put out so nobody can listen to everything. It's become a manufacturing entity very much the way the old studio system of the motion picture companies became a factory. But great records get out through that system as great films got out through that system. I don't think that there is as much attention paid, that the albums are--- that the albums and their marketing, which is really nothing much more than the honorable connection of good music to people who might be interested. Everything is kind of overblown, and when you have so many records being released there is such a generally high noise level out there that it's very tough to get even something superb truly heard. The result is that it's very much like the motion picture business, in that you get an Alanis Morisette, who is a blockbuster, the way you get a *Titanic* or another big movie. But there are so, so many good records that are lost, that do not find their audience because they're put out by independents who may not have the distribution or don't have the marketing muscle or whatever. It's a very tough time in music today, although I think it's easier today for independents to start their own record companies. The internet is a leveling influence. And I would just encourage people who are interested in music to try and tie themselves to an independent record company where they can really learn everything from the ground up rather than working in a large company where they'll just be given a specific job and they'll do that job all the time.

DD: That sounds like the kind of statement to finish up with today. Jac, there's so much music we haven't talked [about] at all. I mean, we haven't mentioned Harry Chapin, Queen, even some of my old favorites like David Ackles and Earth Opera, and of course Tim Buckley and all these records that came out. If you want to find the story of a lot of these artists and their relation to Elektra and the times, *Follow the Music* is available now and is a wonderful history of these times and I'm really, personally, I'm really glad to have this out there. You must be getting some pretty good feedback about this.

JH: Yeah. We're getting great feedback. Today.

DD: Jac Holzman our guest today here on the *World Cafe.*

PART TWO:

1999–2006

THE INTERVIEWS IN THE SECOND HALF OF THIS BOOK ARE FROM THE DAYS WHEN IT ALL GOT EASIER.

After the *World Cafe*'s hundredth affiliate station was on board, the guests came out of the woodwork. Up until this point I'd been running the production of the *World Cafe* by the seat of my pants for a number of years, so it was a relief to have the help of a full time producer with mad radio skills in Tracey Tanenbaum. Under her guidance more second-hour features and themed segments developed, as well as the debut of the one-hour all-interview "Conversations from the *World Cafe*."

That said, we were still shoehorned into our quaint yet serviceable turn-of-the-century red brick mansion in West Philadelphia. Now that we have been in our gorgeous new *World Cafe* studios adjacent to the *World Cafe* Live nightclub for three years, it is hard to figure out how we ever lived without our present deluxe space. But it took the vision of developer and music fan Hal Real half a decade to find the space that would become our new home as well as the venue for his multi-level night club *World Cafe* Live. The *World Cafe* moved with WXPN in 2004, and immediately we were able to book bigger, more involved sessions like Yo Yo Ma and his Silk Road Ensemble, as well as louder bands like Gang of Four.

It was harder to choose interviews for the second half of the book as we have widened the scope of who we want to talk to, adding more classic rock guests as well as alternative acts. The interviews keep getting better, too! Read on!

1999

PETER WOLF

PETER WOLF WAS A TRANSPLANTED NEW YORKER LIVING IN BOSTON

who became one of the great rock front men leading the J. Geils Band. He was also an early DJ at WBCN, one of the pioneering radio stations in Boston. A lifelong music fan, Peter hung out with his idols and, one afternoon, dropped by our old studio to play DJ. Lucky for us we had a lot of the music he wanted to play in our library. I picked out a few things and I got a delightful history lesson. He even wrote me a thank-you note to say he had a great time!

David Dye: David Dye here on the *World Cafe*. Our guest this hour is Peter Wolf from the J. Geils Band. We'll talk with him in just a moment. Here's a track from his new album called *Fool's Parade*. This is "Turnin' Pages."

Peter Wolf recording: "Turnin' Pages"

DD: We started that set out with Peter Wolf and he walked in the door.

Peter Wolf: Here I am.

DD: How did that happen? Good to see you.

PW: Well it's good having me. Thank you, let's do a formal radio handshake.

DD: See? They can see it. *Fool's Parade* is the new disc, and we heard that "Turnin' Pages" tune, which is a good one . . .

PW: Oh, thank you.

DD: . . . from the new one, and---

PW: About "Time is the school in which we learn / How all things flash, how all things burn / What was I that I was then / Metropolitan poetry through here and there / In the parks / The fugitive among us, the motorcars / Time is a school in which we learn / Time is the fire in which we burn / Turnin' pages."

DD: And I want to talk more about this disc, how it came together. You know, the guy who produced this record I ended up meeting on the streets in New York City. I was in front of Bottom Line. Kenny White---

PW: Kenny's done a lot of work with Shawn Colvin, Holly Palmer, Mark Cohn. He's a great piano player, and a producer, and I was honored to have him come in with me and co-produce this thing. And we worked with an illustrious bunch of musicians, and it was a really enjoyable album to make.

DD: One thing I've never--- I don't know the story of Van Morrison after he had his, you know, his first hits--- he ended up--- when he was making *Astral Weeks* living in Boston, right?

PW: Yes, he did. He was in England. He was with the group, Them, and many people know Them with "Here Comes the Night" and "Gloria," or "Mystic Eyes." And then he got involved with Burt Burns, who was a record producer, and Burt gave him this song "Here Comes the Night," and then he recorded "Brown Eyed Girl." Van came to New York and was disillusioned with the whole scene in New York, so he ended up going up to Boston. And he stayed in Boston. When he lived there, I got to meet him because I had a radio show. It was a midnight radio show; it was [at high speed and without pause] "the Wolfa-Goofa-Mama-Toofa show. Welcome to little late tonight, the kid from Alabama keepin' it all hit, all ships at sea, doin' the two and gettin' right through, to havin' a little fun, on the run, give us a call, and don't you stall, we're gonna have some fun, get the work done, and here's a little Muddy Waters, doin' what we oughta," and it would go on like that till about six in the morning. So Van heard that, and he said, "Man!" So he came by figuring some big, old, you know, raunchy blues cat was programming it, and he saw this little punky, white guy sitting there playing all this blues stuff, and we just kind of hit it off, and we did some gigs together. And he was writing *Astral Weeks*, living in a small apartment in Cambridge, and a mattress on the floor with his wife and kid. [He] literally had no money, no telephone, so he'd come by my house to use the telephone, and we've remained friends ever since. It was so great to get to meet him then, and it's so great to see that he's still, *I* think, just getting, like vintage wine, better, and better, and better.

DD: Another thing I've always wondered about is--- people who are fans of Gram Parsons know that on the first Gram Parsons album, he cut a song that you and Seth [Justman from the J. Geils Band] wrote, umm . . .

PW: "Cry One More Time."

DD: "Cry One More Time." And how did that come about? How did he end up doing that?

PW: Well, it's funny. I came from New York, and I went to--- I got a scholarship--- I was going to go here in Philadelphia, the Institute of Art, and I ended up getting a scholarship at the Boston Museum School of Fine Arts. And I was up there, and the first band I had was a band of art students, and we worked with John Lee Hooker at this club. And this young guy, who was going to Harvard University at the time, would come in with this guitar player named John Neuise. And that person turned out to be Gram Parsons. And so he was a student at Harvard, and he was, you know, just still interested in country music, but Boston at that time had a lot of great folk music; Jim Rooney had the Club 47, and people like the Lilly Brothers. So he came, and he--- one of the fellas I befriended was a fella by the name of Barry Tashian, who ended up later working with Emmylou Harris, taking over Ricky Skaggs' place. And Barry heard this song and was playing it, and Gram said, "Man! Whose song is that?" figuring it was some old Buck [Owens] song or something. He said, "Oh, it's a friend of mine." And he said, "Well, let's cut it!" And on the record you're going to play, that's actually Barry singing because Gram didn't make it to the session. He got waylaid and he got sort of lost in the night; one too many, one too fast. So they had this session . . . [and] they cut it, but they later released the record that's out now, *Gram Parsons Live*, where Gram is singing it. So this singing is Barry Tashian with Emmylou, Burton on guitar, who used to play with Ricky Nelson--- but Gram used to do it in the show. But this is Barry Tashian, who was with a group called the Remains.

Gram Parsons (Barry Tashian) recording: "Cry One More Time"

DD: That's "Cry One More Time." That's Gram Parsons' version of Peter Wolf's song, "Cry One More Time," originally cut by the J. Geils Band. Our guest today is Peter Wolf.

PW: Elvis Costello was a huge—and still is—Gram Parsons fan, as many people are. And so, the Geils Band, we were playing in Paris, and Elvis came to see the show, and we're backstage, and we're all staying at the same hotel, and he asked, you know, "Can you come by the room?" And I said, "Yeah," and he said, "You know, Pete, one of my favorite songs is a song that Gram Parsons did, 'Cry One More Time.'" And he said, you know, "Can you play it?" And he handed me his guitar, and it had been like, a long time [laughs]. And you know, we had several bottles of wine. I said, "You know something, I don't quite remember it." And he was dumbfounded; like, how can you write a song and not remember it? But, I mean, his songs got so many words in it.

DD: Yeah, really! [chuckles]

PW: I wonder if Elvis Costello can remember all his songs? But it was funny. But I was very honored that he stayed in Cambridge for a while and then moved on.

DD: Yeah, he, well, he didn't last at Harvard; put it that way.

PW: No, he dropped out kind of early on, and I guess there's a book called *Hickory Wind* that is about the life story of Gram Parsons, for those who want to know.

DD: Peter's picking out some music. This new album's called *Fool's Parade*, and I'm curious about how you cut vocals on this. Did you get a chance to--- I mean, did you get to sing these all the way through, or did you do a lot of punch-in, or how did it work out, because you sound good?

PW: Well, thank you. Basically, this was done pretty much live. I was really into Muscle Shoals records, and there was a particular artist, Arthur Alexander, that did *Better Move On*, and there was a songwriter Dan Penn that did a lot of songs with Percy Sledge. And the records just sounded so intimate, and it was so close, [that] I said to myself, "You know what, this is the kind of record I should be making." And what happens is, you know, when you're making a record, it's like being in the kitchen if someone's cooking, and you know, you figure, oh, well, okay, I'll put in a little bit of this, and I'll put in a little oregano, and then I'll put in a little basil, and then, "Mmmm," it needs something else, and you got some curry in there. Before you know it, you got a big mess.

DD: [laughs]

PW: And so what I did was try to get some really good players, and we sat down, and we just kind of rehearsed the songs, and then we just cut 'em old style; everybody sitting around, lights down low, some nice wine, or, you know, whatever libation somebody might want. And we just sat around and we did, like, a take or two, and everything was cut live. Every now and then I would have to punch something in if I was cueing the musicians like, "Bridge is coming up! Bridge is coming up!," or "Come on now, let me hear your solo!" So, if I did that a couple times we'd punch it in, but basically what you hear is what pretty much went down.

DD: Yeah, it sounds that way; it sounds really great! Uh, you picked out some Bobby "Blue" Bland to get to?

PW: Well Bobby Bland is the man, and is being honored, fortunately—finally—by the R&B foundation out in L.A. I think in about a month or so. And he's just one of these guys that just--- man, he can just scream, and shout, and tear it apart, and he's just the real deal. So, if anybody loves blues--- I mean, a lot of people know about Muddy Waters and John Lee Hooker, [and] B.B. King of course, but Bobby Bland is the man!

Bobby "Blue" Bland recording: "Farther on up the Road"

Junior Wells recording: "Little by Little"

PW: Yes!

DD: Junior Wells, I never heard that one; that's a great one.

PW: Yeah, Junior Wells. That's the late, great, Junior Wells. He passed away a couple months ago, and he was something else. He used to play--- he replaced Little Walter with the Muddy Waters band, and he made a lot of great records with Buddy Guy on guitar. And I got to meet Junior when we started touring with him in Canada. He was just something else. He really kind of carried on the style of Sonny Boy Williamson, too, and he will definitely be missed. He was crazy, but he was unique.

DD: Yeah. Now, your harp playing--- who do you think you're more like with your harp playing?

PW: There's a Dylan-type harp on this last record, *Fool's Parade*, but I mean my favorite harp player's always been Little Walter. But you know, it's funny because what I like about certain artists, particularly like Van Morrison who's been an old friend--- you know, Van had Junior Wells touring with him for a while, and Junior was just sort of playing little, smoky joints, and Van took him around Europe and stuff. And so, I think it might be time to play Van "The Man."

Van Morrison recording: "Rough God Goes Riding"

DD: Van Morrison's "Rough God Goes Riding" from *The Healing Game*, a pick from our guest DJ today, Peter Wolf. He's picking out some music today--- and you've kept up with Van, so you're up with what he's doing nowadays, and does he cut these things live too.

PW: Totally live.

DD: Yeah.

PW: You know, they just sort of rehearse it as it goes down. He's worked with a lot of the same players for a long time.

DD: Right.

PW: And, you know, that's how he makes those records; they're kind of unique. But what's interesting--- once when I was living in Boston, as I mentioned, I had arranged a lunch with Van Morrison and John Lee Hooker, and they both talk so unusual, I think the two of them couldn't understand each other. I couldn't understand a word they were saying. But when I first met John Lee Hooker we were opening up for him and here's, you know--- [to DD] Do you have time for a quick little story?

DD: Hey, you bet!

PW: Okay, so here's the quintessential bluesman and, you know, he--- John Lee, if you don't know him, you know he kind of wears a porkpie hat, and wraparound sunglasses, and pointy—really pointy—patent leather shoes. And he travels by himself, you know, plays guitar and stomps his foot like, [stomping a beat and chant-singing] "I told Mama, told Papa. Ba-doomp, ga-doomp-boom." You know, and we paid homage to him by recording one of his songs called "Serves You Right to Suffer, Serves You Right to Be Alone." And so we were gigging; we were opening up and John and I came up to him and said, "Excuse me, Mr. Hooker. Would you mind if I came by the hotel to visit you, maybe in the afternoon, and we'd just sit and talk?" Because he was—and still is—like a god to me, so--- He says, "Yeah, sure; come on by." [He] told me the hotel he was staying, he says, "Yeah, come by about four o'clock; I'll be getting up." So I'm all excited, you know; all day I'm thinking, "God! Going to meet John Lee Hooker! Going to hang out with John Lee Hooker." And I go to the hotel, and I walk down the hallway, and knocked on the door, you know [knocks on something], you know like [knocks on mic], little knock-knock.

And he goes, "Come on in." The door was open; I walk in, and it was like four o'clock in the afternoon, and it's all dark in his room, and I could see the TV's on, and--- it was one of those rooms with two beds. John Lee's lying out in his boxer shorts, you know. And on the night table he has a pack of cigarettes and a bottle of Ballantine scotch. And on the other bed this guitar's open, you know, like a woman's, you know, lying across the bed. You know in the chair he has his hat—his porkpie hat—and he's sitting there, and he's watching TV. He says, "Pull over a chair." I pull over a chair, and he lights up a cigarette [and] takes a little bit of scotch, you know, and he's watching TV, and I sort of look over at the TV, and I see that he's watching *Lassie.* [laughs] And he turns to me and he goes, "Let me tell you something, Wolf . . . that Lassie is one smart dog."

DD: [laughs]

PW: Oh yeah! John Lee Hooker!

John Lee Hooker recording: "Madman Blues"

DD: John Lee Hooker, an old pal of our guest today, Peter Wolf. Earlier we were talking about harp players, and you mentioned Dylan briefly, specifically his very first record.

PW: Well this is the album that, you know--- when I first heard Bob he was on the radio doing an interview, kind of like what we're doing, but he was singing and playing. He hadn't made this record yet. And then I went to see him, and strangely enough, he was opening for a guy by the name of John Lee Hooker, at Gerde's Folk City. And you know, when you think back--- there's so many people like the new Folkways collection, the Harry Smith collection that came out--- but when you look back at Bob's first record, you know, you got Carter Family songs, some Roy Acuff songs, Bukka White and some great blues stuff, and it's just a really, it was really--- what was coming was already there. But this is just a song I picked--- This is an old Roy Acuff song. I'm not sure if Roy wrote it, but Roy made it popular way back in, oh, about 1940-something-or-other. This is the old "Freight Train Blues."

Bob Dylan recording: "Freight Train Blues"

Johhny Cash recording from *American Recordings*

DD: That's from Johnny Cash, the *American Recordings,* the one that won the Grammy last year and---

PW: Justifiably so. Johnny Cash has been somebody, you know, that ever since I heard "I Walk the Line" I became a fan. And there's a new--- somewhere, somewhere, I just saw it--- new *Rolling Stone* out, I guess with Clinton on the cover, and there's a story that this writer wrote. He came up to Boston to write and we sat around and talked, but one of the things they talk about is--- I went to see

Johnny Cash at the House of Blues in L.A. And he's with his wife June Carter, who comes from the great legacy of the Carter family. And, you know, they're sitting there, and they're talking about how the music moved from Jimmie Rogers and the sort of essence of folk music and country music. But I'm in this bar, and everybody's sitting there, you know, talking, smoking cigars, and no one's listening, and--- What people don't realize is that there are certain great legends that are not going to be around forever. And you know, John Lee Hooker is fortunately left, and James Cotton's around, and Johnny Cash is around, and people like Merle Haggard is around, and Van Morrison, and Dylan, and I don't know, it don't last forever, so--- I just couldn't believe how sort of disinterested many of the people like *came* to the show, more interested in picking up a d-a-t-e than listening to the music. So that just blows my mind but, hey!

DD: So that takes you through a lot of the things that influenced you, and of course that goes back to the Geils Band. I was just sitting here talking about great debut albums of all time, and of course the Geils Band's first album was packed full of just powerfully--- I mean, we've been listening to a lot of how records sound! *That* record was [claps once] right in there, right there.

PW: That's a funny thing because that record was done in less than 18 hours; we recorded it, we mixed it, and it was--- we did it straight through in two blocks, like about seven-hour blocks; seven and seven is fourteen. And then we had an hour for lunch, that's fifteen, and an hour to yak. Basically the producers said, "Okay, Pete. What do you want to do next?" I say, "Well, here's a song. It's an old Otis Rush song that we would do, one called 'Homework.'" And he goes, "How's it sound?" And we would just do it, and that was basically the recording of our first album. But I'd love to play--- a lot of people know "Homework" as a J. Geils song, but I'd like to play where we got it from, and this is the great Otis Rush.

Otis Rush recording: "Homework"

Big Walter Price recording: "Pack Fair and Square"

J. Geils Band recording: "Pack Fair and Square"

DD: Peter Wolf and J. Geils Band, and Peter's with us today. And we heard the original version of "Pack Fair and Square" by---

PW: I mean Big Walter Price. Big Walter down from Houston way and recorded on the same label that Bobby "Blue" Bland and--- When we were playing Texas with my new band, the House Party Five, we were around, and somebody came in with a wheelchair, and there he was—Big Walter. And he said, "Man, thank you for that 'Pack Fair and Square.'"

DD & PW: [laugh]

DD: Man, you must have paid his mortgage for a little while. That's great.

PW: Yeah, that's nice.

DD: We're going to let Peter Wolf catch his train in a few minutes, but want to play a couple more things.

PW: When I went to see an Alan Freed show, and on the show had people like Chuck Berry, Little Richard, Jerry Lee Lewis, Screamin' Jay Hawkins, Frankie Lymon and the Teenagers all on one show. There was a group of young ladies that came out, and they were like 12, 12 and a half, and they just blew the place apart. And you have to realize these three young gals all in these different pastel-colored crinoline dresses, and I don't know--- people don't know what crinoline is; it's sort of like a really hard kind of--- how would you describe it? Help me out here, David.

DD: It's kind of frothy, but stiff.

PW: Yeah. [laughs]

DD: Does that fit?

PW: Okay [laughs]. It's like a lace curtain, but really stiff.

DD: Exactly.

PW: And they had these beautiful dresses, and this young lady opened up her voice, and the place went crazy. And it's one of the great jewels and--- not to name-drop, but when I was on tour with the Rolling Stones, Keith Richards and I would sit back at about three, four o'clock in the morning and listen to this record over and over in amazement—the Chantelles.

The Chantelles recording: "Maybe"

DD: "Maybe," the Chantelles, our last pick from our DJ today, Mr. Peter Wolf. Thanks to Peter Wolf.

1999

BECK

BECK'S RECORDINGS HAVE ALWAYS SEEMED MYSTERIOUS TO ME. Certainly that has something to do with the lyrics. But in person he's funny, affable, and straightforward. This conversation took place in January of 1999 as he was in the studio working on what became the album *Midnite Vultures*. I'm always interested in how people work, and we find out a lot about the nuts and bolts of Beck's craft in this interview.

The beginning? We worked out a way to record each end of our conversation. Beck joined me from a studio in Pasadena and I talked with him on the phone from our old World Cafe studio. I nicknamed the apparatus the "Whispermaphone," thinking a little Dr. Seuss reference might go over with Beck. He played along.

David Dye: Well, when we found out we were going to have an opportunity to rebroadcast some live recordings on the *World Cafe* from Beck and the band that were recorded for *Morning Becomes Eclectic* on KCRW in Santa Monica, we were quite happy. And then we found out we could get some commentary from Beck on those tunes, we were ecstatic. So let me hook up the special transcontinental Cafe "Whispermaphone" connection, set it on Pasadena and uh---

Beck: Yeahhh.

DD: Beck, can you hear us?

Beck: Yes.

DD: We're coming through?

Beck: Transmission received.

DD: Excellent. Welcome back to the Cafe.

Beck: [laughs] Thanks.

DD: Now are you in your studio now?

Beck: Yeah, I am actually.

DD: Hmm . . . are you right in the middle of working on the new album?

Beck: Yes, we are knee-high on the new record.

DD: Is this kind of thing a distraction or a welcome break at this point?

Beck: Well we're just warming up to head into a new song right now so this is après-the-deluge, I guess.

DD: [laughs] I know you're moving forward, but I'm going to ask you to kind of look back a little bit at some of the songs from *Mutations* because we've got these very fine recordings today. Were you holding on to the songs that you ended up using for *Mutations* for a while . . . had some of them been around for a bit?

Beck: Yeah. Some of them had been around for a while. And I tend to like to let songs marinate.

DD: Do they change?

Beck: That's probably the best way to put it. Yeah, they do change, because you write a song, and then you just kind of write it off, and you know you come back to it three years later and then you're like, "That song . . . I guess it's not so bad actually." You know when you're too close to something you can't really see it for what it is, so sometimes it's best to just give it time.

DD: Do you cannibalize things ever, like take parts of one song and---

Beck: Yeah. Oh yeah, that happens all the time. I think that's part of the process. Certain songs are like sketches and then when you're working on the bigger work, ideas from the sketches come into the song, you know? I think it's nice to have a bed of things to draw from when you're going in. Because I like to work a lot off the cuff, and in the studio I tend to write songs as I go. And so I'll draw from other songs I've written . . . ideas, you know . . . notes. Different things will find their way into the song.

DD: One of the things I wanted to say, it's like on *Odelay* and the other albums you kind of play "spot the sample"; on this one you kind of play "spot the influence."

Beck: Uh huh.

DD: But everything kind of gets morphed though. Is that what you meant by *Mutations*?

Beck: I don't know. I don't want to be defensive, but I'm pretty proud of the way the records come together organically, and I don't think I'm any more influenced by other musicians than anybody out there. I'm really always working extra, extra hard to come up with my own sound and my own feel in the music. So you know for me it's not influences. Like I'll give you an example---

DD: Right.

Beck: When this record came out every second or third journalist I would talk to would say, "Oh, I get it; this is Muswell Hillbillies," you know? And I love the Kinks, but I to be honest, I've never listened to that record. I think maybe it makes critics feel clever, but I have to say a lot of them would be just accidents. To me, it would be more influenced by Willie Nelson or Hank Williams.

DD: No, well actually I was mostly concentrating on the morphed aspect of it because it's like, you know, if you would hear "Bungalow Bill" by the Beatles you would say, "Oh, that's kind of a countryish thing," but it's a Beatles track.

Beck: It's their own thing, yeah.

DD: Right, so that's sort of what I meant.

Beck: Yeah, I guess that's what you strive for, but you know it's a hard thing to do, and it's part of the process, and it takes years to develop that. And I think the Beatles were able to do that because they were able to put out two or three albums every year. So by the time they got to that album, they had what, you know, ten, twelve records.

DD: Right. I want to play "Bottle of Blues" from the sessions next, but before that I want to talk about somebody who used to put out two albums every year, which was Johnny Cash.

Beck: Yeah.

DD: Now he recorded "Rowboat" on *Unchained.* How did you first hook up with Johnny?

Beck: The first time I played with him was in January '94, I think. And then we played a show later that year at the Palladium—no, where was it?—the Pantages Theater in Hollywood. And so I just met him a few times and the next thing I knew, I got a call saying he did one of my songs. And I had actually heard earlier that year that he was looking for songs and I went and wrote a few songs for him and I think somewhere along the line just decided they were rubbish and tossed them away, but a few of these songs made it on *Mutations.* One of them is called "Sing It Again." Another is called "Dead Melodies."

DD: What are your inspirations for your live act? Who do you admire?

Beck: I'd say there's equal parts just full-on punk, from the Devo side of just the spaz-rock to the more aggressive, and a lot of it is kind of soul music and I'd say a good half of it probably is hip-hop. We're just, you know, even if we're playing rock songs, we just kind of act like a hip-hop band and we've just always done that because that energy is just so infectious, and I love the naturalness of hip-hop bands. We've toured with several bands, like the Roots. And we just kind of fuse all those things together and then occasionally we'll throw in some of the more folky things, which is where I first started playing music. I was coming up playing folk music, but there's not too much room for that in the shows. You don't want it to be a train wreck.

DD: What is your lyric-writing technique? To me, that's kind of your brilliance, the way you kind of string images together. Do you collect a lot of images and then put them down, or how does it come out?

Beck: It's always different. I think I used to--- earlier on, I was trying to entertain a coffee-house audience more and I would just do something more topical. I'd come up with some idea; I had a song called "Nitrous," where I read a newspaper article where several teenagers had gotten a tank of nitrous. And for people who don't know what nitrous is, you inhale it and it kind of gives you this kind of incredible sensation, this buzz.

DD: Laughing gas.

Beck: Yeah, exactly, and you get giddy and freaked out. Anyway, they had a tank of this and they were running around in a pickup truck and they decided they wanted to get exceptionally high and rolled up the windows of the cab and proceeded to fill up the entire cab of the truck with this nitrous gas. And they, they certainly got high; they got so high, they died. Because of course, there was no oxygen left. But they were so blown out of their minds that they didn't realize it. So I just kind of got into that and tried to get into their minds and that moment where they went from this extreme height and saturation of their intoxication and where that transferred over to the realm of death. You know, that extreme ecstasy, what was that point where it turned over? And so I wrote a song about that, and it's actually called . . . the song's called "Fume, There's a Fume in This Truck." So I'd write these kind of songs and I think I'd written so many of that kind of song, where it was a neat little package. I kind of grew out of it for a while and just started to let the lyrics wander a bit and I got into this thing for a while where I'd just create a movie and the lyrics would just sort of be impressions from the movie. It wouldn't exactly be a shopping list of events and what was going on, and your emotion was this and my emotion was that. And I don't know what you would call what it is. It's just going for the imagery and letting the imagery communicate some kind of emotional space and so also, I just try to make the words musical.

DD: I was going to say, that's one of the things that works best with music, because as you hear things over and over, those impressions add up. It's one of the few art forms that you do end up, you know, using multiple times if you want to put it that way.

Beck: Yeah, I tend to let the music write the words, and there's a lot of times where I sat down and I wanted to say a lot of clever things and put [in] double entendres and, you know, put more into the melody than the melody can handle. Words are heavy and melodies are like air, so you can't saddle them with too much stuff. Otherwise they just fall down, get lying on the ground stuck, you know? You're dealing with gravity, you know, when you're writing lyrics.

RUFUS WAINWRIGHT

THIS WAS RUFUS WAINWRIGHT'S FIRST VISIT TO THE *WORLD CAFE*, AND THE CAFE'S MICHAELA MAJOUN AND HE HAD A GREAT TIME. He had just released his debut and Michaela and Rufus touched on all the subjects that have become part of the Rufus canon. Including opera. In fact Rufus's fame has grown so much that he has now been commissioned to write an opera to be performed at the Metropolitan in New York.

Rufus is the son of 70s folkies Loudon Wainwright III and Kate McGarrigle. He grew up outside of Montreal in Canada and since this album has continued to produce wonderfully eclectic albums. But all that was in the future on this March day in 1999.

Michaela Majoun: Rufus Wainwright is with us today on the *World Cafe*. His debut album, self titled, came out a few months ago on the Dreamworks label. Rufus, welcome.

Rufus Wainwright: Hi.

MM: It's great to have you here.

RW: Rufus Wainwright and band.

MM: And band, who you will introduce at some point.

RW: Yeah. Yeah.

MM: What a glorious album.

RW: Thank you.

MM: It's really wonderful, much drama, direct and implied. Kind of etudes of emotion, filled with a sense of life-changing rendezvous.

RW: [gentle laughter]

MM: You could say. Is that accurate?

RW: Yea, well it's a . . . it could be. That's very philosophical what you just said. Could you repeat it?

MM: [laughs] Probably not.

RW: There's a lot of words in there.

MM: Musically---

RW: Couldn't you just say great?

MM: It's great.

RW: [laughs]

MM: Musically, it's very joyous.

RW: Yeah.

MM: And it seems to be a celebration. Of what?

RW: Ahh, of . . . a celebration of maybe, umm, God, my fabulous life that I've had a chance to live. [chuckles]

MM: Even though you were raised in Canada, there is a lot of American popular music tradition in the songs on this record. Going back a couple of centuries even through the current time. How did you get into that? Where did that come from?

RW: Well, it's funny. I mean, a lot of times Canadians can get away with things that Americans can't. [chuckle] For instance, like singing a lot of American songs and still having a fascination with American song and old American song. Like when I was a kid we used to sing a lot of Stephen Foster songs, "My Old Kentucky Home," and stuff. And we could really look at it as a sort of--- it didn't necessarily become an antique thing or an outdated type of stuff. It was like a--- because we weren't connected to it so directly, it was just interesting, you know. They were great songs.

MM: Right.

RW: We could even--- When I was 12 we used to sing "My Old Kentucky Home" and I'd have to sing things like "'tis summer, the darkies are gay." These horrible lines you could not get away with in America, but in Canada it's, you know, it's whatever. A little more--- there's just not as many people to beat you up. So, yeah, that's probably why I got to know a lot about---

MM: That was very philosophical.

RW: ---the American songs. I never thought of them as old songs, just American songs.

MM: Did you think it was because you were in Canada or because you were from a musical family?

RW: Yeah, being in a musical family, but being in Canada had a large part to do with it. And you could also romanticize a lot more when you are not actually living in the country. And you can really believe that in Tennessee, people really waltz all the time or something.

MM: [laughs] There is also a little bit of English music hall mixed in there.

RW: Yep.

MM: And I've heard you say you've had an epiphany over opera at age 15.

RW: Yes.

MM: Where did you hear opera?

RW: I heard it . . . I always hated opera, like most people ought to, because of its annoying qualities. But, and I kind of wish I still hated it. Because . . .

MM: Why?

RW: Well, loving opera is kind of like loving murdering people. [laughs] Like loving being a mini-serial killer. It's very sadomasochistic or something. But I adore it. But essentially it was an epiphanous experience. One night I was listening to it with my mother and--- she always liked it on the side, she was like a serial killer on the side. But anyways, basically we were listening to Verdi's *Requiem* and also the Quartet from *Rigoletto*. And those two pieces just completely won me over and I couldn't listen to anything else for about five or six years.

MM: You have a song on the album that names a number of heroines from Italian Opera.

RW: Yes. Yeah, it's called "Damn Ladies," and Rimbaud's in it too.

MM: [laughs] How do you figure that?

RW: I don't know. He just popped in.

MM: The very eclectic Rufus Wainwright today on the *World Cafe*. Would you like to do that? It's a great song.

RW: Okay. Great.

Rufus Wainwright performs "Damn Ladies"

MM: Rufus Wainwright on the *World Cafe*. That was beautiful.

RW: Thank you. That was actually the first time we ever played this together, me and my bass player. So.

MM: Lovely.

RW: You made a couple of mistakes there. [laughs] But that's fine; you did it with such panache.

MM: You shouldn't be embarrassed about liking opera. It's just soap opera with great music.

RW: Umm. Right! That's a very good way to look at it.

MM: I don't mean to dwell on opera, but did you ever want to be an opera singer?

RW: Well, I took lessons for a tiny bit. But they didn't like the way I dressed. They used to talk about me behind my back, that I had weird shoes and weird hair and clogs. I used to wear clogs a lot. And it, whatever, it was very weird. I just thought, okay, well, I guess I'll just become a pop star. There's a weird thing with opera singers where there's still remnants of that sort of nineteenth century, you know, if you were an artist, you know, were on the verge of being a whore. [chuckle] A lot of that still exists in opera. So you have to look clean.

MM: I can see you in velvet jackets and ruffled shirts.

RW: Yeah.

MM: I don't know how they dressed.

RW: They used to dress great. Now they just wear bad suits and stuff.

MM: Polyester. Whatever. So, you've been playing piano since you were how old?

RW: Six years old.

MM: How did you learn?

RW: I started with nuns in Quebec. Scary nuns with bad breath. And then I moved up to---

MM: Did they have rulers, those nuns?

RW: Yeah, they wore habits and stuff. One of them did. And then, in Quebec--- and then [I] actually started with an amazing woman for awhile, who used to be Wanda Landowska's [teacher], yeah, who lived in Wanda Landowska's house.

MM: Explain who she is.

RW: Wanda Landowska reintroduced the harpsichord to the world, basically, in the turn of the century. Early teens and stuff. And she--- yeah, she was from Poland. She brought back the harpsichord. People didn't really play it before her for hundreds of years. But, anyway, it was in her house, with all of Wanda's harpsichords there. And pictures of Wanda with Rodin and with Tolstoy, pictured with Tolstoy and Wanda. Like signed pictures with Tolstoy. It was amazing.

MM: What a great atmosphere.

RW: I know.

MM: In the songs on your album, Rufus, there's a sense of being undone by love that comes up over and over again. Why is that?

RW: Umm. God. Well, I've had a very unsuccessful love life. [chuckle] That's why. It's as simple as that. Umm. I don't know. I've . . . partly also related to opera or whatever. I've always put love on a very high pedestal and treated it as an extremely--- And always when I've wanted to, when I felt it and when I desired it, it has always been to the max, you know? I've always loved falling head over heels in love. And that doesn't happen that often. And it's something that you sort of have to wait around for, for a long time. But when it does, it lasts for a long time. I'm not even sure that it is really love, though. I'm beginning to realize it might just be a drug or something. It might be drugs. It may be a type of drug.

MM: That you're seeking?

RW: Yeah, that you're seeking or--- which might not be love. But it is definitely--- yeah, I look for that annalistic relationship thing. I was never a very good relationship person.

MM: One of those songs which kind of sum that up is "Foolish Love," a great song.

RW: Thank you. I'll sing that one for you.

MM: Good. Please.

RW: I have a piano right over here. It's seven feet long.

MM: Now, now.

Rufus Wainwright performs "Foolish Love"

MM: "Foolish Love," the story of his life, by Rufus Wainwright. There are two images in that song—I don't want you to accuse me of being too philosophical again—but there are two images in that song that personally, the first time I heard this, I just went "wow." The whole idea that I don't want to smell you. The notion of smell---

RW: Yeah.

MM: ---which really is a grounding---

RW: A bit putrid, really. [chuckles]

MM: It's a grounding image from that high-flying romantic love that we were talking about.

RW: Yeah.

MM: You've got that fish smell, too, in this song, "April Fools."

RW: Mmmm. I'm a very sensual guy.

MM: I can tell.

RW: Into all the smells and the sights.

MM: Actually, the sun recurs on a lot of different songs on this album.

RW: Yeah!

MM: And almost every song has a religious reference—to God, praying to God. There's Job---

RW: Really?

MM: ---Noah's Ark, Hell, Babel, chapel, holy angels and Zion mistaken for the state of Israel.

RW: [laughing out loud]

MM: What's up with that?

RW: Oh, my God!

MM: You had a big religious upbringing. You said that nuns taught you piano.

RW: I just throw in a lot of History Channel, I guess. Ummm [laughing] I don't know, I think partly what it is--- God, I didn't realize that.

MM: See, you said it again. "God."

RW: I think I could be a latent Catholic in many ways. I think most Quebecers are. I mean---

MM: Were you raised that way?

RW: I wasn't raised that way. I wasn't baptized but I was--- I did go to catechism and I did go to church a lot and sat in the back and wasn't allowed to take communion. And basically was probably really screwed up by it [*laugh*] in the end.

MM: There is also a phrase in

"Barcelona" that may be religious. I don't know what it is.

RW: *Fuggi, regal fantasima*!

MM: Yes.

RW: That's from an opera, actually. That's from Verdi's *Othello* and it's a--- and it means "flee, regal phantasm." It's from the scene where he sees one of the ghosts. Or like Duncan's ghost or something and he freaks out--- Duncan's? One of those ghosts. I don't know. And he freaks out and he goes, [singing] "*Fuggi, regal fantasima*!" [laughing]

MM: So how does it work in the song?

RW: It means--- well the song is--- I mean, it's actually about AIDS, the song. [chuckle] Or it was written from that, thinking about that, more thinking about, you know—I remember I was in my apartment and I was really bummed out that I couldn't go out and have sex all the time. And basically—and in a weird way—I wrote "Barcelona" sort of imagining going to Barcelona where there was--- and that's not really Barcelona--- it's kind of like going to some land where there is no disease and sadness. And "*fuggi, regal fantasima*" I sort of thought of, you know, AIDS as sort of a recurring, you know, spirit or recurring monster or ghost that just sort of shows up and it's frightening when you see it. You think--- because you can sort of put it in the back of your head a lot. But then it sort of pops up [laugh] every once in a while but, you know, it's like seeing a ghost. [chuckle] It really is.

MM: I wondered if it was about AIDS because there was reference to packing and fearing I won't be around.

RW: Yeah, and like rings falling off my fingers---

MM: Right.

RW: ---and stuff like that.

MM: Because of wasting away.

RW: Yeah. So, it had a lot to do with that.

MM: Would you do the song? It's really---

RW: Okay.

> Rufus Wainwright performs "Barcelona"

MM: "Barcelona." Rufus Wainwright accompanied by at least one flamenco dancer and---

RW: And Kevin Hupp. The magnificent Kevin Hupp. On double bass and vocals is Geoff Hill. We've met recently. And on keyboards and also on guitar is Jack Petrozelli.

MM: Very good.

RW: Yes.

MM: Have you played some AIDS benefits, Rufus?

RW: Actually, I haven't played any quite yet. I'm playing one in Canada soon and I'm doing another one New York City. So---

MM: You'll probably do that song.

RW: Oh yeah. I'm going to work that AIDS song!! [laughter]

MM: Oh dear!

RW: Oh dear.

MM: Rufus, did you have trouble getting signed because you are openly gay?

RW: Umm. Not really. No. I mean when I--- I was refused by two record companies, which, I mean, most people are refused by many, all record companies.

MM: True.

RW: [laughing]

MM: Whether they are gay or not, right?

RW: I don't know if it had anything to do with that. But pretty early on, I mean, Lenny Waronker, who works at Dreamworks. Works at Dreamworks?! He *runs* Dreamworks--- an intern--- he---

MM: An intern with power.

RW: [laughing] Anyway, he got a hold of my tape through Van Dyke Parks and just immediately knew that he wanted me signed. And the first thing I told him when we had a meeting was that I'm gay and that I don't really plan on changing anything. Whatever. This better not be a problem and, or this will not be a problem and he said, "Ok, whatever, that's fine." I think he kind of admired it actually. Most people admire it if you're just acting, if you do, if you just, if you're honest with them the way you think.

MM: So you never considered going for the gold first and then coming out like say, k. d. lang did or the Indigo Girls or---

RW: No. No, I wouldn't have been able to, either. I mean, I'm a terrible liar. And I turn beet red, and I did this . . . to get laid anyway. [rim shot in background]I mean, what would be the point.

MM: [chuckle] So, do most songs start with a guy?

RW: A lot of them do. Yeah. Pretty much most of them. Yeah, and a lot of them are guys that I've never met before or don't even know. Like a lot of them I will see for two seconds on the street. And then I'll write four songs about them. That's sort of the way I operate. I don't want to know anything about you.

MM: All kinds of boys inspire---

RW: Yes. Yes.

MM: ---in songs.

RW: All kinds.

MM: You specifically mention handsome Greek boys in one of your songs.

RW: Yes, yes, yes. Well that's from the Trojan War. Greeks bearing gifts. Beware. Even if they're cute.

MM: That was the moral of that?

RW: Yeah, that was the moral of that. And in general, I mean, yeah, especially with this song, I'm trying to work with you here. [laughter]

MM: Maybe you should just do the song.

RW: [laughter] We'll talk afterwards. We'll see what happens.

Rufus Wainwright performs "April Fools"

MM: "April Fools." Rufus Wainwright on the *World Cafe.*

RW: Thank you.

MM: Rufus means red, doesn't it?

RW: Yeah.

MM: You talked about being red faced before and it shows up in some of your songs.

RW: [laughing]

MM: Why did they name you Rufus?

RW: Well, I was actually born with red hair as a baby, like a lot of babies are born with red hair. And they wanted me--- my parents wanted me to have a weird name. Because my father had a weird name—named Loudon. But he was Loudon, the third. And the fourth would have been . . . too much. Too much. So they needed to start a whole new generation, a whole new beginnings of generations of Rufus the first, Rufus the second, Rufus the third. So, now we are in the Rufus era. Dynasty.

MM: Right, but it may stop with you, depending.

RW: Who knows. I was dreaming about having a baby this morning. I was going like: I want to have a kid. Any possible contenders out there in radio land?

MM: This is the *World Cafe*---

RW: Send your photos to---

MM: This is not a dating service.

RW: [laughing]

MM: You know we've gotten---

RW: Life is a dating service.

MM: That's true. We've almost gotten through the whole interview, probably the first time, without mentioning who your parents are. You just mentioned your dad. And your mother is?

RW: Kate McGarrigle of the McGarrigle sisters.

MM: Yes. You've been recently touring with them. Off and on with that McGarrigle Hour project?

RW: Yes. Yes. We've done several shows. And that's a great album that everyone should run out and buy as well. As is mine.

MM: Yes, yours is great too. It's called *Rufus Wainwright.* It features art and a booklet that you put together including some family photos.

RW: Pretty much all the photos in there, in the booklet, are my family. Originally, what I wanted to do is--- because there's this book on Biedermeier furniture and art, which I love, and that's what the other stuff is. But anyway, it's essentially my family as the German and royal family or something. I had little crowns on everybody's heads before but I took those out. I thought that would be pretty ridiculous.

MM: That's your fantasy. That's not their fantasy, necessarily.

RW: Well, it is now. [chuckle]

MM: You're very artistic. You put all these collages together. Is that something you've been doing for awhile?

RW: Yea. I went to art school for a year and a half.

MM: Rufus Wainwright. He does it all.

RW: I know.

MM: And you want to be in films, I guess.

RW: Yes.

MM: Do you really?

RW: Sure.

MM: I could see that.

RW: I want to be in the new *Star Wars.* Ooops. The next *Star Wars.* I want to play Darth Vader as a teenager--- [laughter throughout the studio]

MM: On that note---

RW: ---in the next *Star Wars.*

MM: ---it's time to say good-bye. Thank you so much for being here. What a pleasure.

RW: Thank you.

MM: And continued success with the album. It's great. We'll be right back on the *World Cafe.*

1999

BRUCE HORNSBY

THIS WAS AN UNUSUAL SESSION DUE TO THE AUDIENCE PARTICIPATION. It was also historic because it was one of the first "off campus" recordings at Indre studios, a large funky space in South Philadelphia. The interview concerns the music on his double album, *Spirit Trail,* an album that wasn't well received by many critics. Bruce was primarily warm and supremely intelligent in this interview, but at times his defensiveness comes out.

David Dye: I want to welcome our audience to our first ever Indre Session for the *World Cafe*, as we are extremely happy to welcome Bruce Hornsby and a cast of thousands. [audience applause] Bruce, I wanted to call this "One-on-one at Indre," but then I noticed there was a hoop in the room and that would have been problematic.

Bruce Hornsby: Let's go. I'll go with you. Go to the rack.

DD: We have set this up--- we have a great Baldwin Grand here. You're going to play some tunes for us, but we also have another element of this, sort of *This Is Your Life* element.

BH: What it's becoming, yeah.

DD: Yeah.

BH: Some people know some things about me.

DD: There are people here in the audience who know your past. So, I thought we would start out by delving into your past with random folks and we've asked Jerry--- Jerry, what's your connection here? Tell me what your question is.

Jerry: Two old friends of Bruce. One's from Williamsburg. There's an old song—I thought the title was "Don't Want No Boom, Boom, Boom"—dedicated to Grandmother Keller or something along those lines. Just wanted to know what the story was behind that.

BH: Well, actually, there's no song. That's something that's not quite right. But there is a story behind this "boom, boom, boom" thing. We grew up—our next-door neighbors—we grew up with this older couple, who had grandkids who you're friends with. And we used to play a lot of music in the house. But this one particular night, I had this friend of mine who didn't play anything. But he really wanted to play something. So, I said okay, what's the simplest song I know I can teach him on bass? So, there's this old John Lee Hooker song on a J. Geils recording called "Serves You Right to Suffer" that just goes like this [plays a blues riff on the piano] . . . and just on and on. [singing accompanied by piano] "Serves you right to suffer babe, serves you right to be alone," and you know it just keeps going. So, I taught this guy . . . on one open string and then 5th fret, 3rd fret, really simple. So, I taught it to him.

We played that for about an hour and a half [laughter throughout the room] from about one in the morning 'til about 2:30 or maybe [from] midnight to 1:30 one Friday night, after a high school basketball game, we played. And it's amazing how much you can do one thing for so long at that age and not get bored. Well, poor Miss. Keller calls up about one thirty and says to my mom, she says, "Lois, that steady 'boom, boom, boom' is driving me crazy!" [more laughter in the room] So, my mom, who was very tolerant, she was obviously closer to this "boom, boom, boom" than Miss Keller was, but she was suckin' it up, you know. My mom was just dealing with it, saying, "Okay, let them have their fun and I can deal with it." But she had to come in and tell us that Miss Keller was not psyched. So, there's no song here. I don't know where Billy Geiger is getting his info here, but that's where the "steady boom, boom, boom is driving me crazy" is coming from.

DD: Now, you had another band in high school, Bobby High Test?

BH: We had another band called Schenectady. I'm very excited to be playing Schenectady, New York next week because it's the first time I've ever played in the town that we named the band after.

DD: Why did you do that?

BH: Well, it was very popular to name bands after towns and, Chicago, obviously, being the most well known version of that. But this band Schenectady was a band where, if you knew how to play an instrument, you were not allowed to play it. And we had such great songs as "Man Is the Animal That Uses Tools" and "There's More to Doing Homework than Doing Work at Home." [laughter]

DD: Do you remember any of these?

BH: Oh, absolutely! But I'd never play them for you.

DD: Ahhhh!! [laughter in the room]

BH: But I'll play them in Schenectady, actually. I'll play them probably in Schenectady, New York. We wrote two musical plays named after our band. The first was called "Schenectady," and the sequel was called "Son of Schenectady."

DD: [laughing]

BH: So, I'm excited to be playing in Schenectady next week. But you're talking about Bobby High Test and the Octane Kids, from an old Grateful Dead cover band that my brother had. He was a big Dead head. And I was just little brother playing in big brother's Dead cover band. And that's how I got turned on to those guys. I was the lead singer so I had to learn all the songs, "Jack Straw" and all that stuff.

DD: So it was totally—it must have blown you away the first time you played on stage with those guys.

BH: Well, at least I knew the songs. [laughter in the room] You know, it was . . . I knew the territory. But it was amazing. We started opening for them in '87, but in '90 they asked me to join the band. Which I didn't really join, but I helped them out for about 20 months. And it was really amazing to . . . for all the old Octane Kids followers, the sound people, the roadies, just the people who hung around at University of Virginia in about 1974, to come. The first night I played with the Dead, I just came in off the street and started winging it with them, with no rehearsal—in Madison Square Garden.

DD: Well, the Dead must have been impressed. I mean, you know, you knew every tune they were doing.

BH: Well, actually I didn't. Actually, as it turns out, I knew about 40 of their songs. But it meant that I didn't know about 120.

DD: Right. [laughter in the room]

BH: Because they had a large list—160 songs.

DD: What do you want to start with?

BH: Well, I don't know.

DD: Okay.

BH: Let me just start playing and I'll figure it out.

Bruce Hornsby performs "King of the Hill"

DD: Wow.

BH: There ya go.

DD: That's great.

BH: "King of the Hill." First song. Side one, cut one of CD one.

DD: Now you call this your 6th record but it's kind of your 6th and 7th.

BH: Yeah, I consider it--- I would love for the record company to consider it that way but they don't.

DD: [laughs] The reason why you say that—

BH: Just kidding . . . I'm fine with my record company.

DD: Parts of disc two, like the bulk of it, is all from a whole different set of sessions. Where you were working with a whole lot of—[it] seems like—looped drums and some other little sample things.

BH: That seems to be the part that interests you the most. I heard you mention that before. I thought they were really two very different records. But if I just put out one of them I think it wouldn't give the whole picture. For instance, if I just put out the loop CD that you're speaking of there would be a whole lot of people who'd be going, "Wait a minute Bruce, you developed your piano playing to such a new level that we've been hearing when you play live and it's not on here." Well, you know, the first CD, that's where--- it's on there. So, that's why I wanted to release two CDs. And I know it is a bit of a commercial gamble, but it's really not why I do things. I just did it because it just felt right musically to me.

DD: Now, but, all throughout the 90s, all the albums of the 90s, each one has been stretching out more and more. This one is a little more song-form oriented.

BH: Yeah, this is less, sort of, utilizing the jazz language harmonically.

DD: Yeah.

BH: It's a little more like, "That song is not too much." I mean, sure there are some changes. I started out with--- what's the song I played [hums the song to himself]—"My Romance," and there are few kind of changes in "The King of the Hill," but mostly it's about sort of bluesy gospel. *Harbor Lights* and *Hot House* were more coming from a jazz, sort of swing feeling. This one is a little more rooted in the blues, R&B areas ... gospel areas.

DD: In some of the materials with it, you talk about it being about the South. It's about a lot of great characters, too. There's a couple great ones in that first song. I mean, certainly the big guy, the big man---

BH: With his hands in his pants---

DD: Exactly.

BH: ---leisure suit, thinks he's slick.

DD: But the guy leaning against the fence is a pretty neat guy, too. What about this preacher, this incredible snake handler?

BH: Well, right. There are two songs--- I wrote these two songs, "Preacher of the Ring Part I" and "[Preacher of the Ring] Part II," and they were inspired by a novel. A great writer from Grundy, Virginia, southwest Virginia coal mining country—her name is Lee Smith. And she's written tons of great books. She's not so well known but, typically, she should be. I wrote a song [that] went--- everybody asked me, "What's your favorite song that you've written?" I always have sorta one, or I often have one, on each record, where it seems to stand out to me. My favorite song on my second record is a song called "Road Not Taken," which I wrote out of another Lee Smith novel called *Oral History*. This is a book she wrote recently called *Saving Grace*, which is--- the narrator is the 14-year-old daughter and--- they are just fleeing in droves. [laughter] Lee Smith is really good.

DD: [laughs]

BH: Anyway, this is called "Saving Grace." She's the daughter of a snake-handling preacher, travels around. It was a very intense book. I loved it a lot. And I wrote these two songs based on that. So, there are lots of stories, Boo Radley, sneaking up on Boo Radley, coming up from the old *To Kill a Mockingbird*. I grew up on that novel. I grew up in a small southern town, Williamsburg, with a mental hospital. And we were, you know, typical young kids. Well, typical to us. Who knows if it's typical? We were typical young kids . . . making fun of these patients walking around town who had some various idiosyncrasies. You know, various quirks. Of course we [were] at age nine, ten, eleven—we thought that was just hilarious, you know. Very politically incorrect and all this, but then of course later, we were starting to realize this is a little dodgy, you know? The line goes, "We laugh and sneak around in the night, fun and games, but I know it's not right." So, a lot of these songs are reminders to me about being a better person, about not doing these . . . not doing these things. That's why I call the record *Spirit Trail* because to me a lot of the songs represented collectively, [are] sort of the road to trying to be a better person. "Pete and Manny," a song about me and my friends sitting around laughing at some—like here's the perfect example—laughing at someone and in the end realizing the joke is on us. For instance, "Jimmy went and joined the gym, his posing was a sight. We thought he looked like a clown in tights, but we were the ones home alone at night." Meaning he's the guy who got . . . got the girl.

DD: Right. That has kind of a little New Orleans feel to it, too.

BH: Absolutely. Once again, southern---

DD: Yeah.

BH: That and "Sad Moon" too. "Sad Moon" is also a good—it's a story song--- Good or whatever, that's for someone else to say, but it works for me. I was sitting in downtown Newport News, [in a] real kind of funky, rough section of town eating like a Taco Bell in my car. And all of a sudden, "Bam, bam, bam" . . . this woman bangs on my window. Get my attention. And so I looked at her and she said, "Hey, do you want a date?" She's a prostitute. So, I said, "Well, no thank you. Thanks." "Are you sure?" "Yeah, I'm fine. I'm just having a good time eating my gordita."

DD: [laughter]

BH: So, she walks away and, as she walks away, I think to myself, "I'm watching her walk away. This is the first time I've ever been accosted like this in my home area where I could have, or someone I know definitely went to school with her." So it kind of made me think about this sort of the different paths you go from school on, and so I wrote this song.

DD: So do you want to do "Sad Moon"?

BH: I'll do "Sad Moon." What the heck.

Bruce Hornsby performs "Sad Moon"

BH: Thank you, thank you, thank you.

DD: "Sad Moon." Bruce Hornsby is our guest. We'll be back in a moment here on the *World Cafe*.

DD: We're back on the *World Cafe* with Bruce Hornsby at Indre Studios. I want to talk a little bit more about this album and maybe we'll take some questions from---

BH: Fine, fine---

DD: ---the legions out here.

BH: Whatever you gotta do.

DD: This is what happens when you let somebody kind of study something for a while. You find out things that maybe were meant mad but maybe weren't. Like the end of the first album there is a song called, "Great Divide." And "The Line in the Dust" begins and they are kind of like---

BH: Well, how do you know about the relationship between those two songs? Have you read about this or did you figure it out yourself? I'd be shocked if you figured this out yourself.

DD: No, I just noticed it. I'm not even sure what it is.

BH: Okay. Well, "The Great Divide"--- a lot of the song, the second verse of the song, "The Great Divide" goes, "I heard somebody calling you a bad name, but I didn't say anything to him. Next time I swear it's going to be different. I promise not to be silent again." That's referring to a situation when I would be around friends of mine in my small southern town and, you know, old friends I grew up with. And some of these guys would make race jokes and I would find myself-- well, of course, I didn't like this at all but I would let it go. I wouldn't say anything—sort of not to create a scene or create a funny vibe. But I always was disappointed in myself after the fact, that I would let this go and just, just sort of not say anything. So, "The Line in the Dust" is a song about the first time I actually did do that. Where a guy made this statement and I sort of felt my blood boiling, all of a sudden, said, "Hey, wait a minute. What did you just say?" You know. And, of course, they just [said], "I take that back." You know, once they were called on it. So, the two songs have a relation in the sense that the one song is saying, "I'm not going to do this anymore," and the first time I--- when [I] didn't do it anymore.

DD: So, they are two of my favorites on there. I don't know---

BH: Thanks.

DD: ---if you could do either of those.

BH: What's that?

DD: If you could do either of those.

BH: Ah yeah, I guess I could. Yeah, what the hell. "Line in the Dust" is actually a "synth" song, you know, so it's kind of hard. It's not really a piano song. But I could certainly do "Great Divide."

DD: Is that how it ended up on the second album? Because it's kind of a little more that way. We were talking about it.

BH: Well, the keyboards on there are more like Wurlitzers and a lot of organ—Hammond B3. I wrote most of that second record on the road, on a bus, on a little Casio keyboard. So that's why it wasn't really--- just--- they weren't piano songs.

DD: Is your technique on those instruments a whole lot different from what you do on the piano?

BH: Well, sure. It's no different playing them, but I'm not used to the action. I'm much more comfortable on a piano because that's where I practice. I never practice this. I'm not trying to be a great, you know, Korg M1 wave station player, you know.

DD: [laughter in the room] Right. Right.

BH: [chuckle] Not much. I'm not interested. This is my focus. That's why, I get up and play accordion on my gigs and I'm a terrible accordion player, but it's my punk aesthetic coming out. Sort of the mind-set, "Anyone should be able to play this music." It shouldn't be about talent. So---

DD: It's like that---

BH: ---it's my moment where I have no qualms about getting up in front of anyone and playing the accordion.

DD: But it takes you back to the Schenectady where you would all play an instrument you didn't play.

BH: Well, you see, in Schenectady I was the only guy who actually played my instrument, because then there was a semblance of a song there. But surrounding that was just a complete--- we were the original--- we were the first people influenced by Sun Ra and Ornette Coleman in southeastern Virginia.

> Bruce Hornsby performs "Great Divide"

DD: Little low-end workout there on that one. That's great. "Great Divide." Bruce Hornsby's here and we've got a room full of Bruce Hornsby aficionados. I know. So we're going to throw the thing open to some questions from our audience.

Audience Member: My brother went to UVA and lived on Valley Road Extension. Is the "Valley Road" the same--- any connection?

BH: No, not the Valley Road from Charlottesville. It's the Shenandoah Valley Road, sort of a famous road in Virginia history. So, I grew up in Virginia, where the light bulb joke is, "It takes three to screw them in, one to screw it in and two to talk about how great the old one was."

[laughter] So, it's sort of a place that lives in the past. You know, history is big. So, I thought I would sort of take the piss out of this whole notion--- this whole historical thing--- and make this fabled road into, in my song, this place where people go parking.

AM: Talking about the Valley Road, I think the first time I knew I adored you is when I heard "Valley Road" on Circle II.

BH: Yes. Right. I'm very proud of that bluegrass record.

AM: That was so cool. How was it to work--- you cover so many genres, I guess, throughout your career. How is it to do that?

BH: To sort of work with different people and get . . . ? Well, one of the best parts—thank you, that's a good question—one of the best . . . sort of greatest aspects about my years doing this are the great calls I got to work with other people. [It's] sort of like painting yourself into the mural that you were looking at as a kid. But, you know, so many collaborations that have been so inspiring for me and educational . . . to go into someone else's work and see how they do things, see their process. I've learned so much from it.

DD: That's two for "Valley Road."

BH: Two for "Valley Road"?

DD: I mean two people mentioning "Valley Road" . . . [do you] think that you can do it?

BH: Oh, yeah sure. Okay. That's fine. Yeah. This is played so many different ways but I'll just play it the old tried-and-true. It's kind of hard to play bluegrass on just solo piano.

Bruce Hornsby performs "Valley Road"

DD: Mr. Bruce Hornsby live on the *World Cafe*. Thanks to Bruce and thanks to our incredibly knowledgeable audience, I should thank—

BH: Absolutely.

DD: Absolutely.

BH: Thank you for being so knowledgeable.

DD: [laughter throughout the room]

BH: Seriously. Often I talk on these things and I'm talking about something and I can tell that no one knows what the hell I'm talking about. So, it's very nice. Thank you.

DD: I did want to ask a little bit about you and basketball. Because I don't know your whole history, but you played high school ball?

BH: I played high school ball. Had a couple of small school offers . . . Division II, you know, smaller scholarship situations, but still, offers to play Division II ball. But at the time I was getting much more into piano and sort of went through the motions my senior year. I was very intense about it up through my junior year. Got a little disillusioned with it though.

DD: How so?

BH: Well. I was just in a bad situation. Losing team. Dissension. No unity. Nobody cared about—[a laugh in the room]

DD: Yeah.

BH: Well, what's funny about that? It wasn't funny for me at the time. Maybe it . . .

DD: We're from Philadelphia [laughter in the room]

BH: . . . maybe it's reminding you of a--- I see, it's a familiar story to you here in Philly. Okay.

DD: Bruce, thanks again for coming by.

BH: Okay. My pleasure.

DD: We appreciate it. Bruce Hornsby [applause] here on the *World Cafe.*

1999

JOE STRUMMER

THE FORMER LEAD SINGER AND CO-FOUNDER OF THE CLASH, Joe Strummer only visited the Cafe once, after he released his first album with the Mescaleros, *Rock Art and the X-Ray Style.* We had our co-producer Shawn Stewart talk with him because she was such a longtime fan, and it turned into a witty back-and-forth that revealed a lot about Strummer. He died three years later in 2002 at the age of 50.

Shawn Stewart: I'm Shawn Stewart and we are in the music studio of the *World Cafe* today with an artist that we've been trying to pin down for quite some time, Joe Strummer, and we're really happy to have you here—"The Strummage"—joining us today on the *World Cafe.*

Joe Strummer: Thank you very much.

SS: You're very welcome. Without his Mescaleros.

JS: Yeah.

SS: But I found them to be—when I saw you at the beginning of the tour in July—a really exciting band and I'm wondering if—although they're not here—in their absence, if you can tell us a bit about the Mescaleros.

JS: Okay, well, I really enjoyed being on the road with them, but I fired them this morning for not showing up here.

SS: [laughs]

JS: No really, they're really cool. There's Antony Genn, Scott Shields, Martin Slattery, Smiley Barnard, and Pablo Cook. They're the cats that were making the tunes in London these last few years, so myself and Antony Genn have been talent-spotting them, if you like, so we hope we've got a good band together.

SS: Oh, I thought they were great when I saw them. I am one of those probably many people who come to the shows who have seen the Clash in the past in a different era and I remember with particular songs like "London Calling"—seeing you and Mick and Paul all step to the microphone at once and just attack that song. And I'm wondering if you have any sense of what it's like for the Mescaleros to be performing songs that have so much history.

JS: Well, luckily, none of them were born when these things went out.

SS: They look like they were in diapers when--- I'm serious; they look so young!

JS: Yeah, I mean, it's tough to say. I like the way we play when we play a tune from the past. We play it not xeroxing it, yet not making it sound stupid. I think we've found a good way to play it. We still play it with a bit of flexibility, but it's just right for me. I think we lucked into that—or I have—by picking the right guys.

SS: In addition to working with Antony Genn on this record, you also worked with an artist that you've been sort of trying to work stuff out with for a while—the Grid.

JS: Oh, Richard Norris?

SS: Yeah.

JS: I started trying to make a group with Richard Norris about four or five years ago and "Yalla Yalla" is the remains of that project, or whatever you would like to call it. We were trying to make an acid-punk crossover.

SS: That's pretty ambitious, only because house music tends to be—just dance music in general tends to be—it's not about stuff. It's sort of more about the event—being there and jumping up and down with your compatriots and getting into the moment of the—

JS: What we found out—where it kind of varied was that it wasn't about song. Because punk is more about the song and acid house is more about the track, so we came to blows over the difference between these two words. Now I'm mates with Richard Norris and he's actually done some remixing on this record on some of the singles, B-sides, or what-have-yous.

SS: Right. It really works live which, I think, is extremely hard to do. With acid house, there's no such thing as a band, they don't really perform; it's more of the

DJ culture. But live, it really stood out. I hadn't heard the record; the record wasn't out at the time that I first saw the live show. And it really—it's got a great quality to it.

JS: We make that work because we kinda get into almost like a—you could call it a reggae house groove—so that's probably where punk and acid house could probably meet, in a kind of reggae area of the two. If you imagine three intersecting circles, that's probably where it can meet more easily.

SS: Well, at the dub end of reggae, you certainly have that big, bass sound and I think that's very similar—

JS: Exactly. It ties in, doesn't it? Big sound, big systems.

SS: Yep. Big systems. It's all about the size of your system. So, let's hear that track, "Yalla Yalla," and we'll come back and talk a little more about hybridization.

> Joe Strummer and the Mescaleros recording: "Yalla Yalla"

SS: Joe Strummer is our guest today in the *World Cafe*. It's really great to have you here, Joe. You've always been a really extraordinary singer and I heard that you . . . .

JS: [sarcastically] That was a dirty, backhanded compliment, that one.

SS: No it wasn't. It was really the—

JS: You have to keep on your wits 'round here. It's terrible.

SS: I heard that—

JS: I never felt so insulted. I'm flying home immediately.

SS: Right. First thing. On the next plane.

JS: Cab! Airport!

SS: I heard that you were—maybe this is [a] fallacy, I don't know. Because you hear a lot of things and you don't know if they're true. But I did hear that you were really inspired by the singing of Tony Bennett. And there's actually a line in "Tony Adams," [that goes,] "Tony Bennett eight-track."

JS: Yeah, yeah. Definitely. I'm glad you brought that up because I'm serious about Tony Bennett. For me, it's not some kitsch joke. [laughter] We're not poncing around wearing lounge suits in some postmodernist, avant-garde throwback to purer times. I just like Tony Bennett, full stop.

SS: If there was some sort of decree that you had to choose between Tony Bennett and, say, Frank Sinatra . . . ?

JS: Well, I think even Frank admitted that Tony won it.

SS: And there's another Tony, in fact, the

Tony in the song in which you mention Tony Bennett, Tony Adams.

JS: Tony Adams is the England captain—or was—of the soccer team, which I know no one finds very interesting here, but what the hell. Once you beat us two-nil, so that ought to keep you interested. But anyway, it's just a symptom of the disease rife in modern Britain . . . that nobody seems to know anything about anything. And this is one of the---if you consider Britain as a sick patient, then the fact that Tony Adams has been demoted from his rightful place, as I see it, is a symptom of our national demise or national delinquency. And so the song is really about being lost in a world and Tony Adams is like a cipher for me, personally, although this is ridiculous that we even should be discussing this, but there you go. Life is strange and um, Tony Adams is noble.

SS: Well, it's a great song and we should hear that song.

JS: Okay, thank you.

SS: "Tony Adams" from Joe Strummer and the Mescaleros.

> Joe Strummer and the Mescaleros recording: "Tony Adams"

SS: Joe Strummer and we're really happy to have you here. You may or may not want to answer this question, I don't know, but quite a few years ago—maybe, like, five years ago—I had, I got to interview Mick Jones and it was a gas. I had a blast. I asked him—he was anyway, very forthcoming at the time about his life in the Clash—and I asked him if he had to name one, what was his favorite all-time Clash song.

JS: It's so predictable I can guess.

SS: Go ahead.

JS: "Should I Stay."

SS: No.

JS: I'm just kidding.

SS: Come on; guess again.

JS: Well, my favorite of his would be "Stay Free."

SS: It wasn't his; that was what I was gonna get to. "Stay Free" is a beautiful song.

JS: Yeah.

SS: An extraordinary song. But I think this was one of yours. I just read in a book that you had written it. In fact, I think you wrote it for him—"Spanish Bombs." Is that right?

JS: "Spanish Bombs." Yeah, I didn't write it for him. . . .

SS: Does that surprise you?

JS: Yeah. I'd a thought he'd picked one

of his tunes.

SS: [laughter] That's flattering, isn't it?

JS: Yeah. It's nay bad, that tune. But we're not gonna spin it, though, are we?

SS: You don't want to?

JS: Well, isn't there anything else? Let's think.

SS: Well, there's quite a few. *Sandinista* is a three-record, you know—

JS: That was quite a good intro, though. We better spin it because it was a perfect intro.

SS: Well, it's a perfect song, so we might as well, right? "Spanish Bombs" on the *World Cafe*.

The Clash recording: "Spanish Bombs"

SS: On the *World Cafe* today our guest is Joe Strummer and we just played a track from the classic *London Calling* disc, "Spanish Bombs." Now, first of all, you never did answer the question because I had heard that you wrote "Spanish Bombs" as a gift to Mick. But there's a lot of myth that comes—you know, I think that was in a book that was written by your roadie at the time—so there's a lot of myth that comes into play when it comes to the Clash.

JS: Yeah, and a myth is very difficult to deal with because your defective memory can also detrain a myth when it was, in fact, a truth, so let's just--- Can I be diplomatic and say I don't remember that? I don't know where this myth came from—or this prospective truth came from.

SS: Regardless, we did, as we said, we got a great song out of it, and that's incredible. So there's a lot of stuff sort of circulating right now about the Clash because there's this new documentary, which is great, and all of you participated in [it] and I really enjoyed [it]. There's a new live record, as well. In the documentary, sort of towards the end—in fact, at the very, very end—you talk about the disbanding of the Clash. It really looks on your face as though it caused you a lot of pain. It seemed like, for all the dust-ups and the drama, that you and Mick really loved one another. I'm wondering what's your relationship like now?

JS: I would say our relationship is sort of touchy-feely with the emphasis on "touchy."

SS: [laughter]

JS: That's the best I can come up with.

SS: You know what, I'm not even going to probe any further. But I will ask a few more questions about the Clash, if you don't mind.

JS: Sure, no, I don't mind, really.

SS: Really?

JS: Yeah.

SS: Good. So tell me your personal favorite Clash memory.

JS: Okay, we just played *Saturday Night Live* in New York and, at the end of the show, it's sort of traditional that all the performers come out and sort of wave at the audience as they roll the credits. And I found myself standing next to Eddie Murphy and then I saw Paul Simon giving me the nod and I understood immediately what he meant. So I got down behind Eddie Murphy on all fours—immediately behind him without him seeing—and then Paul walked up while we were all waving at the cameras. Paul walked up and went, "Hi, Eddie," and he pushed him in the chest and Eddie fell backwards and fell over me and hit his head on the stage.

SS: [laughter] You know, I don't remember that moment, but it's *your* personal favorite memory, so that's all that matters.

JS: It's there in the archives.

SS: Yeah, I'm sure it is. I'm surprised they didn't dig that one out when they did their 25th anniversary this year. Let us finish out with another song from the new record, *Rock Art and the X-Ray Style.* But you know what? Before we do that, tell us about—because I think it will actually lead into this song really nicely—tell us about the title of the record. I understand it has something to do with geology— "rock art."

JS: Yeah. I just borrowed a book off a neighbor and there it was, as it is. It just said "Chapter 6: Rock Art and the X-Ray Style." And I went, "Well, that's my title." And when I read the book, the x-ray style is about when they did cave paintings and they began to paint the bones visible through---

SS: Started with the shapes, like the big wooly mammoth, and then began to paint the bones?

JS: Well, on the album, the artwork is by Damien Hirst, but all the figures—every single figure on the whole album—is actually taken from cave paintings, probably a hundred thousand years ago, approximately. So all of those figures were painted probably a hundred thousand years ago and I kind of like that, because there's a lot of fun going on if you study those figures. I mean, there's a lot of fun to be had checking out what's going on in those cave paintings because, first of all, they're having a five-keg party, that's for sure.

SS: [laughter] Yeah.

JS: They're running around naked wearing weird costumes and they're raising their hands in the air like hockey supporters. Whatever we're doing [now] they were doing back then, I'm sure of it. But one tune, are you going to spin, let's spin "Road to Rock and Roll," because

I've got an amusing anecdote about that. Rick Rubin put the word out to all the writers that they were having a song roundup for Johnny Cash's sort of comeback *American Recordings* album. So I sent this song in, "The Road to Rock and Roll," and they didn't use it. Then we went to L.A. and I saw him play an amazing show in the Pantages Theater on Hollywood Boulevard—an amazing show. I'd never seen Johnny Cash before; it was fantastic. And then afterwards, we kind of met and then Rick Rubin whispered in his ear and said, "Hey, that's the guy that sent in that song." And he turned around and he leant right over me—he's a tall; he's a very big man—and he just said [in a southern accent], "You really confused me with that song, boy." And I went [choking sounds], "Oh, sorry, Mr. Cash." And then, when we began to make this Mescaleros record, [we included it] because it was a song on a personal note—that I met my wife just after I'd written it and I used the song to woo her, so it was a personal thing.

SS: You were pitching some woo.

JS: And also my wife kept rubbishing the mixes we were doing of that song until we had it right.

SS: Well, she would want it to be the best, of course, because it was very—she's very personally attached to the song.

JS: So she gutted it when we were doing rubbish mixes of it or whatever from fatigue or whatever. She kept saying, "No, no; you've ruined it. Keep it real; keep it simple." And so we've tried to put it down in a simple way and we're playing it quite well live, as well. I'm enjoying playing it live. But anyway, we figured, "Hey, let's record it."

SS: So we have two love songs and we're going to hear the one you used to pitch the woo and now you have the follow-up, I guess, [which] would be "Nitcomb" because now it's going to take a nitcomb to get rid of you.

JS: [laughter]

SS: So we'll play "The Road to Rock n' Roll" on the *World Cafe.*

> Joe Strummer and the Mescaleros recording: "The Road to Rock n' Roll"

SS: "The Road to Rock n' Roll." I'm Shawn Stewart and I'm in the *World Cafe* studio with Joe Strummer. Joe, thank you so much for being here today.

JS: Okay.

SS: It's really been a great pleasure to have you.

JS: All right.

SS: The record is *Rock Art and the X-Ray Style.* It's out now on Hellcat Records. We hope you'll pick it up and we'll be back in a moment on the *World Cafe.*

BJÖRK

WHEN THE SATELLITE RADIO SERVICE SIRIUS FIRST STARTED, long before Howard Stern became their most famous personality and before they were even broadcasting, the World Cafe began supplying them with our interviews and using their wonderfully equipped studios in the heart of New York City. At the time, whenever I had an interview at Sirius, I would hop on a train and go there to do it live. I was particularly delighted to talk with Björk, the Icelandic singer, about her album of music from the film *Dancer in the Dark,* in which she played a character named Selma. The album, *Selma Songs*, was unusual, as you might expect from Björk, and she was as quirkily charming as you would imagine.

Sirius had given her the full star treatment, complete with beverages and fruit in the studio for our conversation. Before we started recording, we posed for photos using the grapes as earrings. Then we turned on the tape.

Björk: [humming] Do you want some coffee?

David Dye: I have some, thanks. What a perfect opening for the *World Cafe*. Will you have some coffee? Björk is our guest today. We're eating food and talking about *Selma Songs* or *Dancer in the Dark*, or both of them, as they relate. The new album, which is the soundtrack to *Dancer in the Dark*, is called *Selma Songs*. Did you re-title it to make it more of your project?

Björk: Well, it felt straight ahead that what this film seems to be very much about—it being a musical—[is that] it's sort of reality versus fantasy. Reality is kind of when the humans talk and when they have to do work, all the sort of daily mundane things. And then once in a while they break into a song and the fantasy takes over. So I guess, like all musicals, this film is very much about the duality of that. And it seemed like putting just the songs out on the CD, on their own, without the film, without the reality element, it sort of was just one of the worlds. So, I decided it was *Selma Songs*. It's more the fantasy element, you know?

DD: And you originally came to the project to write the songs. And then you were talked into being Selma? How did that work? How did your acting in that come about?

Björk: Well, [the director] Lars [Van Tier] thought I should be Selma, and I always just found it quite peculiar that people with [a] similar sort of job as I have are always getting film offers. And, for some reason, people think that if you're okay in managing in front of a microphone on stage, you must be a terrific actor, which I don't think is right. I think actually, in a lot of ways, these two jobs are quite different. To cut a long story short, one probably is very extrovert and the other one is, actually, quite introvert. But I guess after a year, after I'd written all the music from her point of view and sort of felt like her. I guess I, sort of a little bit fell in love with her and felt like defending her. So, after a year, Lars said, "So, are you going to act it?" and I said, "No," and he said, "Well, then, we won't make the film." And then I said, "Oh, no, that's not possible." And then I ended up acting and being her. Yeah.

DD: What parts of her did you most identify with?

Björk: I guess being an introvert myself, especially my childhood, up to [the age of] like 20 years old. I spent quite a lot of time on my own, walking the mountains in Iceland, and the hills, and just hearing music in my head, and kind of just being very euphoric and very [much] on a high and very self-contained and self-sufficient. And then once in a while, going to school and doing these kind of things and trying to take part in conversation with the other humans and just finding it a bit boring, really. And a bit . . . of not making a lot of sense a lot of the time because people were saying one thing and then they did completely different things. They loved some people and hung out with other people. So, I kind of ended up always going back on my hill, singing sort of things. So, I guess that sort of escapism, sort of introvert universe . . . I can really identify with. And also, I guess because a lot of people think that people that are a lot on their own, that they are sad, you know, like loners. And I always thought that it was the opposite, because if you are very self-sufficient, you don't need anything, you know? It's sort of an introverts united thing.

DD: A lot of people listening right now are cheering. You've spoken for them. That's great. No, I totally understand where that feeling comes from. And it seems like you couldn't be more perfect for Selma, in terms of how her life is expressed and lived, for that matter. I mean, the interior *and* the exterior come together, is that my understanding, in the film?

Björk: I guess we do have a lot in common. I guess what we have not in common is [that] all my dreams have all come true and then some. A lot of dreams I didn't even think of. Whereas her dreams, I guess, none of them, sort of . . . well, not very many of them at least, came true.

DD: [This music] stands on its own as an album, but it shouldn't be perceived as the next Björk album—or should it?

Björk: No, not at all, I think, because I've been doing music since I was a child. I did put out three albums under my name, which I guess were quite self-indulgent and all about me, but I think that if you look at all of the music I've done in my life, that's a minority. Most of the music I've done has been about other people. I guess I just felt ready with this project to sacrifice myself for the cause of someone else, you know. So, I would definitely not call this my music. This is Selma's music.

DD: Björk is here, and we're here listening to the music from the film *Dancer in* *the Dark* as written and imagined and composed in her head by the character Selma, that Björk played in the movie and won the Palme d'Or, which must have just been--- You must have just been floored by the fact that [with] your first acting experience you won this [award].

Björk: Yes. It was a little bit outrageous because I definitely did not even think of that. I guess that my whole thing was that I went on this journey for three years. I didn't do anything . . . for three years, except this film. Like, I felt like I was having an affair from music to film. I felt guilty because [music] is the biggest love of my life and it's something I've been married to from birth and has never ever let me down. [Through] all my hardest moments, music was always there for me. And then to cheat on it with film, I felt very guilty and very dirty and I wasn't so sure that music would welcome me back. And then I started writing music again and music forgave me. Then suddenly, like nine months later, I am invited to France and I go there and then that other world, that film world, that I visited, acknowledged my visit, like by giving me this award. And, it was very, very outrageous, very special.

DD: Selma, a lot of the music she hears has to do with musicals. And I was thinking about what would prepare you for that and, of course "It's Oh So Quiet" came to mind. Did you think of that at all as you began to work on this because, it obviously didn't stay in that direction?

Björk: When I was a child I wanted to make musicals. I would kind of come to my relative's house or into a situation that maybe was not very fluid, like people were not communicating in a good way and maybe not very happy or something. And I kind of . . . wish[ed] I had the power to sort of jump on top of the kitchen table and do a bit of tap and kind of get everybody to sing along with me. They didn't need fancy orchestras or Hollywood and be rich and famous and handsome. They would just have—they could use the spoons and the forks and their hands and whatever. You know, magic is with you all the time. So I guess I had [these] kind of naïve thoughts as a child and wanting to do a musical all my life. Then hooking up with Spike Jonez, who did the video with me for "It's Oh So Quiet." We shared those thoughts, and very exciting to throw ideas back and forth. What we wanted [was] to take a very real situation, you know, nobody looking fancy or anything . . . everybody was just feeling ecstatic and great. I guess with every song we started off being very truthful to each situation. Like for example, this song happens in jail. She is in isolation and she's just about to--- Hope I'm not giving anything away here.

DD: Be careful, be oh, so careful.

Björk: Yeah, oh so careful, yeah. So, every song we went and recorded--- say in the jail, we would record all the noises you could possibly make in a jail, you know? Kind of if you slide your finger through the rims of bars, if you kick the floor with your feet, the echo inside those rooms, if you thump your palms on the bed, you know? This was the only noise we could use. This kind of stood for the reality Selma was trying to deal with. And then, if she was a good girl and had a big faith in magic, she would get orchestral squirts once in a while from fantasy. She's doing a walk there, one hundred something steps.

DD: I love the way you describe sounds. You describe arrangements as orchestral squirts and my understanding is that you're also working on a new album. And, how has making this affected the sounds that you're hearing there, 'cause every time you make an album, Björk, it just makes a leap sonically. And, it's always so exciting because it's always new territory for a listener. It must be--- Is it nerve-wracking for you to try to start with a blank slate?

Björk: Thank you. Um, I guess because I come from Iceland and I was always going to live there. And then realizing I had to travel abroad to do this music, I'm always very aware that it would be a waste of time and energy and probably money and [other] stuff if I would just repeat things. And then the only . . . reason for me standing up and actually taking an airplane from everything I love, is to do something that's never been done before, a pioneer style. I guess the album I'm doing now is very different. I started working on that before I did the soundtrack to this film, so I guess that is more a continuity, like a reaction, of *Homogenic*, to a certain extent, the opposite of that. I guess, then, writing the soundtrack, inside . . . working on two projects at the same time, I guess affected [it] in some ways, maybe, but not really. Musically it's very opposite. In the film, you've got a person born in 1930. The film happens in '63. She's been brought up in Czechoslovakia by American musicals, so her sound world is--- you're talking about something very, very different there. We could use electronic noises as long as you could hear them in 1963, which, of course, is a lot of noises. It's like refrigerators, all sort of hums, you know, toasters and you know. But you couldn't use any of this kind of high-tech, sort of more micro, sort of laptop, sort of [imitates sound] "*kthsss kskksk*" these kind of things. It was more kind of [imitates sound] "*wrrrrrrr*," like drones that we could then chop up and kind of . . . yeah! So in that sense, it's very different. I guess it's maybe too early to say now, but it seems to me that it's the whole drama and the darkness of the film. She's suffering quite a lot. You do that sixteen hours a day in the film studio and you come home in the evening and all you want is a nice cold glass of water. You just want something very simple and very refreshing and happy and peaceful, like no fuss, you know? And, I guess the album is a little bit like that, very, sort of quietly ecstatic.

DD: Sounds wonderful, thank you very much, Björk, for talking with us.

Björk: Thank you.

2000

DAVE CARTER & TRACY GRAMMER

DAVE CARTER WAS A SONGWRITER WHO CAME TO PROMINENCE TOO LATE AND PASSED AWAY TOO SOON. Originally from Oklahoma, Dave met his music and life partner Tracy Grammer in Portland, Oregon in 1996 and the two began a fruitful collaboration that was sadly cut short when Carter died suddenly of a heart attack in 2002, just short of his 50th birthday.

I wanted to include a portion of my 2000 interview because of Dave's description of his songwriting process, which is unique in my experience. I started off asking him about a song called "Happytown."

David Dye: The album starts out in "Happytown" and ends up in the "Bitterroot Valley," which I think is pretty interesting, but "Happytown" is, you know, it's not necessarily a happy, happy song.

Tracy Grammer: [chuckles] That's right, yeah.

DD: But it also features a reference to something that I think you better explain, which is "Occam's Razor."

Dave Carter: Well yeah, you know, "Occam's Razor" is basically the philosophical notion that the fewer elements incorporated in a theory, the more likely that theory is to be true and our CD--- Well, I will just say that "Happytown" is really a song about philosophical and religious artifice. It's a little bit of a song about the new age, although, I don't want to get into writing just another song that's putting down the new age, because there is a lot of great stuff that I think has come out of that. It's gotten to be, unfortunately, a modern cultural cliché that anytime anybody makes any kind of reference to mysticism or the deeper way of thinking [then] they're accused of being a shallow new-ager, but this [is] a little bit of a song about the philosophical conceits that people take onto themselves. Every song on the *Tanglewood Tree* CD is about piercing through illusion and the very first illusion that the person sort of pierces, who's making that journey from "Happytown" to "Bitterroot Valley," is that of that religion is not really going to quite do it for them. Although it's also not like it's attacking religion or anything like that, the song says, "Well, it's going to take you to a certain point, but you must walk that 'Occam's Razor' way ultimately, between the priests and the circus clowns, and the good things, and the bad things, the true and the untrue." Yeah, that's kind of what that song is about.

Dave Carter and Tracy Grammer recording: "Happytown"

DD: Dave Carter and Tracy Grammer on the Cafe today, with that seemingly simple but dense little song called "Happytown." Wow, you know, I was wondering--- You were talking about the lyrics to that song in a way, but sometimes when I listen to your stuff it just scans so beautifully and the words just sound so great together. Is that a part of writing for you?

DC: Well, it's--- I'll tell you. I'm really into Carl Jung [laughs] and so I write from the archetypal level. I like to write essentially first with deep inspiration and a deep strong idea about what I want the song to be about, but instead of writing literally about that, I try to put myself in touch with the various archetypes so that the images spill out in a certain order. It's kind of like stringing beads. If you want to make a string of beads, you go to a bead shop or a bunch of bead shops and you just find for whatever gut level you'll think the next bead ought to be. You know what I mean?

DD: But then you have to edit it.

DC: And then I come back through, a lot of times, like my method for writing that particular song. Now this isn't the method I use for all my songs at all. I mean sometimes they just pop into my head and it's a very quick process, but this song I had an idea what I wanted the song to be about. I had an idea of what the melody sang to me, because the music came to me first on this particular one. And so what I did was, I went on a 20-mile bike ride. I do this sometimes. And on that bike ride, I would pedal with the rhythm of the song and I would let the words just sort of flow and flow and flow, and then I'd sleep on it. And I went through like a two- or three-day process of this and I wrote down five or six pages of just images and rhymes and whatever came to me, and then I literally scanned it like you would very quickly scan a newspaper article that you didn't want to read in depth. I would sort of take this process of scanning through all the lines and from that emerged—really it was really predictable that it would, but the fashion in which it would was not predictable—emerged to me the way the song should really come about. And then once I had like four verses to the song that I knew I really, really wanted, I began to edit those songs and deliberate over exactly how I wanted to say this and exactly where that should come in. But the cool thing about writing like that is that someone can listen to the song in a deep way and get the literal meaning or they can just like sort of hear it on the radio and they hear this bombardment of images, which on a gut visceral level makes sense to you even if you don't want to go to the trouble of picking through the whole thing.

DD: That's the key, I think. That's really what's important. So, Tracy, at what point do you hear these songs? Does he unveil them before they're done?

TG: Well, usually I read about them. Dave will send me the lyrics in [an] email and I'll write back and, unfortunately, I'm one of those people that the first version is always the best version to my mind, you know? So he'll send me . . . for instance, we have a new song, called

"The Raven." He sends me a version of "The Raven" and I love it, and then he sends me, "No, No, No, Version 2" and I'm thinking, "Why did you change anything?" But yeah, usually that's my first input and I might bring up some issues that . . . you know, maybe things don't make sense. I'm a really literal person, so if it's just really out in left field I might say, "I don't get it." You know? Although, oftentimes I have to say I do and then basically it's just [a] matter of Dave coming over and we sit in the living room and he plays it for me and I just start--- I pick up an instrument and we start working it out.

DC: I should say also that nowadays, for the past two years all my writing, I hear the voice of Tracy and the voice of Tracy's instruments. I hear our voices together, that's the voice in which I hear this song framed, so simply, just even the presence of Tracy in my life and work is a big, big influence on every single thing that we do.

Dave Carter passed away in Tracy's arms in July of 2002 two years after our interview.

2000

STING

STING HAS BEEN A GREAT FRIEND TO THE *WORLD CAFE* OVER THE YEARS. He even contributed one of his performances on the program to our *Live at the World Cafe* series, which was a first for him. His initial visit came in 1999 in this intimate and revealing session with the World Cafe's Michaela Majoun.

Michaela Majoun: We're here on the *World Cafe* today with Sting at the Tower Theater in Philadelphia after his sound check. He's performing tonight on tour for his new album, *Brand New Day*. Welcome, Sting.

Sting: Nice to be here after so many years.

MM: After so many years?

Sting: After almost 20 years. I haven't been in this dressing room in 20 years.

MM: Wow, and it is great to anticipate a show in this small a venue. It's a delightful surprise.

Sting: It's a very nice way to begin a tour. To begin in a kind of nurturing, human-scale environment and not a huge stadium that dictates the music. The theater is somewhere where you can be musical. And that's my intention.

MM: Since you started releasing solo

records back in 1985, you've been known for bringing many different kinds of musical influences into the pop matrix of your songs: jazz, world rhythms, even classical music. What new directions have you explored in making *Brand New Day*?

Sting: [chuckles] Umm, nothing terribly self-consciously, or even consciously. The album was made in a sense of fun and joy, mainly to amuse myself. And to amuse the people I work with, to surprise myself, and entertain. There are elements of, perhaps, things that people haven't heard before. There's an element of rai music, which is a North African-based music.

MM: That's "r-a-i," not "w-r-y."

Sting: "R-a-i"---

MM: Yes [chuckles].

Sting: ---and it's very, very popular in France, mainly with Algerian singers, North African singers. But it's a great hybrid of North African, pop, reggae, flamenco, French cabaret. It's a very good milieu that I feel very comfortable in. It's not a pure music form, so I enjoyed it very much.

MM: And it seems like your process was a little bit different this time around in terms of jamming with people, getting things distracting . . . .

Sting: I didn't try and change the process. It's, you know, there's no one way of cutting this cake. There's so many different varieties of angle you could take to, to the work. And this time I just made music. I didn't think about lyrics, or song titles, or even an agenda, or a plan. It was just to have fun. It was only after maybe 6 or 7 months that I admitted that maybe I had a record there, and I better write some lyrics. So this was a slower process, but an interesting one.

MM: And that record is *Brand New Day*. We're talking with Sting on the *World Cafe* today. The first two songs on the album seem related in a way. The first one is called "A Thousand Years." Let's listen to it, and then I'll tell you what I'm referring to.

Sting: Okay.

Sting recording: "A Thousand Years"

MM: That was "A Thousand Years" from Sting's new album *Brand New Day*. The song, Sting, speaks of the many lives of a soul over eternity, and through it all the soul keeps saying, "I still love you, I love you still." It seems to me that the "you" implied there is the same ambiguous "you" that Rumi, the Sufi poet from the 13th century, writes about.

Sting: Mm-hmm.

MM: And that is to say, the "you" could be another person, but it could also be "the divine"—either "the divine" within or a larger---

Sting: Yeah, I think romantic love is often an analogue for more philosophical longing, something greater than ourselves even. And so, yeah, I'm not a stranger to that idea—romantic love and ontology. [laughs] Can I use that word?

MM: Yes, only with *our* listeners. [chuckles] So you believe in reincarnation?

Sting: No, not logically, not rationally. I don't think it can be defended. I think it's a beautiful, poetic idea and, therefore, has a truth. And to live one's life as if it is true will do one no harm at all. In fact, if anything, it would make you live better, in my opinion. But I certainly wouldn't get into defending it logically or saying that that is actually what happens. I can't do that. But you know, for me, faith exists in the creative imagination, therefore, there is a truth there. And logic and rationalism have nothing whatever to do with it.

MM: The second song of the album, "Desert Rose," umm . . . I don't know, I read into it the same kind of longing, the same kind of ambiguous love that could be—that could cover a lot of things.

Sting: Yeah, I agree. I mean, I'm talking about earthly love, if you like, or romantic love, but also the Garden of Eden rears its head at some point. And a sense of philosophical, umm, "longing" is the word, you know? The interesting story is that I wrote this song, but I didn't tell Cheb Mami what it was about. Cheb Mami's the Algerian guy who sings on the record. I asked him to sing some lyrics to this countermelody I'd written, and he had no knowledge of what *I* was singing about. He came back and started to sing, and I thought it sounded very good and very authentic, and I asked him what he was singing about. And he said, "Well, I'm singing about longing"---

MM: Ahh.

Sting: ---which is an interesting sort of confirmation of the process, you know? The music was telling us what to write.

MM: The song is "Desert Rose" from Sting's new album, *Brand New Day.*

Sting recording: "Desert Rose"

MM: I love the last line of "Desert Rose": "this rare perfume is the sweet intoxication of the fall." And, of course, that brings to mind Adam and Eve, especially since you mentioned Eden---

Sting: Yeah.

MM: ---in the song.

Sting: Well, I think that's--- We do have a kind of recollection, almost, of perfection, of a time when there was happiness. I don't know whether it's an illusion or not, but it's certainly in everyone's head. We have this idea of perfection; whether we can realize it or not, I don't know.

MM: You mentioned Cheb Mami, the Algerian singer who works with you on the album. You have some of your standby, wonderful musicians on this record, too, like Dominic Miller on guitar and Vinnie Colaiuta on drums, but also some great guest artists.

Sting: Well, we have Branford Marsalis; he's a very old friend of mine, who's been on every album so far, I think [chuckles]. And Stevie Wonder played harmonica on one of the tracks, which is really an homage to *him.* That song "Brand New Day" reminded me very much of him, and I thought it'd be a great idea to have him play what I consider to be the happiest sound in the universe; that harmonica is such a signature. And he very kindly agreed to come and play, and it was a great honor for me. James Taylor, who was one of my teachers, if you like—just as Stevie was—agreed to sing on the album, but not sing as James Taylor; I wanted him to sing as a character, as a very arrogant big shot with a big car and a fancy diamond ring. Not like James Taylor at all. So, a lot of people haven't recognized him on the record. He doesn't sound like him, but he was directed not to [chuckles].

MM: That's an interesting song; it's called "Fill Her Up," and it starts out as a very country song about a kind of loser and a thief, but then you bring in a church choir, and it ends up being an ode to marriage.

Sting: Well, it's—it was actually inspired by a painting by Hopper. It's a famous painting of his of an old gas station in a pine forest—I think it's a Mobil gas station—with a guy holding a gas pump. And I just sort of climbed into the picture and invented this story about that guy. You know, he didn't seem to have much going for him. And he's tempted to steal the cash box and take his girlfriend to Vegas and have a good time. But something happens. Something happens in the woods as he walks back home.

MM: And it's all there in the song, "Fill Her Up."

Sting recording: "Fill Her Up"

MM: Sting, you started the record in Tuscany at your house there. I was recently in Italy, and so many people said, "Sting has a house here."

Sting: [chuckles]

MM: They were so happy that you're at least a part-time resident there. How has Italy affected your process, or your work, or your music?

Sting: Well, I've been going to Italy for 20 years now. And, like a lot of Englishmen, I've fallen in love with the diametric opposition to England in many ways . . . you know, its weather, its outlook, its philosophy. And so I've been looking for somewhere to buy [a home] for many, many years and never quite found the right place, but I think I've found the place now. It's near Florence and Siena and it's very beautiful. And, can you recognize it on the record? I wouldn't say so. I think all you could recognize . . . is a spirit of joy and good living [chuckles] that Italy engenders. You know, it was nice to spend a year there . . . all the seasons, and with my colleagues, and my family.

MM: Your website says that *Brand New Day* is devoted to the theme that love conquers all, but a lot of the songs are about breakup, the loss of love.

Sting: The loss of love or, or--- I'm not so sure about that. I think there's an optimism in just about all of the songs—that love actually transcends not only lifetime, it also transcends breakups. You know, there's meaning in a relationship even if it doesn't last. It's been a profound and useful part of living. Even the song about the transsexual, you know, there's a pride in the way he/she sings about his/her life that I found very engaging. I like that. It's a song saying, "Don't judge me. I'm not asking to be forgiven. I'm making a living."

MM: The song is called "Tomorrow We'll See," and it is a transsexual hooker's point of view. Where did that come from?

Sting: [chuckles] Well, it's pretty far removed from my experience, I have to admit, except that my wife made a documentary for the BBC about transsexuals in Paris, and how they made a living, and why they did what they did. And what came through that documentary was that it wasn't just commerce. They actually were, to themselves, in a branch of show business in that they cared passionately about the way they looked and the way they presented themselves. They're very proud and exotic creatures and, you know, the world would be a dull place without them as far as I'm concerned. The story is essentially tragic; a lot of them end up in a very bad way. But you know, they've chosen to live that way and I think they should be respected.

Sting recording: "Tomorrow We'll See"

MM: The song "Perfect Love Gone Wrong" on *Brand New Day* features a French rapper named Sté—Sté and Sting together! [laughter] And you've written in French before. Sté does some rapping in French.

Sting: Well, French rap interests me a lot because it's very political in the real sense and very erudite. It's also been taken by French culture in a very big way. It's not ghettoized like it is here [in the United States]. And in France they're very proud of their rap music. And for me, I didn't use it entirely gratuitously. I'm singing from the point of view of a dog.

MM: Literally?

Sting: Literally. And she is my mistress, and I'm very unhappy that this relationship we have has been broken up by a man. And so I'm complaining and then she's complaining about me. But I wanted it so that we didn't speak the same language. I'm speaking dog, and she speaks in French. So we don't *quite* meet. That was the intention anyway.

MM: I wasn't sure if it was literal or figurative, but that's great.

Sting: No, I'm definitely a dog.

Sting recording: "Perfect Love Gone Wrong"

MM: That was "Perfect Love Gone Wrong," a song that's on Sting's new album, *Brand New Day.* We're talking today with Sting back stage at the Tower Theater in Philadelphia on the *World Cafe*; more in just a moment.

Sting recording: "A Thousand Years"

MM: Well you certainly have a different point of view in "Big Lie Small World" in which the protagonist--- there's a very lively samba beat that contrasts with the singer's sense of doom and loss of the loved one, but still it's a very funny song.

Sting: Well, this character has turned up in my songs a number of times. He's the same character in "Seven Days," a sort of hapless, romantic, hopeless person. You know, he can't quite get relationships right. He's always saying the wrong thing or he's never on time, but it's a sort of tragic, comic story of a letter that was sent, of bravado, but then he tries to get it back off the postman. And then he gets into a fight and ends up in prison. It was meant to amuse. It amused me.

MM: It's amusing and very cool at the same time with Chris Botti's trumpet and your vocals.

Sting: Well, Chris is imitating Miles Davis, another one of our avatars.

Sting recording: "Big Lie Small World"

MM: "Big Lie Small World." It's very hard to imagine. I know you're playing a character in that song, but as Sting it's hard to imagine any woman leaving you, so that's—

Sting: Well I've been left, for good reason [laughs].

MM: What was the reason? [laughs]

Sting: We won't go into that now. [laughs]

MM: How has new technology affected your process of composing?

Sting: Well I was--- I would imagine I was one of the first people to begin to use digital systems to compose on computers about 15 years ago. And I've used it as part of my process in all of that time, but never so you would notice. There's an electronic undercurrent in all the music I've done. But it's usually played against real musicians. So it's layered over by real musicianship. And I find that very interesting. It's not entirely organic, but there's a tension between the real musician and the mechanical nature of computer-generated sound, you know? So I've always found that interesting.

MM: Are you still doing yoga?

Sting: I'm doing yoga now even as I sit here.

MM: Oh my!

Sting: [chuckles]

MM: Are you sorry that you did that article in *Yoga Journal* a few years back, talking about tantric yoga?

Sting: No, I didn't. I didn't talk about tantric yoga in that journal. I talked about it in a drunken session of *Q* magazine. And why would I be sorry?

MM: It comes up a lot, so to speak.

Sting: It comes up a lot. It's hilarious. I think it's very funny.

MM: Does "Ghost Story" tap into something that's essentially male, do you think?

Sting: Male? It's about my father, actually. That song is very much about my relationship with my father now.

MM: Now that he's dead?

Sting: Now that he's not--- he's left his body.

Sting recording: "Ghost Story"

MM: You were recently profiled on *60 Minutes*. There's a reference to you going to the Amazon in the current *House & Garden*. What is it like being a cultural icon and trying to have a normal family life?

Sting: Well, I have a very normal family life. I don't bring the celebrity home. My kids wouldn't tolerate it, nor would my wife. I try and be as normal a father as I can be, the only difference being that I travel a lot, and I'm away from home a lot. But when I come home, I do monitor that celebrity guy. He stays outside.

MM: It's a good trick if you can do it. I just have a couple more questions. Sting, you're known for your vocal agility, for being able to go from a very intimate vocal stance to great soaring over the music. How did you discover that and develop it?

Sting: Selling newspapers. I used to sell the *Evening Chronicle* in my hometown of Newcastle and I developed a singing style to get over traffic. Want to hear it?

MM: Yes.

Sting: Eve-ning Chronic-le! [calling like a newsboy]

MM: I can hear that in the---

Sting: You can hear it, can't you?

MM: Yes, I can hear it in your music now.

Sting: Sort of [a] yodel—and it worked; I sold a lot of newspapers. And I had a milk round in the mornings. I was always very hard working.

MM: You've acted. You've had this extraordinary musical career. And you certainly have been involved in some important causes, social causes: Rain Forest Foundation, Amnesty International. Is there anything that you haven't done yet that you really want to accomplish in your life?

Sting: [chuckles] Well, I mean, the only regret I have is my athletic career. I never played soccer for England. I was a runner as a young man but, you know, in the next lifetime, if such a thing exists, I will be an athlete.

MM: That thing that you don't believe in—the next lifetime.

[laughter]

Sting: It's not that I don't believe in it, I can't *defend* it.

MM: Sting, it's been such a pleasure to talk to you. Thank you for being on the *World Cafe* with us.

Sting: Nice to talk to you too. Thank you, Michaela.

2000

DAVID CROSBY

DAVID CROSBY'S MUSICAL LINEAGE IS IMPECCABLE: The Byrds; Crosby, Stills, Nash, and Young; solo albums, and even a new group with the sons he never knew. He also produced Joni Mitchell's first album, a landmark recording.

In April of 2000, armed with a DAT machine, I traveled to the Four Seasons Hotel in Philadelphia to sit down with David and talk about the recent Crosby, Stills, Nash, and Young album, *Looking Forward*. With his history of drug problems and his relatively recent liver transplant, I was relieved to see a flannel-shirted Crosby looking robust and in love with life.

Anxious as Crosby was to promote the band's recent album, we did find out a lot about the inner workings of the foursome.

David Dye: Crosby, Stills, Nash, and Young are just about halfway through the CSNY2K tour, this leg, and we have a chance to sit down and talk with David Crosby about how this has been going. And if all reports are right, are you having as much fun as it looks like you're having?

David Crosby: I am having as much fun as you can have with your clothes on.

DD: [laughs] And I say "you" particularly. People are singling you out as being somebody on the stage who is beaming and having a great, great time.

DC: Well, you know, I don't know, I think

we all are. You know I mean, we all show it differently, you know? Steven's a little more of a stone face than I am, [and] man, he's having a blast, too. And you can tell by the way he's playing. And Neil, God, playing with Neil is like sticking your finger in a wall socket, man. I have never had so much juice, you know, so much energy committed to the music in front of me and driving it. So, I mean he's better than he was, and he was really good. I think that's true of all of us, you know, Nash too. I think we're actually better than we were then. We're not as good looking, but everybody's better at what they do than we were even the first time around, and we were pretty good then.

DD: Now what I want to know about is I want to talk a little about how you guys initially got together with the album. But before that, I want to find out--- you've got hundreds of songs from all different variations, solo, all your albums, the Crosby, Nash, whatever. How do you put the set together? It has been changing, hasn't it?

DC: [laughs] It's very difficult. It changes in between songs. As a matter of fact our crew came to us. The guy who does the house mixing, Tim Mulligan, who is a brilliant guy, fantastic mixer, came to us last night and begged, "Please guys a set list, and then play that set list. Please, please I'm begging you." 'Cause he's got millions of presets and things that he has to change you know for various instruments. And he'll look up and see me playing a guitar that's not the guitar he's got on, because we just switched and instead of doing "Long Time Gone," we decided that night we were going to break in "Eight Miles High" after one rehearsal.

DD: Yeah, now how did that come up?

DC: Oh man, it's just a fun song, you know. We're at a point now where we're pretty comfortable with the set and we're confident in ourselves. You're going to see a lot of that. You know, any good song from any one of those four bands or any one of these writers is fair game and anything else. There's no rules, you know? So on any given night we may wind up playing "In-A-Gadda-Da-Vida," I don't know. There's certainly--- there's nothing to constrain us. If we can think of it, we can play it.

DD: Well it's not going to sound like this if you go to the show, but this is how it sounded originally.

The Byrds recording: "Eight Miles High"

DD: "Eight Miles High," the original Byrds version, not the CSNY version that you'll hear from a--- What's interesting I find about it is, it's kind of a stripped-down stage. It's the four of you guys and just a rhythm section, but what a rhythm section. Talk-little bit about what Duck Dunn and Jim Keltner bring to this.

DC: Well they are master craftsmen. Duck, you know, has a song sense; he knows what a song needs. He's been supplying that essential element to songs all his life. He knows where the bass is supposed to go the way a master craftsman knows when he's carving a seal out of a piece of stone. He knows what isn't seal, you know, well---

DD: [laughs] That's a great way to put it.

DC: Duck knows, you know? And I've never had to tell him anything, the entire time that we've been playing together here. I've never had to say, "Duck, could you play the root there instead of the fifth?" I've never had to say word one. And some of this music was pretty weird to Duck, you know? He listened to *Déjà Vu* and said, "Are you sure you've got the right guy?" [*laughs*] He thought that was pretty outside left field for him, but he mastered it, totally. And Keltner—you know Jim, I mean—Jim is this incredibly strong player, but completely outside the rulebook. Whatever you thought he was going to play, it isn't, you know? And yet he's playing in a pocket, a groove the size of the Grand Canyon. But he doesn't do it the way other people do it. He's constantly feeling it; he never plays anything the same twice; it's constantly a flow for him. He's right there in the moment, you know.

DD: One of the high points of the first set, and I'm wondering if it kind of surprises you, how people are reacting to "Almost Cut My Hair."

DC: [laughs] Well, you know, it does go down great. But in a feeble attempt at modesty, I'll say that a lot of the credit has to go to the fact that both guitar players really love to play it. And they start to, you know, that's where they start to rip. And people--- I mean one of the reasons they love this band is the songs, but the other reason is that they love it when those two guys rip. They are two completely one-of-a-kind guitar players; there's nobody like them. At that level it isn't better or best, you know? It isn't Clapton or Hendrix. It's different. And those two guys are different. Particularly Neil; there is nobody like Neil. But there isn't anybody like Stephen either. He has fluidity and a sense of melody and power that's just--- he's graceful on the guitar, man.

DD: And they're playing off each other, too.

DC: Oh they're having conversations all the time, you know. Either one of them is the best rhythm guitar player the other one could ever hope for. So, as they shift back and forth in the conversation the thing, it's really tough for me as a rhythm guitar player to--- I have to be very spare and sparse, but I do get my licks in now and then.

DD: You know, you do all manage to satisfy all the songs people want to hear.

DC: Come on, every night somebody's just "What about 'Wooden Ships'?" or "Where's 'Déjà Vu'?" or "Can't you do [singing], 'Only castles burning'?" When we started out, Joel Bernstein, who's our dear friend, said, "Well you guys have

900 songs." And we said, "Ridiculous. You're out of your mind." He says, "Well, 480 of them are Neil's, but you do have 900 songs." And we said, "Well, obviously we're not going to pay any attention to that," so we looked at about 50 to 60 songs. Now, that's about a six-hour show. Even we can't do a six-hour show.

DD: Well, one of the things I wanted to mention is that 10 of those, or at least 10 of those, every night, seem to be from the new album, which is really, kind of daring in a way, you know? I mean there's some of those songs not everybody knows like they know all the other ones, and they're going down really well.

DC: Yeah. They're going down well. And again in a feeble attempt at being modest. [laughs] That's one of the most crucial parts, man. You have to understand, we're not the kind of guys who could just come out and do our hits, and take the money, [and say], "Thank you and goodbye." It either has to be vital, actual, real band that's currently got forward motion and is alive, or none of us really want to do it. And the only frustration about how good the new stuff is going down is that we're playing all of it better than we did it on the record; and that is frustrating. "Dream for Him" is four times as good as we did it on the record. "Seen Enough"? Man, "Seen Enough" is a brand new song and Stephen is delivering it so well live, that people are applauding the punch lines. And you know that means they're hearing the words.

DD: Absolutely. Well talk a little bit about "Dream for Him," because I think that's a really great song. It's got a lot of the--- it's got kind of the jazz feel that's been underneath a lot of what you do, and lyrically it's really great. That's about your new son, as opposed to--- I mean there have been a lot of fatherhood discussions around you.

DC: [laughs]

DD: But certainly about Django and James too, so, you know there's something. It's about Django?

DC: Well, you know, I love it because if you've ever loved any kid, even if you don't have a kid of your own, if you've loved any child, you've asked yourself some of these questions. You've said, "How the heck am I going to explain this world and some of the things that go on here to my child?" You know, there are some glaring discrepancies and inconsistencies, and there are also parts of it that are very tough to explain to a kid. Very tough. And I don't want to lie to my kid. I love my kid; I don't want to lie to him. So you're caught there between two very strong forces: the need to tell the truth, and the need to explain some really pretty amazingly strange stuff, behavior of human beings. And I think I caught it in that song pretty well, but the way we're doing it live. Jesus, if I'd had the brains to get Stills to play the bass on the record it would have been three times as good, and we did it too fast on the record. It's just much better live.

DD: This is "Dream for Him."

Crosby, Stills, Nash, andYoung recording: "Dream for Him"

DD: [laughs] Now think back to when you guys first got together for this new album. Was it a little tentative this time around?

DC: You know, the truth was, it was the oddest experience. Before when we would get together, there would be these long negotiations between managers and lawyers [grumbling] and stuff, you know. Or even between us. You know everybody would say, [grumbling] "Well it's got to be this way for me and you can't have that," or "I must, and you have to---" All wrong stuff [sigh]. And this time, Neil walked in, had a Gretsch under his arm, and he said, "Oh, that's a nice song, man. Can I play on that?" And we said, "Yeah, sure. Go ahead." It was "Heartland," and we said, "Do you want to hear some more songs?" He says, "One at a time." And then we played him another song, and he said, "Yeah that's cool. Hey, can I play on that?" We said, "Yeah, sure." Eight songs later, you know, we were all--- We all just decided we weren't going to talk about it; we were just going to do it.

DD: Is that what's changed?

DC: It's one of the main things. No expectations, no, you know. Just focusing on the moment, when none of us are saying, "Oh gee, and next month we'll tour Europe, and then after that we'll conquer the world, and then we'll invent electricity." We're just taking it a day at a time. You can guess where I learned that. And focusing on trying to do the very thing that we're supposed to do right now, the very best we can do that particular moment. And that's working for us like a champ. It's really, really working. I couldn't be happier with it as a method, as a modus operandi. It keeps us focused on the art and not on peripheral stuff.

DD: Well I want to close out with "Guinevere." And I wanted to ask you a little bit about this song because, how far in advance of this album did you write this song? Because I've heard that when you were working with Joni Mitchell on her album, that song was sort of there.

DC: Well Joni Mitchell was one of the women that I wrote it about. The last verse, "golden hair" and "down by the bay," you know, that was me being in love with Joni. And yes, I had for quite a while. I started writing it, gee, right after the Byrds threw me out, I think.

DD: It sounds like that period of time.

DC: Yeah it was.

DD: Well, their loss. This is a great song, and thank you so much for talking with us.

DC: Yeah, it's our pleasure.

DD: This is "Guinevere."

Crosby, Stills, Nash andYoung recording: "Guinevere"

2001

AHMET ERTEGUN

AHMET ERTEGUN PASSED AWAY IN 2006. We did this interview originally for broadcast on Martin Luther King Jr.'s birthday, as part of a show on race relations in the music business. Now we wish that the interview hadn't been quite so focused because there are so many other stories he could have told. After the interview was over, I heard Ahmet tell his assistant over the phone, "Oh, I wasn't very good." Read on and you'll know he was wrong.

David Dye: Our guest is Ahmet Ergetun, the co-founder and co-CEO of the Atlantic Records Group. He is also a founder of the Rock and Roll Hall of Fame. In fact, when you walk into the museum in Cleveland, you walk into the Ahmet Ertegun Wing. Ertegun's father was a Turkish diplomat, and the family landed in Washington, D.C., when Ahmet was twelve. He followed an early love for jazz and blues music to founding a little independent record company called Atlantic in 1947. That independent record company has evolved into one of the most major of the majors. Atlantic's early success in soul and jazz music was followed by equally impressive success with British rock, with groups like Yes, Led Zeppelin, and the Rolling Stones in the 1970s. Today its impressive roster includes Matchbox Twenty, Jewel, Tori Amos, and many others. I spoke with Mr. Ertegun and asked him about his musical education that kind of paralleled his formal one in college, and about a little record shop in the Washington ghetto called Waxy Maxy's.

Ahmet Ertegun: Well, when I first came to Washington, I went to the big record shops, the ones that sold only the RCA Victor and Columbia releases and their Steinway pianos, and I asked for a Louis Armstrong record and they looked at me like I was crazy. They said, "Well, you can't get that here." So I quickly realized that I had to go to the black section to find the kind of records I wanted to buy. And I became friends with Max Silverman, who had a radio repair shop in the black section, but who also had a few thousand used records that he kept on the side, and they would sell three for a quarter, ten cents each or three for a quarter. They were old jukebox records. Many of them had been worn out and so forth, but among them were some very good old jazz records. My brother and I were jazz collectors, so it was a great place for us to find jazz records and blues records by singers like Bessie Smith and Ida Cox and so forth.

DD: Did people hang out? Was there a scene at the store?

AE: Well, you know, the store eventually became a record shop from having been a regular repair store, as records--- After the World War, America went into the Second World War. There was a tremendous increase in activity in the black community, in the sense that more people were employed and there was much more money and there was suddenly demand for rhythm and blues music. There was a shortage of rhythm and blues records because there was a shortage of shellac, which was being used for the war effort, and the major record companies were only pressing records by their biggest stars. And there emerged hundreds of small labels that specialized in "race music," as it was called then, "race" or rhythm and blues music as we know it now. So there emerged all these little labels, which filled a void, and we were among those, and released our first records in 1948.

DD: When you created Atlantic back in the early days, and you signed mostly all black acts, were you thinking of them as primarily for a black audience, or did the idea of crossover enter into your thinking?

AE: Well, the idea of crossover, I always thought, would eventually come about, because I knew that the R&B music that the black people were buying was like all black music, historically, has always appealed to white people. Vice versa is not true, but continues now with rap, and it's a continuation of the music which somehow doesn't fail to cross over. Your black music crosses over no matter what you do, and I tell you, they tried to stop it very, very hard.

The Chords recording: "Sh-Boom"

AE: When I first started making black records, we were making records for the black public, but when we'd make a record like "Sh-Boom" by the Chords, there was an immediate hit, and not only a hit with black people, but it also hit with a big white audience. But the white stations would not play it until a Canadian group made an exact imitation of what we made, and that went over and over. But eventually we broke through. And even more than us, it's Motown that broke through the barrier point going from R&B to pop.

DD: How did Atlantic's approach to trying to break through differ from Motown's?

AE: Well, we were much before Motown. We started twenty years before Motown, so we went through the hard part, when there were no white stations playing black music. They may play the occasional Mills Brothers or Nat King Cole record, but they didn't play R&B music. But, you know, there were stations that were black music stations, and those stations somehow could not be segregated in the sense that they only played black music. But they were on the same dial on the radio, and the white listener could just switch it on, and they did switch it on, and one of the people who switched it on was Elvis Presley. He listened to black music and he started to make it, and that revolutionized the whole concept of R&B music.

DD: Let's talk about some of the heavy hitters that you signed early on. I understand you bought Ray Charles's contract for $3,000. Was that a lot of money for Atlantic back then?

AE: Well, it was. We started our company with a capital of $10,000, so we'd been in business a couple of years, and we somehow were still alive, miraculously, and it was about that time that I first heard Ray Charles. He was recording for a label on the West Coast called Swingtime, and I was knocked out by his singing and playing, and eventually we had the opportunity to buy his contract, which, for $3,000, that was quite a bit of money. We used to be able to make a recording session, including studio time and musicians and everything, for around $500.

Ray Charles recording: "I Got a Woman"

DD: Talk a little bit about the atmosphere at those sessions, those early Atlantic recording sessions. We had a situation where it was mainly the white producers and the black artists. Did race matter in the studio?

AE: No, you know, because we never thought in those terms. We also made a lot of white records, not many of which became great hits, but very often we had mixed orchestras, you know. We had both black and white arrangers, and it was just a matter of digging the music, and in those days we had a hard time finding songs. Our artists, for the most part, were not songwriters, so when we couldn't find material for the recording sessions, I'd have to write it myself. I became a songwriter out of necessity. I was not really a musician, but I knew the kind of songs that we needed to break through, and so I wrote songs for many of our earlier artists, including the Clovers and Joe Turner, Big Joe Turner, and Ruth Brown and Laverne Baker and Ray Charles.

DD: Just look for that Nugetre name, they'll know it's you.

AE: [chuckles] That was my name spelled backwards in those days.

Recording: "Corrina, Corrina"

DD: I've always been kind of interested in what happened at Muscle Shoals Sound in Alabama, where you had such an attuned set of studio musicians, black and white writers, but mostly black singers once again. Did you get a chance to attend those sessions?

AE: Oh sure, I made records down there. As a matter of fact, the first sessions that we made were the Rolling Stones. When I first signed up the Stones, Mick was complaining about how many people would hang outside the studios in Los Angeles. I said, "Mick, when we start to record for Atlantic, I'm going take you to a place where nobody will know who you are." We went to Muscle Shoals and we were recording there, and we were staying in a Howard Johnson's Hotel; maybe it was a Holiday Inn. Anyway, nobody had any idea who the Rolling

Stones were, who I was, or anybody else, and we had a great time working in that studio.

DD: Now, Aretha Franklin is one of the artists who greatly benefited from Muscle Shoals. When she was with Columbia, did you have a vision as to what her records were going to sound like when she moved over to Atlantic?

AE: Well, we certainly did. I tell you, the person who's really responsible for Aretha's success at Atlantic Records is Jerry Wexler, who was my partner. He was a great fan of Aretha's while she was a singer at Columbia. We all loved her singing, and we could see that she had really great feeling for the roots of black music, but somehow she was put in an atmosphere which was much more sophisticated at Columbia. When she came to Atlantic, Jerry Wexler took her down South and it was like going back home, the music was there, and it just happened.

> Aretha Franklin recoding: "Chain of Fools"

DD: In the 50s, you were working mostly with urban artists from the North, but in the 60s, if you look at Percy Sledge and Sam & Dave and Otis Redding, there were a lot of people from the South. Was that a conscious decision on your part?

AE: Ah, yes. You know, we really wanted to make soulful American black music, and in New York it was very difficult, because in the 40s in New York, the musicians who were in New York were very sophisticated musicians who had been working in large orchestras. They were all very good readers; they were accomplished, well-schooled musicians. When we tried to make blues records for the southern market, they really were not--- Not only didn't they want to play that music, but I don't think they could play it in the same way that Muddy Waters' band was playing in Chicago. The Chess Brothers, who started about the same time as we did in Chicago—that label was called Aristocrat, the first label, and they eventually changed it to Chess—they had the influx in Chicago of all the Delta Blues musicians. Vee-Jay and Chess had all those blues players who had come from the Delta. There was one on every corner. In New York, you couldn't find a blues singer or player to save your life. It was very tough for us to break into a market that was looking for soul music. Now, by the time we could afford to travel and to look for musicians outside of New York, which was several years [later], the music had evolved, and of course we really hit it very big with some of the people you mentioned, starting with Ray Charles, and Wilson Pickett, and Solomon Burke, and Don Covay, and Otis Redding, and on and on.

> Otis Redding recoding: "I've Been Loving You Too Long"

DD: I don't know if you can speak to this, but do you have a sense of what the ex-

Front of initial *World Cafe* promotion postcard announcing our new show in 1991.

In September, listen for the debut of:

World Cafe • 10 a.m-noon • Monday-Friday

Host David Dye brings you the music you've grown to love on WXPN in a new national program—a mid-day mix of diverse music for the musically aware listener, including rock and acoustic, R&B, world music, reggae and folk. Plus live, on-air performances by such artists as Blue Rodeo, Michael Penn, Indigo Girls and Ben Vaughn; music reviews by recognized critics; and profiles of music's most visible artists.

Musician's Day • All day September 19

We're turning the tables on your favorite musicians. Throughout the day they'll play *their* favorite artists in a pre-recorded program. Among the special guests: John Wesley Harding, Marshall Crenshaw, The Horseflies, The Brand New Heavies, and Peter Holsapple & Chris Stamey.

Non-Profit Org.
U.S. Postage
PAID
Philadelphia, PA
Permit No. 2147

Back of the postcard.

Our original cramped *World Cafe* studio on the third floor of the red brick mansion at 3905 Spruce Street in Philadelphia, looking toward the equally cramped control room.

Sure we had soundproofing–from stacks of vinyl albums. The original *World Cafe* studio was also the record library.

Our first guest, Bruce Cockburn, during a later remote interview. Note the uncanny resemblance to host David Dye. (Mark Vogelzang, Vermont Public radio)

Rodney Crowell.

Rickie Lee Jones performs on stage at World Cafe Live.

David and Richie Havens.

Leo Kottke, David, and Phish Bassist Mike Gordon at a later *World Cafe* appearance.

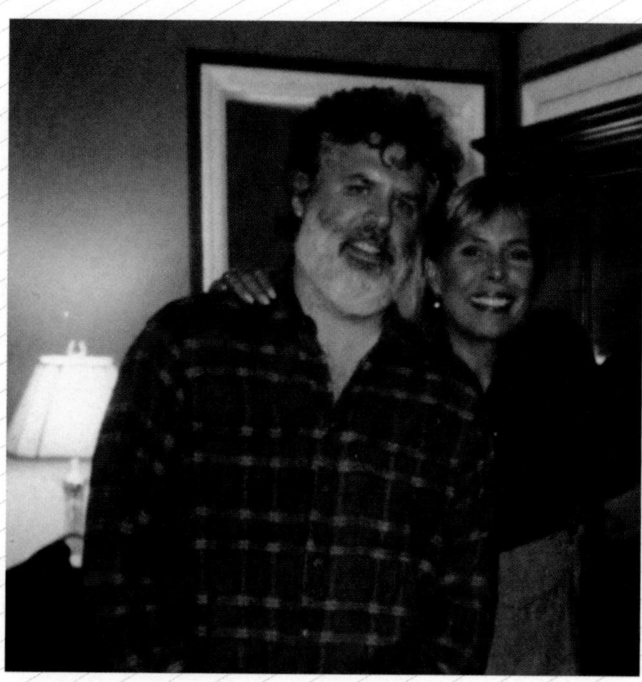

David Dye and Joni Mitchell at our first off-site recording at a New York hotel. (Bruce Ranes archive)

Elvis Costello, David Dye, and keyboardist Steve Nieve at the infamous session with the borrowed Casio keyboard.

Laura Cantrell, Elvis Costello, and David Dye. (Museum of Television and Radio, New York)

Sarah McLachlan and David.

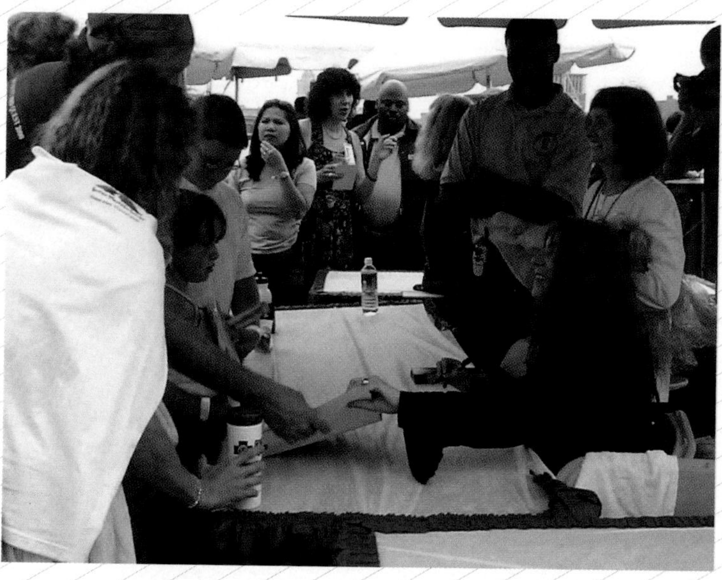

Patti Smith signs at WXPN's summer music festival.

David Dye and Bruce Hornsby.

Björk and David at Sirius radio in New York City.

Sting and Michaela Majoun recording their interview backstage.

A very young John Mayer makes his first *World Cafe* appearance.

Lyle Lovett.

David and Neil Young captured by David's cell phone camera in Nashville.

Jackson Browne and David. (Museum of Television and Radio NYC)

Sonic Youth in the performance studio.

Hall & Oates perform on stage at World Cafe Live before their interview.

Jazz trumpeter Hugh Masakela and David Dye.

Rosanne Cash performs at the *World Cafe* 10th Anniversary Concert.

The 10th Anniversary cake!

Eric Burdon signing our wall of fame.

Dave Pirner of Soul Asylum and David.

John Hiatt, Sonny Landreth, and David.

Lindsey Buckingham and David.

New performance studio. Compare and contrast with our first studio!

[NOTE: All photos from *World Cafe* archives except where indicated.]

perience of some of the Atlantic artists was, touring in the segregated South in the 60s?

AE: Oh, yes. Well, I can tell you horror stories beginning from way before. Do you know that one evening, my brother-- this was in 1939 or 40 in Washington, D.C.--- Benny Carter, who was a great saxophone player, jazz saxophone player, and Duke Ellington were in Washington, and my brother and I wanted to take them out to dinner, and then we suddenly realized that there was no restaurant in Washington which would allow us to sit together and have dinner, and the only one that we could go to was the restaurant in the train station, in Union Station, which is where we wound up having dinner. I mean, it's just unbelievable today to what extent there was a Jim Crow law all over the South, and the capital of our country was a southern city, with Jim Crow laws when I grew up in it.

2001

JOHN MAYER

AS YOU CAN TELL, THIS WAS JOHN MAYER'S SECOND VISIT TO THE *WORLD CAFE*. We had him on once before, on a show about the Aware series of samplers. Aware was a record company that focused on putting out samplers of young singer-songwriters to college students. Their track record with people like Five for Fighting and John Mayer has been pretty darn good. John Mayer has continued to be appreciative of our early attention, and his music continues to grow. I just wanted to include this brief excerpt from the beginning of our 2001 interview because, well, we make a fair comedy team.

David Dye: Well, John Mayer is back at the *World Cafe* today, and he's an artist that--- We started pretty early on with you, John.

John Mayer: Yeah, you guys actually came over to my house when I was four.

DD: I know, and we feel very good that we gave you that guitar at that point.

JM: Yeah, thank you, it was great. You guys used to drive me to school when my mom was working long hours.

DD: Well, your mom and I go back. She didn't tell you, probably.

JM: No, no, she did, and you were---

DD: I'm actually your father, John. [laughs]

JM: You are actually my father, but you are one of the few people who knew the secret code word to pick me up after school.

DD: That's right, that's right. And I even emptied all the contraband out of your backpack before I'd pick you up.

JM: [laughs] Thank you, thank you.

2002

JACKSON BROWNE

THIS WAS A THRILL FOR ME AND IT IS ONE OF MY FAVORITES IN THE BOOK. I am a longtime Jackson Browne fan and, as I say in this interview, I was a fan of his writing even before he released his first album. It was also fortuitous that Jackson was in the mood to talk about his early career. At the time of this discussion, he had recently released his album, *The Naked Ride Home*. This interview was recorded at the Museum of Television and Radio in New York City.

David Dye: That Gibson looks ancient to me, that one you're holding.

Jackson Browne: Yeah, this is from about 1935.

DD: Wow.

JB: And I've got newer ones, but I've got a couple that are about this old, like this. And it kind of changed my whole idea about guitar playing when I found these, because these were made to be played like Hawaiian guitars on your lap and they have these massive necks. And nobody wants them but me because no one will put up with that.

DD: [Laughs] That's right, it's a Roy Smeck. He was kind of the master of that Hawaiian thing.

JB: That's right; he was a radio instrumentalist that had a show and played banjo and mandolin and Hawaiian, and played all kinds of different styles. He was sort of the first--- maybe the vaudeville-era David Lindley.

DD: Well I was wondering if "The Night Inside Me" works on that one.

JB: Yeah. Let me show ya.

Jackson Browne performs "The Night Inside Me"

DD: That's "Night Inside Me." Jackson Browne is playing live for us today and that's one you've probably heard already from the new album, *The Naked Ride Home.* That song kind of stops and you say, "Maybe I should go back to Spain." What does Spain represent there?

JB: Well, in the song I'm talking about all the things I'm trying to escape, you know? Just the day-to-day grind, obligations, and maybe the sort of predictable nature of our lives, and I spent a long time writing—a certain amount of time—writing this song in Spain before I came back to the United States and had to face these things. The thought did reoccur to me, "Well maybe I should just go back there rather than look for this in the night," you know? Make them go where I have this all the time but, as my girlfriend pointed out, we feel that way about Spain because we are kind of on the loose when we're there. We are sort of momentarily reprieved from our greater responsibilities.

DD: Time out. That song has a certain amount of looking back and there's another one, "About My Imagination," that kind of looks back toward the beginning of your life and stuff. I just want to talk a little bit about growing up and what your life was like then. You grew up in Orange County?

JB: Yeah, I grew up, well, I went to high school there. I moved to Orange County when I was about thirteen, I guess, and by the time I was about eighteen, I was pretty much headed to Hollywood every night and I could get there and--- where friends of mine had record deals and had houses and sort of lived communally. Well, we all lived that way in Orange County, too, but somebody would rent a house and they'd be filled with everybody you knew and there were only a few houses but lots of people.

DD: What did your parents do?

JB: My parents were teachers. My dad was also a printer. During my early years, he had a print shop and his father had been a printer. My dad also taught college journalism, but he was trying to make it as a printer. You know, a small print shop not too far from where we lived and he worked really hard doing that. I mean, you're up all hours when you're trying to print things that have to go out in the morning like newspapers and things. My grandfather had printed the Occidental College newspaper and had built this house that was, sort of a hang [out] for various eclectic-minded people.

DD: So you were used to that. [laughs]

JB: Yeah, my father also--- well, he's a musician but not a professional musician. He never thought of himself as professional. He always thought he kind of stopped short of really--- He was in a band that played all the time and he had several bands when I was growing up. Dixieland jazz--- And he'd have these jam sessions at our house that were really wonderful happenings. I mean, when the whole world is nothing but short of kneecaps and you have the hems of people's garments and people are the size of redwoods, but it was around music. I remember my father sitting at the piano with all kinds of people playing instruments . . . mostly horns, and the Dixieland stuff.

DD: You're one of the few artists that we now know, that I've learned your songs before I ever heard you sing them. I mean, like "Shadow Dream Song" and all those early ones that Tom Rush did and those other people. How did that happen? And I'm just curious about that period, the pre-first album period and where did David Geffen---

JB: That was a long period. [laughs]

DD: [laughs] Was it? Did you feel like you were struggling?

JB: Yeah. I was trying to learn how to sing. I was trying to get comfortable with the act of singing, but it's really been a long--- I'm pretty comfortable now, mainly because I stopped caring that intensely. And there are times--- I mean, I'm always--- I continue to work towards trying to discover a kind of way of singing or discover my voice but I'm more comfortable with it then I used to be in those days and I was always trying . . . well, trying too hard actually, you know? So I had interest because my songs had interest from record companies, but there was always a sort of speculation going on as to how long it would take me to get it together and--- for instance, I had been signed to Elektra Records, you know? We were talking with some friends the other day or just a few moments ago actually about the fact that I've been on this label longer than anybody who works there.

DD: [laughs] It's true.

JB: But I was on it before I was on it, because I was on Elektra and then the record I made with my friends wasn't going to be released and they let me go. They cut me loose, which is also a testament to the generosity of the founder of Elektra Records, Jac Holzman, because in the old days they never let anybody go. They might not release your record, but they didn't let you go. They'd sell you to somebody, you know? They sell you a contract or they sell you, you know? They wanted to get their money back. But he let me go and let me have my publishing back and, a few years later, I was signed to Asylum Records. And then a few years after that, Asylum merged with Elektra, so I was back on Elektra Records. But yeah, it was a long period of writing songs. I always originally just wanted to write. I didn't really have aspirations to sing or play in front of people. But all the people singing my songs were having such a good time doing it, I had to sing them in order to write them and to play them. And although I had a really good friend named Greg Copeland who also wrote songs. But [he] didn't really sing, although I did eventually make a record for him of his songs with him singing for Asylum. And he began singing them.

DD: Well there are two questions that spring off of this. One of them is this whole concept of writing for yourself, which is something. I've never had the feeling that you wrote to commercial purpose. And I'm curious if you ever did try that.

JB: I did once because somebody called me and said, "Do you want to take a crack at writing this song for a movie?" Actually, it was David Geffen, and he said, "Do you want to--- Jim Brooks is making this movie. It's called 'I'll Do Anything' and he needs a song called *I'll Do Anything,* and a bunch of people have tried and it hasn't really---" you know? Knowing that I couldn't really goof anybody up too bad--- I was being called at the last minute; I wasn't their first thought, and I thought, "Well, I'll try it." What I've always wanted to do is reduce people's expectations. I didn't want to say, "Oh yeah, I can do that." I turned down a lot of projects just thinking it'll get to a deadline and I'll ruin someone's project by not having the goods when the time comes, you know? But I wrote this song called "I'll Do Anything," and it was a song that I thought, "Okay, I read the script," and it was for a character. It was for Albert Brooks; he was a movie producer singing to a test audience in this musical comedy about the movie business. And he's singing to them this absurd sort of plea to like his movie, "Just think of all we've always meant to each other!" He's really the most false, insincere person in the movie. He's sort of one of the great comedic characters. And I thought this would only work if it was really a serious song. I mean, let him be funny, but let the song actually be a real heartfelt plea to someone that you think of as like a lover or a partner, you know? And if he's singing to this test audience, it'll be funny. And in the end, they took all of the music out of the movie and didn't use my song or anybody's for that matter. But there were great ones. Prince had songs in there, I think. Sinead O'Connor had some songs. It was going to be a great movie but--- And I think it was actually a really cool movie. It just sort of---because he took all the music out, it was kind of neither a musical nor really the movie that he would've really made if he started that way, but it turned out to be as much about me as anything I've ever written. Even though I wrote it for another character in a completely different picture.

DD: You don't remember that, the song, "I'll Do Anything"?

JB: I don't really know how to play that well actually. [tries to plays some of the song] No, I don't remember it. [laughs]

DD: [laughs] The other question I was thinking about, about the songs that preceded you, was the fact that on your second album when you got around to doing "These Days," you credited Gregg Allman with the version that you did of that. And I'm curious as to how you did it before.

JB: Manny, get me a capo. Yeah, Gregg was a friend of mine that I had not seen in a long time. I mean, I knew Duane and Gregg from the Allman Brothers. They were just great guys. They were these southern, totally committed musicians and some of the most dedicated musicians I had met to that time. And they kind of thought playing acoustic music was a little strange. Duane said, "What you need to get yourself is an electric guitar." As of a matter of fact, he lent me his spare guitar for a couple of weeks once and said, "Go figure this out. You know, you need to play with a band." But it didn't really work; it didn't really happen then. And I wound up not playing with any musicians on my songs until I made my first album, until I was in the studio doing it. But when I ran into Gregg, he remembered that song, but the way he remembered it--- This is that songwriter's filter. I mean, the way he remembered it was completely different. It was slow; it was genuinely sorrowful sounding and it wasn't necessarily that sorrowful the way I had done it. But one of the reasons I decided to sing them myself was that very often, people did do them differently or [would] interpret them differently and I thought I needed to at least be able to sing them the way I had intended. I'm going to take the moment to get this thing on here so I can play this version of "These Days" that---

DD: Cool.

Jackson Browne performs "These Days"

DD: Jackson Browne, "These Days." Thanks for doing that. You know, that song has such—I'm sorry—an "old man" feel to it, that resignation. What were you? Eighteen?

JB: Sixteen.

DD: Sixteen?!

JB: Yeah. Well, it wasn't quite--- there were some words that were different too and there was something I considered a distinctly young point of view. At one point at the last verse, I said, "I'll stop my dreamin'" and---

DD: Hmm.

JB: And I don't think an old man would ever say that. [laughs]

DD: No.

JB: [laughs] But yeah, I don't know. I

think I was--- Well I was a big blues fan, you know? I think most of my heroes were really quite a bit older. I mean, I wasn't playing the pop music of my day, although there was some nice, bright, young music that I liked. It was like Mississippi John Hurt, who I really listened to---

DD: You were a big Ash Grove [southern California folk club in the 1960s] kind of guy?

JB: Yeah! My dad took me to the Ash Grove when I was probably about thirteen or fourteen to see Lightnin' Hopkins and he also took me to see Barbara Dane, whom he loved and whose accompanist played piano, but played piano and trumpet at the same time. He'd like comp chords with his left hand and pick up his trumpet and play a solo from time to time, which my dad just loved because my dad played horns too. I mean, he had a house, we had all these pegs in the wall and horns like sousaphones and French horns. And he played them. As a matter of fact, he got us to come for dinner when we were playing in the neighborhood. He would get out on the front steps and play the trombone or like he'd play *Dragnet* on the sousaphone. [laughs] You know, we were known as that family in the neighborhood that lived in a weird house that kind of looked like a church and the old man stood out on the front with the horn, you know? [laughs] My dad was a freak.

DD: Well, as long as you're kind of warmed up finger picking, there's a song that actually Keb' Mo' helps out [with] on this new one---

JB: Oh yeah.

DD: ---called "For Taking the Trouble." How did Kevin [Keb' Mo's real name is Kevin Moore] get involved with this?

JB: Yeah, I asked Kevin to play on this song and I had a track that I had cut a number of times and kept trying to make into this really kind of big rock track. And he played on it, and he played really well, but when he was through, he said, "Okay, well we got that down, if that's really what you want to do. But maybe you should turn off the drums, turn off the bass, turn everything off but your vocal and your guitar." And let me . . . let me . . . the words he used were "throw a monkey wrench in it. Let me just throw a wrench in it. I want to turn this thing around for a minute." And he wound up playing it in such an intimate way and he did sort of turn the song inside out, which is to say that the vocal became the most out of the thing. But he put a groove into the song to make it a very intimate song. And I'm glad that he did. And at the end of the day, everybody was sort of dancing to this in the studio, as opposed to thrashing around listening to this huge backbeat. Well, that version exists somewhere. Maybe I'll go try to resurrect that at some point. But this is called "For Taking the Trouble."

Jackson Browne performs "For Taking the Trouble"

DD: "For Taking the Trouble." That's kind of cool; the album version and the live version from Jackson Browne. He's our guest here on the *World Cafe.* We'll be back in a moment.

Jackson Browne recording: "These Days"

DD: We're back talking with Jackson Browne today on the *World Cafe.* That kind of segue thing we did there, that's reminiscent, of course, of "Runnin' on Empty" where you did that.

JB: That's right; we did that on Danny O'Keefe's "The Road."

DD: Right, which was kind of cool. I didn't realize how well that album sold. I didn't realize that was a huge-selling record.

JB: Oh yeah, it was massive. It was a big surprise. Yeah, I really was just trying to make a live record to sort of give me time to write some more songs, since most people don't put that many new songs on live records. But it just sort of took off amongst us two. We started listening to what we were doing and we thought--- well, it was Kunkel's idea actually. We were listening to everything back and he said, "You know what, why don't we just put out a single?" I mean, most double records could've been better single records. There aren't a lot of them, but more is not always more.

DD: But you also played around with the whole thing of what a live record is, with the backstage stuff.

JB: Yeah, I always felt that there were a certain amount of--- It'd be two in the morning in a hotel room and I'm thinking, "God, if only people could only hear this. This is so amazing; something about this structure." You know, something about [the] structure of a show is it's formal. It's great because people rise to the occasion and they present, in a way. And when they can break down the formality of the thing and really achieve intimacy with a big audience, that's always commendable. It's still not what really happens when people are, you know, unguarded and by themselves.

DD: This is going to sound like a total name drop, but I don't mean it that way. Earlier this week, I had a chance to talk to Peter Gabriel and one of the things he talked about was how he had been talking to fans about how certain [songs of his] have gotten them through emotional times of various sorts. And he talked about writing songs to put in the emotional toolbox. And I was thinking about your songs and many of them--- "For a Dancer," what a beautiful grieving song. And the album for me was *Late for the Sky* in that that was a, I believe, a particularly tumultuous time in your life. Is it cathartic for you to write these things as it is for us to hear them?

JB: It's healing to write them, if I understand it, cathartic sometimes. But what it is, it's a way of focusing your response. It's very much like the blues. It's very much like someone saying, "I don't feel good, and this is why," or it's coming to terms with what is bothering you or [thinking], "I may be in this kind of shape now, but tomorrow I'm going to feel better, and this is how I'm going to get there." If it were just wallowing and despair, it wouldn't work. But if during the course of the song, it pulls you together and you somehow by the end of that song are focusing on how you're going to get where you want to go. And it serves that kind of function and, yeah, I always just tell people [that] I'm glad it worked for them the way it worked for me. It's not an evangelical thing. It's not like I'm holding out for those uses necessarily. I think it's what we really use music for in so many cases. It's hardest to write a really happy song because that sort of has to sum up or sort of depict a thing that is so important to us. It's hard to kind of nail it down.

DD: I was just thinking, "Walking Slow" is on that album, which is happy. So you got some in there. [laughs] Would you be able to do one from that era?

JB: Yeah. Let's see. Which one? I can do "Walking Slow." I actually haven't been singing that song for many years.

DD: You don't travel with a jug player. That must be it. [*laughs*]

JB: Yeah, that's what it is. A jug. People are like, "What is that? A whoopie cushion?" We talked about jug bands earlier. The guy playing the jug on that record is Fritz Richmond, who was the jug player and washtub bass player for the Jim Kweskin Jug Band, whom I used to go see. I used to go see them at the Ash Grove. And he was the engineer on that record. He was the one who assisted Al Schmitt, the great engineer/producer.

DD: Well, try it.

Jackson Browne performs "Walking Slow"

DD: That's kind of brave [laughs], considering all the stuff it needs to kind of propel it along there.

JB: [laughs] Yeah. "Oh, you mean you played it in Albert Hall without the jug?"

DD: [laughs] Well, thanks a lot for talking with us today. We truly appreciate it.

JB: Thanks!

DD: Jackson Browne is our guest today on the *World Cafe.*

2002

BONNIE RAITT

I'VE HAD THE GREAT PLEASURE TO TALK TO BONNIE RAITT A NUMBER OF TIMES OVER THE YEARS. A lifelong Quaker and political activist, Bonnie and I hit it off when I told her that I, like her, had gone to Quaker camp as a kid. This interview was particularly informative as she talks a lot about her guitar style and different influences on her playing. And heck, she's hot!

David Dye: I'm David Dye. Bonnie Raitt has just released *Silver Lining*, her new album. We had a chance to talk with her a couple of weeks ago when she had just gotten her star on the Walk of Fame, and as you can hear, Bonnie is in a great mood, and I mentioned that. Wasn't that coming up?

Bonnie Raitt: Actually, let me clarify. Today I put my hands on my star [in Hollywood] which they unveiled this morning while my dad was singing, "Oh What a Beautiful Morning." I mean, how cool is that? Right in front of the Capitol Building.

DD: You're one of the few native Los Angelenos. Is that how you get on the Walk of Fame, does it have something to do with being from Los Angeles, or is it being famous?

BR: No, I think it's being famous, and in my case it's being on Capitol Records because it's just Garth Brooks and me out front that are actually on the label and I'm right near Joan Crawford and Roy Rogers! It's pretty exciting for a radical partier like me to end up in cement and still be able to walk around.

DD: That's so great. This new album, towards the end of the liner notes you call this a true band record, and I wondered, is that different for you? Is that a different experience this time around?

BR: You know, it's always a function of the chemistry between the great musicians that we pick to make the record, and I would have to say the first and second and third albums were as much band records as this, but it's just in this instance that this particular band has gelled for me in the last couple of years. This particular combination when George [Marinelli] rejoined the band after he had taken a break after road testing. Ricky [Fataar] and Hutch [Hutchinson] have been with me off and on, Hutch for 20 years and Ricky since *Green Light* and then came back for *Nick of Time*, but this unit of people with George in it, George Marinelli and then Jon Cleary, who in himself is a great New Orleans legendary solo artist and piano player and funkster as well. This unit---there's just something about the chemistry, the range of these guys. They're intellectually astute, they're well read, they're deep people, they're real funny, they can play anything from African to Celtic to the funkiest blues I could ever throw at them without batting an eye. So

I think I've finally found a suit that fits the best to be as spontaneous, as deep as I want and they'll follow me.

DD: And they do with this record. It goes all over the place, one of the strong, strong points about it. Let's talk about some of the tunes because there're so many cool ones. Let's talk about John Cleary's song to begin with; "Fool's Game" starts things off with a bang. I think I've heard his recording of this. That's on his record, right?

BR: Yeah, it is. I've just heard him do it live so much he's really--- For those of you who don't know who he is, he had a great record a couple years ago called "Moon Burn" on Virgin Point Blank and he has a new album coming out. I don't know which label yet because he's in between deals but he is an Englishman from Kent originally, in his late 30s now, but [he] moved at 17 years old. He flew and emigrated to New Orleans and lived in the back of the famous Maple Leaf bar so he could soak up every note that James Booker played. In exchange for painting the club he got to live there for free, so in the off hours he shed and became a real aficionado of the Professor Longhair and James Booker style, but he's a secret Johnny "Guitar" Watson and absolute funk fan so he sings and writes and he's treacherous on the guitar as well as the keyboards. He has a great band that's going to be opening for us for the next three months on our tour and his band is called the Absolute Monster Gentleman. Check it out because his record is going to be out soon too.

DD: Well, this is his tune. This is "Fool's Game."

> Bonnie Raitt recording: "Fool's Game"

DD: "Fool's Game" from Bonnie Raitt. We're getting a chance to talk with Bonnie and go through the new album *Silver Lining* today on the Cafe. The process of finding songs--- You're a good writer but you're not as prolific, so you're always looking for tunes from elsewhere. Is it getting harder or easier for you personally to find songs that you fall in love with?

BR: I think after the first batch that I kind of stashed when I was making one record a year in my 20s, I made six albums in seven years, and I look back at that and I think, "How the heck did I ever find enough songs?" And a lot of that was just songs that I stored up, that I learned and that I taught myself on guitar when I was in high school. And eventually, like most people, you end up running out of songs around the second or third album, because I don't write my own and I get a great thrill of mixing Motown songs with calypso songs with reggae songs with Randy Newman songs and I can't even conceive of wanting to fill a whole record with just my point of view. I would just be bored. So for me the songwriting got more developed in the last 10 years because I got more time off the road and more sober time to actually think about what I want to say. And feeling basically that the search for great material is not getting any easier. It's probably getting harder because an awful lot of songwriters, from whom I draw my tunes, also need their new songs for their own records, so there's less of them floating around. And I spend years going through publishing demos and old record collections and calling up people I know for tips on who the new up-and-coming songwriters that are under the radar are. That's how I finally piece together what I think is going to be a great record, and when I get enough to find something that would actually get played on the radio to help get the record across, which we call our singles. When I got those songs from Tommy Sims, "I Can't Help You Now" and "Time of Our Lives," I knew I could go in the studio, so I would probably say it's getting harder.

DD: I want to talk about "Silver Lining" because you just nailed this song.

BR: Oh David! Thank you so much, I'm so proud of that one.

DD: This is the goose-bumps tune for me. Tell me how you came to do it.

BR: Well, I love David Gray. I had been asking some friends I worked with to let me know of some singer-songwriters from their circle, you know, and I sort of rely a lot on people from different demographics and age groups and myself to let me know who's up and coming, if it's African music or Celtic, or the new baby Tom Waits coming up around the corner or great guitar players. David Gray's name came up about three years ago and I got his record *White Ladder* and some of his earlier stuff and fell in love with him as I did with Paul Brady when someone turned me on to him. And lo and behold within six months his record crossed over and he became a huge explosion over here in the States with the help of Dave Matthews and a really good campaign and I was thrilled for him, thrilled to have that level of musicianship getting that kind of acclaim. And I was also praying secretly that "Silver Lining" wouldn't be a single because I knew even three years ago, when I first heard that song, that it was very, very special and I was going to call my album that. The actual arrangement was built around--- You know, I usually just take a song and play it on guitar, [and] whether it's a Jackson Browne tune or a David Gray song, it ends up being in my cadence as well as key, which is already different enough. But that little organ part that I came up with is kind of a Celtic harmonium part in the beginning. That was something that just flew into my head, because I really hear it in that evocative kind of Celtic tone, so I'm hoping David Gray likes it when he hears it. I sent him off a record, I'd be thrilled to hear whether he enjoys it or not.

DD: This is "Silver Lining."

Bonnie Raitt recording: "Silver Lining"

DD: "Silver Lining." Our guest today is Bonnie Raitt, and that is the title track, the David Gray song, that is just so incredibly beautiful on her new album. I guess now's a good time to talk about your singing voice, because you sing that so incredibly well and I remember early quotes from you making disparaging remarks about how, "Oh, I've just got this little soprano," but what have you done over the years to work on your voice?

BR: Oh, I think just aging. Over the years--- Thank God I can sing a blues song and stomach listening back to it. I'm sure my lifestyle of rock and roll to the max, well to the max after the shows anyway--- I was never going to do anything to jeopardize my career. I think getting older and probably using it more, and I'm certain the accelerated wear and tear I put on it by being on the road, and my earlier years smoking and drinking, put a nice sloppy veneer on the gravel. And I think now a lot of it is informed by my heart and my soul and being more experienced and wise, filtered through that same instrument. It's just a process of time, I think.

DD: Wow, that's very similar to how Carlos Santana once talked about playing the guitar, talking about how it's in his fingers and kind of flows through him. It's very interesting. I was looking through at the Afropop Worldwide website one day and I saw you in Mali and that looked like a really fabulous trip. There's a couple of really wonderful African tunes on here. Talk a little about that journey. That must have been wonderful.

BR: It was a fantastic opportunity for me to delve into a kind of music that has always thrilled me since I first heard Miriam Makeba as a kid, when she had her big hit, "Pata Pata." I majored in African studies in college and I was always fascinated with going there and everything about African culture and politics, especially the liberation struggles in the 60s. The idea they would try to find a new way of doing a combination of capitalism and socialism and all that stuff I studied in school became endlessly fascinating to me. Interestingly, I didn't connect my level of rhythm and blues and blues to my love of Africa. They didn't seem that connected, although they're certainly--- the roots of the blues are in West Africa. Later on when I was exposed to Ladysmith Black Mambazo and *The Indestructible Beat of Soweto* in the early 80s, I just went crazy for that township jive music, having Ricky Fataar from South Africa since the *Green Light* album exposed me to a tremendous amount of music that I wouldn't have found otherwise. And our resident music college is Hutch, our bass player. Hutchinson turned me on to Oliver Mtukudzi and I was already a big fan of Habib Koité through Jackson Browne. And myself, you know, being a nose to the grind on listening to the *Morning Becomes Eclectic* and different global village shows out here in California, being exposed to some of the great

African artists coming out and going on tour. That would cut to an interview I did with Sean [Barlow] and Banning [Eyre] from Afropop, asking me how in the world I heard of Oliver Mtukudzi from Zimbabwe, when I co-wrote a song on my last album with him long distance and explaining that. They then told me that, "Oh, you haven't heard our show? We'll send you a bunch of tapes and by the way we're going to Mali in 2000, if you'd like to join our excursion," and I'm going, "Oh great, celebrity joins a thirty-member troupe" and then I went, "You know what? I should be able to join one of these trips just like everybody else." So I went a week early with Sean and Banning and I played guitar and visited all my heroes of Mali and guitar music in their homes, because of Banning's connection with those guys. And I had sent ahead my *Road Tested* live video so they knew who I was, and they accepted me as a pure guitarist and it was a life-changing event. I spent three weeks traveling around and hanging out and jamming and dancing till dawn and all these incredible parties. The purpose of this trip was to get the musicians to perform in the villages where they're from, so they get to make money. We as the fans get to see where the music is from and how the instruments are made and I can't recommend it more highly for a music fan to go on one of these excursions, because it really was what opened me up to such an incredible world of great music over there in person.

DD: Now the Oliver Mtukudzi song you do on here has a kind of a feel of township jive to it.

BR: Oh, definitely and most of his music doesn't have that flavor really. He's got a unique type of writing and I really relate to the way he relates to the way he writes on the guitar. Oliver Mtukudzi has released I believe 39--- he's on his 40th album. He's a couple years younger than I am but he's a legend in Zimbabwe, which is going through such hard times now. It's been devastated by AIDS and alcoholism and just the whole economy and political situation is a nightmare, and Oliver has been renowned as a shamanic figure. He has reached levels of almost Nelson Mandela proportions in that country. That gospel tune is so infectious [that] it became the theme song tune to the late-night drives on the tour bus on my last *Fundamental* tour. And eventually I said, "Ya know, I have got to play this on the end of my sets for the rest of my life." Somewhere in the night I want to be able to play this song because the jubilation of saying to God, "Hear me, I'm feeling low," and having that music attached to it is just relentlessly fantastic.

DD: "Hear me Lord."

Bonnie Raitt recording: "Hear Me Lord"

DD: "Hear Me Lord" is a wonderful addition to *Silver Lining.* We're having a wonderful chance to talk to Bonnie Raitt today about this music. I want to talk a little about Fred McDowell because there is such a resurgence in the northern Mississippi--- the hill country blues, and that repertoire is all Fred's songs, the songs we know from Fred McDowell. When you met him what was that scene like? I know you were good friends. Did you get a chance to visit him at home and go into that area?

BR: I did, I did actually. I was only through for a couple days. Most of my interaction with Fred was on double bills or traveling with him to blues festivals and sort of road managing and we just became fast and furious friends early on. He got a big kick out of the fact that I was a young white girl playing that guitar and we doubled up a lot. And when I finally had some time off I took a trip down to Kokomo, Mississippi. I mean it was a fantastic pilgrimage and he had just the life of Riley in terms of being appreciated in his lifetime and I've really taken a lot from the way he's lived his life and what people have gotten from him. It's as much about how to live and how to look at life as it was guitar playing, and he's one of the, in my mind, along with Son House--- It's not a comparison here between Muddy and Wolf. If I had to compare or decide who my favorite was I couldn't do it. I'd have to say the one closest to my heart is just nobody who cuts as deep to me.

DD: Would you call him the biggest influence on your slide playing?

BR: No, I don't know about that because there's--- I'm a huge Ry Cooder fan. And Lowell [George], who I met after I heard Ry Cooder's record--- And I heard and met and hung out with Lowell long after I developed a style, but my style evolved after Lowell showed me that using a compressor with your amplifier could make your note sustained longer. Nobody's ever been able to duplicate what Ry does 'cause he's just unique to himself. But the long language lines of electric slide and the heartbreaking slide that Ry Cooder plays--- Not that I want to sound like I imitate him, but he moves me in terms of his emotional range. But in terms of groove and soulfulness of his own music, Son and Fred and Robert Johnson are just the masters. Because I can't separate my friendship and closeness with Fred and my love for him and grief for losing him so early in '72, right before we were going to do a duet together of "Kokomo." He's fresh in my mind and in my heart and there are nights on stage when I really feel that he's with me on my left hand. And my bottleneck wiggles a little faster than usual and I just feel I've had moments where Lowell seems to be [playing] through me and there's times when there's Fred right there. It's a very mysterious and magical legacy that those guys have left. They touch me a lot.

DD: Speaking about a couple guitars going at it, I wanted to talk about the duet you and [guitarist] Roy Rogers had.

BR: Oh! Thank you! That is my favorite track I've ever cut.

DD: It is so great! Talk about writing that song. Was it just written there in the studio? How did it come out?

BR: No, actually I called Roy and--- I've been such a fan of his particular style of guitar playing, which is unlike any others of the slide genre. He's just put out massive amounts of great music, as well as producing John Lee Hooker's *The Healer* album, which I got to guest on. We live near each other in northern California and I told Roy, I said, "Can I come up and just jam with you? Because I've basically taken the blues genre as far as I could take it with my band and me. And I want to play off of what you do." And so my impetus for working with Habib Koite and Roy was to play blues with their guitar style. So Roy said, "What kind of thing of mine do you like?" And I went, "You know, that *thang*, that *thang* you do!" and he said, "You mean this?" and I said, "No, no." I felt like Goldilocks. And then eventually he started doing this thing he does on a couple of songs. And I said, "Hold it right there." I got my guitar out and just started to play and it was such a tailgating shuffle against a straight eight-time, which is the root of rock and roll to me. Chuck Berry built his whole foundation around it, you know, whether it's "Nadine" or "Maybelline" or Johnny Johnson's guitar part or Earl Palmer's drums on a lot of the New Orleans stuff. You get this push-and-pull feel. "Thing Called Love" of John Hiatt's, which *makes* me and the boys, which makes *Green Light*, and "I Believe I'm In Love with You." All those songs of mine have that real rock and roll feel, that's not rock. It's the in-between of the rock and the roll that makes this group happen. So I told him I wanted to write a song about a couple that had been together for a while and still having the hots for each other, because--- never to my knowledge had a man and a woman played a head to head guitar duel--- throw it down and give it back like that. This is the first time that we've actually had that kind of warfare going on between a guy and woman. And the song is about, "Get your 'you know what' home. I can't wait!" [That's] combustion to the youngsters. Well, get in line, baby. This is the hottest time of my life and people got to be celebrating the fact that people in a long-term relationship or people at our age are still as hot as ever.

DD: This is "Gnawin' on It."

Bonnie Raitt recording: "Gnawin' on It"

DD: "Gnawin' on It," from Bonnie Raitt's new album *Silver Lining*.

BR: Woo! Get a towel, get a towel!

DD: I love the contrast of the styles of your guitars. It's just--- he does all the short phrases and you do the longer ones. It's so cool.

BR: I mean Roy's been married to a wonderful woman, Gail, now for many, many years now and it's a tribute to their relationship, but I got to say that my duet with Roy and with John Lee Hooker are the two right up there with the penultimate erotic experiences I've had, because that track was just smoking!

DD: The rumors about Bonnie and Roy. Bonnie, I've got to ask. My wife saw this album cover and she couldn't get over how great you look. I have to serve as a stand-in for her [and] for older female and male fans everywhere. And it's about your shock of white hair as a symbol to be celebrated, and kind of become your trademark. In fact, two people have asked me if *Silver Lining* that was what the title was about.

BR: Oh, God! That's what somebody called to my attention the other day and it didn't even occur to me. I've had this since *Street Lights*. You can see the little beginning of it. It just sort of appeared on my head when I was twenty-four and then it sort of grew and you can watch different subsequent album covers. It's still in there and eventually the rest of the front of my hair started to go, so the only real color on my head is that streak. But I definitely imagine the way it used to be when I was a bright redhead. I was too old to do the white-haired thing that Emmylou pulls off so beautifully.

DD: Yeah, she does that great. Well, it's a shining beacon. Thanks a lot for talking with us.

BR: Hey, I'm glad! Tell your wife I'm so glad she thinks I'm hot because I feel hot, baby!

DD: [laughs] Bonnie Raitt, our guest today here on the *World Cafe*.

2002

SONIC YOUTH

SONIC YOUTH ON THE *WORLD CAFE*, WOW! Their record company called us and we jumped at the opportunity to talk with the band that was seminal to the New York City punk and noise scene. Husband and wife guitarist Thurston Moore and bassist Kim Gordon, along with guitarist Lee Renaldo, drummer Steve Shelley and collaborator Jim O'Rourke, who would go on to work with Wilco, played live at Indre Studios and we had an enlightening conversation about New York City rock and roll.

David Dye: My guests today are Sonic Youth, a band from New York City who just released their latest album called *Murray Street*, which was recorded in the band's home studio in downtown New York City, very, very near the World Trade Center. In fact, they had already been doing some recording before the collapse of the Twin Towers and then went back downtown and I asked Thurston Moore what that was like for the band.

Thurston Moore: It was a completely different environment because it was such a hectic area and now it was completely desolate. The only people really working down there were the service people, fireman and policeman, and us. We got special papers from the city so we could actually get through the barricades and get down there. We weren't nine-to-fivers, which was kind of suspect to the police guarding the boundaries, like, "Nobody's working down there." Visually, it was like this alien landscape of huge klieg lights and this kind of dusted air. It was very weird but we felt really connected to it. I mean, we felt like this is our neighborhood and we felt really good about doing what we were doing, because we felt that we were doing something kind of positive and creative in the face of this ruined environment.

DD: All the reviews I'm reading of *Murray Street*--- I guess when you put it on you hear--- The word "accessibility" is being used next to Sonic Youth, and I'm wondering what your relationship is with that word. Is it something you had in mind, how you feel about it, and does it mean anything to you?

Kim Gordon: When I think of accessibility, I think of a CD price people can afford [laughing]. I mean, you know, what's the point of making an accessible record if your CD's priced at like nineteen dollars. I mean that's a little discouraging. But I think the fact that this record has more crafted song structures then our last two records, I guess, makes it immediately more accessible.

TM: We're going more pop. [laughing]

DD: How does something like that happen within a band's framework?

TM: It's a group decision. We just sort of said, "Let's go more pop."

KG: Britney was a big influence, I guess.

TM: Oh yeah. No, I don't know. I think in a way, the last few years, the last few records, we've really sort of been trying--- I mean, not trying. We were just really going out and really expanding on a lot of different ideas and, you know, it's not like we tire of anything. Everything is very just sort of intuitive and you do a record. You don't really concept it out like, "What kind of music are we going to make?" Basically, it's just the music that was written. I mean, these were the first seven songs that we did and it was like, it was very sort of obvious to us that it had this real immediate, kind of thematic, you know, finality to it. It's like, "This is the record."

DD: I'm always uncomfortable with that question about how an album, you know, thematically, how it comes together because the whole concept of a CD and album is [that] it's sort of a construct upon the music anyway. But is it a snapshot of where you are at that moment? Is it made to be an album? It's always a good question.

TM: It's funny to me. It's always interesting critically listening to somebody's new record, because you can really sort of get a sense of theme from anybody's record, even though it's not really what was intended, if there was, indeed, anything intended. And I've always found that to be . . . something really special about the fact that people do records, because it is an abstract, in a way, for a lot of people. But the records sort of take on a certain quality that a lot of people will relate to or they'll sort of impress upon themselves and they [will] read other things into it. I mean, I've had a lot of people listen to our records through the years [and] they create these scenarios about where we were coming from or what the record's pronouncing or whatever, which are completely new to us, but they are great ideas. So in a way, I really like that it kind of takes on this life of its own, that's kind of personal to each listener. I mean we certainly--- Everybody does that with their own [record].

DD: Absolutely. But it's always interesting to see if the band really shares any of that. Thurston, I wanted to talk to you about how this band began. I guess everybody, but I'll start with you, because I had a visual kind of cue over the last summer when I saw this wonderful exhibit of album cover art that's been traveling. I guess it started in New York, but I saw it in Pittsburgh at the Warhol Museum and one of the walls is a black and white wall, which comes from your collection. And visually it's really kind of cool, but when you start looking at what's on there, you start just marveling at how deep you got into certain genres, at what must have been a pretty young age. And I was curious as to how you ended up delving so deep. I mean, I could probably ask anybody in the band this question, but how did you get into this music so young? What was your path to it?

TM: Yeah, I was just reading rock and roll magazines as a teenager in a rural, Connecticut environment in the 70s. But responding to . . . these kind of images, especially coming out of New York City, images of Patti Smith in a black-and-white photograph, you know, in like a men's white shirt and tie, or a singing image of Iggy Pop in the audience spray-painted silver, or things like this. I mean . . . all these kind of images really resonated with me in a way, as opposed to the images I would see of the Allman Brothers Band or Yes or Emerson, Lake, & Palmer, which were kind of the vanguard groups of that time. So there was something going on in the culture that was kind of fringe and when I got to hear the music that was being made by these musicians, which was not easy because you'd really have to go out of your way to find it. It wasn't in the local Sears, where you'd buy your records. Luckily, you would find them in discount bins, because nobody was buying them. I mean, like the first Stooges album. There were stacks of cutouts of them in Woolworth's for 49 cents in the early 70s. Same with the MC5. Same with Can and all these kind of German underground bands. And so this kind of more, sort of, obscure underground music was there really cheap and I think, in a way, that's sort of what turned on a lot of the punk generation was that it was--- There was a certain economic factor involved. [laughing]

DD: Accessibility.

TM: Yeah. I mean that was true. Accessibility; exactly like Kim was saying. And the music was way more challenging, in a way.

DD: What about the jazz end of it, I mean, I remember I think there was some Oliver Lake things there and some, umm . . .

TM: I mean, Kim sort of turned me on to classic jazz after we met, from John Coltrane to Charles Mingus. But then when I started getting into [the] more fringe of that and finding out about sort of European improvisers, et cetera, and finding out that they were making these records on these labels that were far more radical and independent than any punk rock label. And the music was even more . . . you know, beyond categorization a lot of the times.

DD: What's the oldest relationship in the band? Is it you and Lee or you and Kim?

TM: Me and, yeah, me and Lee. Right? I knew Lee before Kim. I knew you? No . . . I knew Lee. No, Lee and I used to play together in different bands at weird CBGB's audition night things.

Lee Renaldo: But probably within a year the three of us knew each other.

TM: We knew each other. I remember Lee trying to sort of--- I was in a band called the Coachman and Lee was in the Flux.

LR: We'd go to each other's gigs.

TM: And we played at an audition night and Lee was--- I remember the first time I met Lee. He came back in the dressing room and he was trying to pressure us off of our position.

LR: Off what?!

TM: "You guys playing second?" I was like, "Yeah." "Oh man." And then he was like, "Well, we're going to play first or fourth; why don't you guys play fourth and we'll play second." I was like, "Nope."

LR: Wow, I don't remember that at all.

TM: That sure was a start [laughing].

DD: What made you---

TM: If you want to play second, you're going to have to play with me [laughing].

DD: So that's how it formed? No?

TM: That's how we got together, yeah [laughing].

DD: What was the musical attraction that made you—I guess we'll start with you three to begin with—start playing together?

KG: Well, Thurston and I started playing together. We were both playing with this woman Miranda, and she introduced us actually. And then Thurston and I started playing together with this girl Ann, who Thurston was also playing with. So, that's kind of how the beginnings of Sonic Youth started.

TM: It coincided with this new visual art world that was going on down there.

And the music that was coming out of CBGB and Max's at the time, and creating this whole other, kind of, music scene there. We got involved right at the outset of all that and we just--- Everybody sort of knew each other from the neighborhood. There was no MTV, there was no . . . none of that.

LR: It was a very localized scene. I mean, there were no labels, there were no national press on any of it. You know, it was really just if you were living in New York. It was a very exciting scene, but it was very localized in New York and a lot of that music in a lot of ways never really left New York.

DD: Which brings a point about having this music be able to be underground and to be music for--- [that was] not exploited in any way by the media, not exploited by record companies, et cetera, while it developed is really important. And can things happen like that without---

TM: Yeah, I think that was sort of the success of punk rock anyway . . . to establish an alternative means of---

DD: Communication.

TM: ---of work. Yeah. And that happens successfully. You can work independently and you can make it work and it's a modest existence. It's not based on any--- It's not a model of celebrity and wealth, which is, you know--- What does that have to do with being a musician or an artist anyway?

DD: One of the things that always interested me was that back when Ragged Glory came out, when Neil Young picked you guys to tour with him, because sonically, that kind of works—there's a lot of feedback and a lot of noise and what both you guys do—but where you're coming from was really different and I was wondering . . . what your feelings about that were, how you reacted to doing that tour. How did it feel?

TM: Well . . . you know Neil and his manager Elliot Roberts had asked us to play. I remember they had a short list and we were on it. And they had all these kind of really radical things on it. It was like us, Public Enemy, Einstürzende Neubauten [laughing] and I just thought . . . it would have been great if you got Public Enemy and Einstürzendes to go on this tour, because the fact that we got booed ninety-five percent of the time we were playing by this audience, who went out once a year to see a classic rock concert, [to] see something like us because we were obviously wrong. We were getting it wrong for a lot of these people and they didn't like the discord or these non- [or] anti-song ideas. And so we were kind of flipped off a lot of the times and although you saw sort of pockets of people, who were aware of us, or people who were into it, there were enough people there who wanted to . . . throw something at us. I can't imagine what would have happened to something like Einstürzende Neubauten or Public Enemy or whatever.

KG: Yeah, I think Neil wanted to challenge his audience. [chuckles]

TM: But Neil generally really liked us. I mean he would come back and was really into what we were doing.

DD: I would think so, yeah.

TM: That was kind of cool. And so we really connected with him and for us it was strange because, for any band to be on a tour like that, it would be this real ticket to say, maybe converting people to what you were doing, where we had really no interest in that so much. [W]e were more interested [in] our own sociological research as opposed to like--- We knew better than to think we were actually going to win these people over. It was obvious from the outset that that wasn't going to really happen so much. Specifically, you're an opening band in an arena gig like that and we'd done them before with R.E.M. and we'd done them recently with Pearl Jam, but you go on at eight o'clock. Most ticket buyers don't really want to see anybody else and so you get this kind of, you know---

DD: Empty seats.

TM: ---half filled audience at best and so it's . . . it's not that rewarding performance-wise.

DD: Thurston Moore from Sonic Youth.

The interview was followed up by a live set recorded at Indre Studios.

2003

THE CLASH

THIS INTERVIEW TOOK PLACE IN A NEW YORK CITY RECORD COMPANY CONFERENCE ROOM. I set my equipment up and nervously awaited bassist Paul Simonon and songwriter and guitarist Mick Jones of the Clash, arguably the most important rock band of the last quarter of the 20th century. Yeah, I was nervous. But as you can see, the dapper gentlemen in bespoke suits that soon entered the room were eager to talk and I steered them through an overview of their career. In hindsight, it was an amazing afternoon.

David Dye: The Clash may have broken up some 20 years ago, but most recently a lot has been going on in the Clash's world. Last December we were saddened to learn of the death of Joe Strummer, one of the original members of the band. At the Grammys recently they won an award for best long-form video for "Westway to the World" and they've recently been inducted into the Rock and Roll Hall of Fame, plus there is a new *Essentials* collection of their work recently released. When I talked in New York City to Mick Jones and Paul Simonon of the Clash, I asked them if they were comfortable with all this attention and all this looking back.

Paul Simonon: No, it's like revisiting your past and it's, I know, our sort of nature to look forward to the next day and keep moving forward.

Mick Jones: And I think with so much going on right now, in this particular minute now, and you know, what's happening the rest of today and tomorrow, I can't even think about it half the time . . . I mean because there's so much to say about today.

DD: Well and of course hovering over all this is even while you were working on the *Essentials* the sudden passing of Joe---

PS: That's right.

DD: ---which has got to make this extremely difficult for you guys.

PS: Well, it's a member of the family really and the only thing to do is sort of keep going forward.

MJ: Or I haven't had that much time. I haven't had much time to really reflect upon anything.

PS: It will probably take a while for us to come to terms with it. It's just really strange. And even more so going over our past and the way it sort of--- It's very strange.

DD: Now all three of you worked on the *Essentials*. Did you sit down in a room and argue about songs or how did that work?

MJ: No, we didn't do that. We did it by fax. We've always done it by fax since we've . . . stopped working together on stage.

PS: Yeah, we just send illustrated notes, and exclamation marks, and . . . you know, stars by one's "yes." And you know, I don't know that that's a healthy way for us to communicate.

MJ: But towards the end of it, Joe passed away and so we had to kind of--- We tried to really put in all his—what we thought [were]—his favorite songs, made sure they went in there, but there wasn't any kind of disagreement.

DD: It's 40 songs. It's 40 songs summing up a career.

MJ: It's going to be good for people who are sort of getting into the band or something. For people [who are] new, it's convenient for them. I mean they can just get all the good songs. Of course we have to bring out the inessential Clash now, with all the rest of them.

DD: I wanted to play "White Riot" to start, and, Paul, I think it would be great for people who don't know the story that you and Joe ended up at the carnival, and what happened . . . what the "White Riot" story is.

PS: Well, yeah, I mean it's pretty much a situation in London. We have a carnival each year and it sort of happens in the West Indian community, and, you know, everybody comes along who gets invited. And . . . because over the years there were quite a few problems with the police situation, there is a thing called "suss," which means you could be picked up with no questions. And really, with the concentration of police and revelers . . . it just sort of caused a friction to start up when the police tried to arrest a couple of suspects and the crowd got incensed and then you had the whole riot on your hands. I mean a lot of it's due to sort of police insensitivity to the local community.

MJ: It was 1976.

PS: Yeah. And so me and Joe got caught up in it.

DD: And how fast did that song get put out?

PS: Well, sort of like a couple of days [later] to be honest. I mean, at the same time there was a reggae star called Tapper Zukie, and he had put out a record two days after the carnival called "Ten Against One," which is quite a famous tune and it was all referring to the carnival and you know that was--- So it's like a musical newspaper really.

DD: And this is that original single. This is "White Riot."

The Clash recording: "White Riot"

DD: That's "White Riot." Our guests today . . . we're talking with Paul Simonon and Mick Jones from the Clash and we're trying to digest the *Essentials* disc and trying to put what's an amazing career into a few songs. Talk a little bit about the connection, where you guys were, with punk and the reggae scene at the time. Obviously you got a lot of credit for bringing reggae into what you did for releasing "Police and Thieves." Was it something that was in the air in London everywhere, were you just reflecting what was going on? Or was it unusual?

PS: Well it's--- I mean, put it this way. Chrissie Hynde from the Pretenders, she said that . . . reggae was such a dominant force in London at the time, that she thought by the next year the whole world would be playing reggae and nothing else. So that just shows you what a strong influence it was in London at the time. And also because there was no punk records, really British punk records had been released. So . . .

MJ: There wasn't that many or there wasn't--- So we used to go to this place, the Roxy . . .

PS: Yeah.

MJ: . . . and the DJ was Don Letts and he used to play like a lot of his reggae records as well. Plus Paul and I grew up in South London, where there was reggae music around all the time or its predecessors, ska and blue beat, you know. But you can see our progression very clearly through the whole record, but that's the same with our albums, you know? You can see the progression of the band.

DD: Oh totally.

MJ: Like the first one . . . we don't know

what we're doing, and we know a little more on the next one and et cetera, et cetera. We got a bit more to say.

DD: Did you guys argue about politics?

PS: Not really. We did with the thousands of drummers we tried out.

MJ: Yeah, some of them didn't really get it.

PS: Some of them sort of said, "But I want to be in a group, I don't want to be in a political party."

DD: Terry didn't--- In other words, Terry [original Clash drummer Terry Chimes] didn't particularly get it.

PS: Not really. Well, I don't know. We sort of asked him what he'd like to do with his money, and he said he'd like a Lamborghini. But, you know, that's fine if he wants a Lamborghini. But unfortunately it didn't quite suit where we were mentally. I mean, I don't think it was necessarily if he really wanted the Lamborghini; it was more about sort of an open debate really. It was . . . like a mini-political party in some ways, but this is sort of something [where] Bernard Rhoades sort of instigated these discussions so . . .

MJ: He was our manager at the time.

DD: Yeah. Bernie Rhoades was one of your first managers.

PS: He was our first manager, yeah. And you know he sort of played quite an important part in the beginning of the groups.

DD: Did he see that as a hip-ness factor, as a total punk thing, or did he believe that as political—

PS: No, it was just that . . . it was, I suppose in the traditional sort of like folk music--- You know, it's like Bob Dylan, Woody Guthrie, or in the Jamaican scene like Joe Higgs, or Bob Marley. It's like communication . . .

MJ: It's like talking about what . . .

PS: . . . about what affects you in your life.

MJ: . . . about what affects you in life, really. But a lot of people can understand that and relate to it, you know, because they know what you're talking about.

DD: And this was something that was *so* vital and at the center of punk in England, and I've often wondered if that was one of the reasons why you guys had a bit more trouble breaking in over here. That there wasn't that political thing going on here; punk was more fashion here it seemed.

PS: Well, it was more of an art scene over here, like in New York. Which is fine, and maybe in some ways in England it was a bit more of a social—

MJ: It was a big social thing, yeah. But the thing is also . . . we didn't break it in America because the first album didn't sound like anything else. Not only was it not talking about stuff you hadn't heard, but it [also] didn't sound like any other record that you'd heard at the time . . . you know, it just sounded really rough. But that's the beauty of it, you know? And so it didn't come out for a while and it came out after the second album eventually, with a bunch of stuff taken off and a bunch of singles stuck on to make it a bit better for American people.

PS: Airplay was one of the major problems we had really, I think.

MJ: We didn't have enough payola. We couldn't get enough together. And we couldn't get around to enough shops to buy the records. The thing is though, I got to say, that even before I came on tour here we came here to record and [in] every city we went to there was like a punk scene. It was just starting, you know? I went to L.A., and I went to San Francisco, and I came to New York, and you could see in every place that it was going to--- You know, it just took a lot longer here.

DD: It's interesting that the album that Bernard saw as--- You know, he got Sandy Pearlman to mix and dub differently to get on the radio in America. *Give Them Enough Rope* didn't really do it as well as obviously *London Calling* [did]. Well, I've read Mick that you actually studied Sandy Pearlman at work. Here was a producer that you thought you could learn some things about sound from.

MJ: Very much so. Yeah, sort of watching--- Well, ever since we first went into the studio, I've always been trying to pick up what I could from that, like learning, seeing how people did it. Well, [on the] first record we didn't really want to know anyway, you know?

DD: That wasn't the point.

MJ: Yeah, exactly. We just wanted to get this stuff out, and down, and get it out. But [on the] second one definitely I learned a lot. Well, I learned a lot from all the people we worked with. You know--- I owe them all a great debt.

DD: Somebody who was really concerned with sound like Sandy, or somebody like Guy Stevens, who was into the vibe . . .

MJ: Yeah. Exactly.

DD: . . . but you were really into the vibe on *London Calling* too, weren't you? I mean---

PS: No, of course. Yeah, I mean---

MJ: Very much so, very much so.

DD: Yeah. Describe those sessions a little bit to people who don't know about [them] or at least the period whole surrounding it.

MJ: I don't think you can have a session like that anymore.

PS: It's like . . . suddenly Sandy coming into the room and screaming and chucking chairs up against the table while you're trying to record a song. You know that I think [during] "Death or Glory," he came running in and just started throwing chairs around the studio which sort made us laugh and try to--- It was quite difficult to hold it all together but it was . . . exciting.

MJ: Other production techniques included wielding a full-size ladder in a circle round the room while you're trying to record.

PS: And there's another technique called wrestling the engineer over the engineering desk.

MJ: And then when the head of the record company came to visit, Guy went out and laid in front of his limousine in the driveway and he wouldn't let him go until he said the record was fantastically great . . . and he would [not] let Maurice Oberstein leave.

DD: [laughs] What were you guys listening to when you were making that record?

PS: Well, I mean for me it's probably quite easy to say, 'cause I just sort of generally listen to reggae all the time, so I don't think I probably steered off that track too much.

MJ: I think what happens with our band . . . we all brought something different to the mixture. We all brought out our own specific part. Paul brought his reggae interests and he used to have his own mix tapes and stuff, and I had all my kind of . . . rock and roll thing going on, you know? And Joe had his kind of R & B kind of rootsy kind of thing.

DD: Right, right. Paul was "Guns of Brixton." Your first one that got recorded on that one.

PS: Yeah, it's the first song that I made and it's quite difficult when you've got two giants, two songwriting giants to fight against, but I did show Joe the lyrics and say, "Well, you know, what do you reckon, Joe?" and he said "It's great. You've got it all there." Because I thought maybe it needed something else but he said, "No, it's fine. It's all there." And Mick . . . in rehearsals Mick sort of really quite liked the bass line, 'cause it had sort of an interesting lilt and yeah--- So I presented that, and then they said, "Yeah, but you've got to sing it." And I had no intention of singing it in the first place because I was just offering it.

DD: Well, it's a great song, and let's play that as one of our picks here. This is "Guns of Brixton" from *London Calling.*

The Clash recording: "Guns of Brixton"

DD: We're talking with the Clash today. We're talking with Mick Jones and Paul

Simonon, who are about to become members of the Rock and Roll Hall of Fame. I don't know, I guess you get a locker or something there. You'll have to go see your space in Cleveland.

MJ: I think they're going to mount an exhibition, you know afterwards, so we're going to loan them some stuff. So Paul's—

DD: What are you going to contribute?

PS: Well, they've got my--- I loaned them the smashed-up bass from the *London Calling* album cover, but somebody told me they saw it and they said--- I don't think they quite realized that they've actually got the actual bass from that album's cover shot, which is broke, a broken bass.

MJ: Or otherwise they may not know that, and it's like when they see it they say, "Oh my God it's broken" and then "Is it insured?" and then you can say, "What do you mean you've broken it?"

[Laughter]

PS: Actually, I was thinking it'd be quite a nice side on it just to get loads of Fender basses and smash them up and put a certificate of authenticity [with them] and send them around the world. It could be quite novel.

DD: I've actually never heard you talk about this. On *London Calling*, of course, "Train in Vain" was not listed and I've actually never heard you say why you didn't list it. I mean, it's a little Jackson Five-y compared to the rest of the album, but I'm wondering what your thoughts were.

MJ: It was a late addition and the artwork had already gone to press.

DD: Oh it's that simple? [laughs] Hmm . . .

MJ: Well, it's not quite that simple, but that is basically what happened. But we originally were going to do the track and we were going to give it away with this English music magazine NME, so we recorded it—the last thing that we recorded for *London Calling*. And then when we recorded it, I thought, and everybody thought, "No, this is a bit too good to give away." So we decided to put it on the album as a last-minute addition.

DD: Of course *London Calling* has been--- Rolling Stone called it "the greatest album of the eighties," even though it came out in 1979. But how did you feel about it when you finished?

MJ: Well, it came out in 1979 in London but it didn't come out until 1980 in America.

DD: Oh okay. How did you feel about it when you finished it?

PS: Well, I think we felt pretty good because, first of all, the added thing was that it was like a double album and because of the price of records were going up, we decided to put out the double for the price of a single. So we thought, you know, that sort of--- I don't know, we just thought it was a very good idea to do that. And also there's . . . the beginning, which sort of led you on to *Sandinista* really, I suppose . . .

DD: Yeah.

MJ: Yeah.

PS: . . . which is three for one.

MJ: Three for one. [laughter] But also at the end of every album we'd have a listening session to the whole record, you know? I mean because when we finished the whole thing and it's all done and we put it all together--- And then we'd sit in the studio control room, all of us. It'd just be like the first time we hear the whole thing and if I remember correctly we decided, "We got to have four speakers here. We can't just have the two." So we had two in the front and two in the back.

DD: When was the band the most fun for you guys?

PS: Always. I mean the thing is, from day to day--- You know, at the end of the first day or the third day, I was surprised that it lasted as long as it did because it was so day-to-day that at the end of the evening you would go home and go, "Blimey, it's amazing we got through today and I'll see you more tomorrow and see if we manage tomorrow." It was famous like that, but, you know, sort of like all relationships. It goes up and down and it goes wobbly at times, but it's, you know . . . it was good.

MJ: I'd say, in the modern vernacular, "It's all good."

PS: I mean we're all pretty much a bunch of misfits anyway, so being together was sort of like creating a family for ourselves, which maybe we didn't really have in the first place, you know?

DD: It's totally a moot point with Joe gone, but you guys always resisted getting back together. Was there a reason why?

MJ: It's like kind of---

PS: We're romantics.

MJ: Yeah, we're idealists.

DD: You can't return. You can't go back.

MJ: Well it was such a . . . [sighs] you know, I mean it's a thing when it--- It's fine, 'cause it was great when it was so.

PS: And I think it's more of a powerful statement that we didn't get back together, because firstly I think it backs up what the group was about, and what the songs were about, and possibly for any new group it's sort of . . . an inspiration hopefully.

MJ: It's like we did our job.

DD: What's life post-Clash like, I mean, for both of you? Paul, I know you paint, and what else are you up to?

PS: Just painting really. I mean I was painting before I was in the group, but, you know for the past . . . I don't know . . . probably twelve years. [A]fter the Clash I did have a group together for a short time, for . . . I don't know . . . two years or something, but unfortunately the singer got cancer and he died and then--- So I went straight back to painting, and I'm sort of getting ready for a show in Tokyo this year so . . .

DD: That's great. And of course Big Audio Dynamite and what else--- What are you up to now, Mick?

MJ: Well, like Paul is a painter, you know. I'm a musician. And so I'll just do my music and I do a bit of production. I've been producing this new band in London called the Libertines, and I've been doing my own stuff and just basically carrying on really. And even if I don't have anything out, I still work in a way, and just find out new stuff, learning about and just being into my music basically.

PS: Mick's trying to be and look like Beethoven, and I'm trying to be like Van Gogh.

[laughter]

DD: I see it. We should actually get to the end of this *Essentials*, and talk a little about *Combat Rock*, which--- I'd love to get your feelings about that album because there are some critics who look at it as—just because it sold in a way—the Clash sell out, you know, just because it sold. And I never have seen it that way at all.

MJ: Well, we've always had to struggle with that. As soon as we signed a contract, we've always had that struggle, you know, "What are we going to do now? We've got some money and is that--- How compromised are we?" You know, and it's been a constant struggle. We've always had to deal with that duality, but in the end we think we probably did the right thing because we wouldn't have been here now, or even been heard of if we didn't . . . choose that path, you know? I mean, it's not for anybody else to say we did it the wrong way. We did it the way we thought was best and that's how we did it, . . . because otherwise probably people wouldn't have heard about us and it was really important for us to try and get out our stuff to as many people as we can. But I can say that that never made any difference to us about the record company; that was only a side issue. We were the main event, you know what I'm saying? So that was only one of the things we had to deal with, but it wasn't the main thing that we were about.

PS: I think musically "Rock the Casbah"--- I mean, it's sort of quite interesting how to the ear it's probably a lot more accessible, but the good thing is that once you've got everybody on the dance floor and they're grooving to the music, then there are times when they go home and they do wonder, "Well, I wonder what the song was about." And then you're communicating, and that's sort of, you know--- I think that's quite valid.

MJ: The music is like a vessel that takes your message, you know what I mean? So the nicer a tune it is, the better you've got a chance—

PS: Better pal you've got really.

DD: Absolutely. Mick Jones, Paul Simonon. Thanks so much for talking with us today.

MJ: Thank you very much.

PS: All right, thanks, yeah.

2003

MERLE HAGGARD

PEOPLE OFTEN ASK ME IF I AM NERVOUS BEFORE ANY INTERVIEWS, and actually, while I can admit to being excited, I'm not usually too anxious. This interview, though, is an exception to that rule. Merle Haggard is a superstar by anyone's standards, and I was worried he might be crotchety if maybe I didn't know enough about his music. It turned out that I had nothing to worry about. As you can see, he was extremely forthright in our conversation backstage at the Keswick Theater in Glenside, PA.

David Dye: The name of Merle Haggard's new album is *Like Never Before*, which is true, but it also could have--- Merle, it could have been called *Like Always*, I think, because you've got everything you do on here. You've got some topical songs, some honky-tonk tunes, some weepers. After all these years, is it kind of hard to figure out what direction to go when you get ready to do a new album?

Merle Haggard: Well, it's a different world that I live in, and the world changes rapidly, and so there's always material for my kind of a writer that writes off of the situation. I try to write something that's about current events, and so there's some truth to it rather than just something that you make up to rhyme.

DD: Well, one of the things on--- I've always said that you were a pretty fair barometer of how people were feeling around the country and you've got a great song on here called "That's the News," and I'm wondering how this song is faring with people in the audience when you play it.

MH: It's about 85-15. I think 15 percent hate me for it because they don't understand it, and they think I'm trying to put somebody down or something. All I'm asking is that we pay attention to see what [it is] we're being told, and it irritates me and I'm frustrated and all those words about the media and the insinuations that are made and the hypothesis sold at prime time. We got 150 countries with men and women in harm's way and we're going to talk about whether or not Laci Peterson is guilty. And at 5:30, you know, it seems to me that there should be some time of day that there's a Cronkite situation that comes about, where everybody's talking about what's going on, whether what runs the ratings up, you know. And that's what that song's about. Maybe I'm saying it—I hope I'm saying it right.

DD: Oh, I thought you were saying it right. Well, it's interesting because people might say, "You're against this, you're against that," but then later on in the album you've got "Yellow Ribbons," which is certainly a song that's pro-soldiers and what they have to do and "That's the News" is totally—

MH: Well you know the latest—talk about "That's the News"—the latest news is that the soldiers in battle, the ones with uniforms on, are unhappy with decisions that have been made. And you know, that's not me, that's them guys that I'm all for and you're all for and all Americans are. And I think every American wants GW to succeed. You know, I think if he'd come out and just say, "Look, we need that oil, and there's a couple of guys in the way and we have to take them out, and it will help the country in the process," everybody would throw their babies in the air and he'd be the greatest president since Abe Lincoln, you know? It's just time we quit dancing around real problems and come with the truth and see if the American public can stand it.

DD: Go right at it.

MH: You know, that's the way I feel about it.

DD: Well, tell me a little bit about this guitar you're holding, first of all. It looks like it's got some years on it.

MH: Well it's a good guitar and it's been used a lot and I don't worry about it [plays chord] sort of like Willy's Trigger.

DD: Right. Except it doesn't have a hole in it.

MH: It was given to me by—well nearly—but it was given to me by Randy Travis, about 15 years ago or so.

DD: Can you do a version of "That's the News" for us?

MH: I think I can.

Merle Haggard performs "That's the News"

MH: That's a little--- We call that an acoustic version.

DD: Absolutely. It's one you'll find on *Like Never Before.* Merle Haggard is our guest today and this album is out on your label, on Hag. And you did a couple on Epitaph before, which before you arrived was probably seen as a punk rock label. You certainly broadened things for them, and I can see why they would want to have a Merle Haggard record on their label. What were the advantages for you, being on Epitaph?

MH: Well, they were interested. First of all, they had honest interest in my music, and there was a lot of—or a lack of—that in a lot of directions. Maybe that may be the low of my life, having—gauging interest. And then it was not a long low, or not a long valley, but it was there for a little bit and they came along with a lot of interest and sort of gave me inspiration to make a couple of records. And there was another thing that occurred in my life. I ran into the guy who played guitar for Lefty Frizzell, who was my hero in my young life, and he was living about 12 miles from me and it was like finding Babe Ruth was living down the street, you know?

DD: Who was that? What's his name?

MH: Norman Stevens is his name. He'll be with the show tonight, and he's---we're the only band on the road that carries nurses instead of roadies, you know? He's got emphysema and everything, but I got him out of the bed, got him playing guitar again and we made that roots album, the one that you're talking about. Yeah, and he and I inspired each other. We both should be probably in a nursing home or something but we're still out here and you know they've got a fix for the taxes and everything you know? They're gonna take all our money anyway, you know that. I mean, I thought GW was going to abolish that. That was a thing that I thought he was gonna fix was the death tax. Does us no good to try to make any money, they're gonna take it.

DD: That didn't happen yet.

MH: So we're out here for the music, and maybe that's why it's good, because it's honest. I really don't care what they do to me. They can put me back in the same old cell if they want to. I've been there and I know how to do that. I can do time, they can't take my mind and they won't change my mind.

DD: Well, could we talk a little bit about Lefty Frizzell? Because there are some turning points in your life and one of them was when you saw him at that concert in Bakersfield and you got a chance to meet him and play your music for him.

MH: There was an immediate bond between I and Lefty. I was sixteen years old and he was passing through town and saw some promise, I guess, or something with me and he let me go out and sing with his band and his guitar and everything and that's like the greatest thing in the world that could have happened because when I saw that his audience liked me, then I knew that I had a solid chance. It was a bit of an evaluation for me. And years went by and then I met Lefty on a different level. I was having hit records, and he said, "You're that kid from Bakersfield, aren't you?"

DD: He remembered that.

MH: Yeah, and we went on to become real close friends, which is something that happens, what one out of 10 million times. Who gets to be friends with their hero? You know?

DD: Seriously. Yes. Do you remember what you played for him? Was it any of your own songs?

MH: I think so, Let's see. [singing] "I was a stranger passing through your town/ Lord I was a stranger passing through your town/ When I asked you a favor/ Good girl you turned me down . . . " Called "I Was a Stranger," a Jimmie Rodgers tune. And I did another thing. I think it was [singing] "I woke up this morning in a terrible mood/ Talk about a woman treating a good man rude/It had me talkin' to myself---" He stopped me and he said, "Listen now, would you like to go out and sing this with my band?" You know, and then handed me his guitar and it changed my life.

DD: Just hearing you do these songs brings to mind one of the reasons why I love your music so much is, there's something about being from California—the California and the country music—and your interests in music, be it Bob Wills, Jimmie Rodgers--- There is this whole influence of blues and jazz, on what you do.

MH: Yeah, and it was instilled in my young life by my parents. They liked a wide array of music and we listened to everybody I think that most everybody was listening to. It had no boundaries like it does now, you know? You listened to Crosby, and Louie Armstrong was with him and Jack Teagarden and, you know? And that's what I heard as a child. I remember Bing's records being big and Bob Wills and Tommy Duncan and they were actually in the studios out in the West, you know, when records was considered a less than acceptable software, you know, and the old 78s--- Well, they would actually make broadcast transcriptions in the mid-40s, and stuff of that nature and I can remember those real broadcasts—and they were . . . telling about where they're gonna be in Fresno the next night, Modesto, and somewhere else and Bob would talk and they--- You know it was like listening to Li'l Abner or Lum and Abner, and all that, you know? It was just unbelievable. Everything was live. What's the guy's name . . . Arthur Godfrey, to sit there with a guitar and do, basically what we're doing here, just rambled around and playing music, and he was live everyday. It was like Rush Limbaugh with a guitar, you know?

DD: [laughs] That's a good way to put it. That's so exciting to me. Now did you have a chance as a kid or did your parents have a chance to see--- Would Bob Wills play dances? Come to the valley and play?

MH: Oh yeah . . . they did but only a part of my family would go because they were religious you know, and dancing was considered sinful, and so only somebody in the family who was 18 or 20 years old that snuck off to dance was able to come back and tell us about it. And I was probably—before 12—I was wishing I could go to the dance, and I think I rode a bicycle out to one of Bob's dances, when I was about 11 or 12. And they had these little canvase windows that you could hold up. They're like shutters, like storm shutters. Well, that old dance hall was way up high above your head, but I could stand on my bicycle and look inside and I seen Wills and the Playboys, you know, and it was back in their heyday, you know, and he had this great band, and it was--- I'd slipped out of the house and my mother thought I was asleep you know, at night, and I went out there and watched him through that window, 'til somebody ran me off.

DD: Merle Haggard is our guest today on the *World Cafe*. I kind of made some notes about some turning points and people in your life that were important to you, and I guess everybody knows you spent time in San Quentin and kind of . . . how did your life turn around there?

MH: Only 'cause they wouldn't let me out [laughs].

DD: [laughs] Yeah. Well, a guy, Caryl Chessman, who was in San Quentin--- and my understanding was he helped kind of set you towards where you're in your life.

MH: Well, without him knowing, he really influenced me in the right direction. He was I think wrongly executed. He was supposedly the Red Light Bandit that was--- You know his history?

[Caryl Chessman's case was a high-profile anti-death penalty issue in the 1950s. He was convicted of a series of robberies and rapes where he would stop cars with a red light attached to his car. Hence the name "Red Light Bandit."]

DD: M-hm.

MH: And at that time he hadn't killed anybody. You know, it was like a misrepresentation, and he really wasn't tried fairly and would never have made the death sentence had he been represented properly. But anyway, it was really controversial about them executing him and when they did, well, the whole prison, you know, was the closest to him and everybody had watched him walk back and forth from his cell to his lawyers, and this and that and we'd all got sort of--- Part of "Sing Me Back Home" comes from that, watching that guy fight for his life. He wrote a couple of books, did them in ingenious ways like wrote it on the back of carbon paper and got it out, you know, without them knowing it. And [he] had taught himself, had got a degree in law from inside the cell, and was really a useful citizen and they executed him for political reasons, and, you know . . .

DD: How did he become an influence to you? Just talking to him?

MH: I was on the--- I'd got busted for making beer.

DD: Inside?

MH: Inside the joint. And I had a pretty good business going in there.

DD: Now how do you do that?

MH: Well it's a big place. There's 5,000 men and there's a kitchen, there's everything you need to make beer. And they do it right now, you know, there's better beer in there than there is Budweiser. [laughs] But we made beer and it was a lot stouter than beer that you drink out here. It was "eight-day beer" we called it, and we had it in milk bottles. We was walking—milk cartons, you know, like a quart milk carton. We'd walk around the yard, little cocky kids, and drink this beer, [and] look at the guards. They didn't know we're drunk. So it was a big deal back then. And I wound up getting busted and falling in a urinal, and the cops drew down on me from up on the guardrail with a 30-30, and they arrested me on the yard, and put me in what you call "The Shelf" for seven days. And "The Shelf" is located in the building on the north block, right at the top, on the very opposite side of death row. And in between death row there's a plumbing area that you walk between, and then that's all that you can hear, the death row prisoners, talking because they're not on a silent deal, but people on "The Shelf" are on a silent deal. You can't make a sound and they'll come in and whoop your . . . So I could hear, I heard Chessman say to a friend, he said, "Hey, you'll never guess what I got in the mail today." And the guy said, "What'd you get?" and he said, "I got a life insurance policy." And you know he was a big political issue at the time and on everybody's mind and talked about every day in the news and he gets this life insurance policy. And I recognized who he was from that. And I spoke to him through the vent in the floor, and I said, "Hey, I'm up here doing seven days for drunk." And I said, "I just want you to know you've got a lot of support on the yard," you know? And that's about all I remember saying. I don't remember what else we talked about.

DD: Moving on to some other things, you--- In the sixties, I mean such a string of hits for Capitol and Capitol had a whole West Coast setup, so you didn't ever really have to deal with Nashville at that time?

MH: You know Nashville, it really wasn't—I don't think—as big a deal as it is now, you know? And we were having--- We were producing a different kind of music out there. We were producing a barroom . . . . and dance music, and that was not even allowed in Tennessee. You know, I mean the other side of the river was pretty white, you know? They just didn't understand what we were doing. They didn't use drums. They didn't use horns, you know? And I really don't know how I got into country music back there. But they accepted me as a country music artist and always had and they paid me a lot of respect there and I had a lot of friends, but it was not for me. I went back, tried to stay there two years and my record sales went down and soon as I left they went right back up. So I was probably selling to a lot of people in the industry there, and it got to be like old homeboy there and they had me playing on everything all over town and singing harmony with this guy and it became a fiasco and I just left. But it's a different music altogether from the coast and I don't think there's many similarities between me and Porter Wagoner.

DD: No.

MH: Even though I like his stuff and he likes mine.

DD: Yeah. Well that's—you just brought up a good thing, a good question to me. I always felt that you could have been a rock and roller, you could have been a kind of a folk musician in a way, in that you were singing [about] things that people were dealing with. There were topical songs all along the way, and as you said there was barroom music there was honky-tonk. And it's interesting that the whole California country, you and Buck Owens, it was harder rocking. I mean Telecasters, you know, that was your instrument.

MH: We were playing serious rock and roll, when I broke into business. We were making a living at night in places where they expected that kind of music. And for whatever reason, I'm not sure, they put us in the country department at Capitol Records. I don't know why, and I guess it's good that they did, but you're right. I was doing Elvis's songs, and Fats Domino, and Chuck Berry, and all that stuff at the clubs, and [I'd] do a Lefty Frizzell song, too. You know, but you had to know everything in order to work in Bakersfield, 'cause it was like Nashville wanted to be. You go to Nashville and all there was, was a Grand Ole Opry had one show a week. We had 15 to 20 nightclubs and a television show that was reaching over maybe 3 million people. At the very infancy of television, we were in their houses at the time that Cronkite was fixing to come on; prime time in the evening. And stars in Hollywood—actual movie stars like John Wayne—was watching our show, and you know, they'd shake our hands and say, "Hey, we're big fans." You know we'd go down there and do a couple of films over the years, and these guys were more blown away with me than I was--- And I couldn't believe what the impact we'd had in those early days, but that's how we got going out there.

DD: Oh, totally. Jumping a little ahead to that, the song obviously that made you a household name for people who didn't even follow your music at all had to be "Okie from Muskogee." And a song that was an ironic song for you to record and kind of—

MH: It really turned a lot of fans off of me.

DD: Of your fans from before.

MH: Yeah. And a lot of them didn't get it. Like, you know that song was about my father, and he was the Okie from Muskogee. I was born in California. And there was a time when nobody knew anything about that Vietnam War, and it irritated the hell out of me for people to be acting the way they were acting. And I'd been to prison, I'd lost my freedom and I was disgusted and appalled by the way these kids at the time were doing [to] the flag and I thought, you know, "They don't know what they're doing. They've never lost it." And it really was an attempt to describe what I think my dad would have thought had he been alive at the time. So that's where that came from.

DD: Now the first time you played that apparently it just galvanized the audience right away. Were you surprised?

MH: They came out of the audience. It really wasn't a good test the first night because we were in Fort Bragg, North Carolina, playing for an officer's club or something. And we'd had 8 or 9 hits. We had 8 or 9 number one records at that time and we were starting to go over into the pop field and they were playing "Take a Lot of Pride" and Dean Martin recorded it and everything. I was about to become a pop artist.

DD: Hmm. [laughs]

MH: And when I did that song it really jumped out there and went right straight up through the Beatles and sold two million pieces in 90 days. Back then that's a lot of records. But it also lost the liberal side of my fan base and it's taken me a lot of years to realize [that] there's more to me than "Okie from Muskogee," you know.

DD: Well, I've always seen you as a populist, and I think that's--- That probably sits pretty fair with you. You're . . . for the working man.

MH: Yeah, yeah. I try to say things I think that people really want to—the majority of the people believe in. I don't try to go off one way or another too far, you know, unbelievably far to the left or right either way. Try not to be an extremist with my music [laughs].

DD: Even though we all saw it coming, did the death of your good friend Johnny Cash kind of catch you by surprise?

MH: You know, I was doing interviews for my new record. I was doing about four or five hours a day, trying to get airplay, which is hard to get for me anymore. So I was doing interviews and talking to everybody already and I'd been on about three or four major television shows just about the time that Johnny died. And it just went from what I was trying to promote to Johnny Cash. There was no use trying to promote anything 'cause all they wanted to know was about how well I knew him and what did I think about his death and his life. And I'll tell you that Johnny Cash and I were very close, and he was like a big brother to me. And there's 2 or 3 of us in the business that know where we're at and have been here a long time. Willie Nelson and I are good close friends, and Johnny Cash and George Jones, there was--- We talked. We knew who they were. There was 4 of us, and now there's 3. He was one of the most beautiful people inside I think that I've ever known, and most--- Maybe the most influential Christian in the world. He may have led more people to Christ than Billy Graham.

DD: That's an interesting point. That is a good point.

MH: Yeah. Yeah.

DD: Merle Haggard is our guest, and the title of this new album is *Haggard Like Never Before.* And there's a song that begins this, which makes me--- I mean, I've seen you on stage and you always get into and always have a great show, but are you in a place where you expected to be at your age, to be out working as much as you're working?

MH: I went bankrupt in '93, and IRS came down on me and, oh, it was a terrible thing. And also at that time was gifted with a son. The day I went into bankruptcy, my wife delivered a boy to me. And my little girl was 3 years older then, so she would have been 3 going on 4 when Benny was born. And so all the sudden I had this little two-piece family going, you know, and a beautiful wife, and my values all changed and I was broke. And there was really nothing to do except just what I've always done. Turn to the music and see if I could scratch my way back to something where I could make some money, you know, in the last--- I was $14 million in the hole, you know, and everybody was after me and all that stuff. So I just went back to the thing that worked before and all the way back to where I'm at now. And I've got the $14 million paid off and I'm in the black and the IRS is paid up, and I've got a good album.

DD: Hm, so yeah.

MH: So I'm flipping the bird to 'em.

DD: [laughs] Well now, so you went back on the road. And I'm wondering . . . I always had an idea that you had an idea who your audience was. You knew who [it was that] you were singing to. But I suspect you're seeing some different faces out there nowadays.

MH: We played for an audience last night, I'm trying to think exactly where we were, somewhere close by in the D.C. area but . . . and it was all young people. And they were, just beautiful. Just courteous as they could be and as knowledgeable--- They knew everything, what songs they wanted to hear, and treated me with the utmost respect and I like to say they were new. They were all new. There was a little girl [that] met me when I got off the bus [and] she had a bouquet of flowers and her mother said, "Well, here he is," and I could see that Momma didn't really--- wasn't there for me; it was the little girl.

DD: That's nice.

MH: That's really nice. Yeah.

DD: Merle, thank you so much for spending some time talking with us.

MH: David, this is a wonderful show. This is sort of what I want to do with the rest of my life, set in some place and interview other people.

DD: [*laughs*] Well you can ask me questions afterwards.

MH: You got to come on my show sometime.

DD: Sounds good.

MH: Okay.

DD: I'd have to learn how to play though.

2003

THE WHITE STRIPES

OFTEN WHEN BIGGER STARS COME TO THE *WORLD CAFE*, IT'S AN ENTOURAGE-FILLED WHIRLWIND.

That was what it was like when I talked with Jack White and the Raconteurs. I'm so happy that we had an opportunity to sit and really talk with Jack White and a bit with Meg White of the White Stripes, right in the midst of the success of their *Elephant* album. Here is a very thoughtful musician at the top of his game.

One a side note: Early on in this interview Jack refers to Meg as his "sister," perpetuating the myth of their relationship. A minimum of research shows that indeed they are former husband and wife.

David Dye: Our guests on the *World Cafe* today are Jack and Meg White. The White Stripes, rock and roll band from Detroit, who are really at the top of their career right now. They've just been nominated for four Grammy Awards for the album *Elephant* and also for the song "Seven Nation Army." We start the interview as I ask Jack a question that he's seemingly gotten before. I'm going to start up with the difficult question that you probably think about in some form every day, which is "Why us? Why now?" And can you ever be prepared for the attention that comes with this kind of success and keep your integrity? Do you think about that?

Jack White: Well, that's funny. It's a popular question to ask us, I guess. I don't know. It's okay because we had done so much at the beginning where we had just toured and played in front of five people in Cleveland or whatever for a long time and we'd made lots of records. And even at that point there, it was success to us, because we didn't have a day job anymore. We were just touring and making records. So that was sort of success to us because anything after that was sort of gravy on the potatoes, you know?

DD: Right.

JW: We--- After a while, I mean, it became mainstream, or whatever, attention on the band, which was fine with us because, whatever. It was just another thing that we hadn't experienced before, and we never changed our attitude to what we were doing. We never stopped and reconsidered what was going on and like, "How can we maintain this?" or "What's the next step we should do to maintain this and to become more popular or sell more records?" or whatever. We just always made--- I think *Elephant*, the last record, it seems to me--- [I'd] be pretty sure that that record still would have been made whether there was anybody liking us any more than the first album.

DD: I think that maybe part of the appeal is that people can sense that you're just doing what you do. And so much today is kind of manufactured that I think that's part of the appeal. I guess you kind of anticipated my next question. What were your expectations right at the beginning? Were there any beyond "Hey . . . " when you sat down with Meg for the first time, ". . . this sounds great"? I mean---

JW: Yeah, I think we assumed that the type of music we were making, that it would have a limited appeal from the get-go. And that was freeing because there was no ambitious thoughts in our head like, "Oh, well we'll take this to the masses," or "We'll bring blues music to the mainstream," or anything like that. I mean, we never sent out demos to record labels or tried to get signed because we assumed that--- I mean, how ridiculous it would be to walk in and say, "Oh, yeah. Me and my sister have this two-piece band and we play sort of really raw blues music or rock and roll and we're centered around the number three and we have everything revolving around childishness and these colorful motions . . . " and someone would've just [said], "What are you talking about?" If we did that in '99 or something . . . it would've been hilarious.

DD: Is the scene you came out of in Detroit still intact? And have you been able to help bands in that scene with your label?

JW: It's very much intact. Those bands are amazing. I think it's the best town in . . . probably the world because we've been everywhere. I've never seen a scene of so many good bands. There's like twenty, twenty-five amazing bands in

Detroit, always happening. Sort of like a revolving door thing, these bands sort of morph into other bands and a lot of people tried to give it attention the last couple of years. And some of it caught on, and a lot of it didn't. And it seemed to me like . . . the bands that didn't really catch on . . . those were the best ones. And maybe one day people will look back and realize that they're something, but there have been--- We've always taken our friends' bands with us on tour, whenever we've gone from Detroit, because it's just the music we love the most and those [are] the people we want to be with the most. So there are so many good ones happening now, like the Dirt Bombs, and Blanche, and the Wax Wings, and The Detroit Cobras. There's just so many, I just--- It's really cool.

DD: You know, I know a couple of musicians from Detroit so I'm going to make a raging generalization here, which is---

JW: Mmm-hmm.

DD: Something I've really been impressed with is that they've got this incredible broad-based music knowledge. Like the black guys I know are big country music fans, and the white guys have . . . Andre Williams' singles collections.

JW: Yeah.

DD: And is there a reason for that? Is there any particular reason why people . . . why pop music in its broadest sense is so important in Detroit?

JW: I think there's just a collective of people that like really the best out of in any sort of genre, whatever it is. They're just such huge music fans. It kind of comes from a little bit of a record-collector obscurist mentality on one side and a little bit of music snobbery on one side. But on the other end, it's just people who really love good music. And you'll see it, no matter what . . . if a gospel group came and played at the . . . museum, it'd be the same people who were there to go see the punk band at the bowling alley. Because you can tell they love good music. And you'll see sometimes these really kind of hardcore sort of punk rockers. They go see the Clone Defects, this punk band in Detroit. And you'll see them DJ at the bowling alley and they'll play . . . "Here Comes the Night" by Them and . . . it's just . . . wow, it's just a beautiful disease, I think.

DD: Meg, if you were to take somebody to Detroit and kind of give them a feel for the Detroit you love, what would you show off? Where would you take them?

Meg White: I'd have to take them to the Motown Museum, probably. That seems to be the first stop for everyone, I guess, and maybe just a walk through downtown where you see all the empty skyscrapers. I think that would give you a pretty good feel of the city. Maybe to a couple good bars with really good jukeboxes.

DD: Sounds perfect. Well, I'll tell you what. Why don't we do a tune and we can talk some more. What do you guys want to start off with?

JW: This song, "Lord, Send Me an Angel." This is a song Blind Willie McTell used to sing and [I] sort of transferred it to my hometown and used it to talk about myself. I just changed his location from Atlanta to Detroit.

The White Stripes perform "Lord, Send Me an Angel"

DD: "Lord, Send Me an Angel," a version done today by the White Stripes, who are playing live for us today. That kind of leads me into something I really wanted to talk in depth with you about, which is country-blues, and these personalities, these guys that I know you're big fans of, people like Robert Johnson and Son House. Did you discover them when you were a kid, or, when did you first discover their music?

JW: No, I didn't know. I was completely ignorant of blues music growing up. I only knew rock and roll and probably the closest thing I knew [to the blues] when I was eight years old is like . . . , someone told me "The Lemon Song" was a rip-off of some blues artist or something. And I'd say "Oh" . . . you know? I didn't know what that meant or whatever, and I think at some point, when I was only about fourteen or fifteen, there was a Howlin' Wolf cassette. Like 'The Best of Howlin' Wolf' cassette ended up in my bedroom somehow . . . whatever, and I really started to get into that, like his song, "Sitting on Top of the World." And I learned how to play that, and that was sort of the first blues song I learned how to play. And that was a nice step because it was something that I could relate to at that point, because it was electric musicians playing with him, like Hubert Sumlin on the guitar, and everything. And I got into it a couple years later. I bought a Silvertone guitar with the amp and the case and that, and then I look and I saw a picture to Hubert Sumlin, who was Howlin' Wolf's guitar player. He was playing on a Silvertone amp and then I think just things just started to roll around. Like you start . . . you get those . . . tiny little pieces like that start to fit in, and you start to get more involved in it and then all of a sudden . . . you go to the store and I bought like a Robert Johnson or a Son House record or someone played me those and I just . . . it was like the whole world just blew up, you know? And that was--- I seemed to want to abandon everything else I liked about music at that point. I didn't want to listen to any rock 'n roll for a while there. I just wanted to listen to nothing but this folk music. And I'd been listening to Bob Dylan and his early things and coming off of all the old folk musicians he would've been listening to, like the Smithsonian anthology records, and everything started to make sense. And I started to want to know more and more about where the truth was, instead of the followers for the last forty years or fifty years or whatever it was. I just wanted to go down to where they were getting it from, and where those guys were getting it from. And learning about that tradition, you know? All these songs that Robert Johnson was doing were the same songs that people around him, like Tommy Johnson and Son House, were playing first. Then you just want to join that family and you just hope that that family still exists and these traveling minstrels of musicians around the world are there instead of this horrible white-boy blues band in the bar in town or something. There are actually people involved in some form of folk music.

DD: I understand you all went looking, and you actually found Son House's grave.

JW: Yeah, it's in Detroit and yeah, it was a nice pilgrimage for me and Meg to go there. And I remember there was a sort of a homeless lady walked up while we were looking at the grave, me and Meg. And she came over having this kind of attitude like "Humph! What are you looking at?" And I said, "We're just here to see this man's grave." And she's like, "Who's that?" I said, "His name is Son House. He was a blues singer from a long time ago." And she yells, "Humph!" and walked off. It was like a little ghost, and I don't know, I just started laughing.

DD: And there are empty spots on either side of his grave, I heard?

JW: Yeah, that's right. Yeah. Last time I been there, there were.

DD: Hmm . . . make a reservation, I guess.

JW: I guess so.

DD: Hmm . . . well I'll tell you what. You want to move over to the piano and do one there?

JW: Of course. Yeah, this song's called "I Want to Be the Boy to Warm Your Mother's Heart."

> The White Stripes perform "I Want to Be the Boy to Warm Your Mother's Heart"

DD: The White Stripes are our guests today and that's one that is on *Elephant*, the new one. You have said this in the past [and] I'm wondering how this sits with you. [T]here is only a limited life to this band and I think you said something about five albums being it. Does that sit well with you about how the band is progressing or is there a lot more room for you to grow?

JW: It's very hard for us to tell. We sort of were asked that a lot, because I think everyone--- Say when *White Blood Cells* came out, I think . . . you sort of get this mainstream attention. People were starting to say, "Oh well, it's okay. It's good." Or "But how long will it last?" And I was like, "Well, I don't know. Maybe a couple more albums then we'll call it quits." And I didn't want to beat this into the ground, and neither does Meg, you know? And of course when *Elephant* came out, and it was another huge international smash hit success . . . we of course knew it was going to be that people said, "Oh, well how long can it last?" And I was like, "Geez, what the hell do you want me to do?" "What's for breakfast?"

DD: Well let's talk about somebody who has a career that's lasted more than four albums. Let's talk about Loretta Lynn, because I know you all are big fans. You dedicated the album to her.

JW: Yeah.

DD: But I understand you've had a chance to spend some time with her. What is she like? What does she think of your music? And how do you guys interact?

JW: We've become just best friends. I love her so much and we have a lot of affection for each other and the thing she said about--- I think only the real comment that stood out in my mind about the White Stripes she said was that she heard--- I guess she was at home and the "Seven Nation Army" video was on TV . . . and she said "Well, that sounds like someone breaking into a bank!"

DD: [laughs]

JW: I still don't know what that means, but I love that. Yeah, we've become real cool and I was offered the opportunity to produce her new album and we just finished that up recently, and I can't wait for it to come out. I mean, all the songs are all written by Loretta and some of them are thirty years old that she never recorded and some of them she wrote a few months ago. And she's such a brilliant songwriter. She just blows my mind. I just don't understand where the--- She just has this cleverness in her head that you'd swear when you talk to her that—she's so funny—you'd swear that she would never think of these things. But she thinks of these intricate little plays in relationship, plays that are so bizarre that I just--- It's like "Wow! Where did that come from?" I can't believe, even at her age, she still thinks these same things, about like when people are teenagers in love . . . you know? She still has those same thoughts in her head [and] that's really, really inspiring to look forward to in my life.

DD: It's encouraging. How do you as a producer--- I would be intimidated. You don't want to get in the way of this, right? . . .

JW: Yeah, it's kind of . . . sometimes, it's very funny. Sometimes when we're doing things with people like that—the couple times we have—it's very funny how the . . . sort of the ball ends up in our court or in my court, or whatever. Like we went and did a set of Yardbirds songs with Jeff Beck in England. And I called and we're talking and I said, "Well, what do you want to do? What songs should we do?" and he's like, "Well, whatever you want to do is fine with me." So me and Meg were sitting there and we had a couple days to practice, and we said "All right." So we picked ten or twelve songs we liked by the Yardbirds. And we went there and it was like, "Do you want to do this?" when we rehearsed it with him. And we only had like two hours to rehearse or something . . . [and] I said, "Well do you want to do that one?" He's like, "Yeah. That's fine with me, if you want to. Yeah, sure. Sounds great." And it's kind of the same thing with Loretta Lynn. She had all these songs here and she--- I said, "What ones do you really want to do, Loretta?" And she's like, "Whichever ones you like, Jack. Let's just do those, you know?" And it's really--- It makes you intimidated because I don't feel like I have that sort of taste enough to know what they want to express or something like that. So it's a very difficult job to get a handle on it. You have to really connect with them, I guess. I'm talking too much about it, I'm sorry.

DD: No, no, I would totally agree with that. Now I'm interested about you and Jeff Beck. He would be a guitarist I would put on a list of people that . . . the sounds they get out of their instruments, you get . . . somewhat out of yours, too. Are there other people you've looked to . . . to take sounds from . . . take ideas from? Rock and roll is a stealing business, isn't it?

JW: I suppose so, but there was a time where we started to play shows . . . or started to go to shows, and see garage rock bands in Detroit and stuff, and the thing that really upset me was that I didn't like [it] when people, on purpose, ripped off old music. And purposefully did that, and then just changed the words and called it their own.

DD: Mmm-hmm.

JW: And I would get disappointed. I would hear a riff or something by a band and I thought, "That's so great," and then a couple months later, I'd hear the song they stole it from and I'm like "Aw, man . . . ." And it would just disappoint me so much. And I thought, "I'm never, ever going to do that." And no matter what, I mean you're going to write songs and people are always going to say it sounds like something; it sounds like this or that. And you cannot avoid that. There's no problem with having influences, but I always try to avoid purposefully stealing from other people, you know? But I never really had one sort of guitar player that I always looked up to and I wanted to be like them. There's always--- I like little snippets of things here and there, like a different tone here on some old record or the way an amp sounded on this record or something like that. And I just try to--- Those things just pop up in my head. When I was a teenager, I really got into Dexter Romweber from this band, the Flat Duo Jets. I was really not too crazy about his tone. I was just crazy about his attitude towards the guitar. The attitude was to not really care that much. And I was trying to balance that with the fact . . . [that] when I saw Detroit garage rock bands,

[in] a lot of them I never saw a guitar player, in Detroit, really stand out. Like if he did a guitar solo . . . [he'd] like pop above the band and break through the monotony of the riff, and break out and do something like that. And that made me really concentrate on tones. So I was sort of balancing my attitude towards it and tone. It's like when you don't want to do something perfect, you know? It's like trying to be an anti-perfectionist, but you're really--- It's really perfect by not trying to be perfect, I guess.

DD: Well, the Flat Duo Jets are a great example of somebody with that kind of an aesthetic too.

JW: Mmm-hmm.

DD: And in some ways—I've been thinking about this—you're kind of a conservative rocker in a way. I mean eight-track, analog, no computers.

JW: Mmm-hmm.

DD: Is it all about sound? Or is it, as you kind of express there, kind of about a philosophy of keeping things closer to the bone?

JW: I suppose it's both. I think that when you are given the job to do something, or you take on a task being creative, you want to do [it] the best way you can do it. If you're a painter, I suppose you'd want to find the best oil paints that suit what you're doing. So I think when I was like, "I'm going to play guitar, I guess. What's the best amp I can find?" Well, I like a Silvertone amp. I like a Fender Twin Reverb and there are not really any better-sounding amps. And I've played a million of them, and I never found anyone better, and those amps are forty years old, you know? So why bother? The same thing with recording microphones, recording tape and old recording gear. I think they never really surpassed it so there's really no point. I mean, if this sound is that good for Frank Sinatra or the Beatles or something, then there's really no point in trying to "improve" it. I've never been a gadget man. I never had that sort of male mentality to want to get the brand new toy that came out just because it's new. It has some new little trick to it; just 'cause it's digital doesn't mean it's better, you know?

DD: I've been reading something [that said] I guess when . . . this album came out that you were happier with this album than any album except for maybe your first. And was it just because that was the first, or you really got the sound you wanted finally on a record then? Or . . .

JW: I think you never get that moment back, you know? You never get that moment you had when you were makin' your first record. I think the same thing when we made our first 45; there was an attitude there that you'll never get back and that's just something that that first album . . . just the way it came out, it just, for me and Meg, it felt blessed to us because it was exactly what we wanted on tape. And you just never get that moment back, and we never wanted to try and recreate it either. So it'll always be the best because it's always my favorite in my mind.

DD: So you want to do something from that first?

JW: Yeah, we'll do . . . this song's called "Big Three Killed My Baby," which I originally wrote for Andre Williams. [laughs]

DD: Really? Really?

JW: Yeah, but he wouldn't sing it.

DD: Well, we should tell people briefly who Andre Williams is, because he's a name you can't drop everywhere.

JW: Oh yeah. Well he's an old sort of soul singer and producer from the 60s. He worked for Fortune Records, and he wrote the song "Shake Your Tail Feather" and he produced the first version of "Mustang Sally." And he worked with people back there in Detroit. He worked with Stevie Wonder a little bit, I think, early on and Ike Turner a little bit. I was in a band called Two Star Tabernacle for a short time and we made one 45 with him. And he said he wanted to do--- And I said, "What song should we do?" and Dan, a singer in the band, asked him, "What song should we do?" He said, "Oh, well, it's got to be controversial."

DD: [laughs]

JW: And I said, "Well, what do you mean?" And he's like, "Well, something like . . . 'Well, what if I was gay? / would you love me anyway?' . . . something like that!"

JW: And so I went home and I had this idea in my head about . . . [how] I wanted to write something against the car companies and I said, "Oh, that'll work for what he was talking about maybe . . . " So I wrote "The Big Three Killed My Baby." And I showed him the lyrics and he's like, "Ah . . . you sing it." So we did a version and I sang it and then he would just say, "She's dead!" in the background over and over again. It was very funny. But it ended up--- It wasn't very country, 'cause it was a country band we were playing with . . . [and they] wanted to make a country record so it didn't work out. So it ended up popping up on the first White Stripes record.

DD: Well, Andre's not here but this is "Big Three Killed My Baby."

> The White Stripes perform "The Big Three Killed My Baby"

DD: "Big Three Killed My Baby." The White Stripes are playing live for us today on the *World Cafe.* We got time for maybe a couple more. What do you guys want to do next?

DD: I have a couple questions that I wanted to get your reaction to. Number one was the cover that Joss Stone has done of "Fell in Love with a Boy," which . . . she turns . . . into something completely different. What did you think when you heard that?

JW: It was beautiful. I loved it. I loved it the first moment I heard it. I thought it was amazing because . . . in R&B nowadays, you get glimpses of people with really, really strong voices. Like someone like Mary J. Blige, I think is just a beautiful singer. But again, a lot of times nowadays, in R&B, this technology is so encroaching on . . . the soulfulness of it. And when I heard that track, I said, "Oh man, they're getting a lot closer to what's going on with what it should be," . . . in the soulfulness of what was happening in "Days Gone By." So it was cool and the Roots played on that track with her. I guess they produced it. So those guys are really talented. I was blown away. I thought it was really cool. I started to . . . want to play that song like that from now on. It sounded a lot better than what I did.

DD: I wanted to ask about the picture of Cole Porter that's inside the jacket to *Elephant.* I've seen that picture before, but I'm curious as to how it ended up . . . why you put it in there.

JW: I was just looking through that book. A friend had given it to me and something just struck me, because I had been thinking about dedicating this record to the death of a sweetheart. And when I turned that page and I saw that one where it's Cole Porter lying in a sarcophagus on his trip to Egypt, something . . . the smile on his face and the person he was . . . pretending he was dead seemed to be the perfect image for what I was thinking about for the record. So I said, "It has to go in there."

DD: Definitely. It's a great image too. Hey, Jack and Meg, thank you so much for playing live for us today.

JW: Thank you for having us.

MW: Thank you.

DD: The White Stripes, our guests here on the *World Cafe.*

ISAAC HAYES

I'M NOT SURE WHY WE GOT TO INTERVIEW ISAAC HAYES; I believe he was promoting a couple of albums he put out in 2003. All I know is that I was sitting across from a formidable man with a bald head and cool shades. As you can see, he was very forthcoming in his storytelling about his days as both a songwriter and producer at Stax Records in Memphis in the 1960s. Along with Dave Porter he wrote all of Sam and Dave's early hits like "Hold On I'm Coming" and "Soul Man." He then went on to become a giant star with his own records. Although it's not in this interview, at one point I remember Isaac leaned in and said, in that low Isaac Hayes voice, "You know I'm very popular with the African American women." That's a fact you can take to the bank!

The interview begins with Isaac talking about how he came to work at Stax Records studio in Memphis. It wasn't even easy for *him* to get inside!

Isaac Hayes: I came there several times trying to get inside, auditioning, and each time Jim Stewart said, "Well, I don't think that's what we're looking for." [laughs] I came with doo-wop groups, I came with a blues band, I came with a gospel group, and you know, I didn't get inside until I joined Floyd Newmann's band, as a keyboardist. And Floyd Newmann's one of the staff musicians here playing baritone saxophone, and he was up for a recording. And I came here with Floyd, we worked, we created some songs, and Jim Stewart eased up to me one day and said, "Young man, uh, Booker T is off in Indiana U in school." [That's] Booker T of Booker T and the MG's. He said, "So we need a keyboard player. Would you like the job?" "You kidding? Yeah!" So I was brought on as a staff member. I was so excited! And the staff was integrated. That was unheard of during those days.

David Dye: Talk a little about that because obviously, the Stewarts, who own the place, were white but it seemed to be a really great mix. If you look at Booker T and the MG's you get the idea.

IH: That's right! You know Jim Stewart, that's where the word Stax came from. His sister [was] Estelle Axton, Stewart and Axton, so he came up with the name Stax. Perfect! We were all mixed there. We were a family. We were a family. And that's a testament of the power of artistry, because it has no boundaries. Music has no boundaries. It's a human process and that's what brought us together.

DD: Now I'm looking through the complete singles, the Stax box set, the first one I see you getting a writing credit on is a Booker T tune called "Bootleg." Is that accurate?

IH: Yeah, you know Booker came to me, [and] he said, "Isaac, you know, Paul McCartney, one of his favorite tunes is 'Bootleg.'" He said, "I'm going to have to tell people, because BBC is going to interview him." He said he's going to have to tell them, "I didn't write that. Isaac Hayes did! He played on the record!" So, you know that's very ethical of Booker to do that. But, you know, we did what we had to do to get everything done. You know, David Pulleys used to sing with Booker T & the MG's. He was our vocalist. One time I pretended to be Booker T because they got some dates mixed up, you know, bookings? And Booker went somewhere in Kansas, I think, and the MG's, we had to go to Pennsylvania. And I'm up there on organ and the guys, people down there said, "Hey, look at Booker T. He ain't got no hair!" I said "Oh my god, what am I going to do?" and I jumped up and started doing some routines with David. [*laughs*]

DD: That's funny.

IH: Oh yeah, but one thing; we did what we had to do to get the job done.

DD: Well, of course the big partnership for you was with David Porter. And the first Sam and Dave single you all wrote together was "I Take What I Want."

IH: Yeah, "I Take What I Want." And the third writer on that was a guy named Teenie Hodges, who worked out of High Studios with Willie Mitchell. That was Teenie playing guitar on "Love and Happiness." [sings riff] That's Teenie. So, like I said, that whole Memphis thing was a big family. I explain this by saying we were wonderfully incestuous [laughs] because we worked all over town together. Competitively, but it was a heavy competition because it added to the growth and development of the whole Memphis thing.

DD: All right, the first song Sam and Dave did of David Porter and Isaac Hayes along with Teeny Hodges is "I Take What I Want."

Sam and Dave recording: "I Take What I Want"

DD: That is Sam and Dave doing "I Take What I Want." My guest today is Isaac Hayes. Well, when you started doing solo albums, you made kind of a party album and then you made *Hot Buttered Soul.*

IH: Yeah my first album was called *Presenting Isaac Hayes* and, you know, I didn't take Al Bell seriously because he wanted a producer, so I said, "Sure." There had been a party, [at] Stax and we had been drinking champagne and eating cake—it was somebody's birthday. So at the end of night Al said, "Let me cut some on ya." I said, "Yeah, okay," went into the studio, cut the tape on, let it roll man and I commandeered Duck Dunn, Al Jackson and I was at piano. Booker came in a little bit and did a little something I think. We just let the tape roll and I started doing tunes, doing tunes. When I finished, I said, "I think I got it!" about an hour or something later. And it was called *Presenting Isaac Hayes.* I didn't think he was going to do it. He said a couple weeks later, he said, "All right, you got an appointment with the photographer." "For what?" [I said]. "For the picture of the album cover." "Oh you serious?" So I went and did that. It had moderate success. It was held critically by the writers. You know, writers for publications and things like that. But I knew I didn't have my best foot forward because I was under the influence of alcohol! So the next opportunity came when Al Bell said, "Look Ike, we got a big sales meeting next spring," which was in '68, spring of '69. "We got a sales meeting. And I want some albums out. Help me produce some of these albums." I said, "Okay, I'll help you do that, but Al, can I have an album?" He said, "Yeah, you can have one!" "Can I do it like I want to do it?" "Yeah sure, you got a carte blanche whatever you want to do." So that's when I cut *Hot Buttered Soul.*

DD: And how did he have the idea to do the extended tracks, because that was *totally* unusual at the time?

IH: Well, one thing about it, since I felt no pressure, there was 26 albums released, so I didn't' think mine mattered. So, I was under no pressure. So, I did it selfishly. I could do what I wanted to do. I was given the permission to do that. So I felt like what I had to say could not be said in 2 minutes and 30 seconds. So that's why I got those extended cuts.

DD: And it certainly took off right away . . . [that's] my memory of that record. Did that change your life? Here you are a guy working in the studio, doing the writing, very much behind the scenes. It must have really changed things for you.

IH: Oh it did, it did. I was thrust up in the forefront and, you know, I'd been performing but not on that scale. That whole nervous area, all that stuff, man it was--- But they supported me too. So it was a big deal, a big deal.

DD: That period of time, Isaac Hayes was one of the biggest things in pop culture in this country. I mean your figure, used on your album covers, taking back chains in a way. You wore them in a completely different way. It was a symbol that I think stretched into certainly all branches of black culture and I think through culture in and of itself. Were you very conscious of how you were portraying yourself at that time?

IH: Yeah I was. You know, I was always on the cutting edge and I would always go where other people feared to go. And I put the chains on because the chains represented power. Once chains represented captivity and slavery for a black man in this country. It represented power. And some took it even further than that and said it was sexy, but I didn't do it for that. But it symbolized power; that's why I did that.

DD: You also--- Of course, anytime you appear anywhere, the orchestra is going to play the "Theme from *Shaft*." And that was, of course, a huge, huge record and backing up a huge movie. Did you get the idea at that time that you wanted to do acting yourself?

IH: I did. I wanted to act then. I'd always

wanted to act because in high school I was a member of [the] speakers and writers club; I was the vice president of that. But you know, I'd never thought I'd get a chance to act, but when the *Shaft* thing came up, I said, "Hey man, y'all cast this yet? I'm going to try out for the lead role." "Isaac Hayes, you can't do the movie, you gotta do the music." A couple weeks later had passed, nobody contacted me, I had to come back home to Memphis. "Gimme a shot, gimme a shot at the role, man," "Hey Ike, you got that call yet?" "No!" Okay, so I went, called 'em up, "Oh Mr. Hayes, haven't you heard? They've already cast a guy by the name of Richard Roundtree. Oh, but remember you gotta do the music!" "Yeah, yeah, yeah, I'll do the music." Best thing that ever happened to me!

DD: [laughs]

> Isaac Hayes recording: "Theme from *Shaft*"

DD: In the mid-70s you and Stax parted ways. How was that situation resolved?

IH: Well, you know, some of the same people are here. But as time passes you don't labor on sour grapes. Time moves on and let bygones be bygones. I fought to keep Stax. I didn't want them to grow as big and rapid as they did because I didn't want the production department just to be over here . . . and move the administrative thing somewhere else. I wanted it all to stick together. But I think I lost that battle.

DD: Now I understand that if you walk into the museum your 1972 El Dorado is right there as you come in?

IH: No, not as you come in. You gotta go through the whole tour and you go back through and you see it there. It's a section in the museum. It's mind boggling. It blew me away and I hadn't seen it in a long time, but I didn't realize, "I did that?!"

DD: Describe the car to people, what's it like?

IH: Well, it's a color that I think General Motors called "Shout of Turquoise." I love that color. I have two cars previous to that color. Where the chrome is on a regular car, it's all been dipped in gold—gold plated. It's got super fly headlights. It's got oval-shaped windows behind the regular windows on the side. It's got a TV, a bar, and no door handles. It's all automatic open with a press of a button on a remote thing; the door pops open.

DD: Isaac Hayes, could you drive that car on the street?

IH: I couldn't back then. I drove it a few times, but I said, "No, I gotta park it," because it was such a distraction. People were having accidents, wrecks and things, looking at the car. So, I had to park it at a garage. The garage had to be well secured because the car was insured by Lloyds of London and that was one of the stipulations. So we had to have a special garage built to house the car.

DD: What a great symbol of the 70s, though.

IH: Yeah! Platforms, all that stuff. It was great. It was fun.

DD: Certainly, well here we are in the next century. There's a certain amount of younger people who know you better as Chef [animated character on *South Park*] I think than anything else. That's been a wonderful thing. Are you continuing to do that?

IH: Well, I am. In fact, we did our last episode of our season a few days ago. Matt and Trey needs a break. So, we'll be back. We just completed our 6th season, 6 years. So, we'll come back.

DD: *South Park* will return. Well, Isaac Hayes, thank you for your work over the years. As we go out here, could you pick maybe one of yours and David Porter's songs that we could go out on, that you think is one of the best.

IH: Okay, it's got to be a Sam and Dave tune, let's say, "Hold On I'm Coming"

DD: All right, this is how it sounds, this is "Hold On I'm Coming." Isaac Hayes thank you very much.

IH: Okay, thank you.

> Sam and Dave recording: "Hold On I'm Coming"

2003

JOAN ARMATRADING

David Dye: We're down at Indre Studios once again, and we are very excited because Joan Armatrading is returning to the *World Cafe*. Last time she was here she brought a little string section with her and it was absolutely fantastic up in our studios, but we've expanded things a bit tonight. She's got her full band that she's out touring with. She has a wonderful new album out called *Lovers Speak*. We're going to find out about that, and here's some tunes. Will you please join me in warmly welcoming to the *World Cafe*, Joan Armatrading.

> Joan Armatrading performs "In These Times" and "Physical Pain"

DD: Ah, there's a place to break, after the song "Physical Pain," which is--- We've been actually getting a little preview of the tunes from *Lovers Speak*. Joan Armatrading is live today on the *World Cafe*. I want to talk about the song you did before that, the "In These Times," which seems pretty pointed to our times. Did you write that in post-9/11?

Joan Armatrading: I wrote it well before September the 11th, but it does seem to kind of sum up that time and the time we're in now, and it's really a song for people who [are] in any kind of desperate times; it seems to express that kind of feeling that you have. But I did write it first of all as a poem about how people feel during wars. I wrote a song called "If Women Ruled the World" and it was talking about--- hypothetical, of course, because women don't, in the government sense, I mean---

[laughter]

JA: And I wrote it because I was thinking, "What would it be like if, in the government sense, women did rule the world?" Would they just be more willing to sit down and have a chat about how things need to be, or would they be just as aggressive—can I say that?—as men, you know, and want to go to war, or maybe feeling war is the right answer? As I say, it's hypothetical because you never know. When you're in certain situations, you don't know what you have to do to make the thing work. So "In These Times" is like a continuation of that; now you've gone to war, this is how it feels, and . . . how you feel when your loved one isn't there and things like that.

DD: Hm. Well segueing from that, "If Women Ruled the World" you not only produced this disc, but you ended up playing--- I mean, the entire cabinet was Joan Armatrading. You played every instrument on it except for the drums, right?

JA: Yeah, I played everything apart from the drums and the horn section, but, you know, it's something I do anyway. When I'm doing my demos I tend to do that anyway, but I just hadn't done it on an album. So I thought maybe it would be quite nice at some point to do it. I don't say that this is what I'll do . . . on every album because I really enjoy working with, you know, musicians. Like we've got Gary Foote playing saxophone, drums, and flute, and we've got Spencer Cousins playing the keyboards, and—

[applause]

DD: You also, you've worked with so many of the, you know, so many great producers over the years, Steve Lillywhite, Glyn Johns, and I wanted mention Gus Dudgeon, because there's a dedication on this to Gus.

JA: Yes, the album's dedicated to Gus, because he was my first producer, and I couldn't have had a better first producer. He produced—if people don't know who he is—he produced all the Elton John albums from the kind of the beginning of his career even up until the 90s. So all those great songs you know, "Candle in the Wind," you know, "Daniel," "Yellow Brick Road." All those things, he produced, and he was one of those very, very involved producers who knew every aspect of production, arranging, how to treat the musicians properly, how to bring the best out of everybody. But the thing that was fantastic about him was that when I started he didn't say, "Okay, I'm the person that knows everything and you're the new guy, just sit back and let me tell you what to do." He appreciated that I had things that I wanted to bring to my songs, and I was very definite about arrangements and things like that. And he encouraged me to do all the things I wanted to do, which was fantastic, because the second person that I worked with, the second producer was the total opposite, who--- I have to say was probably the most unhappiest period of my career, was doing that second album, but I learned a lot from him as well, all the things not to do.

[laughter]

DD: And isn't that your favorite cover picture though? You got that on *Back to the Night*.

JA: *Back to the Night*? It is because you don't see my face.

DD: Aww.

JA: Yeah [laughs].

DD: That's totally "aww." It's totally pretty. I was thinking about those earlier days, and in fact one of the things, there's a sticker on the front of Joan's new album where it says, "Voted top 100 most influential women in rock," from VH1, to which I say, "Duhh." But there's another aspect to that which is, top 10 most influential women to other performers, I think. I see certain performers as people who arrived kind of whole cloth, and you can't really see where their influences came from. They just are who they are and they do what they do, and I am curious as to when you were starting out back then, when you went in the studio for the first time. Who [and/or] what got you excited about music? What other performers got you thinking that, "Gee, I can do this." Or was there anybody?

JA: Well no, there wasn't actually, because when I started, there wasn't somebody playing the guitar in the way that I played or writing the songs or singing the way I sing, and I didn't think, "Oh, there's a niche. Let me fill that." It was just, "This is what I do." It was very natural. And sometimes people say to me, "Oh, but you must have been—it must have been Joni Mitchell, who made you start." But of course I started writing when I was 14, and I don't think Joni Mitchell had had a record then. Although saying that, I think Joni Mitchell is--- She's in that group that you just mentioned, the most influential people, and she's a phenomenal talent, but I think, her like me . . . I think we just kind of did what we do, you know? There's no major influence. The reason I started to write was my mother bought a piano and put it in the front room . . .

DD: Hmm.

JA: . . . [I] thought it was a good piece of furniture, so I just started to play it [laughs].

DD: And when did the guitar come in? Did you want that right away?

JA: Well, the guitar came in not long after that, and in the corner of the room there--

- It's quite funny. In the corner of the room there's a safe thing, and in my house, when I was growing up, my father had a guitar and he used to play that guitar, and he used to--- When he'd play he'd play a song called "Blue Moon," which I thought was beautiful, how he played it. But every time he finished he'd put the guitar away and he'd hide it, and he'd hide it in this room that had a safe, like that safe in the corner of the room, with this huge door, that as a young person, once that door was closed there's no way you're going to open it. He used to hide that guitar in there and on the top shelf. And I think it's that kind of, you know, "You mustn't touch this. Don't even look at it," thing that made me want to play the guitar.

DD: [laughs]

JA: So, I saw a guitar in a pawn shop, and I said to my mum, "Can I have that?" But it cost three pounds and she said, "Well, we don't have the money, but if they'll swap the prams . . . " (You call them strollers). "If you swap the prams for the guitars then you can have it." And that's how I got my first guitar.

DD: Wow. In doing research for this, I kept reading all these bios of you, and the first line in a number of them is, "Joan Armatrading was the first black, female, British, singer-songwriter to kind of be on par with a lot of white folks." And I'm curious as to which was harder for you, being from the West Indies, or being female, when you were starting out, do you think?

JA: None of those things are hard. They're quite easy to do.

[laughter and applause]

DD: I thought it was a curious way to begin a bio.

JA: [laughs] No, my parents went to England, and they left me in the West Indies, saved up the money, and then sent for me, and I made that trip from the West Indies to England on my own. And people say, "Well, didn't you miss the island that you were coming from?" Well no, what I was happy about was seeing my parents, and I grew up in England. So I've lived there since I was seven, so my whole culture for me is English, and I feel very English. My traits are very English. All my influences—conscious, subconscious—are all from there, so although I know that the West Indies has Caribbean music, reggae—and I do play reggae—but I think it's a kind of a white-tinged thing [laughs].

DD: It's the British version.

JA: It's the British version. That's right, that's right, but I do it very well. [laughs]

DD: As do a lot of other British people. Joan Armatrading is our guest; do you want to continue on with some more new things?

JA: Yeah, we're going to play "Tender Trap."

Joan Armatrading performs "Tender Trap"

DD: "Tender Trap." More with Joan Armatrading live from Indre, when we get back here to the *World Cafe*.

DD: Joan Armatrading live from Indre Studios, this is "Love Bug."

Joan Armatrading performs "Love Bug"

DD: Joan Armatrading live on the *World Cafe* with some of that British reggae we've been talking about. Joan, I love—I really like that song. It's on the new album, but I kind of love it against my will...

JA: [laughs]

DD: ... because it reminds me of that Disney movie, *Herbie the Love Bug*, and I—

JA: [laughs]

DD: You should have timed it. You could have had a song in a Disney film. It would have been--- Anyway, a couple things have happened in your life since we last talked and I'd love to hear about them. One of them was [that] you did a song in tribute to Nelson Mandela and you got to play it—explain the situation—in concert?

JA: Yeah, I was asked to write the tribute song in England for Mr. Mandela by an English M.P. and that was great. I was able to write the song, and when I was asked I didn't say, "Yes," straight away because it felt [like] a bit of a responsibility. You have to kind of get across the flavor and essence of the man in this very short time.

DD: Yeah.

JA: But I said yes and wrote the song. In fact the lyrics were written—the beginning of the lyrics—were written in New Jersey [laughs]. And I then went back home and one night I was asleep [and] about three o'clock in the morning I was woken by—there's a little riff in the tune—and I was woken by this little riff so I got up, went downstairs and wrote the rest of the song, wrote the rest of the lyrics and then went back to bed. It was very quick, but I spent ages, ages thinking about it. By the way if anybody does want to hear that song you can go to my website, www.joanarmatrading.com and you can download a copy for free. But I was able to send the song to him and got the word back that he liked it. And then a while later, he was coming over to England to do a private function and they asked if I would sing the song to him there. And I recorded the song with a choir called the Kingdom Choir, so I sang that to him there, which was brilliant, and he danced on the stage the whole of the song, and he's not too nifty on the pins—

[laughter]

JA: But he was absolutely brilliant that he did that, and then I got this massive hug at the end of it.

DD: Aw.

JA: So it was just fantastic, definitely a highlight of my career.

DD: Aw, that sounds wonderful. The other thing you did, seems like an incredible accomplishment considering that you're, you know, doing this full time and everything, is that you got your degree in June of 2001, you got your B.A.

JA: Yeah.

DD: How did you do that?

JA: It wasn't easy. It was a five-year thing, and, as you say, I did it while I was on the road, but it's something I really wanted to do. I've always wanted to have a degree. It was in history, or is in history. And my name's Joan Anita Barbara Armatrading so that's JABA, and with the B.A. at the end it just . . . rounds it off quite well; JABABA, and really that's what I was aiming for.

[laughter]

DD: Did you do a thesis? Did you do a paper on something?

JA: Well, I did. My history was history between the wars, [the] First and Second World War, and comparative history of America and Britain.

DD: Well congratulations, that's great. One of the other things I don't think I've asked you about before is, there have been some wonderful covers of your songs recently or at least ones we like; Melissa Etheridge did a great cover, and are you familiar with the Two Nice Girls?

JA: Two Nice Girls have done a great version of "Love and Affection." They covered that with Lou Reed's "Sweet Jane."

DD: Right.

JA: And it's definitely a brilliant thing I think.

DD: They kind of changed up your chords a little bit to make it work.

JA: Yeah, but it really works. I think it sounds really good, and Melissa's version of "The Weakness in Me" is pretty special as well, I think.

DD: Well gee, I noticed you were very careful to have a drummer who could play the saxophone, so is maybe "Love and Affection" possible?

JA: "Love and Affection" is possible. I don't know if that's--- Gary is very versatile; I think he plays probably the most instruments of anybody that I know. So he's a saxophone player who plays the drums, who plays the flutes, who plays percussion, who plays guitar, who plays piano who plays . . . [laughs] Not that I'm plugging Gary here.

[laughter]

JA: So this is "Love and Affection."

Joan Armatrading performs "Love and Affection"

JA: Thank you, now we're playing the title track "Lovers Speak."

Joan Armatrading performs "Lovers Speak"

JA: This is our last song.

Joan Armatrading performs "Me, Myself, I"

DD: "Me, Myself, I" finishing up our set today. Thanks to Joan Armatrading, this great band, and our audience, live at Indre Studios, here on the *World Cafe*.

2004

DONOVAN

IT WAS A DELIGHT TO TALK WITH DONOVAN IN 2004. It's always interesting to see how some musicians, whose heyday was in another era, continue to strive for relevancy.

In Donovan's case he went back to his roots in the world of Beat culture of the 1950s with his album *Beat Cafe*. Of course, what we're usually interested in is our past, so I had a set of my own questions. Donovan was very affable and provided insight. I had recently watched the D.A. Pennebacker film of Bob Dylan's tour of England in 1965, and there is a scene where a very callow-seeming Donovan has an audience with Bob. It seems like Donovan was the butt of a joke he may not have been in on. We get Donovan's view on that moment in this interview.

David Dye: Donovan is our guest on the Cafe today. His new album harkens back to the days of the Beats in the 1950s. Could the folk revival and the hippie music scene of the 60s have existed without the Beats? Donovan thinks not. Let's begin with this performance of his song, the title track of the new album, "Beat Cafe."

Donovan performs "Beat Cafe"

DD: Donovan is our guest and that is "Beat Cafe," which is the title track of this wonderful new album that explores-- You know it's funny, everybody sees Donovan as sort of the spokesman for the hippie world, but there would not have been a hippie world, I don't think, if there wasn't a bohemia before that.

Donovan: It's true. In the 40s and 50s [there were] three seminal figures, poets always, Jack Kerouac, Allan Ginsberg, and William Burroughs. And Kerouac especially with his book, *On the Road,* but Ginsberg effectively reintroduced the power of the word and these poets were resisted, as all bohemian events are. And then the walls were broken down and they were accepted and Bob Dylan, and Donovan, and definitely the Beatles were informed by these three poets and the work they'd done. So I think the 60s freedoms, the doors of perception, wouldn't have been opened without bohemian efforts from these three poets and many others.

DD: Now, you were born in Glasgow?

D: That's right.

DD: And when did you move south?

D: Ten years old, a good time, 1955. My father actually took me to see *Rock Around the Clock,* this breakthrough rock and roll film. But before then, he'd read me poetry in Glasgow and he had a great library and he read me poetry from the age of one. I heard the rhythms and the rhymes and the cadences of poetry. His library [was] full of revolution and hobo poets, of all things; Robert Service, W.H. Davis, and these hobo poets he read to me and when I was 14. Of course, I heard the sounds and songs of Woody Guthrie and the book *On the Road,* by Kerouac, and all these elements came together.

DD: And this would have been when you were in London, at that point?

D: Yeah, it wasn't London. It was 20 miles north. My father had come down, as many families did in the mid 50s, out of industrial cities. The war was over, the rebuilding was happening. So we lived in a town 20 miles north of London, which put me in the diaspora of everything that was going to happen in rhythm and blues and folk and culture in the 60s.

DD: It's interesting that you're creating it with an historical context nowadays and your historical context is sort of the 50s bohemia. I wonder if you see it existing nowadays.

D: Yeah. Where is bohemian cafe now? Where is the Beat cafe? It's on the Internet. Now, there still are cafe societies attached, usually, to university towns and this is where it usually gets connected to the arts. Art schools are still producing new groups of musicians and writers. These are also breeding grounds. But where is it now? It sounds like a historical thing. In North Beach and San Francisco, they've turned their old haunts into restaurants. And of course, all that period is gone. But there is, on the internet, a thing called getunderground.com, and when I went in there I found it was a network of resources of bohemia all over the world.

DD: Donovan is our guest. If you would love to pick another one from *Beat Cafe*, the new album, that might be a good one . . .

D: Okay. Umm . . . these doors that were opened out of bohemia allowed to be presented to the pop culture at large, movements. One of them was a feminist movement, one of them was anti-war and social concerns and protest, then psychedelia. One of the elements on *Beat Cafe* that I explored was the absence of goddess cults. Out of bohemia came powerful women who said, "The balance must be tipped. It's too male." The Native American Indians even say the white race is too much male and this can only bring suffering and destruction. So, I wanted to introduce a song about the goddess, about the feminine principle of the universe. And so I wrote "Lover, Oh Lover."

DD: And let's rejoin another live performance of "Lover, Oh Lover."

Donovan performs "Lover, Oh Lover"

DD: Yes, that is Donovan performing live for us today, and that's another one from *Welcome to the Beat Cafe*. The new album is out on Appleseed. That is "Lover, Oh Lover." Donovan playing live. There is a--- I'd love to get your viewpoint on something that I've had the chance to see. There were a couple of films made of Bob Dylan going over to England in, I guess '65 or '66 or right around that time. And you're in one of them and you make Bob Dylan look like--- You look like the fair-haired boy from the country and it's hard to tell what he thinks of you. And that was right about the time when all this unfortunate, you know, "Donovan is the British Dylan" was going on. And I was wondering how that encounter felt for you because it's so funny that we can all watch that if we dig up that film.

D: Yeah . . . a lot of people think that Bob, sort of, treated me badly in the film. But friends of mine have looked recently, and I have looked and, actually in fact, he was very welcoming. And in that sequence where I'm singing my song, "To Sing for You," he is full attention; not taking one drag of his cigarette . . . listening intently. And in the newspapers he said that he loved what I was doing. The press made much of it and it was difficult as a young man to know what to say because we came from the same root. Woody Guthrie, Kerouac, and we'd hitchhiked around. We loved hobo poetry and it was difficult then, but I realized that the similarity was more amazing than people realized, because here was I and here was he, bringing this poetic sensibility back into pop culture. The film is a wonderful document. It's unfortunate you don't see many of the other times when I was up in the suite, with Bob and Joan and Allan Ginsberg and all of us talking, and so you're missing all of that. But I find it a very positive film now and it's an amazing meeting for me because I knew

I had to be there. And it's extraordinary that people are still talking about this meeting that happened 36 years ago. But it is momentous. It was a momentous meeting. It did mean that poetry would be introduced to pop culture and I guess we were the conduits for that.

DD: We were just moving into a media society, where moments like that could be documented and I think that had a lot to do with it. You've had such an amazing career with, we mentioned earlier, a string of huge songs that became popular all over the globe in a short period of time. And yet along with those very much produced songs, you made lovely live records and you would go out with the flute player, I guess [it was] Harold McNair, and really stay with your roots. Was it hard for you to keep centered during that period of time?

D: It was easy to dream and to experiment because I'd absorbed, in my bohemian days, pretty much everything from jazz, blues, folk, world music, poetry, art cinema, painting, sculpture, pottery, Zen Buddhism . . . I was a sponge and that all started coming out. And the painter in me would start painting through the lyrics. And when I spoke to John Cameron, the arranger, and Mickey Most, my producer, I said, "I want to paint and I want to make soundtracks to these songs." So it was very easy to be creative. The difficulty was the fame and how we so swiftly, my pals and I, lost our privacy, when we weren't able to go buy a book anymore or get a cup of coffee on the corner because it was just so manic and super fame. That was the difficulty, not the music.

DD: Could you do one more live, and I'd like to request something older. I don't know if you want to do something from way back or . . .

D: Well, people call them my old songs but they're my young songs and you can select if you like. What do you got in mind?

DD: Well, umm . . . that "Hurdy Gurdy Man."

D: I can do that. I love doing that solo. Here it is, dedicated to George Harrison, beautiful George, [whom] we've lost, but his music goes on forever. I wrote this in India, mostly in India, and George gave me the tamboura that's on the recording of it, the Indian instrument. So I'll be thinking of George.

DD: So let's go back to the stage and this version of "Hurdy Gurdy Man."

Donovan performs "Hurdy Gurdy Man"

DD: And recorded live on stage, that's "Hurdy Gurdy Man." Donovan, our guest today on the *World Cafe*. Now you and George and--- Were all the Beatles involved in that trip to India?

D: Yeah. What happened was we had read the books. I should say it wasn't the first time we knew about meditation. George had given me *Autobiography of a Yogi,* by Yogananda, and I'd given him *The Diamond Sutra.* We had sort of funny little chats about how he was a Hindu and I was a Buddhist. When in actual fact, we were both Celtic. So, when we went to India it was extraordinary because we turned our back, the world thought, on our fame, but we needed it. We took acoustic guitars. I always had an acoustic guitar. So there was nothing but acoustic music there. George brought in sitars and tamboura, and tablas for Ringo. And for the first time, those four guys and me and one Beach Boy, Mike Love, were separated from our fame and we actually got our bohemia back. In a strange way, we had our life back. And the press of the world, and the media of the world, and the paparazzi came from all over the world and parked themselves outside, but soon they wandered away and we were left to ourselves and we were in the jungle. And they wrote *The White Album*, and I wrote *Hurdy Gurdy Man*, and it was an extraordinary return, in a way, to being a teenager again and just making music for no reason other than doing it.

DD: Later, they seemed to turn away from the Maharishi. Was that your experience?

D: Oh yeah. There was a bit of a controversy, yeah. John sort of wrote a couple of songs about Maharishi touching up the girls or something. I never saw anything about that or have any proof that it happened. And anyway, George was very quick to say it's not the teacher, it's the teaching. So if there was any disillusionment it's always projected onto teachers and it's never the teaching. We learned a lot. The reason why [we] were there, we really did want to save the world. We really did want to make a difference. But we realized that exploring with sacred plants or revolution or protest wasn't getting at the true root reason for human suffering. There must be a reason and we went down into meditation to find it. And it's true, it was found down there. Conditioning of race, family, state, and religion had conditioned the world into these extraordinary conflicts and so we found the true reason and we brought it back and in a way, I guess, we promoted meditation all over the world, which is a good thing.

DD: Did you ever own a hurdy gurdy?

D: You know . . . no, but I nearly ordered one and they're made in Belgium, France, and Italy, and for people who don't know what it is; it's an antique wooden instrument. You turn a wheel and it goes across some strings. It's very droney and modal. I never bought one, but I know exactly where to get them.

DD: [chuckles] Thank you so much and thanks for *Beat Cafe* and playing live for us.

D: Well, thanks for inviting me down the to *World Cafe* and I'll be hoping to see you again.

DD: Hope it doesn't take eight years [laughing].

D: Perhaps next year I can come and we can share my birthday. I'll be forty years in music next year and that brings with it a book and a documentary and a continuation of *Beat Cafe* around America and I hope to come back and join you again.

DD: Thank you very much. Donovan is our guest and we'll be back sooner than that here on the *World Cafe.*

2004

JOE SAMPLE

JOE SAMPLE WAS THE KEYBOARD PLAYER WITH THE CRUSADERS, ONE OF THE MOST SUCCESSFUL INSTRUMENTAL BANDS OF OUR TIME. In 2004, Joe came out with a solo album called *Soul Shadows* and an accompanying stage show, featuring him on solo piano. In many ways it was a kind of "lecture" on some of the most important music of the early parts of the last century. This interview became Joe's fascinating take on early jazz piano players, although we got to talk about his work, particularly with Steely Dan. We started off talking about the song "How Ya Gonna Keep 'em Down on the Farm after They've Seen Paree?" a big pop hit in the wake of the first World War.

Joe Sample: It was actually written as a theme song of the New York regiment of the French Military, renamed and renumbered as the 369th Hellfighter's Regimental Military Marching Band and that theme was "How Ya Gonna Keep 'Em Down on the Farm after They've Seen Paree?" My father sang that song to me as a child. He was a cook of General Pershing's staff in World War I in France.

David Dye: Wow. So a lot of signficance to that.

JS: It was a haunting melody and I always sang it as a child, a teenager, and I began to discover the songbooks, I would say, in my 20s, and then I realized the significance of the song. It was the very first civil rights composition ever written. That's how I feel about it and it was the theme song of the African American soldier in World War I.

DD: So as Joe turns to the piano, we're going to hear "How You Gonna Keep 'em Down on the Farm."

Joe Sample performs "How Ya Gonna Keep 'em Down on the Farm After They've Seen Paree"

DD: Joe Sample is playing live for us today on the *World Cafe* and this is music that is on his new album called *Soul Shadows,* which features him pretty much as you're hearing him today—at the piano playing a number of compositions that go back to the first part of the century from jazz traditions. It's interesting—and I know there's a Scott Joplin piece on here—how formal those pieces are at the time and how music moved through that era.

JS: At that particular time, I was amazed at what I call the harmonizing of the Tin Pan Alley concept of music, which was all based on the classical system of harmonies.

DD: Strong left hand, strong bass line and all these things, that in particular, real two-handed piano playing.

JS: The concept of music at that time, going from the beginning of the rag era during the 1890s, all the way to the bands of the Clef Club . . . I believe that the New York society and that the high society elite organizations all along the East Coast had gotten into dancing. Basically, the white folks of that era decided that it was actually a very nice and wonderful thing to move their bodies in a similar fashion to the black dancers in Harlem.

DD: And actually people do forget that the popular music of the era was jazz. It was--- I mean, Tin Pan Alley and then the influence of jazz. It's funny, you talk about dancing, and I've just gotta ask you--- This is one of my favorite compositions of all time; the "Jitterbug Waltz." Talk about the significance of Fats Waller. I'd like to have you talk about the musical significance, because I see him as a really strong personality figure.

JS: Well, when I listen to the stylings of Fats Waller, I detect right away that he was a very, very musically superior individual with great skills, great talents, and I believe that he developed all of the other—his show-business attitude—because he wanted to survive in a world where he perhaps felt that just being the musician and a writer was not enough. I think that he was a born entertainer and he demonstrated that. He was an awesome singer and I do believe that even Ray Charles learned from Fats Waller what soul singing was all about. He came out of his father's church in Harlem. He was the organist in his father's church. So he was just an amazing player and I describe him as a Formula-One piano player.

DD: Aren't there some recordings of him playing jazz on a pipe organ?

JS: Yes, there are. Yes, there are many, many and I have seen footage of him once and I have heard audio of him where he was playing the piano, he was singing, and he was telling jokes at the same time—an amazing individual.

DD: I'm not going to ask you to tell me jokes.

JS: Please don't.

DD: But can you do "Jitterbug Waltz" for us?

JS: Yes.

Joe Sample performs "Jitterbug Waltz"

DD: Fats Waller's "Jitterbug Waltz." [A] really nice version played today by Joe Sample, and that's one of the piano compositions you will find on *Soul Shadows*, his new disc. When you started out playing with the Jazz Crusaders, your instrument was the piano and as the band evolved, you moved over and started playing more electronic keyboards and actually today's music people don't talk about playing piano, they talk about playing keyboard. How do you feel about that transition now and what are your feelings about those various electric pianos that were available, things like the Fender Rhodes and--- I don't know what else you played. Did you play the Wurlitzer?

JS: Yes. I played the Wurlitzer. I never went into the synthesizer world because of the lack of resistance in the keys and there was no way I was going to undo basically 30 years of trying to learn how to play the piano. The advent of the keyboards came about because the life in the world of the piano player was completely ridiculous. The pianos that I encountered throughout the jazz clubs of the United States as a Jazz Crusader during the 1960s were a joke. I believe we all welcomed the advent of the electric piano in the late 60s.

DD: So in other words, it was a necessity—a boon—in that way. But it also really changed the sound of music. Clearly, the sound of the Crusaders didn't change because you changed keyboards. You meant you changed the sound of what the band was about. I've heard you talk about a little bit when you were just introducing this album [about] how important it is to go back and look at past music. A lot of "jazz" has really gotten away from jazz. If you listen to what they call the "soft jazz" radio stations nowadays, you'd be hard pressed to see any of the elements that we considered jazz, including, in some cases, improvisation.

JS: If you listen to the Crusaders—the *Crusaders 1* and all of those albums in between all the way up to *Streetlife* and maybe *Rhapsody in Blues*—I look at that as a very, very wonderful and incredible period that I now just describe as the Wild West in all forms of music, because [we] were constantly hearing something that we had never heard before. What I hear in all forms of today's music, which seems to be the downfall of today's music, is that it is all under the control of those who insist that formulas are used. Once we have gotten into formula, then the incredible age of American music—all forms of American music—have actually come to an end.

DD: Now relate that a little bit to what you see as the mission of this record. It's just wonderful to hear you talk about these players, their artistry, in a lot of cases, forgotten.

JS: Well, the significance of their music--- First of all, I believe that the music of the first half of the twentieth century is the most important period because, without what they did, no one in the middle of the century or the rest of the century would be doing what they did at that particular time. We have become so terribly distant from the origins of American music. Again, I hear whining men. I don't hear men singing anymore. I don't hear men singing or telling stories that would interest another man. The whole game of music has turned into a tremendous soap opera. I hear that everywhere. It all has to do with personalities that are capable of being videotaped. I believe that the younger generation today has actually lost the ability to hear and to feel. They now use their eyeballs to detect what music means and when they say "music," they have visual images that they relate to music.

DD: Joe Sample is our guest today and I'm going to let you pick another piece to do.

JS: Well you know what? That's right. I did some Fats Waller. You know what I'm going to do? I'm going to run through--- This particular piece isn't really on the album, but it is one of my favorites and it was one of the most incredible periods of Harlem. It was during the Harlem Renaissance. The rent parties were the social life of Harlem and all the musicians converged to the rent parties during the wee hours of the morning or the late night, and if you wanted to work in Harlem, you had to be able to play this particular hit song, "Carolina Shout" by Mr. James P. Johnson.

Joe Sample performs "Carolina Shout"

DD: James P. Johnson's composition as played by our guest today, Joe Sample; "Carolina Shout." Now that would've been from the 20s?

JS: The 1920s. I've heard recordings of Harlem bands at street parties, at parks and that was a hit during the 1920s. Yes.

DD: Boy, beautiful, beautiful song. It's kind of self-effacing, this album, in a way that you are really concentrating on other people's styles over the years. I would be remiss if we didn't--- There's one element of your career that I know our listeners are really going to find interesting, and that is the work you did over the years with Steely Dan as one of the real signature players in the Fagen and Becker stable of people, working on their albums. Was that a rewarding part of what you do, was it a creative part for you? Or was there—one wonders how they made the records—a lot of control into your parts that would go on from them?

JS: Steely Dan would record the same song numerous, numerous times and from one recording session to the other. I never really knew if I was going to be on the final release or not. And basically, they knew when it was right and they knew when it was wrong. What they needed help with was, "Why is it right and why is it wrong?" If they had had that expertise in the studio with them at the time—and it was actually sitting there, but they never requested anyone to address it. Because it was like, "Well, if we don't get it today, we'll bring in another band tomorrow." Now there's one way to address it, but I knew what the problems were and unfortunately, they spent a lot of money. The musicians made out; they really helped to support us, but they spent a lot of money in the creation of the recording.

DD: It's interesting how that all came out in those recordings. You've got a number of your compositions on this. Do you want to maybe finish up with one of yours?

JS: Yes. I probably would like to play "Spellbound" for you, a very meaningful recording in my life. This recording signaled the end of the nightmare of the 1980s. "Spellbound."

Joe Sample performs "Spellbound"

DD: A solo version of "Spellbound," Joe Sample, our guest today on the *World Cafe*. I'm sorry, it's my job not to let statements like that just hang. Tell me about the end of the 1980s, what you meant by that.

JS: In 1980 I was very happy about what was going on in my life. In that same year, a major corporation came in and bought ABC Records, and when I finally went to the offices of this corporation, I realized that I was not in the music industry anymore, I was in the marketing industry. And by 1983, I was being told by everyone around me that I could not do what I had been doing. By 1984, I was beginning to lose my confidence. I fought very, very hard for two years to regain my confidence. I look at it as the worst period of my life. I was out of the contracts. By '88 I was recording with Tommy Lipuma and Warner Brothers. At the end of '88 into '89, the *Spellbound* album was proof that I had not lost anything, and I was amazed that that sort of pressure on me actually resulted in me losing my confidence in myself, which was unbelievable because I knew that in order to survive I must be very confident in myself. I lost it for nearly two years, but I certainly proved them wrong, and I was right with the *Spellbound* album.

DD: What a lesson for people about the effects on performance, on one's confidence. What an amazing little lesson. It's terrible that you had to go through that.

JS: I was being told, in 1982, that black music was finished. I just looked at people and I said, "This is a dream. This is a nightmare. How could that be possible?" They were telling me that country and western was in, pop was in, black music was out, and, "We have a contract with you," and "We will just figure out the best way of how to get out of this, but you know, black music is over, finished, and done." You know, that was when everybody vanished and Motown finally gave out. In '80, what was it, '87, Berry Gordy finally sold the Motown label. No one, no one knows that. Amazing.

DD: I can't believe anybody would make a statement like that. It's also interesting to me, because however one wants to define your music, it's always had an amazing appeal to everybody.

JS: [laughs] Well, there's no such thing as black music!

DD: Exactly!

JS: But, you know, it was a backlash. This is the most interesting thing that I know that no one knew—I was in the middle of it, and disco was blamed on African Americans. It actually came out of Munich, Germany, with Giorgio Moroder and I had a conversation with Gorgio about six, seven years ago, and I asked him, "Did you know that African Americans were blamed for the advent of disco?" and he said no. He created it with Donna Summers for the German market. What really was very, very amazing—the backlash began in Chicago. I believe it was Wrigley Field. The disc jockey from the big rock station there had a "burn your disco records" rally, and what it was, it was, "Burn your R&B records," and that was the beginning of the end of the R&B that we know. Right at the same time that they were killing R&B, rap was peeping over their shoulders.

DD: And now look at where we are.

JS: Look at where we are today.

DD: Joe Sample. Thank you very much for talking with us today.

JS: All right, thank you very much.

DD: Joe Sample, our guest on the *World Cafe.*

2004

MAVIS STAPLES

POPS STAPLES PASSED AWAY IN THE YEAR 2000. He was the funky guitar-playing patriarch of The Staple Singers, along with his high aching voice. In this interview from 2004, we get a look at what life was like inside the Staples family from Pops' most famous daughter, Mavis. She's the voice we all remember from "I'll Take You There." Mavis talks about touring with Dr. Martin Luther King Jr. in the South during the civil rights movement and more. I was fascinated throughout. At the time, she had recently released a new album called *Have a Little Faith in Me.* Mavis's career has been in and out of gospel music with The Staple Singers. I asked her about growing up singing and whether the church really was the first place she sang.

Mavis Staples: Everybody came out for the choir, all my friends. But you see, when I started, I was too tiny. I was too small. I was eight years old, you know, and the choir—my older sister Cleotha and my brother Pervis—they were in the choir. See, we had a junior choir.

David Dye: Aha.

MS: Yeah, you had to be a teenager, you know, to be in that choir. So when we started singing, I didn't get a chance to sing in the choir, and I've always regretted that, you know, because that was always what I wanted to do. You know, I did a *Cosby Show*, and he was--- We were in church, and so they had a choir singing behind me, and Cosby didn't want me to have a robe, and I said, "No, man, I want a robe like everybody else! If I'm going to be in the choir, I'm going to be in the choir!" So they had to get me a robe. That was my only time, David, to sing in a choir---

DD: [laughing] Did you spend a lot of time---

MS: ---out of all of these years!

DD: [laughing] That is so funny. I'm sorry; I just find that hard—well, you spent a lot of time in church, though, right?

MS: Oh, I was in church.

DD: Right.

MS: I was in church from a kid. Every Sunday we'd go to Sunday school and then 11:00 service. You know, we came up in church, and then when Pops started us singing, you know, this is what he taught us; gospel songs. So I've just---It's just been my life, you know, minus the choir.

DD: [chuckling] Right, right. Well, you know, the other thing I was kind of curious about, because Pops moved to Chicago, but did you all ever go down to Mississippi? Did you go visit?

MS: Oh, man, yes. My sister Yvonne and I--- You know, it came a time when my mother and father just had too many children, and they couldn't keep us in shoes, you know? So at a time, they would send Yvonne and me down to Mississippi with my grandmother. And we went to school there, and in the summertime we'd come back to Chicago, during the summer. But we had some grand times, and I feel very fortunate that I had that experience. And then my grandmother was really churchy. She had Yvonne and I going to church maybe three times out of a week, you know? And on Sundays we had--- I don't know where that started, but I guess it started down there. Yvonne and I would have to wait [while] my grandmother would invite the pastor over for dinner.

DD: Aha.

MS: [chuckling] And we'd have to wait until the pastor finished eating, and sometimes, he just didn't look like he was going to quit! You know, so, you know me. I'd sneak in there and grab me a chicken wing, piece of cornbread, and run back to the bedroom. But those were the really, really good times that we had in Mississippi.

DD: Well, the way you described that music when Pops and you all started singing together, it was just--- He would play guitar and you all would sing, so it wasn't too far removed from that.

MS: That's right, that's right. And he taught us to sing the way his brothers and sisters---Our sound, you know, everyone's always said that we had such a unique sound, and that's Pops' family sound, you know? There were fourteen of them, seven girls and seven boys. So they *had* a choir, you know, but—

DD: Altos, basses, tenors, everybody!

MS: Everybody! [laughs] And he gave us the voices that they would sing and taught us some of the songs that they would sing and the way they sang them and, of course, you know, then Pops was playing the blues on his guitar.

DD: Absolutely, and the combination we know well. Pops passed in 2000, and we recently were hit with another great loss as Ray Charles passed away. Did you all work with Ray, or did you--- Were you friends over the years?

MS: Oh yes! Oh yes, oh—Brother Ray, anytime he was in Chicago, he would come to the house. He would tell my mother what he wanted for dinner. And he wanted some turnip and mustard greens, some hot water cornbread, and my mother was the best sweet potato pie-maker in the world.

DD: [laughs]

MS: You know, and Brother Ray started eating that sweet potato pie, he told Mama, he said, [imitates Ray Charles] "Sister, you know, we could start a franchise with this sweet potato pie. We could start a franchise!" You know, he said, "We could make little ones, big ones, you know, and we could travel the world with these sweet potato pies!" She would put coconut in her sweet potato pies, and he loved that. And he would just be patting his feet, you know, [chuckles] under the table. I'd say he was at our home maybe three times over the years, yes.

DD: Wow. And Ray's music, of course, is straight out of gospel, so . . .

MS: *Straight* out of gospel, *straight* out. That's the most soulful man in the world. I mean he is the epitome of soul.

DD: Indeed.

MS: Brother Ray Charles. And we are going to miss him, but we are just so grateful—like he *and* Pops, we have their music, where we can listen to it and smile, and I'm sure Brother Ray and Pops--- Brother Ray is on the piano, Pops is on his guitar, walking 'round heaven, spreading' the news.

DD: I would like to hear that.

MS: [laughs] Yeah! Yeah!

DD: I would like to hear that. Now, you won a Grammy back in 2003 for a duet you and Bob Dylan did on *Gotta Change My Way of Thinking*. And I've been reading up on you. Is it true that at one point Bob Dylan asked Pops if he could marry you?

MS: [giggles]

DD: I heard that.

MS: [laughs] Well, well I guess I have--- I cannot tell a lie. Yes, he did!

DD: Aha!

MS: He did. Mm-hmm. He told Pops. He just yelled it out! Everybody was--- We were doing a television show for Westinghouse back then, and all of a sudden he surprised me, you know, because he just yelled out, "Pops, I want to marry Mavis!"

DD: [*laughs*]

MS: You know, and Pops said, "Well, man, don't tell me, tell Mavis!" You know, and---But we were very close friends. We were teenagers together, and we met Bob when both of us were like nineteen; eighteen, nineteen years old. But Pops loved him too. We recorded maybe about seven Dylan tunes.

DD: Right, right, right. Early on, right?

MS: Yup, yup.

DD: Well, tell you what, why don't we let folks get an idea of what this new one sounds like and then we can talk a bit about what you've been up to. What do you want to start with?

MS: Let's start with "Have a Little Faith." That's the title of the CD, and this is a song that we feel is very much needed today. You know, people are down, and burdened down, and they—some people don't feel that they can make it through the next day, you know? But if you have faith and you believe, you can do it.

Mavis Staples performs "Have a Little Faith"

DD: And that's just the beginning, folks. Mavis Staples is singing live for us today, and that is the title track of the new album, *Have a Little Faith.* I would like to get your perspective, because I guess you were in your early 20s when you and the Staples traveled around with Martin Luther King, during the civil rights era. What was your impression--- I mean, was that the South that you knew well when you went traveling, or did you see things you didn't expect to see?

MS: Oh, yes. The South was everything that it is known to be now, back then [chuckles], you know? We had some run-ins, you know, but we weathered the storm. Pops taught us to not to start anything, but don't take anything that makes you feel less than who you are, you know? But back in the early 60s, we were down in Montgomery, Alabama, and this was really the best thing that happened to us, because it healed all of those wounds that had hurt us back then—you know, to meet Dr. King and to work with him. We were woken that night in Montgomery at 8:00, and so Pops called us. You know, he knew Dr. King was there in Montgomery. And he called us and said, "Listen, you all, this man Martin, Martin Luther King, he's here. He has church here and I want to go to his 11:00 service, and would you all like to go?" And we said, "Yes, we want to go." We all went to Dr. King's church, Dexter Avenue Baptist Church, and Dr. King was a young man. Ms. Coretta King was in the choir, and she was holding a baby—I believe that was Bernice—and after the service, Dr. King would stand at the back door and shake hands with all of the worshippers, you know, and I noticed he and Pops stood there and talked a while. So we got back to the hotel, Pops called us to his room and he told us, "Listen, you all, I really like this man's message. I really like what he's doing, and I think if he can preach that, we can sing it."

DD: Hmm.

MS: And we began to write freedom songs. Our first song was "March Up Freedom's Highway," and that was for the march from Selma to Montgomery. Then we wrote "It's a Long Walk to D.C., But I Got My Walking Shoes On." That was for Washington, D.C. And "When Will We Be Paid for the Work We've Done?" "I Challenge You Today," "Why Am I Treated So Bad." "Why Am I Treated So Bad" turned out to be Dr. King's favorite, and every time we worked with him, you know, we would sing first, and then Dr. King would speak, you know. And he would always tell Pops, "You know, Stape, you're going to sing my song tonight, right?" And

Pops would say, "Oh, yeah, Doctor, we're going to sing your song!" "Why Am I Treated So Bad." And Pops wrote that song from watching the news. There were nine black children, and they were called the Little Rock Nine. They were trying to segregate a school down there in Little Rock, and for months they could not board this bus; no one would let them board the bus. And eventually, on this day, the mayor, the president, the governor, everyone had given these children permission to board the bus. And watching on the news, just as they started to board, a policeman put his billy-club across the door. And Pops sit back in his recliner, you know, and he said, "Now, why are they doing that to them? Why are they treating them so bad?" And he wrote that song that evening.

DD: Hmm.

MS: We sang the freedom songs, you know, until we felt that the world was coming together, you know, and we made another transition!

DD: Yeah, I was going to say, the transition *into* those songs was one, and then you made at least *one* more, I'd say.

MS: Yes, we did! That was when "Respect Yourself" and "I'll Take You There" came. See, these were—we called [them] "message songs." So we began to sing—and then, we were singing these songs, you know, we always wanted to reach the youth. And so Pops said, "Listen, you all. I think if we get us a rhythm section, those children will hear that beat, and they will maybe hear what we're saying," you know? Because all these years we had just sung with Pops' guitar. And we got a rhythm section, and we recorded "I'll Take You There," "Respect Yourself," and these songs went across the board, you know, on the rhythm and blues stations. And all of a sudden, the church people wanted to put us out of church.

DD: Yeah, I was wondering about that.

MS: Yeah, yeah, they wanted to--- They weren't listening to the lyrics, you know? They just heard the Staple Singers on the rhythm and blues stations, and they just started saying, "Well, the Staple Singers are singing the Devil's music. They're going to the Devil." You know, but we had to do so many interviews explaining, you know, "I'll Take You There," we're talking about taking you to *heaven.* You know, "I know a place, ain't nobody crying, ain't nobody worried, ain't no smiling faces lying to the races." You know, so where else could that be that we're taking you, but to heaven?

DD: Mavis Staples is our guest today. Mavis, we talked about it—can you maybe do a version of "I'll Take You There" for us?

MS: Oh, sure. No problem.

> Mavis Staples performs "I'll Take You There"

MS: We have enjoyed hanging with David in his Cafe. We hope we're invited back again! David!

2004

TONY JOE WHITE

TONY JOE WHITE'S MUSIC IS FROM THE SWAMP. He is the real deal. He is best known for writing "Rainy Night in Georgia," and for his classic hit, "Polk Salad Annie." It's always a thrill to hear how some of the best-known songs came together, and we got to do just that in this interview.

David Dye: Tony Joe White is in the *World Cafe*'s studio today with his drummer Jack Bruno for a set of music that includes his best-known song, "Polk Salad Annie," and a number of tunes from the new album of duets that he recorded with female artists called *Heroines.* We'll start with this swampy performance of the song "Rich Woman Blues."

Tony Joe White performs "Rich Woman Blues"

DD: And that's the "Rich Woman Blues," as that begins our set today. Tony Joe White is here with us, and it's one of the women that appears on this album. In fact, if you're not singing with somebody, the songs . . . all seem to be about women in one way or another. What was the inspiration for doing this whole record?

Tony Joe White: About a year ago, my son Jody, who works with me and [has] been with me about seven or eight years-- websites and all that--- and then he kind of got into the studio end of it, and he came up to me and he said, "Have you ever thought about doing any duets?" And I said no. "Well, who would you pick if you did?" And I said, "Well, gosh, two or three hundred people out there, you know, that I'd love to hear." And he said, "Well, just start with girls that have recorded your songs and that you've worked with." And so these names just jumped out. Shelby Lynne, Jessi Colter, Michelle White, Emmylou, Lucinda Williams, and all of a sudden there were five and we went. And the songs were already kinda demoed and laid down, late at night, just--- it was only like one take, one very lucky album--- it was like, there was never no problem, you know, so I knew it was meant to be.

DD: Now, I ask all these songwriters about songwriting and how they do it, but you actually have a system. I mean, it may not be a system, but you do sit out there by the campfire and write when you get a chance, right?

TJW: I got--- I don't know if it would be a system, I doubt it would be that, because I haven't got anything in order--- but if I get a line on the guitar . . . then I'll usually go out by the river there somewhere, build a little fire, and sit with a few cold beers for two or three nights, and sometimes I have to come back to it a month later or whatever if it don't come, but I try to let it happen instead of pushing it, so I don't write many a year.

DD: Right. You've got Jack Bruno here on drums, and maybe you want to bring him in on a piece here?

TJW: Yeah.

Tony Joe White performs "Who You Gonna Hoodoo Now"

DD: Tony Joe White's playing live for us today, "Who You Gonna Hoodoo Now." Listening to you play that brings to mind a couple things I want to talk about. One of them is Lightnin' Hopkins, and I understand that it was a Lightnin' Hopkins record coming into your house that was pretty influential early on.

TJW: I was one of seven kids. There was five girls, two boys. I was youngest and he was oldest and Mom and Dad—all of them played guitar and piano daily on the porch . . . when we'd come in from the cotton fields or the river. So I heard music all of my life like gospel and a little country, you know, and then I was about fifteen years old and [my brother] brought home an album by Lightnin' Hopkins and it was just him, an acoustic guitar, and his foot, you know. I was fifteen years old man, and man, it just turned me completely around. And plus about fourteen or fifteen other teenagers around the river there--- we all got into it--- got into Hooker and the blues period from that. From him.

DD: He's influenced so many people over the years. A lot of people I talk to, they mention Mississippi John Hurt and they mention Lightnin' Hopkins and it's interesting.

TJW: I'd say he was probably my favorite guitar player of all the blues people, not to mention his singing, God. But they found out, you know, that I was a big fan of his and folks at Atlantic came out and we was in L.A. together. He was there recording and they invited me down to the studio to play acoustic guitar and a little harmonica on his album called *The L.A. Mudslide.*

DD: What was that like? That must have been great!

TJW: Oh man! It was like when I met Elvis. It was like when I met Tina Turner. It was just like meeting your heroes, you know. I was sitting in the studio. I had gotten there early, you know. I was *really* nervous about it and he come walking in with his wife and he had a paper sack with a wine jug in it and he just come walking on through the control room and walked by me and I was sitting there with the guitar and he said, "You going to play with me, boy?" And I said, "Yes, sir." Then I hit him with two or three of his little licks and he said, "All right, turn it on." So they turned the tape on and he never stopped. He did fourteen songs in a row.

DD: [laughs] Wow.

TJW: And when he got through he got up and shook my hand and said he enjoyed me--- my licks--- enjoyed my playing. We went into the control room and by then the wine jug was emptied so he took the paper sack and his wife held it out and a couple [of] these guys there in suits, they put ten one-hundred-dollar bills in the paper sack. And he folded it up and tipped everybody with his hat and out the door he went. No royalties, no paper work.

DD: That's amazing. The other thing I wanted to ask you about was the first time you got yourself a wah-wah pedal. How that changed things for you--- because so much of what you do is about going through that pedal.

TJW: You know, that is the pedal that was on "Polk."

DD: It is? This one here?

TJW: Mmhmm.

DD: Wow.

TJW: My drummer, at that time, in Corpus Christi, his dad owned a music store. He said, "Man we got a thing in, you need to come down and see how it sounds to you." He said, "It sounds pretty swampy, really." And I said, "Well, what is it?" And he said, "It's called a boomerang." And I thought it was something from, like, Australia or something, you know. But it's one of them things that's like harmonica that you just need a little touch of it here and there. You don't need it just rompin' all the time.

DD: It's funny you mentioned "Polk Salad Annie," and one of the things that always frustrates me about that song is right at the end of it you play a ferocious little lick--- wah-wah lick--- and it just seems like, God, where's the rest of this guitar solo? I want the extended version! [laughter*]* Did it go on in the studio?

TJW: No. It faded pretty well after that. There was probably another thirty seconds of it, but it's one of those things where when you're really into a groove in a song in the studio, it seems like you do something unreal at the end of a song and if you try to copy it later, it don't happen. But always, there's this little lick that pops up, you know. I think it's just the heat of the tune--- pulls it out of it.

DD: Well it's there. It's definitely there. If people know anything about Tony Joe White's career, they may know that you had a song before that called "Soul Francisco" that didn't really happen in the States, [but] happened in France. But then you were back in the States and you were just working in Corpus Christi or something when finally "Polk Salad" kind of broke?

TJW: Yeah, in fact, I was in Corpus just working in the club six nights a week there when I get a call from Paris, the disc jockey on the radio, and he says, "You have a top-three record in Paris, France." And I didn't even know how it'd gotten over there, you know. I was still playing for ten dollars a night in this club. So anyway, I'm doing interviews and everything [and] all of a sudden I take off and I'm in Paris. Just me and my foot and my wah and singing this song, which was about the hippie movement--- the flower children, you know--- and totally an American thing, you know--- it was like this outfit over here--- and all these people and I'm going, "I know they don't know what I'm talking about." And yet they were mouthing the words and moving the woman. I think it's because they felt what I was doing inside more than what I was saying because they've stayed with me through the years. France, Europe, and Australia, it's like some of our biggest sales worldwide are over there. But I think it's just if they dig you the first time and know you're real they stick with you.

DD: And the part about being real is something. If you go to Europe you see that all the time. It doesn't matter what kind of music it is. Be it a jazz artist from back in the day, they stay with people and it's really kind of great. Well I hesitate to ask, but is it possible to get a version of "Polk Salad?"

TJW: Yeah, we can do it if you want. I think we had about a fifteen-minute version of it last night. Didn't we in Baltimore? [laughing]

Tony Joe White performs "Polk Salad"

DD: Little "Polk," little more of that wah-wah at the end there. [laughing] The extended solo. Probably don't have to tell you that's Tony Joe White and if the hair on the back of your neck doesn't stand up then you're not a fan of that kind of guitar playing but, oh boy, it does it here. I'm trying to figure out if there's a thing, because I know you've worked with Elvis--- we're talking about--- there's sort of a southern connection here. And I'm wondering if that's important--- if you find a real connection with, you know, people who grow up in the same part of the country you did? I guess it'd be kind of natural to have it that way.

TJW: Yeah, I did. It was like when he did "Polk" in Las Vegas, he flew my wife and I out to watch him do it live and record it, you know, on stage. And we hung out for two or three days and backstage . . . he always liked guitar and wanted me to show him a little blues stuff and he said, "Man, I felt like I wrote 'Polk Salad'" and I said, "Well, when you sing it, it sound like it man," because he really got out on it. Yeah, it's a beautiful connection when you see a song like "Polk" and him do that and then Brook, Randy Night, and then Tina on the Steamy and things like that. I get off on that as much as when I'm recording it. Maybe more.

DD: Well I want to thank you, both you guys, for playing for us today. A real treat.

TJW: I had a good time, man. Real good.

DD: Tony Joe White is our guest, and we shall return in a moment here on the *World Cafe.*

2004

NEIL YOUNG

TODAY ON THE *WORLD CAFE*, A CONVERSATION WITH NEIL YOUNG ABOUT HIS LATEST WORK, *Greendale.* One of the things he did, as he put it together, was to try to start with a blank slate–a tabula rasa, if you will–trying to wipe out all of his success, all of who he was in the past, all of people's expectations, and even his own expectations of Neil Young. I asked him, to begin our interview, if he thought he was successful with that process.

David Dye: What I'm going to do is, in the intro to this piece, I'm going to set up, if you'll trust me to do so, the characters and kind of the plot to *Greendale* so we don't have to do that now because it will take more time.

Neil Young: Sure.

DD: And then we'll just begin with some questions.

NY: Okay. That sounds good.

DD: Neil, the further I've been getting into this *Greendale* project--- and further is the way to go--- [chuckles] there was the concert tour to begin with, the album, and now the film. And of course you can find out family trees and everything on the website and the whole thing. Neil, what I really want to do is kind of go back to the beginning of this because you've said some things about this that kind of fascinated me. One of them is this whole concept that you kind of went even beyond a tabula rasa, you kind of wanted to lose your Neil Youngness to begin with, like you know, kind of wipe out your success, your past works, people's expectations. To begin with, did you feel you were successful with that?

NY: Umm . . . well, you know I think I was pretty successful with it . . . as much as I had a lot of characters and I was able to speak through the characters instead of through my own direct voice, you know, so I think it was a big success in that way, a big success in many ways. It was liberating to be able to write songs through characters and have dialogue and be able to tell a story. It seemed like I broke through to something else with it.

DD: The characters are pretty rich. The other part about the beginning is I'm curious as to what kick-started the characters' view. Who was first and how did they grow from that?

NY: Well I think it . . . at first, you know, when I first started writing the songs the first characters that showed up were Grandpa and Jed Green. But then right away Sun Green showed up and she's been on--- she was born from an idea that I had that it would be nice if one of these young pop stars that sell so many records and get so much airplay and TV time and is on *Entertainment Tonight* and all these publicity shows and everything--- and instead of doing, you know--- I realize this is a rather idealistic thought--- but instead of doing scandal-based advertising, if they would use some of their clout with the media to actually speak out on things that matter to young people like environmentalism and fairness and truth.

DD: Do you identify a lot with her or--- I hate to be ageist about this--- but I kind of put you in the grandpa mold.

NY: Oh yeah, well yeah, it's pretty easy to do that.

DD: [laughs]

NY: Yeah, I kind of put myself in the grandpa mold by myself there.

DD: Well, a lot of that has to do with, you know, resistance to change. Things we have heard from you before.

NY: Yeah, yeah. Well you know, I'm in all the characters but I think anybody that writes a book, you know, a little bit of the characters are in the author. It's kind of the way it works.

DD: Now, as you went along, there [are] some characters and there [are] some parts of the song like "Officer Carmichael" where you go back and you attend the funeral and we find out things about his life, you know. He becomes a pretty rich character. You talk about how you would write some of the lyrics to these songs, like driving over to the studio and stuff. Did you go back and revisit some of the characters as you went along?

NY: Uhh, not really. I never looked back doing this. I never went back to see what was happening. What happened with Carmichael I think is that you know after the incident with Jed and getting stopped there by Carmichael for speeding . . . I wondered who Carmichael was. So the next song, you know, I opened myself up to finding out who he was. So we delved into it even though his character was already gone and there was not going to be any more future for him, but it felt right to really treat him like a human being and like a regular guy instead of dismissing him as a stereotype.

DD: Cop stereotype. Did, um, when you went to do the film, did any of the characters like expand upon themselves? I mean, they must have.

NY: Yeah, yeah. They all grew a little bit more. I mean, the film pretty literally tells the story that's told on the record because the soundtrack for the film is the record. So the whole thing is one and there's no additional dialogue or anything. But during the instrumental passages, a lot of things are revealed that we introduced basically to kind of give some background on the characters and the ambiance of Greendale.

DD: One of the things . . . I think flows from the music and the tone of the music is kind of the real literal imagery on the film, and on the stage show for that matter. Real simple sets, simple--- you've described it as kind of like a high school play and I loved that because it makes a lot of sense to me.

NY: Yeah, well you know, I think high school plays are--- it's a--- I don't think anybody ever really thought of it as an art form before. That's unique [in] and unto itself, but I think it really is. I mean, these kids putting on these productions at school, they have limited budgets. They build the sets themselves and they're all very earnest and a lot of the students write their own plays and they perform these plays and they really get into it and it's very, very meaningful to them, a lot of the things that they're doing. I found that to be very refreshing. Instead of a career move, they were actually doing what the form called for.

DD: Right. Well, you know, in the past I've seen you as kind of this artistic speedboat driving across the lake with albums coming out in your wake and you're on to the next thing. This is a little different. You really seem to be spending some time on this. What about the story has been so rich for you?

NY: Well, it's a story that works. First of all, the reason that I'm able to continue doing this for so long--- I mean we're into the seventies now on the number of *Greendale* shows that we've done around the world.

DD: Wow.

NY: It's been all around Europe, it's been around Japan, Australia. It's been around the States once--- now is the second time through--- we're just really giving it a reprise. It's the music. A lot of the music is based in, you know, old electric guitar blues themes and it's based on a kind of a Jimmy Reed sound. It has a depth and simplicity. Repeated plays are rewarding. Instead of playing something that is technically complex--- over and over again for eighty shows would be really boring. But playing something that's simple over that amount of shows, it just keeps developing. And the music just keeps growing and it's all very simple and straight ahead and some nights the groove is bigger than other nights. It's all about where you are and who's listening and who isn't and what's going on and so the music has been the richest thing that has kept this going. It's just been a lot of fun to play the songs.

DD: Well, speaking of that, when you first set out last summer, it was before the album had actually come out so you were actually playing for audiences who had no concept of what this was to begin with.

NY: Right, that was a little bit hairy for a while there.

DD: Yeah. But I think in some ways you're rewarding people by coming back this second time.

NY: Well, you know I had to convince everybody that it was all right to do it again. No one wanted to do it again. None of the promoters wanted to do it. The booking agents--- no one wanted to do it. And I said, "You're just locked in a box, folks. I mean, you can't see what's going on here." This is a play. I mean this is a play that tells a story. And plays are different from concerts. People can see a concert and they see it and they hear it and that's great, you know. Now you go see another concert and if the guy comes around eight months later playing with same band playing the same songs, you're really going, "Well I heard that. I saw it and it was cool." And if you really loved it you might go back and see it but why is he doing it again? With this, there was so much in it and so many things going on at once that, especially without even knowing the music, the people would look at it and then afterwards I get the reaction from people that, "Wow, there was so much in that and I didn't even know what you were doing and I didn't realize what was going on. I have to see it again."

DD: Right, Right.

NY: And people said that to me time and time again, they'd say, "I really want to see this again. Are you going to do it again? Where's the next shows, where's your itinerary? Where can I go to see it again?" And people are fanatical about it to the point where, you know, I've got more reaction to *Greendale* then I got from anything I've done in the last twenty years . . .

DD: Wow.

NY: . . . and it was real reaction. It wasn't, you know, reaction from press and magazines and things like that. It was people. So I knew that there was an audience out there that would come and see it again. And I also knew that it was a play. It developed into a play instantaneously as soon as we took it on the road in West Palm Beach, Florida, about . . . whenever it was we started. I mean it was a good six or eight weeks before the record came out but we started playing the show and people were, you know, in shock looking at this thing because they had no idea and they never heard the songs before. But thanks to the fact that there was a stage play, they could sit there and watch it. But they came to a concert to enjoy my music and maybe relive their youth and go through all kinds of changes with their kids and celebrate whatever our music means to them. And instead of getting what they thought they were going to get, they ended up seeing a stage play of totally new music, and then we'd come out, of course, at the end and play a selection of other songs, but the people were kind of in a shock at first. Some people were mad at me and were yelling at me to play "Powderfinger" and play this and that, but I just had to block it out and just keep on going, realizing that, you know, I know what I'm doing and they're just not there yet, but they will be. And now when we do the show, I mean, people are interested in the story. They've heard about it, they know about it and they want to see it, either for the first time, or see it again, or see it for the fourth or fifth time. So, it's that kind of a thing, you know.

DD: Well, a lot of this has--- I mean, I want to go back to one of the first things of this whole concept of reinventing yourself. Going back and the challenges--- You go to a new town, here's something nobody knows anything about and you get an honest reaction. You get what you're going to get. Which would have been like, I guess what it was like, in the early days when you started out. Did Buffalo Springfield ever tour in that way in that you would have got in that kind of a situation back then?

NY: Well, Buffalo Springfield never had any hits, so it was hard for us to go out and play our greatest hits. Almost everywhere we went people were hearing a lot of our songs for the first time.

DD: Right.

NY: And that's what music is all about . . . playing your songs, especially the new ones that you have, for people who want to hear them. And then everyone relates to the song and if the song is a good song the crowd is in tune with it. Then everybody gets off and they have a good time and it's a good experience, and then whatever. If there's a record they go out and pick up the record or they listen to it on the radio or whatever. And that's what makes the world go round as far as I'm concerned as a musician. Playing songs that are fresh and new, that relate to something that's actually going on in the world or to some personal thing that people can relate to, that's what I do. So, the very idea that I would be letting some people down by not playing all my old songs is counter to everything that made me who I am today and it's counter to everything that I believe in. So, the only thing that it fits into is kind of an *Entertainment Tonight* mentality or a *People* magazine mentality of, "Well, stars are supposed to play their hits."

DD: Right.

NY: You know, I don't fit into that. I never tried to fit into it. I'm just not there.

DD: Right. And now the film. If we could just talk a little about the transition of this whole story to film, I mean, absolutely the music is central. It is the film, but this is, shall we say, the best realized of your oeuvre as a director and it must be great- -- you kind of wrote a script for yourself this time which is something . . . you were resistant to doing, maybe, in the past.

NY: No, I haven't been able to do that until now and it came out of the music and the music telling the story. That was the script and so I was able to take the film and just put the pictures to the story and add the characters in, and I think one of the biggest plusses for me in the whole thing is that I'm not in it and that I don't have to lip-synch and fake that I'm singing. I mean, it doesn't work for me. I've done it and I tried to get into it and it just always felt like, "Oh God, what am I doing?" You know? Who are these people?

DD: A lot of artifice in that. I understand that you are continuing Sun Green's kind of echo vision that you are traveling around by bio-diesel now.

NY: Yeah. The whole tour is powered by--- we got seventeen diesel vehicles being powered by bio-fuel and different mixtures depending on the temperature and stuff of the surroundings, but sometimes we are running on 100 percent bio-diesel and it's quite rewarding. We have a, you know--- The tour does a lot less damage to the environment than other tours and it's making a point that if you have a diesel-powered automobile you can use bio-diesel in it and reduce your emissions by up to 80 percent and not damage the ozone layer. Especially in the summertime, you can use what is called B100, which is like 100 percent bio-diesel. And if the temperature is above freezing or whatever you can use this stuff and you just don't do any damage. So if somebody's got an SUV or big truck or whatever with a diesel engine in it, they don't even have to convert it. They just put the stuff in it and away they go.

DD: Where do you load up with that much vegetable oil?

NY: Well, it's not vegetable oil. Bio-diesel is--- part of it is vegetable oil, but it's a mixture of things and they're all basically organic, you know, renewable fuels that don't harm the atmosphere and really it's a renewable fuel cycle that doesn't damage the earth. Things that are grown by American farmers--- I mean it seems so obvious to me that it's a great way to go rather than destroying the Alaskan wilderness to dig holes and find more oil. Why don't we just grow it?

DD: Absolutely.

NY: And, you know, people can go to work doing that. A lot of farmers are out of work and our government pays farmers not to grow vegetable oil so we can keep the price high, you know, so there [are] a lot of things. I'm just doing this to make an example for people who want to make a change that--- hey, you can make a change right now. You don't have to wait for vehicles to make a change. If you have a diesel-powered vehicle or a truck or an SUV or a, you know, a Mercedes or a Volkswagen that has a diesel engine in it, you can run on biodiesel and you can get biodiesel almost everywhere. You just go on the web to biodiesel.com and find out where you can get it and, you know, you can store it in your backyard. You can get a 150-gallon tank or something and put it there and have it delivered, 500 gallons. You don't have to have a special permit because it's not like petrol. It doesn't blow up. It's just, you know, if you dump [it] on the ground it's not going to hurt anything. It's a much better way to go. It's alive, you know, it's like we just grew it. It's not like dead stuff we sucked out of the earth from way down in there and brought it up and then it destroys everything it touches and harms the atmosphere. It's a different way of looking at it. So I'm hoping that some people hearing this--- if one college student has a Volkswagen . . . or they're thinking of buying a Volkswagen and now they decided to get a diesel because they went on biodiesel and want to be a more conscious citizen of the planet Earth, then that's a good thing. That's all I'm trying to do is try to illuminate that there [are] alternatives that are available today.

DD: Neil Young, the *Greendale* concert stage show continues across the country and it's kind of a rolling, city-by-city release of the film that goes along.

NY: Yeah, that's how we're doing it because, you know, in Philadelphia I think you're playing "Sun Green" at the station, but I think there aren't many stations playing it so we don't have any other way to get the message out there other than continuing to do the show and introducing the film as we go around the country. And usually the film follows us into these areas we play and I'm just trying everything I can to make sure it gets out there and that people hear about it. And I hope I'm not wrong but I think your station is playing this record.

DD: We're actually playing "Falling from Above" and "Beat the Rain," so . . .

NY: "Falling from Above" and "Beat the Rain"?

DD: Yeah.

NY: Okay, well my guys were wrong. Anyway, "Sun Green" is the one that we have out now but I appreciate you playing whatever you play. It's great. And we just--- you know, it's hard to get on the radio these days for me. I don't play the kind of music that is generally on the radio so, you know, things have changed. I've gone one way, radio's gone another way, but I appreciate all the help that I can get from you guys and, you know, I just like what I'm doing so I'm going to do it until I'm tired of it.

DD: Great. Well, I think it's really remarkable that you've kept with this project so long and I think you've got the right instincts about letting people soak in *Greendale* for a while because it's very rich and I--- Frankly, we haven't really touched on a lot of the different themes that are in here. There are a lot of family themes and things that are really, really important, like any great story, so I appreciate that you put these characters in and put this together.

NY: Well thanks, you know, it's been very rewarding for me. I got the film. It's gotten excellent response from all the critics and everything. Much better than we ever thought we'd get on a thing like this. It's really a lo-fi film. Kind of guerrilla film, if you will, but it's got something going for it and I'm just glad that some people are enjoying it and it's really fun to get into something different and have something out there like that.

DD: All right, Neil, thanks so much for talking with us.

NY: All right, take care. Thank you.

2005

AL GREEN

AS YOU CAN TELL FROM THIS INTERVIEW, I AM A BIG FAN OF AL GREEN. Few singers have his expressive style and range. His ability to hold tension in a vocal line and then explode is, well, as Al himself says, it's kind of sexy. Although I had been warned that Al was not an easy interview to keep on topic, on this day we had no problem. I just wish print did justice to the swoops and hollers in his speaking voice that mimic his singing.

David Dye: We have a chance to talk with one of the great singers of our time today. Al Green has been singing pop music again after concentrating on his Memphis church and gospel music for years. He originally turned to gospel after a tragic incident in 1974 where a former girlfriend poured hot grits on the singer and then killed herself in his house. He also turned away from working with the producer of all his hits, "Tired of Being Alone," "You Oughta Be with Me," "Let's Stay Together," on and on. That is Willie Mitchell. His new album, *Everything's Okay*, is the second for Blue Note that Willie Mitchell has returned to produce. And I started the interview by commenting that I thought that Al was singing with more abandon on this new album.

Al Green: Well I mean I had to get an understanding of what I was doing and the purpose for my life. I was confused because I was a minister and then again I was confused because I was singing, [singing] "Take me to the river/ Wash me down," you know, and I was trying to say, well okay now, well some people say, "Well you can't sing that because you're a reverend now," and I'm going like "Yeah, but I said cleanse my soul / Put my feet on the ground," and they was kind of like saying, "Well I guess ain't nothing wrong with it, but he's an oddball isn't he?" So I was called an oddball. [laughs] These people are going like, "He's kind of weird but I guess 'Take me to the river/ Wash me down/ Cleanse my soul/ Put my feet on the ground' do go along with the ideology of the Christian teaching that we're talking about, so--- but it's the way he does it and then he's got those little hips up there he's shaking and carrying on," and some of the women said, "Heh I tell ya" and so the men would say--- [clearing throat] and so the women would have to calm down. And yeah, like that, yeah.

DD: Yeah, so it's all about the falsetto. It's about the way you sing them?

AG: Well it's--- you know, our music is sensual, it's just kind of sensual. It's, you know, like the people saying yesterday, "I've got three kids and I know good and well two of them [laughs] was conceived to your music." And I'm like "Ahhhhhhhhhh! What did you say?" And I mean, he says, "Al, I mean the music is--- you know, you be with your lady, the fireplace going, you put on, hey, you know, 'For the Good Times,' 'How Can You

Mend a Broken Heart,' that 'Tired of Being Alone' stuff, and I want to hold--- take you in my arms and hold you--- I mean Al," and he says, "I just, I just, I just." I said, "Skip it, I got it. You just, you just, you just was *you*." And he said, "I'm afraid so," you know. So that's one. [laughs]

DD: You know, you mention those songs like "Tired of Being Alone," those old ones, those recordings, and these are so intimate and I'm curious as to how much of those and these new ones come out of your life.

AG: They come right out of the pages of your life. That's why my old lady says, "Al, don't tell the people everything." And then I'm trying to go like, "Baby, if you just be quiet they don't know what I'm talking about. I mean they don't know that I'm talking about the time I was talking to you at the bottom of the stairs." But she said, "Well just don't be so graphic, I mean, because, I mean, we got to have some type of life." I say, "Yeah, but I got to write about what's happening now with us today, because if I don't, I'm writing about something either in the past or something I don't know that's coming in the future. So I'm writing--- this is real time." And so she's saying like, "I love you." [laughs]

DD: Does it help your performance when you've written something? Because you wrote a bunch on this record.

AG: Yeah, and Willie writes, too, and he's so magnetic in getting these changes and this music choreographed and the horns and the violins got to go--- [sings melody] I'm going like, as the preacher would say, I'd say "Damn! What was that?" [laughs] He says, "Oh, you going to like it, you going to like it." So that's really, I mean, we're just ourselves in the studio. I mean, you know we can be ourself and write and compose. It's just things that's already happening in your life now. Yeah that's right. It's real time stuff, yeah.

DD: I want to play some of these performances for people. I want to do the performance of "Perfect to Me."

AG: Oh, that's a tasty one.

DD: This Mr. Al Green from *Everything's Okay.*

Al Green recording: "Perfect to Me"

DD: And that's "Perfect to Me," one that Al Green certainly gets a hold of on *Everything's Okay,* and we're talking to the Reverend Al Green today on the Cafe. You brought him up and you've been talking about him a little bit. Can you tell us about how you first met your producer, Willie Mitchell? You were already singing pop then, weren't you?

AG: Yeah, I was singing pop, but I was kind of like singing everybody's songs because I didn't have any songs of my own yet, because I hadn't been discovered [laughs] really. I had a song called

"Backup Train" that I cut with Paula James and Ted Majors in Grand Rapids--- course that's why I don't have a southern drawl to my accent because I was raised in Michigan. So I went to Texas. Willy Mitchell was hired for the band, "And I'ma hire this new kid Al Green, and he's going to come in and sing. Y'all work something out at three o'clock, we'll open the bar at ten and y'all do y'alls thing." And so when Willy went to the bar after doing a couple tunes with the band I got up and he says "Well go over the tunes with him," you know, so they started going over the tunes and I started to sing and Willy turned around from the bar and says, "Man! Boy, you got a voice and a half." And I'm going like, "Yeah, yeah right man. Yeah right, right, I just want to make the three hundred dollars." [laugh] You know, I mean like I heard him say that but I didn't like really believe it. And you know, like if you're living life you done heard it all before, you know, so you're kind of like, "Yeah, yeah, yeah right," but I didn't know I'd be with the guy 35 years later, so you know that's just the way life works, yeah.

DD: Now he helped you to discover what Al Green sounded like. Who were you trying to sound like back then?

AG: Oh man, I was sounding like, [singing] "I'm so tired of being alone/ I'm so tired," I was trying to sound like Wilson Pickett, James Brown, I was trying to sound like um--- whoever else was on the market, cause I didn't have no Al Green. I didn't know who Al Green was. So Willie Mitchell kept saying--- he kept cutting the tape off and running back to the beginning and says, "Sing like Al Green." And I'm going like, "Willie, I really appreciate it, but I don't know how Al Green is supposed to sound." He said, "Well, we going to cut until you do." So I got mad. I went outside. I took my Corvette, did donuts in front of the studio. Spin my wheels. [makes screeching noise] I left and I came back about two-and-a-half hours later and Willie starts smiling, says, "Mmm-hm, I knew he'd come back." The guy sitting by him said, "How'd you know?" And he says, "If he's got what I think he's got in him he'd come back." So I said, "Hey man, what about this dang song?" He said, "Don't scream and try to sing something you're not." And so I said, "Okay, just knock the song"--- he said--- I said, "I don't want to hear it. Just knock the song on." I said, "I'm not going to put no feeling in it, I'm not going to put no emotion in it, I'm just going to sing it dry." And so the song came on [and] I said, [singing] "I'm so in love with you/ Whatever you want to do/ Is all right with me." Like that. And . . . Mitchell stopped the tape and said, "That's Al Green!" And I'm going like, "Damn fool, that's hurting my ears!" [laughs]

DD: Well big kudos to him for making you do that, making you know you had that. Now you stopped working with him when you made the *Belle* album. Was that important to you? Did you prove something to yourself in producing that? A lot of people loved that record. It didn't sell as well as some others but . . .

AG: Right. Well, but I had to get out to experience things for myself, to learn things for myself. I had to get some wing space. I had to just kind of--- I need to know if I can do this or not. I built my own studio. I started cutting my own music. I couldn't find anybody to play the guitar, so I played the guitar on the whole *Belle* album. Because I couldn't--- Well you know Memphis is very, very organized and if you're not part of the organization it's going to be hard for you to find a bass player, it's going to be hard for you to find a drummer, it's going to be hard. So me and Reuben--- Reuben is a bass player. Fred Jordan--- he ran a studio. I got another guy, Bill Cantrell from Alabama, white guy, to build a studio and put it together for me, and we cut this song, "The Lord'll Make a Way," which was our first Grammy. And that was a shock to us. Our eyes were as big as bo-dollars because we'd been to the Grammys five times and we never won on "Sha-La-La." Michael and them was winning and we went again and then Lionel Richie and them was winning and after that it was a bunch of other folk winning, so Willie said he wasn't going no more, the hell with that. So you know the old man is, "The hell with it. C'mon, let's go home." And so I didn't know, so I went and cut this little song, "The Lord'll Make a Way," won a Grammy, and I'm going like, "What? That song didn't even sell as much as 'Tired of Being Alone' or nowhere nearly as [much as] 'Stay Together.'" And one of the guys at the Grammys, I don't know who this man was, was standing with his back to us and he said, "Maybe somebody's trying to tell you something." And I took that very seriously but he walked off real fast and I don't know which way he went in the crowd. It could have been an angel, I don't know. But I just heard that and then I know that Willie and I was made to be together, but I just needed to get out on my own. I was eighteen then. And I needed to get out on my own and talk to Francis and them and Juanita and all them other gals, and see what they were doing. And I didn't need Willie around. He's like a parent. So I kind of like--- that's right, like that.

DD: Yeah, you talk about that event--- also at the height of your stardom in the 70s there was a personal tragedy in your life and you at that moment went and formed your church, the Full Gospel Tabernacle in Memphis, and you began to turn away from secular music. Did you find peace during that period?

AG: That was the eight years I didn't sing any secular music at all. And I went to Jamaica, and I finally heard the people said, [with Jamaican accent] "Al, Al, you have to sing the 'Love and Happiness,' we want to hear the 'Love and Happiness,' man." And when I heard that I'm going like, "What do you know about love and happiness? What do you know?" I mean, come on man, this guy . . . he says, [with Jamaican accent] "Please, please, Mr.

Green, Reverend Green, whatever your name is. Please sing 'For the Good Times,' you know, you know, sing the 'Love and Happiness.'" And that kind of woke me up to all these people at this concert. It's 100,000 people out here, we're sitting out on a grass lawn that's surrounded by a fence that I see. I can look way over here and see people coming over the fence. [laughs] It's so many- -- it's 100,000 people out here and the police say, "Hey man, I can't run to every hole in this fence to try to keep people out of here." And so, I kind of woke up that . . . God created the whole world, and, "I also created 'Love and Happiness' and 'Let's Stay Together,' and created Sunday, but I also created Monday, Tuesday, Wednesday, Thursday, Friday, and Saturday."

DD: Amen to that.

AG: Yeah.

DD: You sang a little bit of "Take Me to the River" a little while ago, and on your recording of that you dedicated it to little Junior Parker. He was your cousin?

AG: He was my real cousin, for real, on my Mama's side.

DD: Did you see him perform? Did you know him well?

AG: I never got to see him perform. I got to meet him one time, and shake his hand, when I was little. But I never got to see him, like, take a guitar and perform in a club. I wished I could have. I never got to see Sam Cooke either. Otis Redding either. I really was too poor, I think, and then I was too young. I was like twelve or something so Daddy wasn't going to let us out of the house for nothing like that. Cause Daddy thought that was like, you know, that's worldly music, and we had a gospel group so, "What are you doing listening to it anyway?" So I got put out of the house for listening to Jackie Wilson's "Baby Work Out." [laughs]

DD: [chuckles] And you were . . .

AG: [singing] "Baby work out. Work, baby work . . . Honey work out. Ahhh." I mean, [laughs] Daddy said, "Yeah, while you workin' out, get out!" [laughs]

DD: Now wait a minute, you were in a group with your brothers, the Green Brothers. Did you get kicked---

AG: That's right!

DD: Did you get kicked out of that too?

AG: Well, when you get kicked out of the house, you get kicked out of everything.

DD: [laughs] Oh, okay.

AG: So I mean, hey man, I had to go live with Lee Vergis, who's a friend of mine that I had met that dropped me home, off home from school. And we started a little group practicing everyday at three o'clock in his living room. These four guys, Palmer James, Al Green, Curtis Rogers, and the tenor singer, um gee what's his name, would get together and sing these songs, [singing] "Moon river, wider than a mile," aw whatever man. I mean, you know, we just had this little group, you know. And so that's how I got to go to Battle Creek and meet this man going, [singing] "Money, who needs/ Just to live a life free and easy/ With toothbrush in my hand/ Let me be a traveling man/ Because I'm a road runner baby." And I said, "I kind of like that." And that was Junior Walker.

DD: Absolutely.

AG: And he'd get his horn and start playing that thing. And I said I'd get to scootin' and he'd get to playing that thing, [singing] "Don't want no woman/ To tie me down," I tell you. I said, "Boy, you better go along here," [singing] "I got to keep free baby, to rove around." I said, "Me, too, [laughs] whooo! You making me happy boy."

DD: Al Green is our guest. He's got a new album called *Everything's Okay*. Al, I thought we would play your version of "You Are So Beautiful," and how'd you pick that one?

AG: I love that. I didn't. Willie picked that one and that was his baby for the new album project from--- that was the first song that we cut. He always picks these songs that leads into another arena. And he says, [singing] "You are so beautiful." I says, "Uhh, ah, what are you talkin' about." He says, "I want you to sing it." I says, "Yeah, but a lot of folks done sung it." He says, "Yeah, but I want you to sing it. And say it. And be able to look at her and tell her, 'You're beautiful to me. I don't care if you're ten pounds overweight. You're beautiful to me.'" [She says,] "Well I haven't gotten my hair done yet honey I uh---" [He says,] "You're beautiful to me." [She says,] "Well I don't, I mean, I don't look how I know should I have a---" [He says,] "You are so beautiful to me . . . I don't care about anyone else--- to me."

HALL AND OATES

DARYL HALL AND JOHN OATES MET IN PHILADELPHIA when both of them had records out and they were promoting them on the record-hop circuit. When we heard they were available to do the World Cafe, we jumped at it and they seemed to really relish talking about their history and all the hits–"She's Gone," "Rich Girl," "I Can't Go for That," "Sara Smile," "Maneater," and so many more. We also got a chance to talk about their early days playing sessions for Gamble and Huff, and more. I started by asking Daryl and John where they grew up.

John Oates: Well, I was born in New York City, but I moved when I was four years old to a little town called North Wales, which is about 25 miles north of Philadelphia. Right after high school I came straight to Center City and that's where we met.

Daryl Hall: When I first moved to Philadelphia, even before I met John, I lived, actually, right across from Overbrook High School. I used to live [there] for a while. So, I got to know--- that was rock and roll high there, you know--- so I got to know all those people: Delphonics when they were still teenagers, and Three Degrees and all those people.

David Dye: I heard you cut a single with the fellow musicians from the band, being Kenny Gamble and Leon Huff.

DH: Yeah, that's how we started. When we first started, it was in that sort of dip period between the Bobby Rydell/Chubby Checker thing, and the beginning of what the world knows as the "Sound of Philadelphia." And so we were all part of that. I mean, it was a small group of people. I was a street corner singer, you know, like a lot of guys that were singing then. I won a talent show at the Uptown, and Kenny and Leon produced a record for me with a band I had called the Temptones.

DD: Now, John, what was the difference between the Masters, your band, and the Temptones?

JO: Masters was more of a combo, more of, like, a band with me singing, whereas Darryl's group was more of a vocal group with a backup band.

DH: We were more like a boy band back in the sixties, you know, dancing around and singing, well, like the Temptations, basically.

DD: Now, I know both of you spent time in the studio here in Philly. John, you were playing guitar, playing what?

JO: Well, I brought a tape down to the Record Museum, and the guys at the Record Museum liked the tape and they gave me the name of a guy named Bobby Martin who had a little office on South Broad Street, not far from the Shubert Building. Went down there, played him the tape and said, "We need an arranger, we want to make a record." He said, "Okay, sounds good, we'll do it." And, that's how I got involved with Gamble and Huff and that whole group, 'cause Bobby was one of his main arrangers.

DH: He arranged the first Temptones record, too--- did the string arrangements.

DD: And you did backups on--- for people like?

DH: Well, I used to be, you know--- I worked a lot out of Sigma. And, you know, I did everything. I was, sorta, on the B-team. I was just a kid. But I worked with all the same people: Norman Harrison, everybody, Roland Chambers, Earl Young, Vince Fontana.

DD: And one thing you really note from the people you name--- and this was true in Motown behind the scenes--- people didn't realize there was a black and white thing. It was not---

DH: Absolutely. Completely integrated, racially integrated. It was almost fifty-fifty, in as far as the studio musician thing went. But that, you know, if you look at any regional sound in those days, that's the way it was. You look at Memphis, you see Steve Cropper and Duck Dunn and all those guys. If you look at Motown, you see a white and black thing. It's much--- that's the way it was, you know. People don't realize that musicians are colorblind and that's what it's really all about.

DD: Now, *Our Kind of Soul* is really interesting because you are talking about contemporaries here. And, Thom Bell, there's a couple of Tommy's tunes on here. You did--- you do a version of [the Spinners' song] "I'll Be Around," which we're going to hear a live version of today. This song is so difficult to make your own because the vocals are really distinctive. The percussion track is like, right there; the hook is huge. And you didn't really avoid some of those things.

DH: Yeah. You know, I didn't--- we worked mostly from memory. We tried to not listen to the original recordings because I didn't want to be influenced. They're in my head anyway. We started--- most of these songs are, sort of, keyboard-driven because Kenny, Leon, and Tommy Bell, they're, you know, keyboard players and they wrote the songs mostly on piano. And we decided we were going to start with a rhythm section of being mostly acoustic guitars and right from doing that, you're changing the arrangement. Because when you generate a song from an acoustic guitar as opposed to gospel piano, or whatever, soul piano, it sort of changes the arrangement from the bottom. And then after that, we just said, "Let's try and take these songs as songs, forget about the performers, forget about the arrangements, and make them sound like songs that we would have written yesterday, and make them sound like Hall and Oates songs." And that was the concept.

DD: It totally works. Let's listen to this

live performance of the Spinners' classic, "I'll Be Around."

Hall and Oates recording: "I'll Be Around"

DD: That's "I'll Be Around," a live version from Hall and Oates. We're getting a chance to talk with Daryl and John today on the *World Cafe.* One of those things I found out during your live performance today, and actually going over the liner notes in here, John, is, your picks on here. One of them is "Ooh, Child," which is a great song, but I understand that goes way back to the beginning for you and Daryl.

JO: It actually has to do with the very fact that Daryl and I are together, in a way. As we spoke about earlier, we both had singles out with our respective bands. And there was a record shop in West Philadelphia at the Adelphi Ballroom, and we were both taken there to promote our records. You know, you would lip-sync your single, you know, for the local DJ whoever it was--- I guess it was somebody from DAS. And on the bill was Howard Tate and the Five Stair Steps. We were all sharing this little room upstairs and a big gang fight broke out. We basically ran out the back and that's how we met. We were both going to Temple University and we started hanging out. Then, eventually I joined Daryl's group as a guitar player.

DD: Tell me a little about recording, re-recording, this one.

JO: Well, "Ooh, Child," I just thought it was just a great vehicle for us to sing together. The way the vocals are structured, it's perfect for our voices. And I just felt it was an anthemic song that wasn't done as anthemically on the original. You know, it was very, very kinda linear, just a very simple song, very direct.

DH: And like a lot of songs, I changed all the words. The only song--- the only things that are the same lyrically are, "Ooh, child, things are gonna get easier, things are gonna get brighter." All the verses are completely rewritten. And we took out parts of the song. This is typical of a lot of the songs. We took out bridges, we'd add bridges. We change keys, change lyrics, all those kind of things--- all to make them ours. That's why we called it *Our Kind of Soul.*

Hall and Oates recording: "Ooh, Child"

DD: That's another one you'll find on *Our Kind of Soul,* the new album that Daryl Hall and John Oates have out. That's a version of "Ooh, Child." You guys have been doing pretty well on your own record label. The *Do It for Love* album did really, really well. I was thinking about, getting ready for this, and I was thinking, "Oh, well, we'll talk about comebacks." But your entire career has been built on comebacks. Atlantic Records drops you. You have, you know, a couple of hits at RCA. The hits sort of go away. You have *huge* hits. And then, now here, you've managed to do it again.

DH: Yeah, well, it's almost like, as you say, it's so, it's so part of our career that I wouldn't call it comebacks. It's the way we do business.

JO: If you really never go away, you never have to make a comeback. So, that's kind of how we are, I think.

DH: Well, you know, we have a very tenuous relationship with the record business. We started out here in Philly. Philadelphia is known for its shady business deals. I'll just leave it at that. So we saw it all from the beginning. It just, it affected the way we deal with the record business and we've always been very much mavericks. We do what we do, and we evolve at our own pace and our own rate and we don't really pay attention to what's going on outside of us. And sometimes that clicks big-time with mass audiences, and sometimes it doesn't.

DD: So you don't have that 'eureka moment' when you're working on an album in the studio and you go, "Oh my God, this is going to happen."

DH: No, because we might do our best work and other things that we can't control will keep it from being.

JO: The world may not be receptive to what it is that we are doing.

DH: It's not even the world. It might be because program directors don't want to do it. Or, the media doesn't feel like writing about us this week. You know, there [are] so many factors we can't control.

DD: I want to talk a little bit about--- because we're here in Philadelphia, because this is where we all came in--- about the trio of albums you made for Atlantic. You made one that was kind of a folkie album that didn't really do much. Then you made *Abandoned Luncheonette*, and you made *War Babies* using outside producers. One thing, if you know about Hall and Oates' career, is once you guys started producing yourselves, things started really happening in a big way. But you worked with two guys, Arif Martin and Todd Rundgren on *War Babies*, on those records. Would you say that--- was there anything helpful about that for you? Because you guys had been in the business awhile.

DH: That's two opposite sides of the spectrum in the world of production.

JO: Every time you work with someone, you gain something. You learn something. You learn what not to do, you learn what to do. You learn what works, what doesn't work. Arif was, and still is today, one of the consummate producers in music history.

DH: I would say him and Quincy Jones pretty much changed the face of music and have continued to do so. And they haven't lost a thing. We were so lucky to have worked with Arif in our first two albums. It enabled us--- it gave us a place to go that we could work with a Todd Rundgren and do something completely left field and still recover and keep on moving forward. So, I think Arif was a huge, you know, benefit and influence on us.

JO: And with Todd, we learned how to, sort of--- what I say "learned," I don't know, was to just like, not care, just to do what you want to do and basically go for whatever was in your head, no matter how cartoony it might be

DH: To be a bit more experimental and just let it happen.

DD: You know that *War Babies* is a--- record geeks just put that up there as a great album.

DH: A lot of people say that it's their favorite record. It isn't my favorite, but I can understand why it would be some people's.

JO: It was very adventurous and very experimental and we have that side to us, which, you know, I don't think maybe the public at large, if you're not a true fan and you don't go all the way back, may not know about us, and I guess that's--- but it's still there. It's always an element that's part of what we do.

DH: I would say it's Todd Rundgren, Hall and Oates, Tommy Bell and Gamble and Huff. That's the sound of Philadelphia.

DD: We're with you on that. *Abandoned Luncheonette,* a lot of loving care went into that one, with Arif and "She's Gone." Your version is just an amazing recording. When Tavares covered it, did you go, "Wow this is . . ." I mean, 'cause they used a lot of your arrangement, they used a lot of your stuff. Was that--- did it make you feel good about it or did you say, "Oh, shoot . . . we shoulda?"

DH: I think we had mixed feelings about it, you know. We were glad that we had a number one record. We were not glad that it wasn't us that had the number one record. We knew--- but at the time, you said you were on MMR, you know, what was called underground radio in those days, FM radio, was playing "She's Gone" a lot all over the country. And we were known for that song. And then Tavares made us known to the national black radio scene. In some ways, that may have paved the way for "Sarah Smile" because that was our first real single that broke on black radio. It was a process. I think the Chris Bond experience where we went to California and recorded out there, I think we made some really good music out there, but we were never comfortable. We never felt comfortable with the situation and working in California, being away from the East Coast. It wasn't right for us, but we learned a lot and we made some good music. And we met David Foster also out there, and we recorded with him. I think it was the record we made with David Foster, the *Ecstatic* album, where he turned to us in the middle of the program and he said, "You guys are producing yourselves," he goes, "what am I doing here?" That, you know, half jokingly and half not jokingly. And we said, "Yeah, we are." And that was really the step that we needed to take to get us to the *Voices* album.

DD: And as you went on through the 80s, you managed to take what was going on musically and make it work for you guys, in a big way. Daryl, I've heard you say you always wanted, you didn't want to be an obscure artist, you always wanted to be big. Well, there you go! There it happened.

DH: It happened. I wanted to be big because the only way you can have a life career is by being big sometime. I mean, you know, every career artist is a pop star at some point in his or her life. I don't care who you talk about. And, yeah, so it's something we had to go through and we needed to go through. It was a step that we--- we had to step up to that level and I'm glad that it happened. I don't know. It's one of those things--- you don't know why. I think part of it had to do with us producing ourselves. I think that was very important.

JO: We had hit our stride. We found a band that really got it, and really gave us the musical, kind of, backbone to lay our songs on. And it was the right sound for the time. The time was right for the music we were making. The music--- we were making the music that was defining that time.

DD: Absolutely.

DH: And, MTV happened.

JO: And MTV happened as well and we were right there in New York.

DH: And we rode that wave. And so it was really--- it was our time to get out to the masses of the world.

DD: You guys did a version of "I Can't Go for That" in a set we just heard. And that song, in particular, has gotten a lot of samples.

DH: Oh yeah. I don't even know how many at this point.

DD: Do you remember getting that groove in the studio?

DH: Oh, absolutely. I was sitting---

JO: It happened after a session . . .

DH: . . . I was by myself in the room. We were at Electric Lady Studios, and everybody had gone home except for John. And the engineer was still, sort of, fooling around in the control room. And I sat down and I had this little Korg organ, and I had a Roland CompuRhythm, which, in those days, was an early drum machine. And it had, like, Rock and Roll One and Rock and Roll Two, and Samba.

JO: It had four sounds, basically. It had four sounds and you couldn't use two of them.

DH: I turned on, you know, "Boom, dik dik boom dik boom dik dik boom boom dik," and I started playing on this chord organ, "Doo do doo do do do dum dum," and the song wrote itself. In about five minutes, I had the song.

JO: And, not only that, it was recorded.

DH: The engineer was in there and he started turning things on and I was recording it as I was writing it. And I said, "John, play this: dum dum dum dah, dah dah dah dah dah." And he played that and we had a song.

DD: And that was the song that broke black radio bigger.

DH: We've had a lot of hits on R&B radio over the years. That was number one though.

DD: Totally, with good reason. Well, let's listen to that. You got to get the vintage rhythm machine to do this one.

Hall and Oates recording: "I Can't Go for That"

DD: "I Can't Go for That." Our guests are Daryl Hall and John Oates and they have a new album called *Our Kind of Soul,* and it's great to hear them re-doing a lot of the material that, as we mentioned, has been done by people who are their contemporaries. And, one of the things that we learned today is, Dan Hartman, who had a huge hit with "I Can Dream About You," that was going to be your song, but were you not doing covers at that point?

DH: We had just finished an album.

JO: It just wasn't the time.

DH: I saw him in a restaurant--- we knew Dan--- and he said, "I just wrote this great song. You guys should cut it. I wrote it with you in mind." And we didn't need a song then. I didn't even bother getting a demo or anything because we had just finished a recording. And, about six months later, I was watching MTV and I see these guys dancing around like the Temptations, "I can dream . . ." and I went, "Oh, there's the song. I can tell." So you know, better late than never.

DD: Definitely. Let's listen to a live version of that, "I Can Dream About You."

Hall and Oates recording: "I Can Dream About You"

DD: Hall and Oates doing, "I Can Dream About You." I'm sure you guys have talked about this, about the nature of a partnership. What does it take to keep something like this going so long?

DH: Um . . .

DD: You probably have different answers.

DH: . . . No, we probably have the same answer . . .

JO: You have to really like what you're doing. And, you got to be around people that you respect and that, you know, have your respect and you got to want to do it. And, we're almost compelled to do it. I think that's the thing. We've been musicians ever since we've been born. So how do you stop doing that?

DH: Right, it is literally a compulsion.

JO: You don't want to stop, and you don't stop if you don't have to.

DH: And we really--- were you asking how we do it with each other?

DD: Yeah!

DH: We just start--- I think the story that we're telling right here, that we've been telling, explains it. We started together—we started as kids together. We shared our entire adult lives together . . .

JO: Basically, every experience---

DH: . . . Any important experience in my life is probably the same one that John would talk about, you know. It's just one of those things. And our personalities are different enough that we don't get in each other's way, but we complement each other. So, that's also very important.

DD: Let's play one of the new ones from the new record, one of the new ones you guys wrote, "Let Love Take Control." We've got a really nice version of that. What's interesting, this crowd, listening to this show today, clearly, you know, Hall and Oates fans from way back, fans of the music that you're covering on the new album, but totally took to this song. It's interesting.

DH: A lot of people really like this song.

JO: We wanted to make sure, if we put originals on this record, which we did, they'd stand up. That they would stand up to these amazing songs on this record.

DH: Quite a challenge . . .

JO: It is a challenge and we knew it. And I think it's a great idea to put this album first, I'm sorry, put this song first on this CD so that it kind of leads off by saying, "Hey! we consider ourselves songwriters in the same world as these songwriters." So there you go.

DH: . . . I think the biggest compliment I've had, and it's been said to me quite a few times now, is that they thought that the new songs were just old songs they had never heard before. So that's exactly what we were trying to do.

DD: Let's give credit to another songwriter on this, a guy we've actually had on the Cafe: Billy Mann.

DH: Oh, another Philadelphia guy, Billy Mann, there you go.

DD: I think, a little bit younger than you guys, but certainly came up with a lot of the same stuff.

DH: Billy Mann is--- he, he--- we're his baby food. And he has said it himself. He's a great guy, a Philly guy, and he is quite a strong personality. And when we get together, it's like psychotherapy, and then it turns into a song, so, it's great.

JO: We wrote "Do It for Love" with him, as well.

DD: This is "Let Love Take Control." Thanks, guys, for talking with us.

DH: All right.

JO: All right.

Hall and Oates recording: "Let Love Take Control"

2005

GANG OF FOUR

OUR GANG OF FOUR INTERVIEW TOOK PLACE AS THE ORIGINAL BAND WAS TOURING following the re-release of their debut 1979 album, *Entertainment!* The original album is full of politics and the jittery funky rhythm that so many bands, particularly in Britain, were emulating at the time.

I wish we could somehow let you hear how the band played that day. It was fresh, loud and great. This interview followed that session and found the band eager to set the record straight about Gang of Four, then and now.

David Dye: The Gang of Four are my guests on the *World Cafe* today. Their first album, *Entertainment!* from 1979, has just been reissued. That album, with its funkified-punk sound, has become quite influential in the new century, as bands like Franz Ferdinand and Bloc Party talk about its influence on what they do now. We'll hear them play in the studio, but I start off by asking the band what they saw as their relationship with British punk in 1977, when they formed.

Jon King: Well, I think it's because the key influences on the Gang of Four are more American than British. I don't think that, when people sometimes call us a post-punk funky band. Actually, most of the things that we listened to and loved and revered were from the U.S. It was P-Funk, it was Television, it was Velvet Underground, that sort of thing. And I think that, certainly, if you look at our music, it's probably closer to the music of northeast America than it is to the U.K. And we had very little in common with the Clash or the Sex Pistols, musically.

DD: I'm glad you said that, because that's what I was going to say. People see you as this second wave of punk, and I just assumed that you were a band that happened to come along at that time, but whose influences were far before that.

Andy Gill: Yeah, we could've come along at any time, actually. I think that punk rock facilitated sort of the deconstructed musical ambitions that we had. Punk rock opened the door.

DD: One of the things that has happened through all this is that the first album, *Entertainment!* has been reissued. And one of the things you look for when something like this comes out is, "Where does it stand? How does it fit? How does it sound?" And this album is kind of timeless. The themes may have come out of what was happening with Thatcher in England, but it doesn't sound like it. It's not specific to any of that. The themes are as alive today. The music is as alive today. It must be really gratifying to have an album that holds up in that kind of way.

JK: Often there's a view taken of things that we've done. You'll say there's the music and there's the lyrics, and of course it wasn't really like that. The project was to deconstruct the thing so that leadership and the pole position in each song shifted and moved all the time. Songs like "Anthrax," you've got a lead vocal and you've got a commenter on the lead vocal. Then you've got these sections that drop in and drop out. And there's sections of improvisation and sections of structure which sit outside of, I suppose, of the conventional II-V-I chord sequences that you see in AM pop. So without having that verse-bridge-chorus-verse-bridge-chorus, I mean there are some of the songs that we do have that in them, but by removing outside of what was a straitjacket, both of content and form, you end up with something that sounds like itself. And I guess that's why it's not dated. It doesn't sound much like others. It's not a II-V-I thing.

DD: Jon, there's a nice article that comes in the reissue of *Entertainment!* and one of the things that it talks about is how you guys argued all the time when you were playing and rehearsing. What did you argue about? Did you argue about the stance of the lyrics, or what kinds of things?

JK: I don't think, necessarily, that we argued about the stance of the lyrics. You mentioned earlier on where some of the ideas came from, and the ideas weren't really from an anti-Thatcherist thing. The things that stimulated all of us were a lot of the ideas that came out of Paris in 1968, and the ideas of Situationism, which I think hold an incredible resonance, particularly now. And it's become more and more the case that people see themselves as commodities operating within a commodified society. We've gotten to a point where the only value of anything is the price of it. And you see that in all sorts of things. If value only exists in price, then those are the sorts of things that we kicked around ideas about. And it seems a bit strange maybe to a lot of people who don't get involved in those things, but we would have very fierce rows and fistfights, almost, about some of these things. And we were all very demanding on each other.

DD: Now, you're all doing different things. How have you all changed as people, now that you're back together? That's a big question, I know, but if people have some observations on what it's been like . . .

Dave Allen: It's been a long time, but I think in an odd way our characters have not changed at all. But we've clearly matured--- not just in age, but we've found ways to discuss things without having to climb the mountain, tear it all apart and then have the camp for the storm, et cetera. In my case, cleaning up my act generally over the years has been very good. And then having a family. I've got three kids, and dealing with three kids is actually harder than dealing with these three guys, so it's all a kick.

JK: I think that, moving away from our personalities slightly--- but it's interesting that we're talking about the reissue of the record, *Entertainment!* and that record that you've got in front of you, that CD, was deleted in 1992. So it's rather like those samizdat papers in Russia, under the Communists, where musicians would be passing around this stuff that was kind of banned. We had two singles banned in the U.K., and not that Warner Brothers banned the record, but there was *this* record which most people in music said, "This is something you should listen to," but couldn't be gotten.

DD: So it's good to have it back. How do you feel about this new wave of bands that all the critics are rushing to now praise for sounding, or at least being influenced by, Gang of Four? Is it a compliment?

Hugo Burnham: I think so. I think Andy was just saying the other day that it is. Clearly we wouldn't be having quite this much attention. Somebody said it to me the other day, which I thought was quite good, that they're not seeing this as a reunion tour, where it's the original band as if we've just had some pause, because there's been so much clamoring, or too much mentioning in the press and sort, of almost overburdening about these bands with this tag that, "You sound like the Gang of Four." I'm very pleased that these bands have looked at our catalog and decided to borrow certain elements out of it and create their own thing out of it. It's been quite pleasing, actually. And at the same time, all this press or media awareness which has created this juggernaut that helped us get back together . . . I think we'd all agree, has been a very good thing.

DD: It's interesting that you haven't yet or didn't start the creative part of it again, with writing new things. And I'm curious to what you think about that.

JK: I think when we finally came to think about or agree to do this, there was a collective view that we had to be at least as good as we were at our best. So we decided to look at the material that we'd written and choose stuff that was relevant to when the four of us were together, and that necessarily meant material up to, more or less, '81. We do "We Live As We Dream, Alone," and "[I Love a Man In] Uniform," and a song called "I Parade Myself," from a later period, but we wanted it to be intensely focused about this stuff. So I think that was a key thing for us, to rediscover what it was that made it so intense, that made the music so dissident.

2005

HUGH MASEKELA

David Dye: The South African trumpet player Hugh Masekela is our guest today. He has a new album, *Revival,* at least the thirty-second in his career, and it stretches back to the early 1960s. Masekela left South Africa in 1961 and, with some help from Harry Belafonte and Dizzy Gillespie, settled in the U.S. As a youngster in South Africa he picked the trumpet to play after seeing the film, *Young Man with a Horn.* In talking with him about his early influences, I asked Hugh if Louis Armstrong was one of those influences.

Hugh Masekela: Louie Armstrong took away everybody's inhibitions about singing. When we were kids we'd all walk around singing, [imitates Louie Armstrong] "I'll be glad when you're dead, you rascal," you know?

DD: [laughs]

HM: But when I started my band--- I came here as a bebop player, and you know, bebop players were very cool. We wore dark glasses and hid behind the mic; we didn't show any emotions. And when I was teaching my first group the songs, I had to sing them to them, and they said— and at the time I was married to Miriam Makeba— and they all said, "It's either you sing, or we don't play." And she said, "Oh, so it's either you sing, or I don't marry you." You know, it was before we got married. But everybody said, "You sing so great!" And I was like, "Hey, the last thing I want to do is sing." So the first time--- In fact, it was on that album, the first time I started singing at the Village Gate--- The first day I had to sing, I had, like, cottonmouth. I was sweating and I just felt very, very strange, and when people applauded I was very surprised. I still get surprised.

DD: What you're pointing to is--- I have a reissue of an album that came out in '65 called *The Americanization of Ooga Booga.* Well, you better explain what you meant by the title, because that's like Tarzan language to me.

HM: Yeah, well, umm--- [chuckles] Tom Wilson, the producer of the album, said, "Hey man, what are we going to call this?" And at the time there was a movie called *The Americanization of Emily.* It was a very big movie. And people were still struggling to identify with what Africa was really about, and we were some of the first immigrants to come in, and people used to ask me, "What do you eat?" "Do you have trees?" "Do you live in houses?" and stuff like that. So I always made fun of the ignorance about Africa, and he loved it, and he said, "Let's call it *The Americanization of Ooga Booga.*" And we made fun in the cover too, because I have a *Wall Street Journal* and a briefcase and a Brooks Brothers suit and am barefooted. And a lot of people, actually, like, two or three years later, I met women who said, "Oh, I've always wanted to meet you, but I'm so disappointed, now you're wearing shoes! You've really gotten Americanized." [*Laughs*]

DD: [laughs] Well, the interesting thing about the album is that everybody talks about the fusions of world music, and combining African and certainly other cultures of Western music you did on this album a long time ago, and it didn't seem like it was any kind of a stretch.

HM: Well, I mean, when I came I was, like I said, a bebop musician and a jazz musician. I grew up in township dance bands, and I started music when I was three years old, playing the gramophone. And everybody--- well, Miriam Makeba and Harry Belafonte brought me to school in the States and then they introduced me to Dizzy Gillespie and Miles Davis and all, and I was trying to get a job either with the Jazz Messengers or with Horace Silver, Blue Mitchell, and they all said, "Why don't you start your own group?" And they all advised me, they'd say, "If you're going to be a jazz musician, you just gonna be a statistic like all of us, but if you put some infusion of some of the music or most of the music from your country or from your traditional background, you're going to stand out just like Miriam Makeba or like Olatungi does," you know, and I sort of regretted at the time why I didn't immerse myself more in ethnic and traditional music when I was back home instead of American music. Not that I didn't know it, but I slowly came up with a hybrid, and a lot of it was helped by Miriam Makeba, whose mother was a traditional healer, and who had a major, major anthology of traditional South African music. And between her and her daughter we used to sing all these songs. And I was able to, like, come up with something that people seemed to like, and I've been going back ever since. Now I'm completely immersed in whatever is old.

DD: That's interesting, how you go from being immersed in the American culture to going back and becoming immersed in your own. Let's play the first one, which is your then-wife Miriam Makeba's composition.

HM: "Dzinorabiro."

DD: Yeah. Here he is on stage at the Village Gate in 1965.

> Hugh Masekela recording: "Dzinorabiro"

DD: Hugh Masekela. That's not the new album he has out called *Revival,* but that's a recent reissue of a couple of groundbreaking albums from 1965, which they've re-released under the title of *Lasting Impression of Ooga Booga.* Two albums that came out on either side of "Grazing in the Grass" being a hit. I think one of them was kind of, you know, "Hey, we better catch the Hugh Masekela train before it leaves the station." Can we backtrack just a little bit? Hugh, talk a little bit about--- maybe if you could contrast for people, because you were in such an amazing position---you left South Africa in 1961?

HM: 1960.

DD: 1960, went to England first, and then later came here. Can you describe what it was like for you, just as a human being and as a musician then, and then contrast it to when you went back after apartheid had been lifted?

HM: Well, I left South Africa when it was, I think, at the beginning of the peak of repression. It was right after the Sharpeville Massacre. I had been waiting for a passport for three years, and I was in a very--- well, probably the most famous popular group in South Africa, a jazz group called the Jazz Epistles, and after the Sharpeville Massacre where, you know, 69 people were shot in the back when thousands of people had peacefully congregated at the municipal offices in Sharpeville to protest the raising of the rents and the carrying of the identification passbooks. The first state of emergency was proclaimed and gatherings of more than ten people were illegalized, so we couldn't play anymore, and a month later I got my passport. And Father Huddleston, Bishop Huddleston in England, who had been deported five years before, helped me to come to England through the help of Johnny Dankworth and got me into the Guildhall School of Music. Then Miriam Makeba, the year before just attained major success here, and she was a childhood friend and she was an ex-girlfriend, and she brought me to the States with the help of Belafonte. And I came here during the very, very peak of the civil rights movement and Martin Luther King and the emergence of Malcolm X, and I arrived here when Nixon and Kennedy were campaigning. My mentors were people who were into civil rights, Belafonte and Miriam Makeba, and I was influenced by Dizzy Gillespie and Louis Armstrong and Miles who were all, like, were very much activists. And, long story short, finally things changed in South Africa and they said we could come back. When I came back it was just a wonderful miracle, because it gave me a chance to re-immerse myself in a lot of things that had to be fixed and a lot of things I hadn't been involved in. But I think the interesting part was to see how much damage had been done by apartheid over the thirty years that it had gone, and the population had quadrupled, but you actually saw the effects of the reshuffling of people, the impoverishment of people, and the systematic manipulation of the death of their traditional excellence, because with the impoverished people, if you take their lands away, they cannot practice who they really are and they can be homogenized. And I think of all the things, of the poverty and everything, the thing that really broke my heart most was the homogenization of people. I would say the homogenization of Ooga Booga. And through radio and television and advertising, people have actually abandoned their African-ness, their Africanness and their color, and I think that that was systematic and manipulated by the apartheid government, because they figured, like, if you're gonna separate people then you can't have them admiring each other. You can't have mutual admiration, and mutual admiration was really damnation, and I think what we're all working on, including the government especially, is to, like, re-instill in people mutual admiration and their pride in, like, their traditional origins.

DD: I'd love to talk about what that does to music. One of the things you talk about on this new album, *Revival,* is the rise of--- is it Kwaito?

HM: Kwaito.

DD: Kwaito, yes, which you seem to equate with South African hip-hop, in a way. Does it take any traditional elements, and what about it is particularly South African?

HM: Well, this is really no different from the music we're playing in dance bands and music that Miriam Makeba and the Manhattan Brothers were singing, quartets and girl trios of those days were doing--- although we were influenced when I left by jazz. The influence of rhythm and blues, the influence of disco and then the influence of rap and hip-hop affected the urban music, and basically it's really the old township music decorated with the new influences.

DD: I wanted to play a piece from it, that Zwai and Guffy produced, "District Six." What does that mean, what is District Six?

HM: District Six was an area like Sophiatown. It was one of the areas that was forcibly--- where Africans lived and they were forcibly removed from the center of town to go and live in remote areas, and after we got free District Six was revived and the people who lived there began to come back, so it says, "We're going back to District Six." It's a celebration of that. But what is ironical about that is that the girl who's singing with us is a seventeen-year-old Afrikaner girl who has an unbelievable voice and, you know the Afrikaners were the people of apartheid, and she sings in Zulu here and she can sing soul, she can sing anything, which again shows you that people are forced into categories, even socially, culturally, racially, but most people, I think most children, when they grow up, just want to be human beings.

Hugh Masekela recording: "District Six"

DD: Our guest is Hugh Masekela and that is "District Six," which is one you'll find on *Revival,* a new album he has out, as we mentioned, his first one in three years. And her name is?

HM: Her name is Corlea. Corlea. Corlea Botha.

DD: You know, you're so much connected to what's going on now, I hate to take you back into the past, but there [are] some questions I've always had. One of them is, going all the way back to the Monterey Pop Festival, you played at the Monterey Pop Festival. Were you one of the few jazz groups to play there?

HM: Yeah, well, at the time I wasn't considered--- people were very confused about what I really was, because, being a black artist at the time, I was doing a lot of protests, what was considered protests and social consciousness. I think the only person who was doing that at the time was Miriam Makeba and Bob Dylan and Peter, Paul and Mary and Joan Baez and Harry Belafonte, you know, it was a handful but it was an unpopular thing to do, especially after the McCarthy hearings and Pete Seeger and all those people were blacklisted. People were like, "Why are you doing this? Aren't you afraid?" I said, "I can't be afraid," because it's difficult to come from a people who are oppressed and not sing about them.

DD: Now, was your music--- did it get back to Africa? Even though you didn't, did it get back to either South Africa or Africa in general?

HM: Oh yeah, it got back, it got to all of Africa, and even though it was banned in South Africa, it was smuggled in. What the government used to do is that--- the South African Broadcasting Corporation was the only broadcasting medium in South Africa, and if there was a funny track that they didn't like on the LP, they just scratched it with a nail, they'd destroy that side. But people still could buy copies, it's just that they couldn't be broadcast, but it was--- it had a certain track, it was illegal to get, so people played it privately. And when I went back to South Africa a lot of people said to me, "You got me arrested!" I said, "Why?" They said, "Because I was found with your album." [laughs]

DD: Music: the most subversive of the arts.

HM: I think I still have about twenty albums that haven't been released yet in South Africa. They never even got to South Africa, because they were just banned outright.

DD: Well, I have to ask about "Grazing in the Grass" because I understand for you it was just something that happened at the end of a session, but it ended up--- it's just hard to believe, nowadays, that instrumental pieces can be such huge hits as they were back at that point. You were surprised at its success?

HM: Yeah, I mean, we did an album called, I think it was maybe my fifth or sixth album, called *The Promise of a Future,* and Russ Regan from Universal came in to listen to the finished album, and he said, "You know, I think you need another track here." And the tenor saxophone player, Al Albreu, in our group really was crazy about the track and loved it and said, "Why don't we do that track with the cowbell?" And we did it, we learned it--- because it was very simple, you know, the bass player had only four notes to play, and the drum and all the guitar had to play was [sings guitar riff], and the piano player, [sings piano riff], so I showed them quickly and we put it together and there was an old friend of mine who was playing with Phil Ochs, Bruce Langhorne, and he's a guitar player who, when I was a student, used to come and listen to all the South African music, so he knew it, so I said, "Bruce, can you take a break and come and play the guitar part, we'll overdub this part," and then he held the cowbell and I hit it. And in half an hour we had the song, and in an hour's time we mixed it. That evening we played it for Ross Regan and he said, "This is a smash." But, you know, we'd never really--- I'd never really aimed at singles, I didn't even know how you made them. And this song, he said, "It's going to be a smash." I said, "What's a smash?" [laughs] So I thought it was going to be a flop.

Hugh Masekela recording: "Grazing in the Grass"

DD: Well, that's one everybody knows from my guest today, Hugh Masekela. There's a period in your music that I guess I call kind of a funk period, and I'm thinking of something that's still popular nowadays, the song, "The Boy's Doin' It." What was the origin of that one?

HM: Well, it was less funk than it was fun. I think we were playing at Lansing, Michigan, and I had this group--- Hedzoleh had sort of broken up, and some of the members of Hedzoleh stayed and they got some of their other friends who were in Washington, we were working out of Washington then, and a couple of them were at Howard, they were musicians, and we put together a group and we did an album called *The Boy's Doin' It.* But we were backstage at Lansing, we'd just finished a concert at Michigan State [University] and we were backstage partying, having a great time, and we just started singing this song, [sings] "The boy's doin' it, the boy's doin' it," and we were fooling around, and somebody said, "Why don't we record that?" So we made up more lyrics for it and it became the song that Neil Bogart loved, you know, and he said, "We're going to call this 'The Boy's Doin' It' and we're going to push this song," and it's still one of the most popular songs in our repertoire.

DD: Definitely. Definitely.

HM: But the fun things always seem to take off. [chuckles]

DD: Human nature. Well, let's listen to a little bit of this one that some folks remember, "The Boy's Doin' It."

> Hugh Masekela recording: "The Boy's Doin' It"

DD: We've been talking with Hugh Masekela, talking about music and the many things that have gone on in his life. So, one thing we haven't talked about, and I'd love to hear what you have to say about it, is Paul Simon's *Graceland* tour in the mid 80s. You were one of the first to defend Paul Simon when he was attacked for violating the ANC boycott. What was your reasoning on that?

HM: Well, I first met Paul Simon through Tom Wilson, who produced *The Americanization of Ooga Booga.* And we were sort of distant friends, you know, when we met each other. And then when he was going to record *Graceland* in Johannesburg he was looking for me, but I told him, "Hey, I can't go to Johannesburg, I'm not involved." So when he came back, he said, "Listen, I did this thing and I'm going to get into a lot." And I said, "Well, let me hear it." And I was just really knocked out by what he did, and what I knew from the cultural boycott was that people were not supposed to play in South Africa, but there was nothing about recording there, and for me the people who were promoting South African musicians overseas, you know, and promoting South African music was a plus for us. Because of *Graceland,* by 1987 there was nobody who was recording an album without either having a song about Mandela or an entire apartheid song, so for me, that had a major, major influence on conscientizing the world about apartheid, and I just said, "Anybody who is against this guy has to be crazy," because first of all, he shared the composition credits and royalties with Ray Phiri and Black Mambazo and all these guys. And he wasn't exploiting anybody, and my thing was like, "If we're going to complain about this, then we're going to have to complain about the Beatles, and we have to complain about the Rolling Stones, and complain about Elvis Presley, who also exploited genres that they didn't come from in those people's songs. I have always in my life tried to stick to my beliefs. This is something that I, you know, learned from growing up in the struggle and from Miriam Makeba and Harry Belafonte--- and especially Miles Davis, who never bit his tongue and was always very straight to say, "If you don't like a thing, you just got to say you don't like it, man. You know, you can't try and find out what the advantages are of liking or not liking it because later on, if you're wrong, you're going to be feeling pretty stupid," is how he put it.

DD: Thank you so much for talking with us.

HM: Thank you for inviting me, I'm sorry that I spoke you to death.

DD: Ahh, I'm still alive. Hugh Masekela, my guest today on the *World Cafe.*

2005

ROBERT PLANT

NOW I KNOW THE SEDUCTIVE NATURE OF HANGING WITH LED ZEPPELIN THAT CAMERON CROWE WRITES ABOUT. Reading back over this conversation with Robert Plant–the model for the great front men in rock–and his bandmate in the Strange Sensation, Justin Adams, it takes me right back to the enjoyable afternoon in the hotel room at the Four Seasons in Philadelphia where we did this interview.

Robert had just released the second of his recent solo albums, *The Mighty Rearranger,* which followed *Dreamland*. The two albums reflect Plant's current interest in folk, blues, and especially African and Eastern music.

To me this is a rare moment of getting to hear from a totally articulate artist enthralled by music and his work.

Robert Plant: We all knew that, to go anywhere special with the ambition and the kind of musical tastes that we all each individually have, and had at the time, that we got to do something very special or not bother, because my time is so precious for me. But everybody else's taste buttons are so--- the finger is always ready to press the button and denounce. So we created a sort of, if you like, a judge and jury within ourselves as to how far we can go and how commercial or how, how the root of what we want to do has got to come from a really solid, grounded and imaginative place. And we wanted to create a brand new way of looking at contemporary rock music.

Rock is a dirty word, man. It shouldn't be, really, you know? So we fretted and scratched our heads and lost sleep and lost time and lost a bass player and got another one and the whole thing kind of came round and opened like a very reluctant, beautiful lotus into this great unusual flower, this amazing bloom. And with all great blooms, it takes a lot to get it right. And I think, you know, one way or another we got it right by everybody feeling they could extend themselves without taking over at any particular point. And the greatest compliment that's been paid to us by so many people is that it seems like, from the beginning of track one to the end of the album, that it's almost a seamless marriage of intent, sound and style. Even though we moved through the sort of landscapes of, you know, American desert music, if you like, into African rhythms and the stuff that Justin's brought to our party, and the willingness by everybody to actually take that on and learn like kids and become quite besotted by the whole idea of this huge landscape ahead of us now to explore.

David Dye: I wanted to play a live version of "The Enchanter," which we had a chance to record with you all. Tell me about some of the things that are in this--- what you see rhythmically that is part of this--- from your viewpoint, Justin.

Justin Adams: Well, I started the guitar on that one with luck, a blues tuning, but then sort of finding some Islamic kind of ways to play it with the same blues tuning. And, uh, there's a certain thing I know Robert likes--- this half-tone--- when a piece of music goes up a half-tone and down again. So I put one of those in to see if, uh, that would . . .

RP: [laughs] To see my eyes light up.

JA: . . . To see his eyes light up, exactly. And you know, sure enough that was one of the ones he picked up on and brought to life with the lyrics, really.

DD: Well, this is a performance of "The Enchanter" from Robert Plant and the Strange Sensation.

> Robert Plant and the Strange Sensation recording: "The Enchanter"

DD: Robert Plant and the Strange Sensation. [A] live recording of what you will find on the *Mighty Rearranger* album. Robert, I've heard, I've read some of the things you've said about your first trip to Morocco and, when was it?

RP: I can't remember, really. I think it was about 1971. And I went sheerly as a tourist. I mean, bearing in mind that at the time I'd brought all my life up until — in fact all my life until now, really--- I've lived in the part of the United Kingdom where there's been a big Asian influx. Growing and growing and growing, and the culture's gotten bigger and bigger. You can see how it's happened here in America, that they're very self-sufficient, fantastic music, great color, beautiful people. The whole deal . . .

brought so much flash and reverberation to the kind of dull, postwar United Kingdom. It was--- I mean, we really did suffer at the end of the war. And my parents, it was a pretty dour life that they led--- but always striving. And then the Asians came striding through with this almost pizzicato, Baliwood strings cascading through the dark streets of middle England, you know. And so, I was always intrigued by this and I loved the look of--- I married a woman from India--- I was going to say I loved the look of the women, but I actually--- I tried. [laughs] I still loved the look of the women from India, and the idea of going to North Africa was very appealing because it seemed as if, romantically, it was something I didn't quite understand or know about. And the whole idea of the closed--- what I thought--- shrouded culture at the time, which I found out later I was quite wrong about.

DD: How so?

RP: Well, because Morocco is quite spurned by a lot of the Arab world as being the sort of Maghreb, the land in the west. But, in some maps of the Arab world it doesn't even appear on the maps. It's just like of a little chuck on the west coast of Africa--- west end, where there's not even a name for it. So it's almost, with the Berber influence and Jewish communities and the Islamic the Muslim world, it's much more of a cocktail--- a Masala, than I think you'd find farther east. And it was spectacular. I went there as a tourist with my wife and we stayed in the Holiday Inn in Marrakesh. And the next time I went back the Holiday Inn, the King Hassan, Hassan II, I think, had decided to give it to his wife for a birthday present. So, she then owned the hotel; it became somebody else's hotel. And I began to understand that in Morocco, there was a kind of a whimsical sense of humor where things could change overnight and rapido: you're in another world. You can get that feeling when you just turn a corner of a street and you're on the same block. You're just on the other side of it, and you're back in the 14th century. So I was just blown away. And then my lady went back to England and I started getting Jimmy [Page] to come down and we started exploring. And we took a big Nakamichi portable tape machine up into the Atlas and started recording Berber women in the fields who were singing around. I mean, bearing in mind there were no gigs, per se. There were classical Arab concerts in Casablanca and Rabat and so forth. But down in the south, music was based around weddings, circumcisions, the various times of the year, the equinox and that sort of thing. It was really fantastic, market day, farmer's market in the middle of the foothills of the Atlas Mountains. And it was always something where people were about to clap their hands.

DD: [laughs]

RP: And about to shuffle their feet in the dust. And it was superb. And I just, uh, I bought my ticket for life

DD: Yeah.

RP: I can't get away from it now.

RP: When we were working on *Dreamland*, Justin had already been to Tisdas . . . out into the Sahel, with Tinarawin, and had recorded there. And he said, "I'm going to go back to this festival next January." And I said, "Well if you go, I've got to come with you." So, like eleven months later, you know, we're on a plane loaded up with adventurers and scallywags. And it was all because of Justin's links and, uh, and the sense of adventure. You know, your nostrils flare. And then you do very silly things and you make liaisons with strange people to get to where you got to go.

DD: Justin, you should talk a little about this because this festival is like none other. You look out from the concrete stage and what, what does the audience look like?

JA: Well, there's--- when we played, there was Robert and myself, Skin and two French guys playing with us. And [I] just looked out--- say there were probably seven hundred Tuareg--- the men veiled, the women with fantastic jewelry in their hair, all wearing these beautiful indigo robes, and a lot of guys on camels. That's really how they get around. There [are] no roads. This is serious sand. And they really know how to strike a pose. There's some of the most, the best, posers in the world. And it's all about stature and poise. They have swords and they, they really look like they know how to use them. And these [are] tough, very noble, and very funny people, you know. So, it's incredible.

DD: This is their--- was their festival to begin with, and then they put the music on top of it?

JA: Yeah, basically. As nomads, they need to have festivals where they get together and--- especially for a kind of courting and exchanging news. But there's been a lot of war in the north of Mali in the past twenty, thirty years, and so at the moment there's been a relatively calm little time. And so, the Malian government and the Tuareg local governments were really looking to bring westerners in and to try and open up a part of the country which is incredibly poor and has been closed to westerners for some time. And so, it was originally a French band that I was working with called Lo'jo, who made the original connection. We went out for the first Festival in the Desert which was really, really rootsy, but an incredible experience. I found myself as the stage manager, wandering off to a tent in the dark, where I'd find a load of guys sitting around completely veiled in the dark in a tent. And I'd say, "Excuse me, are you the Griots from Timbuktu, because, if so, could you come to the stage by five-thirty, because, you're needed for a sound check," and trying to explain this to guys who'd never really been on a stage before or such. They play, I mean, they're incredible players. But the whole, sort of thing of a concert, as such, was a new one, really.

DD: Well, probably, more interesting in some ways than your reaction to the music you heard there was their reaction to the band.

JA: Yeah. Well, they love guitar. And I think they completely get it. I mean, you don't, uh--- that's one of the great things about going to Africa or the Middle East for me is that when you're there, you begin to realize that all these kind of separations and ideas that people are really different and that it's all, you know--- it's like going to Mars. It's not, you know. And they, you know--- when Robert starts singing they totally know. They [one] hundred percent know what that's all about.

DD: Yeah.

JA: There was no difficulty. I didn't feel that there was anything they didn't get. They can't understand the lyrics, and we can't understand their lyrics. But . . . you know, they understand dancing and music.

RP: I think the way that we played there and the way that we do play . . . for perhaps forty, fifty percent of the time right now on this tour of the United States, is totally understandable for those guys, for those people. I think the more, the harder, big choral stuff that is part a kind of the tough aspect of the rock and roll influence within what we do, would be too much for them. But I think the--- say with *Dreamland*, "If I Ever Get Lucky," which was one of the songs that we played out there in Timbuktu--- and it works--- because it's got, it's just as I was saying before, it's got that kind of trancy-ambient thing. Which is, when you see these guys play, there aren't a lot of explosions with the Tuareg music. There's much more of that kind of dreamscape musical ingredient [that] works. It works perfectly.

DD: A lot of the things that you can see overtly influencing Led Zeppelin are there in both of these [types of] music.

RP: That's right.

DD: And, um, we have a live performance of "When the Levee Breaks," which is a good example of what you can, how you can, take a song and work it out.

RP: Yeah.

DD: Maybe Justin can talk a little bit about how--- the conversations about redoing this.

JA: Yeah. I mean it's--- when we, as a band, when we sort of take on doing one of the Led Zeppelin tracks, I guess what we're thinking about is how to make it really alive. And, we're very conscious of, okay . . . this is not a covers band. And so, it's trying to find the real spirit . . . in the music, and "When the Levee Breaks" on record is such an incredible piece of work. We felt, well okay, one thing, let's not start it with the same--- let's try and find the power in it from a different source than, you know--- 'cause how could you compete with the drum intro on the record? So we found another way that I think it's got its own power, but it's with acoustic guitar and stand-up bass and singing.

DD: And this is what it sounds like. It's "When the Levee Breaks" from Robert Plant and the Strange Sensation.

Robert Plant and the Strange Sensation recording: "When the Levee Breaks"

DD: "When the Levee Breaks," [by] Robert Plant and Strange Sensation. We're having a chance to talk with Justin Adams, guitarist, and Robert Plant about this music, this band and this journey. And Robert, one of the reasons why we're spending time talking about Morocco and talking about Mali is that these are the things that you had with you for years, that are moving you, and are moving things forward for you with music. And there is a song on here that I think we should talk about, "Tin Pan Valley," which kind of pokes at maybe your contemporaries who aren't--- who aren't as involved. And that must be frustrating?

RP: Well, I don't know. It depends on how you want the sort of--- the ingredients of your life to run, and whether or not there are, you know--- I mean, [it is] very evident that the cycles of life--- you can't predict how they're going to change.

DD: Right.

RP: And I think the essence of what I was trying to get to in the song was that, often, these changes are almost subliminal. And you do move from, you know, you can go back to things later on and say, "Okay, well I--- it's time I didn't do that now. It's time I moved over here." Or, "I've got nice kids and, you know, yeah, okay the marriage has split up, but I've got this nice young girl and she, you know, raises horses or whatever." It's--- and people become, they go into another place. And that's absolutely their entitlement. It's just, I think, if you lose it too quickly or if you're, if you're--- there's a sort of almost an invisible move which dictates the way that your life is going to really slow [down]. And you lose that--- I know so many people who have lost that sparkle. People who are my contemporaries who once upon a time could set the world on fire but now they're playing to their strengths without even knowing it. You know, there's a kind of move into the kind of easy life, and the easy way of doing things. People with great voices who could still rise to the challenge of interpreting great songs without it actually just playing into the sort of floppy underbelly of Americana.

DD: And you're also challenging the audience too, to not keep looking back.

RP: If we, if we were really making a

huge impression, these records that we make would have been--- our praises would have been sung from coast to coast, and you wouldn't be able to hear us for the sound of approval.

DD: [laughs]

RP: But it isn't working like that, because most people do want to hear, you know, a catalog, and a great, you know, library of American songs.

DD: Yeah.

RP: Everybody wants to get, you know, "Moon in June." And I did that with the Honeydrippers to a degree for a bit of a laugh to keep Ahmet Ertegun from nagging at me all the time. About, why don't you get Charles Brown in on the piano and do Drifting Blues, or whatever it is. So yeah, I think "Tin Pan Valley" was, um--- I just want things [to] explode now and again. I just don't want everybody to end up, you know, going for the cantoral at the same time.

DD: This is "Tin Pan Valley," a live version with Robert and the Strange Sensation.

Robert Plant and the Strange Sensation recording: "Tin Pan Valley"

DD: We're back on the *World Cafe* and we have a chance to talk with Robert Plant about music and things around this new album, *The Mighty Rearranger*, which I think he's downplaying. I think for, you know, certainly without singing praises, it's not a number one album. But for people who are doing what you are doing, this album has really found an audience. And I think that is a real challenge from where I'm sitting in radio and this kind of thing. It's a real challenge to make a really relevant record like this. Kudos to the band and you and the whole situation for getting that to happen, and I wanted to play "Shine It All Around," which seems to be a song that seems to keep all parts of this equation happy.

RP: It's also a song, if you like, about celebration. It is about, for crying out loud--- this is what we've got, let's make the most of it. You know, which to me, it's kind of a very simple thing but it actually is, I hate to say, and it sounds so twee, but it is like, it's just, it's laying it down. It's the way I want it to be. It's not always the way it is, but that's the way you gotta look at it. It's got to be, you know. This is the land that I love painted all over, troubled, you know. And it's, it's a strong piece.

DD: Definitely. And I think that's part of what people react to as well. This is a live version of "Shine It All Around" from [Robert Plant and the] Strange Sensation.

Robert Plant and the Strange Sensation recording: "Shine It All Around"

DD: "Shine It All Around," [by] Robert Plant and the Strange Sensation and Robert and Justin Adams. We're getting a chance to talk to them about this music and the new album today on the Cafe. Robert, I had a chance to watch the show last night. I was really happy to see how you carry yourself as somebody of your age as a front man. There's other ways to look at it, you know what I mean? You could go, "God, there's things I can't do anymore that would just make me look foolish."

RP: Well, I do actually, occasionally put my foot up onto the monitor.

DD: [laughs]

RP: And put my shoulders back and do the sort of leonine mane bit and . . . I see people laughing because they know that I'm taking the piss out of the whole rock/vocalist syndrome. And I was the one, one of the first guys ever to wear a girl's blouse with so much skill and style. But I feel really cool about the way I'm doing it. And I also know that because the music is sultry and it does have a certain amount of sensuality about it, especially because a lot of the rhythms and the loops and the stuff that we use—it's pretty sexy stuff. So there's no, you know, it wouldn't be appropriate for me to go clipping along in my stack-heeled shoes, head-banging Clive Deamer's drum parts, which is, I think, what I had to do with Bonzo, 'cause I was so stated and sparing. And also there were long periods of instrumentation when I could actually go off and make a cup of tea in those days and come back a revived sex god. Now I feel very, very comfortable, and it's the way that we've developed the projection now with the way that we move quite naturally. Skin is lurking behind some very, very pink or magenta light, and as he comes towards me, and the light catches his eyes through the--- through the sweat in his hair--- I don't know whether to beat a hasty retreat and leave the building, leaving a trail of hundred-dollar bills on the floor, [laughs] or rugby tackle him.

DD: [laughs]

RP: But there's a lot of lurking and lurching going on, which is great.

DD: And weaving. You weaving out, in and out of the band which is, which is kinda fun. You seem like, more like just a member of it.

RP: Well I am, for Christ's sake. Let's get this right. If the music wasn't here, there'd be no lyrics, you know. And I haven't been so charged up in a continual run of one tune following another, following another. I mean, Justin will bear me out. I said as we began to develop this in [a] very simple environment, and after about three or four months we got--- we were beginning to get this huge catalog of pieces of music to nuance and to twist and turn. And I said, "I've got nothing to sing about." And then I realized I've got everything to sing about. I think it began with "Somebody's Knocking," rather like Dylan did that "High Water Everywhere," that Charlie Patton song. I started moving more and more into the all those great terms from Mississippi. The great, you know--- that black poetry which was never written down but it's so beautiful. You know, that whole deal of that kind of African hocus pocus stuff that--- the whole deal of the magic in the Delta and those old African shadows. And I got it and I opened up again.

2005

RAY DAVIES

I'VE ALWAYS BEEN A BIT OF A KINKS FAN and this opportunity to spend time with Ray Davies, who wrote all those classic songs from "You Really Got Me" to "Lola" and "Waterloo Sunset," was a personal joy. This interview may center around his 2005 solo album, but we really learn a lot about Ray's past.

David Dye: "Other People's Lives" is my guest's, Ray Davies', first solo album after leaving the Kinks since 1963. It's also his first album to deal thematically, almost exclusively, with America. One of the things we learn today is how Ray's obsession with England was at least partially the result of the Kinks being banned from touring the States in the mid 60s and having to stay at home in England. During the making of this album, Ray was living in New Orleans and was actually shot in the leg while coming to the aid of someone who was being mugged. We'll talk about how that experience affected his writing but first off, I wanted to know . . . why go solo now?

Ray Davies: Well, I call [it] stubborn, I guess, people. I wanted to write something different and not go for the same old sounds. So I went through about four or five rhythm sections . . . I did demos with different people. I even got Mick Avory, the original Kinks drummer, to audition. [laughs]

DD: [laughs] That's funny.

RD: [laughs] He failed the audition but he took it well. He didn't even pass the audition for the Kinks actually. I might mention that.

DD: [laughs] What happened then?

RD: It's straying from the subject but he played with the band . . . he came to the first audition when we started out before "You Really Got Me" was a hit. I didn't actually say he had the gig but he got into the band, made albums with us for twenty years, and then he had a falling out with my brother, Dave, and Dave said, "You know, you gotta fire him." And I said, "Well, A: I don't think he should go and B: Why don't you fire him?" I ended up doing it, and I took him to a pub in the countryside in England. We had a few drinks; I think he knew what was on the cards. The story is a bit like one of those horrible hit scenes in *The Sopranos* or something. You take somebody out for dinner and then you blow them away. But I took Mick out for a few drinks. I remember I couldn't drive that time. We went on bicycles . . . two drunk sort of middle-age guys on bicycles cycling through the sorry countryside to various pubs. And just before closing time in the last pub, I said, "Y'know, you came to that audition, Mick, twenty years ago?" He said, "Yeah." "Well, you never got the gig." [laughs].

DD: [laughs]

RD: It didn't work out and he knew what I was talking about. It was just a horrible thing to go through because he said, at the time, even if it didn't come to this, he had had enough of touring at that point. This was in the mid 80s and he wanted to just not tour for a few years anyway so it was welcomed news. But it was horrible; it took more out of me than it did Mick. I saw Mick last week and we're still the best friends and I never thought a drummer would be one of my best friends but he is.

DD: Well, back to the current rhythm section. You've finally settled on some people that have made most of the record?

RD: Uh, no [laughs]. I'm still looking for Al Jackson-and Steve Cropper-sounding people. When I've got a song, I hear it as a record. I think of all the songs, things like "You Really Got Me," things like "Waterloo Sunset," that wasn't a big hit here but it was everywhere else. And even "Sunny Afternoon," I heard it as a record when I wrote that song. So I have this sound in my head for drummers. It started off as a very English record because all my demos were about "Englishness" and I wanted to get away from that. When I had made the demos, I realized there's gotta be music from elsewhere and that's when I came over to the States, to the United States, and started writing songs here. I did a trip here, I played "Storyteller" for the last time in America in 2001 just after 9/11, and that was a pretty horrendous tour 'cause of all the events that went on before that. And it made me realize that there's still so much of America that I still want to discover, musically as well as culturally. And because it was post-9/11, we had to travel by road a lot. We couldn't rely on the flights and we traveled to places that normally we'd hop on a plane. We drove from New York to Cleveland. Normally, it's a flight. So I saw bits of America I think that I missed before. And I started writing a whole new batch of songs on that trip and eventually . . . I had already been to New Orleans, [the] beginning of the year 2000. I ended up going down there again to write more songs.

DD: You actually ended up living there and you're not the first musical artist to kind of fall in love with that city . . . you know, from elsewhere, I should say. What was it, particularly, for you that made you want to make that your home for awhile?

RD: I said to a journalist down there I don't think there's any musical snobbery down there. It may sound strange, someone like me saying that . . . I am still learning my craft as a musician, and people find this difficult to believe. I actually get very insecure about new work. But there I felt there was more openness when it came to music. Nobody expected me to play like Jeff Beck. . . . I felt comfortable in the music and environment more than anywhere else, certainly more than London. And also, culturally down there, America is, for the most part, middle class, I think. Or, the aspirations are. People have their cards and their ideal of American culture that grew up through the 50s and post-Second World War is middle class, what the English would call middle class. And I was drawn by the kind of--- not the poor people, but the more blue-collar approach to things. And I can't pinpoint any part of the community, I'm not a great sociologist or anything, but I'm an instinctive, intuitive person, and I liked the way it felt there. It made me rediscover why I picked up a guitar in the first place.

DD: The other thing, Ray, that we should talk a little bit about, talking about this new album, it's *Other People's Lives,* if you're looking at it from the outside, you've always been an observer. You spent a long time observing British culture and there is certainly some satirizing things and some praising things. How does it differ, looking at American culture, as I assume a lot of these songs now, at least a lot of the new ones, are that way?

RD: I spent so much time touring in America. But the ironic thing about it is that I think we were obsessed by America because [we] were banned from America, for playing in the mid 60s . . . a group of musicians' union groups banned the Kinks for three and a half years. And this was at a time when we had lots of success all over the world, so we missed what they called the "Woodstock era" because we weren't allowed to come. So when we came back eventually, at the beginning of the 70s, we found ourselves playing college dates, small clubs, really building ourselves. We were a cult band. People knew about our hits, but we had no real following because there was no MTV, there was no way the world could keep up with what we looked like and how we sounded without getting radio play, which was difficult even then, without being on tour or on television. *Other People's Lives* itself, and the song itself, came about because it's one of these English demos that I had in the mid-90s, and I just liked the chords a lot. I could play them and I could remember them, and the English tabloids, I don't know if you had that many tabloids here, but the English culture is very in-your-face, it's a very intrusive culture, tabloid culture, and I thought of this idea to make a story up. It's a story about two people who meet in Spain and she comes back to live with him and because of *Hello* magazine—am I allowed to say that—*Hello* magazine really started the tabloid culture, which is really all over the world now. And I wanted to write a song about that, and I really wanted to use the word "vomited" on a track.

DD: [chuckles] Let's listen to it. This is "Other People's Lives."

Ray Davies recording: "Other People's Lives"

DD: That's the title track to Ray Davies' new album called *Other People's Lives.* We were talking about the span of time that a lot of this writing took place in--- and people listen to songs, I was thinking particularly about "After the Fall," and assume that it's about your being shot, assume that it's about the problems of New Orleans. But my understanding is that that song actually came from a while ago.

RD: Yeah, the worrying thing--- I was attacked and shot in New Orleans, beginning of 2004, and [with] a long recovery process. The injuries were more severe than people realized, so I stayed there a long time--- but actually, all of the tracks of this album had been recorded and all of the songs written, so nothing on the record has come from that experience of being injured down there. But the worrying thing is, there's a lot of--- it's almost anticipating--- the songs like "After the Fall" take on a new meaning, and all of the lyrics were written lying in bed in a hospital down there. All those songs went through my head over and over again, songs like "The Tourist," about somebody out there having a good time in an impoverished community and they get robbed. It could have been written after the event, but it most definitely wasn't. And it made the process of mixing the album quite difficult for me, confronting the songs again after the accident. So it took me on quite an emotional journey. It's almost as if the songs, songs that--- these are good songs, okay--- Ray, you like them, what's going to happen because of these songs? And I went down there, and this happened, and almost by perfect casting, it happened.

DD: You have to watch what you write.

RD: Blame it on the music, don't blame the parents.

DD: Let's listen--- actually, either one of those would be great--- but let's play "After the Fall."

Ray Davies recording: "After the Fall"

DD: That's "After the Fall" from *Other People's Lives,* and we're talking with Ray Davies about his first solo album and about these songs that were recorded before any of the events--- the place [where] you actually lived in New Orleans got flooded?

RD: Well, I spoke to the people I stayed with--- really kind people, Bob and Jean down there--- and I phoned [Bob] up on his mobile a few days after, and they had already got out--- they got out early, they went to--- where did they go? Baton Rouge. So, he got out safely, and I'm picking up things--- the doctors that treated me, I got a nice email from one of the doctors down there, because I wrote a piece in the English newspapers to say I was concerned about some of the people I knew down there. They're gradually coming back, like the city itself. It's gradually coming back to normality, if that will ever be the case again. Whatever "normal" is. I just hope that the community can rebuild itself.

DD: One of the first songs we had a chance to hear from *Other People's Lives* came out last year, the "Thanksgiving Day" song--- which kind of became an anthem around many places right around Thanksgiving--- and [it] had me scratching my head a little bit, because Thanksgiving seems like a purely American thing, and what was the inspiration for writing that?

RD: I've been to Thanksgiving dinners on tours. We often wondered why there were no dates at the end of November in the itinerary, and they'd say, "Oh, we can't work on Thanksgiving, nobody goes to concerts." So I ended up going to friends' houses on Thanksgiving. And one particular Thanksgiving in 1999 we went to see some friends in New England, and later on, when I was down in New Orleans, we went to several Thanksgiving dinners there, and it is a special thing. I know perhaps Americans--- people I talk to, I said I wanted to write a song about Thanksgiving--- and they rolled their eyes up and they'd say, "Why would you want to write a song about that?" It seems to me, and this is just my take on it, that it's a very special event, and as much as people are bored by going home, it's a time, I think, when it's a real family event. That's the feeling I get from it. It's a time of unity, and that's not such a bad thing, to do that once a year. So I kind of admired it, and wished--- perhaps Britain should pick up on that and we should have a day of unity. So this song is about the tension of this older person, senior citizen-type character, waiting for the kids to come home, who's going to make it. And in the song, there's a son who's broken up, his relationship has broken up, his marriage has fallen apart, and he's waiting at a truck stop wondering whether he should go back or not. At the end of the song, of course, they all come down the driveway and they all arrive. That's my own fantasy world, doing that. It strikes me that it is a great time to settle, but it's so uncool for a rock musician to write--- to talk this way--- and especially to write a song about a senior citizen, but hey, why not? To me, it's a special event, and it's probably the uncoolest song I've ever written.

Ray Davies recording: "Thanksgiving Day"

DD: "Thanksgiving Day" from Ray Davies, and that's one that was out on an EP but is also out now on *Other People's Lives,* Ray's first solo album. You know, it's interesting, hearing you talk about how you think that song is kind of uncool, but Ray, you've actually--- if you look at it that way, a lot of your view of England, I think some people might consider, have been uncool at the time that some of the things were written. I mean, you were very--- "Village Green," I'm thinking about, some of the other real vignettes about England, have been very nostalgic and very warm. In fact, I bet you've really skewed my view of what England is like, unless you end up in the Cotswolds or something. You seemed to like to romanticize British life when you were writing about that.

RD: I don't think it's romanticizing so much, it's actually--- there are pockets of England that do exist that way. It's what they call Middle England. It's not so much Cotswolds, it's more like the home county. It's more like Kent and Surrey, places just outside London, not really rural, and that still exist. Just last year I had a visit from Prince Charles--- that's Middle England for you. It's caring about your environment, caring about the small shops, little shops. But the interesting thing about the "Village Green Preservation Society" is that it was written during this ban, when we were not allowed to come to America, and I never thought I'd be able to come to this country again. So I immersed myself in Englishness and I thought, I'll write these songs, it doesn't matter if they'll be successful or not, if they're uncool. I wrote a song called "The Phenomenal Cat." What's that all about? Like I said, I was immersed in this Englishness. It was very twee, possibly, on the worst viewpoint, but actually very honest about the way I felt about England, and not written by what I was, twenty-two or twenty-three-year-old, that's the thing. I should have written it now, more advanced in years. And that's another thing, about particularly my songs, not the Kinks rendition, is I was always writing for an older person's approval in many respects. I wasn't really a rebelling teenager. I guess "You Really Got Me," or "All Day and All of the Nights" they were rebellious songs. There have been a few others, many others, but for the most part, I wanted songs that could be sung at family parties, you know?

DD: Well, as that twenty-two or twenty-three-year-old, why do you think you were writing as sort of an older person at that time?

RD: I don't know, I think [it] was expected. I was the first boy in the family of girls, looking at this on a real Freudian level, and I was a really good sportsman. And I was expected to become a professional footballer, and I had a really horrific accident and broke my back and it took me a long time to recover. And I think Father's disappointment at not having a sports star--- and I think in a strange way it was to get approval, possibly, that's all. Also, a family sing-song is a great place--- I advised Clive Davis to do this next time--- play it to your family rather than send it to all these digital companies. It's a great place. A family get-together is a great place to check out new songs and test new things. So it was experimentation, but also to get approval, I think.

DD: Now, I understand that you've been teaching your brother, helping him get his guitar playing in shape since his stroke?

RD: Well, he was really sick last year. It was a bad year because I got shot in January and he had this attack. He's so mean though, because he had this stroke on my birthday and I had to abandon my plans for that day, I couldn't really have a party knowing he was struggling for his life in a hospital, though I did think about it. But I had to abandon that, and we've had good conversations since. And I like to think something good comes out of everything, and obviously he's had to do a lot of soul-searching because he is Dave the Rave, he has unstoppable energy--- party guy, and living life to 150 percent--- and I think he'll look back on this, because he's getting better, as a real watershed obviously in his life, and when he comes back to play again properly, he's going to be better.

DD: You yourself have mended quite well from your long convalescence. From everything I've heard of reports of the British shows, you're really, really enjoying being back on stage.

RD: It's odd to be on stage sometimes with new material, and I still play some of the old Kinks songs and I always will, because as I say in the concerts, it's part of me as a person, and I wouldn't play a song I wasn't proud of. I'm amazed to think of songs like "Tired of Waiting" and "You Really Got Me." "All Day and All of the Night," I still can't believe I've written that. I play the songs with as much relish as I did when I first put them out, so they're very close to me, still very current and part of me.

DD: Ray, thank you for spending some time with us.

RD: Absolute pleasure. It was very good, thank you.

DD: And thanks for *Other People's Lives.* Ray Davies, our guest, here on the *World Cafe.*

2005

STEVE CROPPER

AT THE 1992 INDUCTION CEREMONIES OF THE ROCK AND ROLL HALL OF FAME, Booker T and the MGs made it into that exalted company. I had a chance to talk to Steve Cropper, the guitar player in that band, in 2005. In the 60s and 70s he, along with organist Booker T, bassist Duck Dunn, and drummer Al Jackson, not only cranked out their own hits like "Green Onions" and "Time Is Tight," but also backed most of the big records on Stax from Sam & Dave to Carla Thomas and Otis Redding. Later on in the 80s you may have seen my guest backing the Blues Brothers in the movies. When we talked to Steve he had recently been involved with the production of Shemekia Copeland's, *The Soul Truth*. Rarely have I talked to a more affable man who really gave you a sense of time and place when he recounted the past.

David Dye: As a teenager, our guest today had an instrumental hit with his band, the Mar-Keys, which led to him working in the Stax Studio in Memphis as part of the house band, which became the legendary Booker T and the MGs. His guitar is all over those old Sam and Dave and Otis Redding records--- in fact, he co-wrote "Dock of the Bay" with Otis. Recently he came out of retirement to produce the new album by Shemekia Copeland, *[The Soul Truth]*, and I ask[ed] him what had excited him so much about that project.

Steve Cropper: Well, I mean, pretty much I came out of retirement to do that. I had helped some buddies along the way--- when Jerry Wexler came out to do an Etta James album--- and I rushed to get on that session, you know. Jerry called me and said, "I'm doing Etta. You want to help me out?" I said, "Are you kidding, when and where?" So I got a phone call--- I really didn't know who Shemekia Copeland was--- I knew who her dad was, um---

DD: ---Johnny Copeland.

SC: Through the links of--- Johnny Copeland, great guitar player--- when I found out and I got the call and they were interested in me working with her and I said, "Okay, send me some records," and lo and behold, I'm going, "Wow, here's a lady that just sings her kazoo off, and sings for real." You don't have to worry about--- I'm not putting anybody down, I wouldn't do that--- but in the modern world of, you know, vocalizers and pitch controllers and all of this digital stuff that you could do right in your living room and sound like Barbra Streisand if you want to, or Aretha, here's a lady that could just sit in a room and mesmerize you, and I said, "She needs the real deal." I mean, she doesn't need anything phony. She doesn't need anything that's already contrived where you build a track that you know is radio-worthy and you just put a good singer on it and there you go--- and that's their one and only hit for life. I said she need[ed] to be treated just like we used to do Mabel John or Carla Thomas, or, you know, I can say Aretha, even though I didn't produce Aretha, but she needs that sort of honesty in the studio. Let's put it that way. So . . . all the musicians are there for the purpose of trying to make her sound as good as they could make her sound; make her feel as comfortable as they could make her feel. So basically we cut it live in the studio, unlike, you know, digitizing, or building a whole track with computers or whatever, we actually had live musicians in the studio and she sang live just the way we did Otis Redding. It was fantastic.

DD: Well let's just play a little bit of "Who Stole My Radio," one of the tracks from this very fine, new Shemekia Copeland album.

Shemekia Copeland recording: "Who Stole My Radio"

DD: From *The Soul Truth*, the album produced by our guest today, Steve Cropper, that is Shemekia Copeland and "Who Stole My Radio." And just the latest in an incredible---

SC: ---Where did that radio go? [laughing] Let's put an ad in the paper, you know, [laughs] if we could get on over we probably could find that radio somewhere.

DD: [laughs] Oh man. Steve, I want to actually go all the way back with you. I want to ask you a question that probably precedes anything you ever did in music, which was, you were born in what, Missouri? Your family was in Missouri, right?

SC: I was born in Wellsprings, Missouri.

DD: Uh huh. Now how---

SC: I was real tiny then, too. I was just a little guy when I was born.

DD: [laughs] That's all the way back. And, to use the song title, how did you get to Memphis? Did the family move there?

SC: Well my dad had been in the service, and he was in the air force. And anyway, he was asked to be on the police force in a little town called West Plains, Missouri, which is pretty famous for some country artists. And a guy came through--- I think my dad was probably on the force for a couple years, maybe--- and a guy came through soliciting applications for railroad, for people to go work for the railroad, like the TV show *Railroad Detectives.* And my dad filled out an application and he got the job. So he was a railroad detective for thirty years, you know, he was a gun-toting [laughs]--- he's got many, many great stories--- but he was a gun-toting railroad detective, which I think is great, which moved us to Memphis, and he woke me up. I was asleep in the backseat and he said, "Son, you need to get up and see this." And I said, "What?" And he said, "Get up, wake up, wake up, you've got to see this," and that was the Memphis/Arkansas bridge, which in those days was one of the longest bridges in the world. It was over a mile long, and it was a cool thing, and that was my introduction. So we moved there. I saw my first TV show. About three weeks after we moved there a lady came next door, saw that I was out playing, and she had a young son and she was making cookies and some hot chocolate and said, "Would your son like to come over with my son and watch *Howdy Doody*?" Of course my mom didn't know what she was talking about, and I surely didn't know what she was talking about. She said, "Oh, *Howdy Doody* is coming on at four o'clock on television." Television? What's that? [laughs] So anyway, I sound like a Neanderthal, but I promise, I mean, that's how I started. My first TV show was watching a black and white *Howdy Doody*, you know, and with Buffalo Bob and the whole deal. That was it. And then later in life, later in Memphis, Tennessee, I heard gospel music for the first time, and what can I say--- it attached to me, I attached to it, and it was wonderful.

DD: Well you know a lot of people nowadays, everybody wants to be in a band. Everybody wants to be a guitarist. But back when you were doing it, it wasn't--- musicians were not always kind of looked up to, and I'm wondering what your family thought about you when you finally decided that's what you're going to do.

SC: Well they--- I'm not going to say they did the opposite, but--- and you're right, the stories go, "Hey son, you're going to be a bum the rest of your life playing music," you know, "you need to get a good job in a filling station or work at Walgreen's or something." But anyway, my parents were very supportive of me [and] the band. My dad got off from work to go to a gig. He'd help load the drums and all that. They were totally supportive of that. They never went negative on me about any of that, about, "Well you're not going to make it." Or, "You don't have a chance doing this and if you do then you're not going to be anybody." But they were very supportive. I think that was a big plus, and it helped, and I just moved right along. I was very fortunate. I started getting serious about it when I was fourteen. I wrote some songs, I had a little instrumental that I wrote and I got a buddy of mine at school who actually read music to notate it and I was over at his house one day and his dad, B.B. Cunningham, came home and he worked for Sam Phillips at Sun Records and he said, "Hey what's that?" And [my buddy] said, "Oh, it's a little thing that Steve wrote and I'm making a lead sheet for him. He's going to copyright this song." And [B.B.] said, "Hey that's a pretty neat little melody. You mind if I put that on recorders?" He took it to a guy named Bill Justis, and Bill had just come off of, what, two number one records in the nation? He was big on Dick Clark and all that with *Raunchy* and "College Man."

SC: And he loved it and recorded it; brought me down to sign the contracts on it on a Saturday with my dad. I was fifteen years old, and I got my first royalty check when I was sixteen years old.

DD: Wow.

SC: It's like hitting the lottery so--- I mean it was a small check--- [laughs] I wish I'd saved it, but it was a small check. But to me it was like it could have been, you know, the biggest check in the world, and I went, "That's what I want to do the rest of my life."

DD: Now were you still in high school when the Mar-Keys had "Last Night," which was '61?

SC: We had just--- yeah, we had already graduated from high school so we [were] a little older than we think. [laughs] We graduated in '59 and "Last Night" with the Mar-Keys was '61. So we'd been out there trying to hit it pretty good and been on the road and so we had that record. It was number three in the nation, I think, on billboard. And we did Dick Clark and all that, so . . .

DD: Now that song didn't have a whole lot of guitar in it, right, I mean---

SC: . . . It didn't have any guitar.

DD: [laughs] Yeah, exactly.

SC: And as the history books would write, Steve Cropper didn't play on that because there's no guitar on it. Well, I have to disagree with them. I did play on it. When Smoochie, Jerry Lee "Smoochie" Smith, plays the piano solo I'm holding down that sustaining note on the organ so I was on that session and I helped produce it. I helped write the song the day before, the [humming] and the drum beat, [imitates drum beat] so I was there for the whole thing.

DD: Well let's go back. Let's listen to it. This is back in the era of fantastic instrumental hits. This is the Mar-Keys, and "Last Night."

The Mar-Keys recording: "Last Night"

DD: Our guest is Steve Cropper here on the *World Cafe* today and that's, well, as we've just heard, not Steve's first recorded song, certainly, but first big hit for the Mar-Keys. And that was "Last Night."

SC: How 'bout that sustaining note? [laughs] Isn't that incredible? Get paid for one note.

DD: Well, about that time was when, as people keep describing it, Jim Stewart kind of gave you the keys to Stax Studios, and I think what people may not understand is how much of a mom and pop business Stax was in those days. Is that a good way to describe it?

SC: That's a good way to describe it. And I think the reason I was brought in is just, basically I was honest. And I was somebody Jim Stewart and Estelle both could trust. Estelle actually put me to work selling records up in the record shop, satellite record shop, and of course she owed me a favor because I put her son in our band. We had a pretty good little band working around town with no horns, and he came to me one day at school and said, "I want to be in your band." And I said, "We're not looking for any new members. What do you do?" He said, "I play saxophone." I went, "Well, we're not really looking for horns." I said, "How long you been playing?" He said, "Oh I've been taking lessons for three months." [laughs] Oh boy, this is good--- and somewhere in the conversation he said that his uncle and his mother owned a recording studio and I said, "What are you doing Saturday morning?" So we had Packy, Charles Axton--- his nickname was Packy--- and Packy showed up for rehearsal and God, he was . . . screeching, but you know what, it was music to our ears because every Sunday we used to go out to the studio that his uncle had, and his mother, and we would play, and of course his uncle thought we didn't have a chance in a hailstorm; we'd never make it.

DD: We've talked to a lot of people in different places where there was a house band in a studio that would work on a number of different sessions--- everybody from people in the 60s, like you know--- I had a chance, obviously, to talk with people who worked in the Motown, I guess they called it the Snake Pit there, but also in Philadelphia, people who worked in the 70s for the Philly sound, and about how sessions would go. And some places the rhythm players would be able to do the whole arranging thing themselves. And we heard from Thom Bell here in Philadelphia that no, he would often write out every single note, and I'm just curious from you, what form sessions took when you were producing things at Stax.

SC: Well you hit a--- you rang a bell there with Thom Bell. I'm an amazing admirer of his work, and so was Booker T, and so was Isaac Hayes, and that was great that those guys had the talent to do that. Booker T actually had that talent, but we didn't use it in the studio. We actually had what we called "head arranging," and we would bring a song, the writers would bring a song, or we'd be up all night long teaching it to the artist in the hotel room or whatever, and go in [and] teach it to the band--- [we] want[ed] everybody to learn their part. And even like horn lines, we would just sort of hum the melody that we wanted to be the most predominant melody, okay, and one of the guys would take that--- whether it was on trumpet or on tenor or trombone or whatever--- and then they would work out their own harmony, so we didn't actually write stuff out. Now when it came to embellishment of strings and stuff like that, absolutely we would reach out to people that actually did arrangements. Booker was very good at that. Booker's a fantastic string arranger, and he's shown that through the years, if you want to look at his credits and so forth.

DD: Now one of the things about the

guitar playing on it, and what you do and what you're known for, you do incredible rhythm guitars and yet, you play the fills too. And I understand that was sort of out of necessity because, often you'd be the only guitarist there.

SC: Well, we really couldn't afford a second guitar player, to be honest with you. That's kind of how that started and that's why there's only one guitar on the record, so I was faced with a double problem, you got it. Same thing with Booker or Isaac on piano, they had to play the basic chords to the song for support and then every now and then they [would] have to play the fill and that's kind of what we did. So we had a double job there and it was kind of fun getting off that rhythm and playing a lick or two, but there wasn't room for a lot of solos because if you played a solo the bottom dropped out. I mean, there wasn't room for it, you know. Later, of course, as we got advanced and had a little more money in the budget, and in the kitty, so we would hire other people and we wound up with a couple of different guitar players on the sessions. And then we got, I don't know, we just got too diversified. We had to farm out stuff. We were so busy; we had too many artists--- just got bigger than we could handle. That's all I could tell you.

DD: Hmm. Well I'd like to play a couple things, including, of course, one of your most famous co-writes, which is the one with Otis Redding, on "Dock of the Bay," and maybe if you could just lead us through a little bit of this. I mean, there's some incredible guitar playing on this. [It] just kind of sets the whole tone of the song, and what kind of a co-write was it? How did it work out?

SC: Well, let me just start out by saying that Otis never got to hear the final version of this song. It's very sad and unfortunate. He called me from the airport so excited and wanted to know that I was in the studio, otherwise he would have gone on to the hotel. I knew he was coming in but, uh--- so his pilot flew him in and he said, "I've got this song, Cropper, I just want--- you've got to hear it." So he comes to the studio, they drop him off, he comes running in, "Get your guitar," he says. He called it a gut-tar like I spell g-u-t, "Get your gut-tar," and so we did that and he starts showing me this thing, [hums] [sings] "I left my home in Georgia." I said, "Oh man, this is it." So we sit there, I think it probably took me about maybe twenty minutes to put it together, and I wrote the bridge with him, [singing] "Looks like nothing's going to change/ Everything remains the same/ I can't do what ten people tell me to do/ So I guess I'll remain the same, y'all." And he said, "That's it, man. That's it." So we went in the next day and recorded that song and it was awesome. I played acoustic guitar on the session. I think there's an album out or a DVD or something where there's some outtakes and he's kind of doing--- he wants the seagull sounds and he's going [makes bird noises] and I said, "Man that sounds like a crow; doesn't sound like a seagull." And I had a little---

for all those people out there, listen, he says, "I watched the ships come in and I watch them roll away again." And I said, "Otis, ships don't roll. If they roll, they'll sink!" He said, "No, Crop, that's the way I want it, I want it--- I want them rollin' in." And it took me years to figure out he was talking about the ferries from Oakland over to Sausalito. He wasn't talking about ships; he called a ferry a ship because it was a big boat. I thought he was talking about the big ships out there under the, you know, the bridge over there, the Golden Gate Bridge. But he wasn't talking about that at all. He was talking about the way the ferries come in, you know, how they dock, they roll the water in as they dock so the cars and people can get off. That's what he was talking about. At the time we recorded it I still disagreed with him about watching ships roll . . . and like I said, he didn't get to hear the final product but I know he's still up there listening and very proud of it, and God bless Otis, wherever you are, my man.

DD: Absolutely. Well let's listen to that. Is he the whistler on it?

SC: Absolutely. We had a little deal. He always was the greatest fadeout guy in the world, you know. I mean, he could start a new song on the fadeout. But this time he couldn't remember what we talked about so he just started whistling, and that's the way it came out.

DD: This is Otis Redding with the co-write, with our guest Steve Cropper on "Dock of the Bay."

Otis Redding recording: "Dock of the Bay"

DD: The late Otis Redding, "Dock of the Bay." Steve Cropper is our guest. Steve, we're going to let you head off, but I just, I wanted to set something straight, because I was a little curious myself as to some things I was reading about. Obviously Booker T and the MGs' first big hit was "Green Onions." Well, first of all people have made a point about how quietly important it was that Booker T and the MG's were two black guys, two white guys playing together in a band in the early 1960s. Did that feel important to you guys? Did it feel unusual at all to you guys?

SC: The funny thing is that we didn't know that. That's not what we saw. As far as I know the whole time I was at Stax Records there was absolutely zero color. Everybody came in there equal through those doors. And it literally was like going to church every day, or you know that feeling when you go to Grandma's house, you just feel like, as a kid you go to Grandma's house, you're so safe. You know you're going to get a good meal. You know you're going to get tucked in, and a great place to sleep and all that. So walking through those doors at Stax Records was that feeling. It was like going to church every Sunday. You felt this camaraderie of safeness and everybody was there for the same purpose and everybody was helping everybody out.

DD: Well, that's an important point. But

the point I wanted to clarify was about "Green Onions." I've heard two things: one, that it was a jam to begin with, and number two, that it was recorded after you guys had done a jam and I didn't know which one of those was true.

SC: The second part [is] probably more the truth because we had just jammed on the flip side of that record called "Behave Yourself." We were waiting on an artist to record with, Billy Lee Riley was his name, and he didn't show and so we just, we were jamming on some blues, so Jim Stewart had the tape [al]ready going all out so he just pushes the recording button and records what we were jamming on in the studio. And we get through and we're laughing it off and all that. And I'm sure somewhere in the archives of the tape we can find the first cut and listen to us laughing and carrying on. We had no idea he was recording. So he said, "Hey guys, come and hear this." And we go, "What?" "Just come in here, come up in the control room and listen to this," [he said,] and so [we said,] "You recorded that?" He says, "Yeah." So he plays it and we go, "That's pretty good." And he said, "Well, you guys got anything--- if we put this out, is there anything you could put on the B-side?" And we all sort of look dumbfounded, we're going, "Is Jim Stewart serious or what?" Well, we guess he was. So we all looked dumbfounded. I didn't have anything and I thought about something--- Booker had played me a riff about a week and a half, two weeks prior to that date, and it just came to mind. I said, "Booker," I said, "you remember that riff you played me a couple weeks ago?" And it went [humming]. And he said, "Oh yeah, yeah." So he goes out on the organ and he starts playing this riff, and two cuts later we have "Green Onions" that you know about today.

2006

ROSANNE CASH

ROSANNE CASH IS ANOTHER ARTIST WHO HAS VISITED US MANY TIMES. We have listened to her work change stylistically and mature over the years. *Black Cadillac*, her album written in response to the death of all three of her parents, gave us an opportunity to talk not just about her craft, but to explore the emotions that led to the songs. This was a very special interview.

David Dye: I'm David Dye; this is the *World Cafe. Black Cadillac* is Rosanne Cash's new album, and there's a lot of loss on it. Rosanne lost her father, Johnny Cash, her stepmother, June Carter Cash, and most recently, her mother, Vivian Liberto. Today we're going to hear some live versions of the songs onstage at *World Cafe* Live and talk with Rosanne, and I started off by asking her about how the deaths affected the creation of the songs on *Black Cadillac.*

Rosanne Cash: Right, I'm not the first person to lose their parents, by any means. I mean, it was unfortunate and a bit overwhelming to lose three parents in such a short period, but, you know, this is--- I'm certainly not in a unique position and, in fact, I don't have any friends who aren't going through this in some way or another. You know, it's our generation.

DD: Absolutely. When was the point when you were able to turn the grief you were going through and to decide, "Well, I'm going to make art out of this?"

RC: I don't know that it was ever a--- it was a conscious decision about three months after my dad died that this was what we used to call a "concept record," because I had written half the songs by then, and I saw that this was a single-themed record. But the song, "Black Cadillac," I wrote six weeks before June died, so that song was the first song in the cycle and it was prescient, you know, it was kind of a foreboding--- and then I wrote another that summer. And then my dad died in September, and I wrote three songs in very quick succession, and then realized that it was a thematic piece.

DD: Well, there are two images that are really strong. Obviously the title images, the roses and that Cadillac, and, I think--- let's listen to "God Is in the Roses" first, and where does that imagery come from?

RC: That was the first song I wrote after my dad died and, you know, I was just in that raw state of grief and I just woke up in the middle of the night with that idea that you could find God, or whatever your idea of God is, in sorrow as well as in joy.

DD: It's a beautiful song. This is "God Is in the Roses."

Rosanne Cash performs "God Is in the Roses"

DD: Rosanne Cash is our guest and that is a performance with--- I'll have to mention it right up front— the co-producer of the album, John Leventhal, who is Mr. Rosanne Cash, playing guitar today. Have you done much of this--- acoustic versions of the songs?

RC: We've done a bit of it, you know. John and I have our little George and Gracie folk duo thing that we go out and do, so we've done them a bit. I still--- they're still very fresh to me, though.

DD: It seems the performances are really heartfelt and in that great position of things that are fresh. Various people I've talked to over the years say . . . that songs have a life before you--- when you can perform them and get inside them and then you're sort of just performing them.

RC: Yeah, but then they--- I've noticed they come back around sometimes, like a song like "Seven Year Ache." I got into that place of being automatic about it for a long time, and . . . now it's fresh to me again.

DD: Maybe we can get a performance of that coming up as we look back. Some of the historical pieces in here that might need some explanations for people--- one of them would be the song, "Radio Operator."

RC: Yeah, my dad was a radio operator in the air force in 1954--- this is before my parents were married--- and he intercepted Russian signals, you know, and tried to translate them. And he always said that's why his ears were so good, because he spent so much time with headphones listening for these signals. So I imagined that, and he was writing letters to my mother, who was the girl from San Antone, and I was just imagining a time before they met, and that I was a gleam on the horizon--- and then a time after they're both gone, and maybe they're still sending signals back to us.

DD: This is "Radio Operator."

Rosanne Cash performs "Radio Operator"

DD: "Radio Operator," another one of the new songs from Rosanne Cash on *Black Cadillac.* That song is a great example of something that happens--- which must have been part of your process of coming to terms with death--- is that songs appear before you were born. Songs happen, communication happens after people have died, next generations fit in--- there's even a song that goes back to the---

RC: ---To the seventeenth century.

DD: Yeah. That's a really wonderful concept of continuity.

RC: Well, I--- that was very comforting to me, to try to fit myself into a place, a linear kind of picture, that was much bigger than just my little spot in time, you know, what survives these hundreds of years, and . . . the thing I came up with that I think survives is love, and that a relationship founded on love doesn't end when one person leaves the body, but particularly parent and child, you know, that those relationships have to go on some way. I'm the only one talking right now, and the terms are being renegotiated, but the relationship goes on.

DD: How have your kids dealt with all this?

RC: My kids have been phenomenal. They've actually been a tremendous area of support for me, and I'm aware that as I'm going through grief and losing my parents that I'm also teaching them about when they are going to lose me, you know, that there's a continuum happening.

DD: I think of pictures of at least one of the Cash family homes and I'm thinking about any of us, when our parents die, we have to clean out the family homes. How can you possibly deal with that? That must be---

RC: ---That was very, very painful, the realization that when you lose your parents, you lose your childhood homes and, you know, with my dad and June it was very complicated because the estates and the amount of properties and, you know, everything involved with that.

DD: Was he a packrat, or was she?

RC: June was. Yeah. [laughs] But, you know, they also had a lot of homes and a lot of belongings, and they had designated that a lot of it went to Sotheby's, so it was painful, but--- and I also--- "House on the Lake" got to that point of trying to find out, well, what survives this if you lose all of these tangible artifacts of their lives? What are you left with? Well, you're left with love and memories.

DD: I was thinking of that one or "Burnt Down This Town." Let's listen to "House on the Lake."

Rosanne Cash performs "House on the Lake"

DD: I was thinking about what you do. You're a songwriter, and here you go through this simple and very profound thing that you've gone through--- it's simple because we all go through it, but its profundity just keeps speaking--- and your art form is popular song, which is such a proscribed form--- you've got to have a certain number of verses. You've gotta have a hooky chorus. You've got to--- and you're interested in that aspect of your art, too. You want this to get out there. Did you feel limited by the form at any point?

RC: No, I didn't. In fact, the form itself brought me a tremendous amount of solace because when something feels unmanageable and overwhelming--- that amount of emotional content in your life--- and I'm a songwriter, and I have a structure that I can bring to that, a sense of poetry, a sense of discipline, focus, a rhyme scheme, you know, a verse, a chorus--- that was so useful to me. It made things feel manageable. And a lot of times, in the midst of the confusion and grief, I would start writing and something would be revealed, or something would come clear, something would kind of click into place. Some days, you know, I had a lot of faith. And some days I had no faith. And to write it all out was helpful, to give each one of them equal weight, not go, "Okay, well let me just get through this dark period so I can get to the light stuff." No, but to give the dark stuff equal weight, because it's just as human.

DD: I wanted to play, "Black Cadillac" here, because in terms of song form and all that, this one stands out in a lot of ways. And it was--- as you've expressed--- you wrote this way early in the---

RC: ---Way early, right. Lyrically, it's a little bitter, you know. I mean, I was anticipating the public takeover of grief about my dad and my stepmother, and that was--- I was really dreading that, you know. I felt like I had to share my father my whole life. I didn't want to share him in death. So there's a little bitterness in the songs. They're not all this bitter. But, when we recorded it--- when I recorded it with Bill Bottrell--- as it started unfolding, the arrangement and the approach to the song, I started thinking about the Doors' "Riders on the Storm" and that kind of eerie, you know, ambient thing, so we brought a bit of that to it with more aggression and it seemed to be perfect.

DD: Well that's an interesting way to put it. That's interesting. Well of course none of that is on this, this is the---

RC: The live, yeah, this is different.

DD: The acoustic version of it, of "Black Cadillac."

> Rosanne Cash performs "Black Cadillac"

DD: "Black Cadillac," which is one, as Rosanne Cash stated, of the songs that ended up being produced by one of two people that worked on this album. John Leventhal worked with you on it and so did Bill Bottrell, and you did a performance of one of the songs that Bill Bottrell produced called "The World Unseen," which knocks me out. I just love this song. It's not one, you know, one of the big shiny single-type songs on here, but it's a gorgeous, gorgeous song. And how does that song--- how did it fit in, how did it get written?

RC: It's interesting that you dialed in on that song because that song was really important to me. To me, it's the centerpiece of the record. And just, personally, it's really important. It's kind of almost a manifesto for me, but it's so quiet that a lot of people miss it. That was also written shortly after my dad died. I started writing it and I was thinking about finding the people you love in the artifacts they leave behind and in their geography and in their habits, in their strengths and weaknesses and, you know, are they there--- just that searching--- and I went to Christmas Eve services that year--- he died in September--- I took my kids to Christmas Eve services at the Episcopal church in New York and they sang that old song--- old hymn, "We Three Kings of Orient Are," and they got to that line, "westward leading, still proceeding," and I felt like somebody hit me with a two by four. I wrote it on the program, that line, and I went home and I just inserted it in the song and it was so profound to me, the realization that, well, we're all headed in this direction. Some of us get there sooner than others, but, you know, death is not for the chosen few. We're all going there. And maybe there's a whole world beyond this one that we don't see--- the world unseen.

DD: How did your relationship with faith move in and out during this period, because you have songs here about "I don't believe" and then there are songs, very strong ones.

RC: But that's really human, isn't it? Some days you believe, some days you don't. I really don't trust people who don't have any cracks in their faith and who say they know. I don't know. I believe some things and some days--- I like what Saint Thomas of Aquinas said. He said, "I believe; help me with my unbelief." So at very dark moments, I had absolutely no faith, and in brighter moments, I had a lot.

DD: Well let's listen to this song--- it's a very beautiful one--- it's "The World Unseen."

Rosanne Cash performs "The World Unseen"

DD: "The World Unseen," another performance from our guest, Rosanne Cash. Wow, there's a lot of songs on there, a lot of great songs. When--- have you come to terms with this album, as you said, have you figured out--- I mean, I think it's right up there with *Interiors*---

RC: ---I feel it's up there with my best work, too. I'm still in it. I don't have a lot of perspective or detachment from it, rather. I still feel really close to the songs. They're still—the emotional back story is still very much a part of my life.

DD: It's still happening.

RC: Yeah, it's still happening.

DD: Well, you did a performance of "Seven Year Ache." But are you in touch with that person that wrote that song? I mean, the things that go on in that song--- I was listening to you do it and I was listening to the profundities of the other songs you have and I started saying, "Boy have we all changed." [laughter]

RC: Yeah. Yeah, I grew up. You know what I feel about that song? I feel about it as I would a song my daughter had written. I was so young when I wrote that song, I was 2, and it's come back around to being meaningful to me in a whole different way. It's like singing a song my kid wrote.

DD: [laughter] Well, let's listen to it as we go out. Rosanne, thanks a lot for talking to us.

RC: David, it's always a pleasure.

> Rosanne Cash performs "Seven Year Ache"

DD: "Seven Year Ache." Finishing up onstage with Rosanne Cash and John Leventhal--- an earlier song from a younger Rosanne. The new album is called *Black Cadillac* and it's on Capitol Records, and if you're looking for it you can find it at our *World Cafe* CD store on your web browser at worldcafecds.com.

2006

ERIC BURDON

THIS SESSION WAS A REVELATION.

Eric Burdon and his band on stage at World Cafe Live. Eric Burdon, the original Animal who made "House of the Rising Sun" a world-wide hit, and was one of the hardest-rocking parts of the British Invasion, in the house. I didn't know what to expect, as I'd heard that Burdon could be feisty, to say the least. I was also worried that his latest band of Animals might be a weak oldies circuit group. Turned out I had nothing to fear. He was a master storyteller with a surprisingly good band that burned through two of his hits to begin our session.

Eric Burdon: We're going to start off with a song I learned from Nina Simone many years ago, and it features Eric McFadden on guitar. He's going to do this Español opus at the front.

> Eric Burdon and the Animals perform "Don't Let Me Be Misunderstood"

EB: Now here's a song--- it was a big hit for the Animals from the 60s. We got to get out of here, baby.

> Eric Burdon and the Animals perform "We've Got to Get Out of This Place"

David Dye: Eric Burdon and the Animals playing live today on the *World Cafe*. Eric, the hair's standing up on the back of my neck. I think I speak for our audience today. That was fantastic. And

I'm not easily impressed, mister. Wow. Those two songs I imagine came to you in very different ways. That was originally a Brill Building song, right? Barry Mann?

EB: From the Brill Building in New York, came through the mail . . .

DD: Really?

EB: . . . to our producer.

DD: It's such a perfect song for you. I mean, it's just a--- and the other song you learned from Nina Simone's recordings?

EB: Yeah, I first heard it by Nina Simone and--- I was in New York after it had been a hit record for us in England, and she was at the Hunter College in New York, and Linda McCartney became Paul--- Linda Eastman at the time. She took me backstage to meet Nina. It was pretty scary.

DD: I would think so. [chuckles]

EB: Yeah, and we became the best of enemies from that point on.

DD: But you really did become friends, though. You sent her part of your diary and stuff, I heard. And she had that at one point in her life.

EB: Yes. I had this diary--- I was making notes in [it] and [saving] newspaper cuttings and she asked to borrow it. She kept it for like two years.

DD: [laughs]

EB: I thought I was never going to see it again. And then she returned it and she said, "You know what you are. I figured it out. You're a musical journalist. And that's what you should pursue." And I went on to do things like "Monterey" [and] "San Franciscan Nights."

DD: "Sky Pilot"?

EB: "Sky Pilot," which were for me, off the pages of the newspapers at the time.

DD: Now I knew you and Jimi Hendrix were running buddies. Now did you meet when you were here, or did you meet when he came to England?

EB: I went on a mental sojourn to try and figure out when was the first time I ever met Jimi. And I was in Florida, just recently, and I met a guy who was, in the 60s, was the manager of the theater where the Animals were topping the bill, with support from Little Richard and Chuck Berry and Dionne Warwick and the Shirelles. It was scary, you know, to think that we were going to be topping the bill against these people that we hero-worshipped all our lives. And there was one of these huge elevators backstage which took equipment up and down from the dressing-room level to the floor level. An argument ensued in the elevator because . . . Little Richard had gone overtime. And this guy who I met in Florida, who was telling me that he had to lay the law down to Little Richard, and saying, "Richard, if you go over just five minutes during the next set, you're cutting into the Animals' time, and we're going to have to report you to the union because they're going to shut us down and they're going to fine us $15,000 dollars." And Little Richard went off and into one of his famous tirades. "I'm Little Richard and don't you talk to me that way or . . . !" And there was this little black guy running around with a towel . . . trying to cool him down, "Hey, Richard, it's okay. Hey, be cool, man. It's all right." And that was Jimi Hendrix--- who was playing guitar for him at the time. The argument was settled by a tall black New York cop who stepped forward, opened his winter jacket, and displayed his .38 revolver and said, "If you don't shut up, I'm going to put a hole between your eyes."

DD: [laughs]

EB: And everybody was [whistles], "Oh, okay." Anyway, it was the first time I met Jimi. And the next time I met him was in a mutual friend of ours' house, Zoot Money--- well-known English musician--- and Chas Chandler had brought him there to introduce him to London with um--- for the event that he would be surrounded by musicians and like-minded folks. And he--- yeah, that's the way he was introduced to the U.K. Yeah.

DD: I would think you two would have totally like minds on a lot of things.

EB: Well, I had an apartment on the west end of London which was as west end as you can get. It was just a stone's throw away from the Royal Palace. And I had a great stereo system, and so people would come by, and Jimi would be one of them, and we'd, uh, we'd just avoid the press. Avoid the fans and kick back and discuss horticulture and listen to music.

DD: This new CD is an all-blues album. How did you decide what songs to do?

EB: When we decided to do a blues album, we were in the process of making another studio album with the same crew and producer, Tony Braunagel and many great players. And I said, "Yeah, why don't we do what the people are asking for . . . what are they asking for?" "Well, they all want a blues album." "Okay, so let's go for it." You know, he said, "We'll divide up the work load. You go for the current new stuff that's coming to you via various writers and I'll do some research and go back as far as I can and come up with songs that we can alter slightly and make them relevant for today."

DD: Well, the title song, "Soul of a Man," is great, but then there is a tune in there, I think it's "Red Cross Store," a Mississippi Fred McDowell tune?

EB: Yeah. Yeah, it was written by Mississippi Fred McDowell in about, I think 1929 or 1930. It's history.

DD: It's not entirely inappropriate today.

EB: Absolutely, it's history that's happening right now, as we speak.

DD: We should let people hear it. This is "Red Cross Store."

EB: Yeah.

Eric Burdon and the Animals perform "Red Cross Store"

DD: Eric Burdon and the Animals are playing live today. Live on stage at *World Cafe* Live. Can we go back and talk about Newcastle in the early days a little bit? Explain to the people here in the U.S. what it means to be a "Geordie," what it means to be from Newcastle. What's the myth of it? What's the reality of it?

EB: Drunk.

DD: [laughs]

EB: Um. We loved our hometown football team. In fact, the whole of England does. Whether we're in the first league or the third division, it's like, "Oh man, we hope Newcastle makes it next time around!"

DD: [chuckles]

EB: And it was a town with lots of clubs, fortunately, for a young guy like me. There was like four folk clubs, three jazz clubs, there was a great movie theater where we could see all those great Brigitte Bardot epics.

DD: Was the love of blues unusual in Newcastle? Or--- it seemed to be all over the north of England at that point.

EB: Well, we thought we were the only people in the world that discovered this new art outlet . . . and I was serious about it, man, I remember cutting open my finger and writing blues in blood . . . pretty crazy. But then as I traveled, went to Paris and London, on my way to Paris and London. On the way back, I met Alexis Koerner and Chris Barber and people like that and I realized that all over the world, as far afield as the Communist countries like Poland and places like that, there was this love of your traditional New Orleans jazz or blues and jazz and . . . it was so strong. And at its peak it was like a secret unspoken word that summed up a worldwide youth peace movement. To the point of where most governments thought it was a communist plot. But it was just a bunch of young guys and girls trying to have fun.

DD: Now, when the British Invasion happened and you came to the U.S., was that your first time in the U.S., or you'd been before?

EB: My first time in the U.S. was 1964. I was about to go there in the Merchant Navy and all of a sudden I found myself in the Animals and I came to the States with the red carpet treatment instead of sliding in through the back door. It was all ridiculous.

DD: How did you take advantage of it,

though? In terms of your interests?

EB: Well, because every time we made a stop, I would head for the black side of town. I spent more time up in the Apollo in Harlem and made good friends with Honey Coles, who was the manager of the joint, and he gave me an open backstage pass and I was always hanging out there. I met B.B. King, Rufus Thomas. I found the place where Malcolm X had been holed up across the street in the St. Theresa hotel. I bought a Malcolm X album of his speeches and I could quote these speeches off the top of my head. People thought I was crazy. You know, who was this little white dude? Spouting all this black anger? But I did have black anger. It's easy to explain when your grandpa came home from work at night and he was black--- from working in the coal mines. Fortunately, we could wash it off. And I fell in love with an African girl in my hometown. Ray Charles' record, *What'd I Say,* was heard all over the world. And those lyrics, [singing] "I see the girl with the red dress on/ In Birdland all night long." I walked into a club and there was this black girl, beautiful black girl, with a red dress on. It was like a screenplay that had been written for me. And there was no turning back from that point on, you know?

DD: And was there a special lure to California when you finally got there because you'd been there a lot?

EB: Well, California was a lot different. It was white, first on.

DD: [chuckles]

EB: The cops were an awesome force to deal with. It was different. I could breathe, actually, for the first time in my life. Growing up in Newcastle, it made me asthmatic, and when I got to the dry West Coast weather it was like, wow, I can breathe. And wow, look at those palm trees moving in the wind, you know. And a lot of people told me, "There's nothing going on in LA., it's just a place where they make movies." But in actual fact, a lot of people in the jazz and blues world like myself had moved there to escape the tough times in place like Detroit and New York, [and] down South, you know. So, if you look at blues you can, you can follow the history of the movement of people, and a lot of them, like me, washed up on the West Coast.

DD: Well, you ended up where you were with Jimmy Witherspoon. Wasn't he based there at some point?

EB: Yeah. Jimmy Witherspoon, Ray Charles, many luminaries that I can't come up with their names right now, and Witherspoon took me to--- on gigs to prisons, to work the prisoners. I got--- probably the highlight in my little dream world--- was entering the main yard in San Quentin with Jimmy Witherspoon, Curtis Mayfield, Muhammad Ali and his wife. And that was my introduction to America.

DD: Another introduction of yours in

Los Angeles was you and Lee Oskar getting together with the band that became War. And was that you actually looking for a band to play with at the time? How did that come about?

EB: Well, I'd gone through like three generations of the Animals' bands. And it was really physically tiring and it became mentally devastating when we found out there was no pot of gold at the end of the rainbow. So, I needed help. And instead of going to a psychiatrist, I went to the Actor's Studio for a year in Los Angeles. That was a wonderful experience, and I drove down to Guatemala from California and went--- hung out in Mexico for a year. That was really a great period in my life, and then I was grabbed, sort of, literally grabbed, because these entrepreneurs [were] saying, "What are you doing in the Actor's Studio? You're just wasting your time, you know. If you want to be successful you got to capitalize on what you've already got! And you're the white kid with the black voice, so what can be better than getting involved with a black band?" I thought, "Makes sense." You know. We cruised the clubs in the L.A. area and we found a band called the Night Shift. They were a massive show band with baritone sax, tenor sax, backup singers, percussion, two keyboards. You know, to me it was like a full dressed Harley Davidson, which you knew the engine was, you know, powerful, and it just needed stripping away. You know, and with great difficulty we managed to lose certain members of the band, keep[ing] the rhythm section. So it became viable. It became a band that could travel. And I stayed with those guys for three years.

DD: And I guess, and I never really thought of this, but you listen to your spoken part of "Spill the Wine" that's sort of about you trying to make it in the movies, in a way.

EB: Well yeah, you could say that, but no, actually, it was just my reflections on Mexico. I'd just gotten back from a year south of the border. It was my homage to Mexico and its beauty and its women.

Eric Burdon and the Animals perform "Spill the Wine"

SOUL ASYLUM

THIS ONE IS A LITTLE DIFFERENT.

It took place at our annual visit to the Andy Warhol Museum in Pittsburgh where we go to record a series of benefit shows in front of a live audience for our affiliate WYEP in Pittsburgh. Soul Asylum had been on the Cafe before but we had never had this much fun. The band was playing their first show together to promote their new album, *Silver Lining,* and was in a great mood. We asked a lot of questions about growing up in Minneapolis and the scene there with the Replacements, Husker Du, and other bands.

It was rollicking, and here in this book you get the interview *before* the language was edited for radio!

David Dye: Our *World Cafe* Week at the Warhol concludes today with a ragged but rockin' performance from Soul Asylum. The band's new album is *Silver Lining* and it was recorded by original members Dave Pirner and Dan Murphy with longtime bass player Karl Mueller while Mueller was in remission from cancer. He has since died, and the silver lining of the title comes from the band's reuniting and making the album. In some ways the indie rock band that originally recorded for the hometown Twintone label in Minneapolis never recovered from the worldwide success of their album, *Grave Dancer's Union,* and the single "Runaway Train." We'll hear some stories about those days but first, I asked Dan Murphy to explain the significance of *Silver Lining* as the title of the new album, and to give kind of a timeline of Karl Mueller's illness.

Dan Murphy: Beloved friend and accomplice in crime, and all things great, and some things not so great, and our longtime bass friend, bass player Karl got diagnosed pretty tragically with cancer, and right before we were going to go in to make this record. And then, initially, he got treated with chemo and radiation and he was kind of like the poster boy for cancer recovery, you know, he still kind of looked like a middle-age male model, you know, [laughs] and we decided we were going to make this record. We'd kind of been kind of fussing about that. We didn't really feel an urgent need to get together and record again, and that really kind of became the impetus to get together. And he was in remission for a while and he really wanted to do this, and we didn't know of the complications in the long term, you know, how it was going to affect us, but it seemed like as good of a reason as we needed to get together and make a Soul Asylum record. So that was the initial spark, and yeah, he ended up playing on more than half of the record.

DD: That's great. So he was really the impetus to get you guys--- you were not thinking about doing anything like that?

DM: No, we were kind of enjoying some time off. And like Dave and I started to do a bunch of interviews and everybody's like, "What have you guys been doing the last eight years?" [laughs] You know, like I just kind of--- yeah, you know, it's like it just kind of seemed like a yawn to me. It's just kind of, you know, you kind of let the divas that dance around with headsets kind of do their thing and then, you know the--- you know whatever else is going to happen in music you just kind of watch it and chuckle or whatever, and so there's a million other things in the world that you don't get to do when you do this. I mean, this is not me complaining about doing this. It's more like there are so many other opportunities and events that are parallel, and it was really nice, I think, for Dave and Karl and myself to have a kid, do whatever it is that normal adults do. Live a lot.

Dave Pirner: See what normal life is like, kind of.

DM: 'Cause this ain't so normal, dudes and gals. [laughs]

DD: So what's next in this hootenanny?

DM: Well, I tell you what, it was getting a little heavy for a second there, did you feel that? So let's lighten it up a little bit, you know. This is basically a song about getting loaded. So—

[Audience hoots]

DM: Enjoy!

DP: This is a song off our upcoming release. It's called "What You Need."

Soul Asylum performs "What You Need"

DM: That one goes out to Andy Warhol.

DD: [laughs] "What You Need." That's another one from *The Silver Lining,* the new one from Soul Asylum, our guests today. And we are at the Warhol Museum, and the Warhol museum has a great gift shop, which incidentally is open until 10 o'clock tonight. And—

[Audience laughs]

DD: And the reason why I say that is they lent me a prop for tonight and they said I had to plug them. They have a lot of Warhol-esque music in there: Stones, and Lou Reed, John Cale, Velvet Underground. And they lent me a copy of this album which I'm holding up, which is *Loaded,* and I understand this album had something to do, Dan, with you and Dave hooking up to begin with.

DM: Oh yeah. We got to actually play "Sweet Jane" on that record with Lou Reed when they opened the Rock and Roll Hall of Fame Museum or whatever in Cleveland--- they were like--- they give you a list of people that they think it'd be really cool for you to play with and you kind of go, "Ehh . . . ehh . . . " and then they said, "What about, like, Lou Reed or Iggy Pop?" We said, "Yeah!"

[Audience laughs]

DM: So we got to like, play--- we did a song with Iggy, "Backdoor Man," and we threw a little bit of "I Wanna Be Your Dog" in there. And then we played

"Sweet Jane" and Dave and I were doing the harmonies, like on "Sweet Jane," and he like, turned around, he's like, "I haven't heard those since the Velvet Underground." Because it's like, they're really high. But it was certainly like one of the more memorable things. It was funny, like Lou and Iggy did all these interviews together, and you'd think that they would have been in the same scene, you know, and Lou's like, "I really thought uh, 'I Wanna Be Your Dog' was a really good name for a song." He's like, "Well thank you, Lou."

[Laughter]

DM: You know, they were like--- it was very formal and polite. It was really weird, you know. It was just like, it was very surreal, you know. And Dave and I are kind of sitting there like, "Wow, this is weird," you know. We didn't say a peep. We sat on this couch and let those guys interview each other, you know.

DP: They were wagging their fingers at me not to mix beer and wine, and I was like, "I can't believe that I'm having dinner with these notorious, you know, addicts or whatever . . . "

[Laughter]

DP: . . . and they're going, "Don't mix beer and wine, sonny." [laughs]

DD: Yeah, real dangerous combination for them. Yeah, yeah.

[Laughter]

DM: In the big picture, right, yeah.

DD: I want to talk a little bit about Minnesota music because this year, also, *Closer to the Stars* came out, which brought together Soul Asylum's Twintone--- sort of a best of the Twintone years. And also there's a Replacements' best of, and Dave, I haven't heard this, but there's something about you're involved, you're on the album in some kind of a fight in a club there?

DP: What song is that?

DM: "Kids Don't Follow."

DP: Right, it was the first song off of *Stink*. And it's not--- it's kind of superimposed, so there's this lore that goes along with it and at the--- can I swear?

DD: Try it.

[Laughter]

DP: [laughs] I mean, at the beginning of the record, the Minneapolis police are busting up a party. We used to have these warehouse parties and all the bands would play. It was a reality, you know, back in the good old days. And you just hear this guy in the background going, "FUCK YOU!"

[Laughter and applause]

DP: That was me. I mean, I remember

really particular[ly] we were just yelling it for the sake of doing it---

DM: ---No, because it was like, "This is the Minneapolis police," you know. "Everybody . . ."

DP: ---You know, we were just trying to make noise and yell at the top of our lungs, and when it's superimposed on the beginning of this track, it sounds like the cops are breaking up a party, and I'm screaming "fuck you" at them, and then the Replacements come tearing in with this song.

DD: [laughs]

DP: It really was a great illusion.

DM: The way it really went was the cops broke up the party and everybody went home.

[Laughter]

DM: It wasn't so defiant then. It was like, "Oh fuck, Dave said 'fuck you.'" And they said, "Who said that?" And everybody's like, "All right, we gotta go," and then the party was over.

[Laughter]

DM: You know, but hey, that's show business, you know.

DD: Twintone was one of the fabulous labels, and I always had, I don't know, from the outside it looked like there was kind of like a family vibe to the label. Is that accurate? Would the bands all hang out?

DM: Dysfunctional family. Yes. [laughs]

DD: Yeah, yeah. Well it's the legendary fact that you became the B-team. Now where did that come from?

DM: Uh, Paul Westerberg's mouth.

DD: Oh, oh, [laughs] so we won't go there. Well the B-team's done pretty well.

DM: Well, no it's just, I mean--- but I think the thing about the Replacements was, I mean I went to the fifth floor [of the Warhol Museum] and you look at, you know, pictures Andy Warhol took of Topper Headon and Joe Strummer in the elevator, I mean, that's kind of what their school of thought was, and you know, be outrageous and say whatever you want. And Husker Du and the Replacements hated each other, you know, there was a rivalry there, you know, and I just felt like it was never an issue until I read about it in Japan 20 years after the fact, you know.

DD: [laughs]

DM: You know, "What is the problem with you and the Replacements?" I don't know, you know, you tell me.

DD: Well Tommy was in this band for a little while, right?

DM: Yeah.

DD: And was it also true that to get respect at home, you guys had to actually do something out of town? Because I heard when you guys first toured to New York, that went well. Did that help you?

DP: Yeah.

DM: Karl was kind of handsome so he could get us shows in town. He liked the woman that booked First Avenue, she'd--- like you'd go into her office and there wouldn't be pictures of me and Dave, there'd be pictures of Karl. I'm like, "That's kind of weird." But, so we'd get some gigs. But Minneapolis is kind of like the--- I guess Missouri's "The Show Me State," but it should be Minnesota—-because like, you know, show me what you got. It's like . . . nothing really happens. Same thing with the Replacements and every band. I mean, Bob Mould told us early it's like, "You know what you guys, spend 800 bucks of your gig money, get a van and get out of town." You know, that's like 1983 advice.

Soul Asylum performs "Success Is Not So Sweet"

DD: So Dave, as soon as you get tuned up here, I understand that song kind of came in the wake of the success of *Grave Dancer's Union*, some time back then.

DP: Yeah, it's a funny story because I had written this song and nobody either heard it or liked it. At the time it just wasn't palatable, you know. Nobody wanted to hear that at the time. So we played it once at the little club called the 7th Street Entry in Minneapolis--- kind of, we kind of have a tendency to do an unannounced show and try out a bunch of new material, and I was like, "Fine, nobody likes that song," and I blew it off, and I never heard from it again. And then a guy that used to be my guitar tech found a bootleg of it and brought it in and played it for Danny, and suddenly everybody really liked it. And I was like, "I don't know, you all slept on it the first time, but I guess it makes more sense now or something, I don't really know."

DD: Well, if you're coming right off of that kind of success you guys had, it must be hard to hear that message, you know, at that point.

DP: Bingo, guy.

DD: [laughs] I want to talk a little bit about that because I interviewed you guys around that time, and Dave, I got to say, you were--- it's like you did not want to be in the room. It's like, this is not where you wanted to be, you were like sick of this stuff. And how crazy did it get? What was the most bizarro stuff you guys had to do around that time? Because you not only--- that song was not only a success with rock fans, it became top forty.

DM: Opened for the Spin Doctors, that was pretty bizarre.

[Laughter]

DP: It became very nonmusical for me at some point. I just felt like it was like, "Come on, just stand over here and play your hit song and get on this helicopter, go over there and do that thing blah blah blah blah blah." And you're just like, "Where's the music, you know?" So---

DM: ---I remember we were in Europe one time and we'd been doing a whole bunch of interviews, and there's always a language thing, and you go, "Ah, maybe I just don't get it," you know. They're asking weird questions, you know, like, "Who is watching your cat now?"

[Laughter]

DM: And you're, "Okay, ahh," you know, and so you go, "Ahh." And so then our tour manager was kind of the bullshit detector, Bill Sullivan, who worked with the Replacements and owned a club. He's like, he just throws like these twenty magazines on the table and he goes, "Hey, I just want you guys to know what kind of press you guys have been doing all day." It's like *Popacandy Rock*, you know, it's like the David Hasselhoff, Michael Jackson . . .

DP: ---It was really like these teen magazines where I'm . . .

DM: ---Or draped in an American flag. I walked in this photo shoot, and I was like, "What the fuck is going on here?" You know, it's like---

DP: ---That was the weirdest thing that happened to me because I didn't know why it was happening, but I walked out of a show in Hamburg or Munich or someplace and I got mobbed by these people pulling my hair out and stuff. And this big roadie was trying to hold back all these screaming girls, and I spun around and I tried to fling my beer at the crowd of girls and just hit the roadie right in the face--- and he was trying to help me, you know. And yeah, and that led to, "Why is this happening?" And it was these magazines that were promoting the band just to--- you know, without telling us. [laughs]

DM: I mean, you know, like when your questions is, like, you know, your plants and cats and your favorite color, and, you know, what day is your birthday, and shit. I was like, "Ooh, this is kind of light," you know it's like, "don't you want to hear about the new tunes or anything?" And then, you know--- but I don't know, it just seems like it's just kind of our original plan was to get enough fans where we could pack the shit in a van and go play a club somewhere, and that's, you know, that's . . .

DD: Yep.

[Applause]

DD: Well you did do something in that era which got preserved and put out on disc, which was play a prom, which I thought was just a cool move, absolutely. Was it really fun for you guys?

DM: Eh, we had to wear purple suits for a while. But you know, it's like, we're kind of thinking, like if it's a prom, you want to play some like, booty grabbing or shaking [music] so we did, like, we kind of put together a set . . . of stuff.

DP: We really thought we were going to impress these kids with our Marvin Gaye cover and all this like--- and they're all 15 so they had never heard any of this music.

[Laughter]

DP: And we're like, "What the hell?" And then we finished the first set I remember, and they all went over to the other part of the airplane hangar where we were playing and started listening to Hanson.

[Laughter]

DP: And that's when we kind of knew our goose was cooked, you know. It really was the beginning of the boy band era, and we were just like, "Pshh, man."

DM: If I hear that "Mmm Bop" one more time, I'm gonna kill someone, you know. Be careful what you wish for, I'll tell you that.

DD: Soul Asylum's our guest on the *World Cafe*. And our thanks to our audience at the Warhol, and a great band.

2006

JOHN HIATT AND THE NORTH MISSISSIPPI ALL-STARS

JOHN HIATT IS USUALLY REFERRED TO AS A "SONGWRITER'S SONGWRITER," a well-respected practitioner with hundreds of songs under his belt. He's been on the World Cafe numerous times, but this time in 2006 was special. He was touring with the trio of the North Mississippi All-Stars, including the Dickenson brothers, Luther and Cody, and Chris Chew on bass. They have just made the album, *The Master of Disaster,* together. Hiatt can be reticent in interviews, but boy, not on this day! He had some great stories about high school and juvenile delinquency, among other things. The North Mississippi All-Stars are from outside of Memphis, so I asked Hiatt, who wrote the song "Memphis in the Meantime," about recording the new album there.

John Hiatt: You know that was the first time I ever made a record in Memphis. I went to Memphis, briefly--- I moved to Nashville when I was eighteen and I went to Memphis briefly. Steve Cropper had started a label in Memphis back in the day--- I think it was called TMI records--- and I went to Memphis because Steve wanted to sign me to that label. And I spent a very strange night at Don Nixon's house. Yeah, and he showed me his Nazi gun collection, among other things. Yeah man, what a trip that was. In fact, I think he was putting on the uniforms, dancing around the house. I believe he loaded up a few--- the guy was out of his mind. This is the guy that wrote, what was that song? Oh, "I'm Going Down." And he was, too, man. He was way out there. I wound up not signing with Steve Cropper's label. I can't remember what my reasoning was at the time. I was sure it wasn't anything that made any sense, but I stayed up in Nashville, wound up signing a thing with Epic Records through New York City at the time. But I fell in love with Memphis. I love the whole vibe there. Wound up staying. I had a girlfriend in Nashville and wound up staying there. But yeah, you know it didn't take long to conclude once she started going back to the whole American music thing--- came from, you know, the southern United States. So that's sort of where it all--- to me it was the place to be.

David Dye: Now all you guys are band guys, in a way. You know, John, you're kind of known as the singer-songwriter, but every time you go out you have a killer band with you. I'm not going ask you which is your fave, but I am going to ask you if each band has a life of their own as things go along.

JH: Oh yeah, well you know I've always--- it's funny because I've always straddled the fence. I've liked being autonomous but I've always wanted to be in a band, so I've always sort of played this weird cat and mouse game. But I've always been lucky and been able to play with great people. I've sort of always just been drawn to playing with people that are better than me, and then just wanted to play with band-type players. These guys, North Mississippi guys, really are a wonderful band. It's been a real pleasure and privilege and art to just play with them.

DD: John Hiatt and the North Mississippi All-Stars are our guests. You guys ought [to] play some music as long as you're here. What do you want to start off with?

JH: Uh, well? I don't know, what do you want to start off with? "Wintertime Blues?"

Luther Dickenson: Uh, yeah, that sounds good.

John Hiatt and the North Mississippi All-Stars perform "Wintertime Blues"

DD: That's the "Wintertime Blues," and not exactly what it sounds like on *Master of Disaster*, but a really nice live version from John Hiatt and the North Mississippi All-Stars, who are hanging out today. They've been touring around and you, been revealing stuff in concert and I've been reading a little bit about it on the web, John. One of the things is, I understand, this June [there] were at least a couple of graduations in your family . . . tell us about that.

JH: Yeah, my oldest daughter graduated

from college, University of Denver, and my youngest daughter graduated from high school up in Bath, Maine. And I myself graduated from high school.

DD: Wow!

JH: At fifty-three years of age, I finally got that done.

DD: Applause for that!

JH: Better late than never.

DD: Now when you left school did you leave out [of] a burning desire to do music or just a burning desire not to be in school?

JH: Well, I'll tell ya what. There was some kind of burning there. I'm not quite sure what it was but I was burnt up and burnt out. I just couldn't--- I was a freshman and I just couldn't, you know--- I was just a troubled youth. What can I tell you? I just couldn't--- I just wasn't equipped to handle it, to be honest with you. I was just a mess. I couldn't think straight and it just wasn't in the cards for me to finish high school when I was a freshman. [laughs] I did the best I could and various reasons converged at the same time.

DD: What did you do before you started making music?

JH: Well I was already well into making it at that point. I started when I was eleven and so yeah, it was pretty much, you know, I was pretty much set. But you know my father died when I was thirteen and my mother had to go back to work. I was the youngest boy [of] seven kids and I had my three older sisters at home and I was the youngest boy. I was ready to get out of there. I'm really, kind of, you know it's the old story: a kid was kind of left to my own devices and I was already sorting things out and it was like, school, what? Who needs that? I'm going to play music. It was that sort of thing. The high school experience for me was just torture. [laughs]

DD: Can I get an "Amen" from the Dickensons on that?

JH: Yeah, just torture.

Cody Dickenson: One hundred percent.

JH: But you know what, it's always bothered me that I didn't finish. Just because, just because, I always had that in the back of [my] mind that I couldn't, whatever. I couldn't go on to college, for example. Now I can. The next step is, I wanna take the ACTs or the PSATs or whatever 'cause I'm not just going to go monitor courses. I want to get courses for credit. I want the damn credit. [laughs]

DD: Yes! Now here's a question for everybody who's got kids in high school, and here you go back and you get your GED and you do it now. How hard is it for you now? How hard was it now to do it?

JH: Well, I got to say, it wasn't easy--- particularly the math and algebra. That was a painful experience to know just how little of that I'd retained. It was, you know, I had to study, man. I went to the Williamson County, which is the county I live in, in Tennessee, I went and I had a mentor. I went and hooked up with this lady who is so wonderful and she gave me little pretests to find out what I needed help in--- hooked me up with some workbooks. I went home [and] got my work done. I learned where I was short. Then I took a pretest last December; four hours. You have to pass that to be eligible to take the real test. You know, I did, I barely eked by on the math. Of course on my word skills and all that stuff I did real well. But you know in math I was terrible. So I just barely got by. So I knew I had to study so I got one of those big workbooks. There's about twenty different kinds, studying for your GED. I just got one and I just busted my ass. My girls helped me, thank God. They were explaining stuff to me. I didn't know how to use a calculator. [laughs] I had no idea! Half the math test or algebra test is--- you have to use a calculator. So they showed me how to use the damn thing and I had this whole thing. But this woman, God bless her, man. When the student's ready, the teacher appears. That's all I can tell ya. That's all I can tell the kids. You got to want to learn. Yeah, okay fine, high school's silly, whatever. But get it done so you can go and actually learn something in college.

DD: Well, amen to all that.

JH: Just for the feeling of, "Hey, I did this!"

DD: Absolutely. I am so glad I don't have to try to do that now. I truly appreciate how difficult it must be at this point, too.

JH: Yeah, with the brain cells missing, it's harder.

DD: John Hiatt and the North Mississippi All-Stars are here. One thing about *Master of Disaster,* if you're talking about American music, is it's all over the place. There's this wonderfully folky thing called "Howling Down the Cumberland." I was wondering how that swings with you guys.

JH: Yeah, that's kind of a good--- we're into winter songs on this. Thematically, starting with the "Wintertime Blues." But this is good because this is the hottest frickin week of the tour. It's good we're playing this cool motif. But yeah, "Howling Down the Cumberland" was another wintertime song. Wintertime in Tennessee isn't all that rough, but it's just gray and blue enough to get me down. [laughs] "Howling Down the Cumberland." Let's play that one.

> John Hiatt and the North Mississippi All-Stars perform "Howling Down the Cumberland"

DD: John Hiatt and the North Mississippi All-Stars with "Howling Down the

Cumberland," another song on *Master of Disaster,* the new album. John, there is a song on here, "Thunderbird." Did you ever own one?

JH: I do not. I've stolen one.

DD: Yeah? Tell that story.

JH: Well, I'm not proud of it, but when I was a freshman in high school, when other people were studying to be sophomores, me and a group of kids we were faux punks. We thought we were badasses but we weren't. We played pool and hung around the pool hall and stole cars. We were so stupid we would keep them for weeks at a time and drive them to school and not change the plates--- not do anything--- just begging to be caught. We stole this 66 Thunderbird one very cold February night and kept it for weeks and drove it to the pool hall and shot pool and hung out and, you know, drove it to school in the morning, like idiots. But we were driving home from the pool hall one afternoon and an identical Thunderbird, 66 Thunderbird, stopped. [It] came up alongside us in the far right lane and cut in front of us like it was turning left and spun around right in front of us and these two huge guys jump out. I notice that it had a vanity plate that said "HIS" and ours had a vanity plate that said "HERS." So we realized at that moment that we'd stolen this guy's wife's Thunderbird. He got out and the guy driving, my buddy Gary, he jumped out immediately and took off into the cornfield. [laughs] Me and my other buddy--- I was sitting in the shotgun and my other buddy was sitting in the backseat--- and we had this plan that if any of us were ever stopped, the riders would disavow any knowledge of the driver or the car being stolen or anything--- that we were just hitchhikers. So there was no honor among thieves. So that's exactly what we did. "Stolen? Why we had no idea! We were just hitchhiking! We had no idea this was a stolen car!" Somehow the wife, who was with the guy, she stayed behind with one of the friends while the other two huge guys ran after our friend. And they believed us.

DD: Ha!

JH: We actually talked them into believing us and so we were allowed--- They let us go. I walked home. I was a few miles from home. That cured me of thievery. I'd never stolen as much as a candy bar ever again in my life. I remember walking around for months after, terrified my buddy would've told somebody that, in fact, I was involved in the theft. But I never heard from my buddy again. [laughs] I saw him years later at a show. He came to a show when I was in my 40s and he came backstage and he brought his wife with him. I tried to bring up the incident and he was like giving me the old, "Cut, cut," like his wife didn't know anything about [it] and he didn't even want to talk about it. So I just didn't even say a word. So it was very strange. I was all ready to talk about it. He must've gone away and done---

become a cop. Maybe he'll hear this and chuckle about it. Oh my God. It was just so bizarre.

DD: But I'll bet none of that had anything to do with writing the song.

JH: Well, I make the joke now that this is what I got out of it. I'm not proud of the incident by any means. And on top of that it was like [a] five-below February night and the car--- the lady was going into a pizza place to get a pizza for her family for dinner. She left the car, this was 66, and she left the car running. In those days you didn't think as much about that kind of thing. People did that. Maybe not in New York City, but back in Indiana. And here come these four little scumbags out of the bushes and we took her car. [laughs] I'm an awful person, when I think about, you know. So, there.

DD: All right.

JH: I'm telling on myself.

DD: This is our therapy session with John Hiatt.

JH: Yes, thank you for letting me get that out. I feel much better.

DD: And this is the song that came out of it. This is "Thunderbird!"

JH: What do I owe you, David?

[Laughter]

John Hiatt and the North Mississippi All-Stars perform "Thunderbird"

DD: And that's "Thunderbird," another one from *Master of Disaster.* John Hiatt with the North Mississippi All-Stars playing live here on the *World Cafe.* Do you want to maybe close off with going back in the day? You only got a few to choose from, John.

JH: Yeah, we learned up four or five tunes that we hadn't played last summer. I wanted to learn this one up 'cause I knew we were going to Houston and we were in Houston last year. Well actually, I did a Houston date last year, solo. Rick Linehan, who's an astronaut--- I actually know an astronaut pretty well. He came to a show and he actually took a *Perfectly Good Guitar* CD up with him in 2000, I think it was, or 2001. He went up to repair the Hubble spacecraft--- doing a little repairing, a little space-walking. [laughs] I got to meet him and he told me he took that CD up and he used to play "Blue Telescope" to wake up the other astronauts. I was so touched by that. Then he came to the show last year and I didn't play the damn song! I did everything--- I had tickets for him. I had it all. Everything all hooked up then I don't know what happened in my brain other than nothing right. I just forgot to play the damn song for him. This is the kind of thing, David, that I do in my life. These are the kinds of things I do. If, you know, I've got one foot in my mouth, hey, why not put the other one in? These are the kinds of things I think of on a consistent basis. So I forgot to play the song for him. So this year I was determined that when we went to Houston I was going to invite Rick Linehan and whoever else from NASA that wanted to come, his buddies. I was going to play this song. So we learned up this song. So let's play that song.

DD: This is [the] "Making Amends Tour." This is "Blue Telescope."

John Hiatt and the North Mississippi All-Stars perform "Blue Telescope"

DD: "Blue Telescope" from our guest today, the touring aggregation of John Hiatt with the Northern Mississippi All-Stars. And big thanks to Luther, Cody, Chris Chew, and to John Hiatt for hanging with us today. John, thanks a lot for being here.

JH: Thank you, and thanks [to] the All-Stars for coming out and, you know--- these guys do a set before I play and they are just--- they've been tearing it up across this vast land.

DD: And they continue to. They are among our faves. Thanks to everybody. We'll be back in a moment here on the *World Cafe.*

2006

NEKO CASE

OUR GUEST, NEKO CASE'S MUSIC BRINGS OUT RAPTUROUS DESCRIPTIONS FROM FANS AND MUCH DELIGHT FROM THOSE WHO DELVE INTO HER WORK. Her new album is called *Fox Confessor Brings the Flood,* and we'll find out where that name comes from and more from this artist who made her name in the Pacific Northwest, although she was born in Virginia. She also spends time as vocalist with the Vancouver-based band, the New Pornographers. Her new album comes almost four years since her last studio effort. There was a delightful live album in between, and I ask her if her rumored perfectionist tendencies have added to the time between albums.

Neko Case: Well, *Fox Confessor,* we started recording about two and a half years before its completion, and I just did it in little pieces, so it kind of satisfied my perfectionist streak. But then, also, I made *Tigers Have Spoken* during that time. And also *Twin Cinema* with the New Pornographers, and we toured for both of those records as well, so it kind of freed me up a little bit. I hadn't ever recorded like that before, and what I realized from that recording was I wasn't so immersed in a project that I felt like I couldn't see the edges of it. The nice thing about doing little pieces was I could leave and go work on another project and, you know, when you let your mind go from a certain project your subconscious tends to work on its own, like it has some free time and so your ideas seem better and you have more perspective when you come back and you're able to be influenced by the things, too. I mean, obviously, working with the New Pornographers influences me a lot and as a result, on *Fox Confessor*, there's a lot more vocal arranging because I really enjoy doing that with them. So, it was good. I just went all over the place and just got it done. I gave myself a couple deadlines and then broke those, and after a while I just realized I'll just finish it and then we'll see about the deadlines.

David Dye: Yeah, the vocal harmonies sound great, and it's a note that Kelly Hogan's here today so we're probably going to hear some of those.

NC: She is indeed. We are lucky.

DD: Yeah, that's great. Well, what do you want to do to begin with?

NC: Well, I think we're going to start with "Star Witness," which was one of the first songs on the record and kind of a little tale about living in America.

Neko Case performs "Star Witness"

DD: That's "Star Witness." Neko Case is playing live today for us on the *World Cafe* and Neko, who's all with you today? We mentioned Kelly.

NC: Well, we got Kelly Hogan doing the vocals. We got Tom V. Ray on the bass. Barry Mirochnick is playing the drums. John Rawhouse is playing the pedal steel, the banjo, and the guitar, and then Paul Rigby is playing guitar as well.

DD: When one starts delving into your life, your career, it always seems to me that you've been at it forever and one expects you to be older than you are and you're not and I guess it's sort of because you started so young. You ended up being on your own at the age of fifteen and I'm curious as to how you ended up supporting yourself at that time, how you lived.

NC: I used to steal lots of eggs. [laughing] That was a big source of nutrition. Odd jobs here and there, but mostly, I don't know, the kindness of other people. I don't know, being fifteen, it's really not easy to get a job, and I was trying really hard to finish high school but I couldn't do it because I was very undernourished at the time and learning and not eating just don't really go together. So I kind of had to hustle a little more than go to school, unfortunately, which was kind of heartbreaking. I really wanted to finish high school at that time, which I ended up finishing eventually but, you know, I had to be in the work force for a few years after that to kind of ramp up to it after all.

DD: I know you played drums originally. Was playing in bands kind of a way to survive, of making some money?

NC: No, I never made any money, but I

think it was kind of a way to survive moral lies, you know. I met a lot of other people who were kind of in the same situation as me and we all really stuck up for each other, you know. I grew up in Tacoma, Washington, which is a pretty poor town and, you know, I met a bunch of other like-minded people who--- our town is very poor and kind of industrial and we decided to just embrace that and feel good about it, rather than feel beaten by the whole thing. So we very much loved our town and we loved playing music and, I don't know, I know for a fact that's how it made it all easier . . . because of those people and the music scene there and in Seattle and Olympia at the time. So, it was a good thing. I don't remember much about eating or sleeping or anything at that time, but I'm sure I did.

DD: Clearly, the evidence is here.

NC: Yes.

DD: Now, I know you played in punk bands then and that's sort of a background to what you do but there's--- people often label you a country singer, but really there's a whole wide range of roots that is involved in what you do and I heard there was one specific recording that was sort of an epiphany for you. What was that?

NC: It was a record called *Swing Down Sweet Chariot* by Betsy Griffin and her Gospel Pearls. My best friend and my neighbor downstairs, Miss Laura Woods, found the record in a thrift store and she loaned it to me for about a month and it was the greatest record ever and, you know, there were many other things that were an impetus for wanting to be in a band and wanting to be a singer, but that one particularly kind of stuck out, just because those ladies were so much more passionate about anything than I ever heard and, you know, punk rock was really at an all-time low in the mid to late eighties. It was very macho, and there was just lots of political rhetoric and there weren't that many ladies and I wasn't really finding any sort of voice, you know, that I could relate to--- that I thought represented me in music. And even though I wasn't a religious person, and being really closed minded and thinking I was really punk rock, I thought all religion was really bad, too, you know, like "religion sucks." But then finding this gospel record and just finding some sort of compassion for this kind of music, I don't know, it just opened up so many doors for me, that record. Just the way those ladies sang, the proof was in the pudding. They were not kidding and religion wasn't about some weird strict rules for them. Religion was about love and about power and about making the best of what you have and that really moved me and, you know. Even though I'm still not a religious person now, I have such endless respect for that and those ladies were more passionate about, you know, their love of life and their love of God than anybody in rock and roll or punk rock singing about sex or love or cars or whatever, you know. They had them beat by a thousand, so, I don't know. It just made a real impression on me and I gained a whole lot of respect and that's, you know, when I learned the life lesson, which I'm sure everybody kind of learns around that time. Some people don't, I suppose, but there's so many sides to everything, like everything cannot be black and white. There's all kinds of beauty everywhere and I just am so grateful to those ladies for opening my eyes to that.

DD: Had you been doing any writing at that point?

NC: No, I just was playing drums in bands at the time and singing along with records in my apartment. And going to shows as often as humanly possible, and working really crappy jobs.

DD: When did the writing start?

NC: I played in a band called Mao when I was going to college in Vancouver with my friends C.C. and Toby, and we just started all writing songs together for our band. And then I just started writing more and then I started writing songs that didn't really seem like they'd work in that band, but the Canadian thing is kind of--- the Canadian music scene is very small even though it's one of the largest countries in the world. And so everybody, you know--- there's a big focus on the scene in Canada right now because of all the bands that are huge up there, but basically everybody was in all kinds of different bands so it didn't even seem remotely weird to be in that band and then also start my own band as well. And then eventually I had like four bands. [laughing]

DD: And then, yeah, be in two or three other bands at the same time.

NC: Exactly! It just wasn't weird at all, so you know, [I] just went ahead and did it.

DD: And for our listeners, at least one of the two or three other bands we're talking about of course is the New Pornographers, which is a pretty incestuous band in and of itself. People from all other bands helping out there.

NC: Yeah, exactly.

DD: Neko Case is our guest today and let's move on. You want to do another tune? What's next?

NC: I think next we're going to do "Maybe Sparrow."

Neko Case performs "Maybe Sparrow"

DD: "Maybe Sparrow," a live version of that, which you will find on *Fox Confessor Brings the Flood*, the latest Neko Case album, and we're really happy to be able to hear some live versions. That's one of my personal favorites on there. That's a great song, great song. Where did it come from? Tell us about it.

NC: I'm just pretty obsessed with animals in general and birds pretty specifically and . . .

DD: They're all over the covers, yeah?

NC: . . . They are. They're everywhere. I've always been very close to animals and, I don't know, I think it was just a little rhyme that wouldn't leave me alone and I ended up making it into a little fairy-tale story.

DD: I want to talk about reverb . . .

NC: Let's do it!

DD: . . . Because it has a little something to do with the way the live album sounded and a bit [of] a way of how you sound today, and even makes a way onto the album. You love singing into that void, it seems.

NC: I do.

DD: What about it?

NC: I think a lot of the old recordings that I really enjoy have a lot of that, and it's incredibly unpopular right now. You would not believe the opposition that you're up against when you want to put a bunch of reverb on there. There's a couple bands out there that love it. My Morning Jacket have been really instrumental in promoting reverb in this day and age so maybe there's me and them right now. I don't know [laughing]. But I don't know. It kind of— on the live record most of the reverb is natural, and that's one of the really great things, and I guess one of the influences I can cite for that is live Tina Turner records. Live Ike and Tina records where Tina Turner would be singing and then she would go into some very passionate chorus and you could hear the reverb change because she actually changed the way the air moved in the room, because she was that powerful, and that's what reverb is. Reverb is, you know, the way sound is echoing inside of a natural structure, and it's an indication of the way air is moving, et cetera. It's very physical, and so taking a breath before you sing something, [she takes a deep breath] the ramp up to that is very gone right now in radio music and so, I guess I'm not that worried about being played on the radio or I wouldn't have reverb or leave breaths in. But I think that's such a powerful thing. Like, I always think about "She's Got You," that song that Patsy Cline did where she goes, "I should hate you the whole night through." The breath she takes before the phrase, "I should hate you," is so much more powerful than what she actually says right afterward. It just breaks your heart. And that's the part that makes you cry. Like, you should be able to hear the physical space, I think, and reverb is that to me.

DD: So there's kind of emotion in the air and in the physical space. That's certainly what you're saying about Patsy.

NC: Yeah, exactly. And that's the difference between going to see a live show and hearing a record. That's the reason why you can make the same amount of sound with five people live as you can with, you know, with seventeen on a recording, because it's more two-dimensional on a recording so you have to kind of build it up, but--- well for me personally, I mean, everybody's different with the way they record, but, you know, I like to hear that air and I like to hear it moving and me, I put a little bit extra on just because I like it so much. It's like people who put extra sugar in their coffee, I guess. So some people are kind of thrown by it and they're like, "Are you trying to cover something up?" But if I were trying to cover something up I would use auto tune, [laughs] which I am very proud to say I do not.

DD: Well, okay, we'll crank up the reverb a little bit for what's coming up next. I have a list of things you might want to do. Is "That Teenage Feeling" possible?

NC: Teenage Feeling is--- it can happen right now. [laughing]

DD: Excellent.

Neko Case performs "That Teenage Feeling"

DD: "That Teenage Feeling," a live version from *Fox Confessor Brings the Flood* from Neko Case, who's our guest today. Animals [are] certainly involved in all of this. *Fox Confessor Brings the Flood* is from a fairy tale?

NC: The Fox Confessor himself is from a fairy tale. There isn't one specifically called *Fox Confessor Brings the Flood,* but I just borrowed him from some Ukrainian and Russian folklore just because I liked him as a character very much, and Ukrainian/Russian folklore had a lot to do with a lot of the things on the recording. It's funny because when you make a record you're thinking about the songs and you're thinking about getting the bed tracks down, and whatnot, but the themes don't always become apparent until about halfway through, and I definitely work that way. And so about halfway through the recording I realized how obsessed I was with things like loss of faith or Ukrainian and Russian folklore or just literature in general and, you know, living in America, I was thinking about how we don't really have fairy tales anymore. We have movies and things like that; that's kind of our folklore. American movies these days are pretty much standard and usually you get the answer at the end of the movie. It's not very open ended, and what I really loved about Ukrainian and Russian folklore is that they're not overly moral. The interpretation is pretty open, and they're also very dark and they're very funny and, much like Native American folklore, they rely, or not even rely, but they respect animals on the same level as people. They don't separate human beings from nature and I think that I'm very obsessed with why we don't have things like folklore or why we do separate ourselves from nature every single day. Like, there's this big void in between, even though we're natural beings, and so I think that obsessing about that--- I don't really have a language for it--- but maybe that's why I have to write songs about it which hopefully doesn't sound too overly hippie, but [laughing] it's true.

DD: Neko Case is our guest on the Cafe today and it's funny, we're talking about the folklore and the various themes and I wanted to talk about probably the most kind of confessional song on [*Fox Confessor Brings the Flood*] which is "Hold On, Hold On," which you've described it that way. This is more you?

NC: Yeah, it's kind of a just a tongue-and-cheek song. It's kind of silly. Just about, probably, being thirty-five and not being married or having any kids and living with a dog, you know. Your peers around you are all married with their kids and stuff and you wonder if you're just floating in a sea of not belonging or something, but, you know, really there's nothing wrong with that. And I don't know, I still feel like I'm nineteen years old and all the possibilities are wide open, I suppose. So I'm just going with that because it feels good. [laughs]

DD: And you can do a version of that?

NC: Yes, we can do that right now.

Neko Case performs "Hold On, Hold On"

DD: "Hold On, Hold On," finishing up our session today with Neko Case. Another great one from this album. Neko, thanks a lot for singing for us and talking. It's been fun.

NC: No problem. Thank you for having us back. I really appreciate it.

2006

LINDSEY BUCKINGHAM

ONE OF THE ADVANTAGES OF BEING OF A CERTAIN AGE IS THAT A NUMBER OF THE PEOPLE I TALK TO ARE SIMILARLY SEASONED!

Doing an in-depth, sit-down interview with Lindsey Buckingham at the height of Fleetwood Mac's success with *Rumours,* was not only unlikely to happen, it probably wouldn't have had any of the insight this conversation from 2006 has.

He was calm, tan, and completely open and at ease in talking, but a little obsessed with how his acoustic guitar sounded in the live music portions. Right in character. We got to talk about his personal life now, and in the Mac days, and got some insight into a number of the old recordings. It was a great afternoon.

David Dye: Lindsey Buckingham is my guest today. He has a new solo album called *Under the Skin.* He and Stevie Nicks joined Fleetwood Mac in the 70s after releasing a duo album on their own, and their input rejuvenated Fleetwood Mac and led them to their greatest success. He has been in and out of the band, reuniting for the *Say You Will* album, which was a success. All along there have been experimental, inventive solo albums. I began by asking him if it was freeing for him to work alone, as he did on the new disc, compared to balancing all the egos and ideas and in the group, Fleetwood Mac situation.

Lindsey Buckingham: Well, it was. I mean, as you may or may not know, much of the material that I had been intending to get out as a solo album over the last ten years or so ended up on *Say You Will*, the last Fleetwood Mac studio album. So when that found a home, suddenly I found myself in a frame of mind to really want to do something different. I had gotten married and had kids in that interim. And, I wanted to make something that felt intimate. And I think, also, you know, I had had experiences on the road with some songs that had transformed themselves from ensemble pieces to single guitar pieces, and those seemed to be very effective with audiences. So, it just got me thinking about how to make an album that is, basically, presented that simply. And I think, you know, as you say, the reason it doesn't sound like other acoustic albums is because there are production techniques applied liberally, and I think that's the point of departure.

DD: Absolutely. Lindsey Buckingham is our guest. Why don't you do the first track from the album, if you could, because it's a really good one, and people might understand why I say that word "visionary" when they hear this.

LB: Well, this was actually a song that came about because I saw a piece by Bud Scott in *Rolling Stone,* who somehow had reason to want to refer to me as an underappreciated visionary, and it got me thinking about motives for what you do for long periods of time, and how it lines up with the present, especially when you have children. So this is called "Not Too Late."

Lindsey Buckingham performs "Not Too Late"

DD: "Not Too Late" is the song that begins *Under the Skin*, Lindsey Buckingham's new solo album. And, yeah, you're right, there are almost too many questions and things that come up in that song. You got a lot in there. I'd like to center in [on] the part about having kids. My response to having kids was [that] it made everything I'd done before in my life seem like prologue, and that it was kind of starting now. I wonder what your vision was when that happened.

LB: I think, to some degree, that there's almost a biological imperative that that would be the case. And I certainly experienced that same thing. I think the irony, you know, comes when you have sort of chosen to conduct your life in a way that's very focused on very few things. You know, I had a lot of my friends in the earlier days who were parents and were not really present, were not really there for their kids, and the kids suffered. I swore I would never do that. I wanted to honor the upbringing that my parents gave to me. So, by the time it seemed possible, it didn't seem particularly probable. And yet, you know, I did meet a beautiful woman, my wife Kristen, and we've had three children. And so all of that which is all about the present, you know, lining up with the product of maybe twenty,

twenty-five years of work, you know, this album which is also in the present but is as much about the past--- I mean, there's an irony there. You have to ask yourself about the motives that, maybe, led you to this point. And, of course, there's the part at the end of the song where I'm talking about my children looking away, they don't know what to say. You know, my two older children have seen Dad on stage with Fleetwood Mac in front of a whole bunch of people. I think my son called it "showing off." So, you know, he understands. He has a healthy skepticism of the pretense of all of that. So you know all of it--- there is a great deal of irony to all of that.

DD: You were talking about doing one that goes back, I think, to *Tango,* which was the album you made before you kind of left. What were the circumstances of recording this the first time? Did you get what you wanted?

LB: Yeah, sure, at the time, you know. That album was a bit chaotic. I think probably the main reason that I produced the album and went through the process, and then left before the tour, was because it was extremely chaotic. I think that point kind of represented the apex of everybody's, you know, personal lives hitting the wall in every way. And you know the road is usually times five, or whatever, of that. So, it was a kind of a survival mode for me. But sure, that song, "Big Love," was the first single from that album. And, at the time, just to get through it, you know, was the triumph. And you know, to be able to come back to the song and restate it, not consciously--- it was just something that happened, you know. It, sort of, has been the springboard for what I'm doing now, in a way--- the psychology of that.

DD: Cool. So, we can get a version of that?

LB: Yes, "Big Love."

Lindsey Buckingham performs "Big Love"

DD: The big acoustic guitar version of "Big Love." Lindsey Buckingham is here today. That sounds fabulous. In reading up on your life, one of the things I read about was when you were a kid you not only noticed pop music on the radio, but you claim you noticed, like--- you were interested in production as a kid. I mean, you knew what that was? You figured out what a record sounds like?

LB: Well, not in those words. After I became skilled at knowing how to listen, how to take things apart to understand what makes something sound the way it does, I remembered that even before rock and roll came into the household, that when I was drawn to my parents' 78s, I would be listening to *Nutcracker* suite or *South Pacific* or Patti Page, for God's sake, and asking my mother, "How! How did they make that sound? I mean, what is the concept behind that?" And my mom, not always being able to tell me--- but, yeah, there was a train of thought towards trying to take things apart even back then. And then, of course, when my older brother brought home "Heartbreak Hotel," as I'm sure is a fairly common story, I was just, that was, you know, just a revolutionary thing for me, and I started spending hours in my brother's room listening to his 45s.

DD: One of the things I also noted: your life has been a series of coincidences, things happened that were just fortuitous along the way. You met Stevie, you ended up going to L.A, you got some kind of an inheritance from somebody you didn't even know, that allowed you to do production work, and that led to being in the studio. I mean, a series of coincidences . . .

LB: Yeah, that's right. It really is. You're right.

DD: . . . Do you ever wonder, "Gee, if I'd taken a turn this way . . . ?" But you were always drawn to production. You were always drawn to music. Obviously, it was always there.

LB: Yeah. All of that seemed like a very natural series of things. I met Stevie when she transferred to my high school when I was a junior, and she was a senior, and then she graduated and I finally got in a band. Somehow, we hooked up the following summer. All of that seemed like it was kind of a natural progression. The only thing that I've ever thought about, now, in terms of what might have happened had we made a different choice was, after we did that one album, Stevie and myself, we were in the studio and working on--- we were in the back studio at a place called Sound City. And we were working on some new material and I walked into Studio A and I saw this big, tall guy listening to one of our songs, "Frozen Love." He was rockin' out to the guitar solo. And, of course, that was Mick Fleetwood, and a week later he asked me to join the band and I said, "Well, you gotta take both of us." But it was not a clear idea, you know. They had had many incarnations since the Peter Green days, since the Danny Kerwin days. And we had had a strange kind of phenomenon that had begun to happen even though our album hadn't sold and was not on the charts. We were, somehow, able to play for four or five thousand people, headlining in places in the South. And it was a sort of a calculated move, weighing the pros and cons. But, what might have happened if he hadn't done that? You know, it's an interesting thing to think about.

DD: You want to do another older one? What are you doing next?

LB: Sure. Yeah. You know, it was interesting--- the big challenge being in Fleetwood Mac in the early days was, of course, as everyone knows, Stevie and I were a couple, and John and Christine McVie were a couple. And somehow, we, the four of us, ended up, you know, being four people instead of two couples, and were still having to fulfill what appeared to be the destiny that had been laid out for us. And that was a hard thing for me, you know, as a producer, to be able to go in every day during the process of the making of *Rumours* and craft songs for Stevie--- basically make hits for Stevie--- that were allowing her to move even farther away. It was a tough, emotional challenge, and I think we all got through that . . . to some degree on, you know, maybe not the best means--- probably to some degree, a certain amount of denial, a certain amount of compartmentalizing of feelings. You know, you come up with songs where you have the illusion there's that old adage that says, "When you're happy, you think you'll never be unhappy again." And I think this song was, basically, about a point where I had kind of gotten a little bit down the line with closure with that, and I thought maybe, you know, there would be never be another emotional strain in my life.

DD: So you're going to do "Never Going Back," huh?

LB: Exactly. So, "Never Going Back Again."

Lindsey Buckingham performs "Never Going Back Again"

DD: Live, acoustic version of "Never Going Back Again." Lindsey Buckingham is with us today on the *World Cafe.* You know, you talk about all the angst and everything that was going on in the making that album. Everybody has heard about it all these years. Do you wonder, "Would it have been better without it?" Or, did it fuel it, the creativity?

LB: No, absolutely; it was inseparable from it. I don't think we understood it at the time. I don't even think that we were that in touch [with what] we were writing--- such clear-cut dialogues back and forth to each other. I think they appeared, at the time, to be way more generic than they really were. It was really the audience who made us aware how true they really were, and how specific they were. It's one of those things: you do your work and you try to get through it. Sometimes you can't be objective about it until you get other people involved, get the audience involved. And in this case, the album, the effect of the album, the success of it, certainly, was not strictly about the music. It was about people buying into our lives and possibly, if you want to look at it, our heroics, if you want to see it that way. It brought out a bit of the voyeur in everyone. I can't see that it was inseparable from the music. That was part of what made it a phenomenon at that time, I guess.

DD: And yet, now when you hear it, it's the songs that last. And there's something about--- they're great songs. I have to ask one more Fleetwood Mac-era question, and that's about *Tusk,* which was seen at the time as--- because it didn't sell twenty million copies, and in fact, only at the time, sold two million copies--- as seen by some people as a failure. Yet, over the years, *Tusk* has come to represent one of the high points of the band,

and certainly towards your work on that--- if people are going to call you a visionary, that's part of where that comes from, is people's idea about that album. How did you feel at the time, and how have your feelings about the album changed?

LB: Well, you know, that was an interesting process. To go through the kind of mega-success that we experienced on *Rumours* is not something too many people get to be on the inside of. And certainly it was a great experience. And yet, as with anything else, it had its limitations. It certainly gave us the artistic freedom--- it gave us some financial freedom; it gave us visibility. But, you know, I think there is a kind of tendency to follow that adage, "If it works, run it into the ground." And I think that there was pressure from the record company and, probably, to some degree, there would have been a tendency from within the band as well to try to make "Rumours Two." But the band was still way behind it, and so was I. It was only when, as you say, it did not sell sixteen million copies or whatever it was, that there was a kind of a backlash from within the band. And that was something like, "Well, Lindsey, we still want you to produce but you can't do this anymore, you can't do this anymore." So, that left me sort of dead in the water in terms of knowing what to do, you know. I mean, you can't consciously go back and be something you're not. That was sort of the beginning of the end for me. It was certainly the beginning of making solo albums, which I probably never would have made if we'd somehow been allowed to include that more left side of the palette. So, you know, at the time it was kind of heartbreaking for me. But, as you say, in retrospect, now I have Mick Fleetwood and Stevie both saying, "Gee, that's our favorite album now."

DD: Lindsey Buckingham is our guest today on the Cafe. Thank you so much for coming in.

LB: My pleasure. Thanks a lot for having me.

2006

TOM WAITS

I'VE BEEN AT THIS SO LONG THAT I ONCE SAW A BRUCE SPRINGSTEEN SHOW IN A COUPLE-HUNDRED-SEAT COFFEE HOUSE AND TOM WAITS OPENED FOR HIM . . .

or maybe I've been at this so long I dreamed that. Nonetheless, I had to wait until the sixteenth year of the World Cafe to talk to Tom. He was in California and I was in Philadelphia and I was nervous. Mr. Waits does not suffer fools, or so I thought. Maybe he suffered me, or maybe he's just a nice guy.

Look at the way his mind works. You can certainly hear it in his songs, but you can read a lot of the twists and turns in this piece. He just has a way with language. The forty-five minutes flew by.

David Dye: One of the most important figures in American popular song is our guest today. And a true iconoclast, Tom Waits, joins us for conversation and we'll hear performances from his recent *Orphans* tour. Waits is from California and brought his boho persona and style to the southern California scene in the 70s, dominated by the country rock of the Eagles. In fact, the Eagles recorded Waits' "Ol' 55." A change in his music took place in the 80s following his marriage to Kathleen Brennan, who became his collaborator. His audience followed into a strange, more dissonant and often beautiful world. A lot of songs that didn't find a home in many of those post-1980 albums, plus film soundtrack work--- Waits has developed a second career as an actor--- and new songs all live together on *Orphans*, his new album. I asked Waits if he had any concerns about making the songs from various places all work together.

Tom Waits: Well, that's always a concern. You know, it's like editing a film or anything else. You know, after you create some kind of meaningful experience out of all this raw material.

DD: You've been talking about it, or least mentioning it since, I guess, 2004. So, did it really take that long to put it together?

TW: Well, you know, it's like taking chickens to the beach, you know? They ran off in all directions. And I don't really have an archive, and so it's kind of hard to get 'em all in the same drawer. So, some of them I had to, had to buy from a plumber in Russia, who actually keeps better, takes better care of my songs than I do.

DD: Yeah, I read about that. How do you know how he got ahold of them? Or you didn't ask?

TW: I didn't ask. You know it's kind of like a cloak-and-dagger thing, you know. It was just, there's this guy and he had a translator and everything and the kind of muffled voices and weird sounds. You know, we made a deal. I sent him a cashier's check, you know. It was all very--- no, it was like 007.

DD: Yeah, you didn't have to meet on a freighter in the Baltic Sea or anything, did you?

TW: No, but I would have. [laughs]

DD: That would have been fun, actually. [laughs]

DD: Let's talk about some of the pieces on here, because there's some really, really interesting things from all over the place. I want to talk about a couple of the spoken word things, or sort of spoken word things. There's a, there's a Jack Kerouac song on here.

TW: Yeah.

DD: Now, where the heck did that come from?

TW: Well, you know he, he recorded it on a little reel-to-reel in a closet in the middle of a party one night. And his--- one of his nephews, Jim Sampas, got ahold of it and put it on a Kerouac compilation. So, I heard it and--- yeah, he was singing. It was really nice to hear--- hear Jack singing. I think it worked really well in that sequence after that Bukowski thing about the kid on the bus in North Carolina. And it segues into this piano--- that's that "Home, I'll Never Be."

DD: Yeah. That's one of the points where the *Orphans* get along really well. Tell ya what, why don't we just listen to that sequence; because I was gonna talk about Bukowski anyway. So, let's put those two together.

> Jack Kerouac recording: "Home, I'll Never Be"
>
> Charles Bukowski recording: spoken word piece

DD: A couple of pieces that were not written by our guest today, Tom Waits. Jack Kerouac's song, "Home, I'll Never Be," and Charles Bukowski's spoken word piece in there as well. I understand at one point people were looking to you to play Bukowski in a film?

TW: Oh yeah, in "Barfly," yeah. I was a little too out of money, I thought--- although Mickey Rourke did a great job in it. He was--- Barbet Schroeder asked if I was interested in pursuing it and I was working in Zoetrope at the time and--- yeah, I wasn't really that confident as an actor, to be honest with you. I thought it was a little too much for me to take on at that time. But, you know, [I'm] a great admirer of Bukowski's and all of his incarnations, you know.

DD: Well, so much of his work has actually made it to the screen, in one form or another.

TW: That's true, yeah, yeah.

DD: Speaking of Kerouac and the Beats, one has to assume that they were a huge influence on you early on. I know this is probably going way back in your mind, but do you remember when you were introduced to them?

TW: Teenager, I guess. I was a doorman at a nightclub and the guy who owned the club was a--- read Kerouac--- and he gave me a book and got me *On the Road*, I guess. I got glued to it. You know, sittin' out there on the door, half in the rain and half out of the rain--- it just spoke to me. You know, it's like hearing a song on the radio or something that all of a sudden, it's just everything winds up, and just, the recipe is just right. So, a lot of those guys kind of became father figures for me and I, you know, they were real buccaneers, you know.

DD: I guess Ginsberg would have been one of the ones you were able to meet.

TW: Yeah, I met Ginsberg a couple of times and I did that song, "Home, I'll Never Be," at a memorial for him. That was done in Los Angeles on--- yeah, he's one of the great ones.

DD: Another one of the people I guess from a similar era, probably a little earlier, is Leadbelly. You do a version of "Goodnight Irene" on here.

TW: Oh yeah.

DD: And "Fannin Street," which is your song, but isn't there a Leadbelly---

TW: ---Yeah, he's got one with the same title. He died the day after I was born.

DD: Wow.

TW: And [of] course I read a lot about him and, you know, heard a lot of the records. And yeah, I really--- he really speaks to me. And I had a chance at one point to be a part of a compilation on Leadbelly. Pick a Leadbelly song and his--- one of his distant relatives had his guitar that had been beneath her bed for the last fifty years or whatever, and she was gonna let everybody on the record play his guitar and do a song. But I guess--- I don't think they could get clearance from Alan Lomax, who has a lot of his songs tied up. I guess that whole Lomax estate, you know--- so it's kind of a mess, legally.

DD: Was it a big ol' twelve-string or---

TW: Yeah, yeah.

DD: Oh.

TW: The same one.

DD: That's amazing. Tom Waits is our guest on the Cafe today and we're talking about some of the *Brawlers, Bawlers, and Bastards*, which are a part of *Orphans*, the sprawling, shall we say, new release. One of the songs I'd heard before was that one that was in the film, *Big, Bad, Love*, "Take the Long Way Home."

TW: Oh yeah.

DD: And did you, did you write that for it, or were they looking for a song, or how did that work out?

TW: Yeah, yeah, they wanted a tune. They didn't know what they wanted. But, but yeah, so you know, it's--- sometimes a song is really at a right angle to what the film's about and you don't always hit it right on the money. You don't always want to. So, left of center is usually the best way to go and--- yeah, the mind will make sense out of just about anything, you know. If you show somebody a film clip of a shark attack and then you play a little snippet of, you know, "That's Life" with Frank Sinatra, you know, people will make sense of that. Your mind will go, "Okay, shark attack. That's life," you know, "Okay, I got it." So sometimes you have to kind of create a riddle. I think those are the songs that last the longest; are the ones you don't necessarily understand. Not that that's one of those songs you don't understand. That's pretty clear. You know, "Take the Long Way Home," you know. But sometimes, if there's a little nagging misunderstanding--- or it helps glue the song to the pictures, you know . . . because a song is really a complete item in and of itself. It's really a movie for the ears. So, you don't want to be redundant.

DD: Well, this one stands up pretty well on its own. You can take it out of the context, obviously and it works, as well. And this is "Long Way Home" from Tom Waits.

Tom Waits recording: "Long Way Home"

DD: "Long Way Home" from Tom Waits, a song that some of you may actually know. Norah Jones ended up covering that one as well.

DD: You know, it's such a huge question with you about covers. I don't even know where to begin, because so many of your songs have been done by other people. Is it still flattering or is it---

TW: ---Oh yeah, sure man. Yeah, of course. That's really--- I mean the idea that you can do something that someone else finds interesting for themselves to sing is--- and they find it meaningful, that it's not overly personal, and to you yourself, you know, they can find a place they can sit down . . .

DD: ---Right.

TW: . . . in the song. Yeah, that's kind of what you are looking for. I had a song covered by Johnny Cash. That was like a huge thrill for me. He even changed some of it. I thought, "Oh boy, well, I guess he must've thought it needed some changing." I should have talked to him before I finished. Probably could've helped me. But--- and then you know--- yeah, it's interesting. You hear songs recorded by a, you know, a band from Finland, or Norway, or Thailand or Tokyo. It's a--- I love it.

DD: Well, I wanted to go in a completely different direction with this next thing, because I guess I'm kind of enamored by some of the spoken word things here, because I love it how you use your voice to conjure up things.

TW: Oh yeah?

DD: This is one I think combines a couple of your scientific interests and--- I'm talking about "Army Ants."

TW: Oh yeah, yeah.

DD: I just kind of wait for the beep on the filmstrip on this one. It's a--- how did you and Kathleen come up with it?

TW: Well, most of that is from the Audubon Society Field Guide for Insects, you know. So, you know I think we both like the arcane minutia of life and the little things that hold this all together and--- I don't know, those are, those are fascinating facts. I guess I'm hooked on fascinating facts. Like, did you realize that in Texas, you are considered legally married if by publicly introducing a person as your husband or wife three times?

DD: Wow. That could be useful. Or not.

TW: It could really hurt. It could really get cha. But, I don't know. I thought those were interesting things about the insects because they do live parallel lives with us, I guess.

DD: Well, let's listen to a little of the "Army Ants."

> Tom Waits recording: "Army Ants"

DD: You did almost, I mean, if you look at the credits on here, a whole lot of these songs are ones you and Kathleen worked on together, your wife, Kathleen Brennan. Who says, "Come on, hon, we need to go to work?" Is that--- How does that work?

TW: Gee, I don't know. It kind of--- you throw down the gauntlet, you know, for each other. I don't know how you get started. You get started with a deadline, usually.

DD: Yeah.

TW: "We only got another three days on this, baby. We better start working," you know. I'm one of those people who likes to write in the car on the way to the studio. And she'll do that, too. She's a good sport. You know, she's quick on her feet, and a remarkable collaborator. And so she, she's, you know--- if two people know all the same stuff, one of you is unnecessary. I think when you come at it from two different angles, you know--- she's got the rumbas and the bossa novas and the Gregorian chants. And she had one of those record collections. At one point I said, "Baby, I don't know if I'm marrying you because I love you or just because you just got such a great record collection." You know? It was a little bit of both, I think. All my records were like, you know, out of their sleeves, and you know, in pizza boxes. When she--- she keeps it all together. But we have a lot of fun writing together. It's a hoot. You know?

DD: Your life changed so dramatically when you met her. You had, I mean, obviously you had kids.

TW: Yeah.

DD: I guess around that time you stopped drinking--- a certain domesticity--- which some say can kill art. But you know, it certainly didn't in your case. But there was also a kind of real major change in your music, kind of a second act, although kind of hinted at before, I guess. It was pretty dramatic. Can you kind of pinpoint or even draw kind of a large circle around, around that change, and how that happened?

TW: Oh God, geez, I don't know. [laughs] I don't know about that. I think those things are like fevers. You know? Gee, when did I get that fever? How long did that fever last? How high was that fever? I don't know. I think you start out early on by kind of imitating and doing bad impersonations. And slowly you evolve more into yourself. So---

DD: ---Well, amen to that. One of the things we're going to be doing today is listening back to some of the performances from the *Orphans* tour this past summer.

TW: All right.

DD: A tour that was a remarkable lovefest by all reports. You seemed to enjoy it. And I know people who flew in from the East Coast where we are to any of the various 'villes you played in: Nashville, Louisville, Akron, or whatever. You had a great time? Do you like playing live? How do you treat it after doing theater? Did you treat it as a theater piece at all, or how is it for you?

TW: Well, there's usually a lot of technical things that have to be dealt with and I--- sometimes it ruins the whole experience for me. It's like, you know, it's kind of like, it's like open heart surgery. Now we're going to move it, you know, we got to take this whole thing. We're in mid-operation and we're going to move this to, you know, Alaska. So, it really bothers me at first and--- I had a lot of great people working with me. And the whole gang went out: my son played drums and--- so yeah, it was really good, it was really good. I actually had a good time, in spite of myself. Surprised myself. I'm usually pretty grumpy out there and--- you're dealing with physics all the time. And a lot of people like the fact that it's different every night. And I don't know, of course, if it was the same every night, you'd stop doing it.

DD: Well, I want [to] maybe ask about a couple of tunes we're going to hear. And one is a song that you do live a lot, is one of the earlier ones. It's, it's "Tom Traubert's Blues."

TW: Oh yeah.

DD: And this may just be a really dumb question, but I was trying--- is there any--- is Tom Traubert somebody that you made up, or is there a Tom Traubert, or what do we know about him even if you did make him up?

TW: He's a friend of a friend of mine.

DD: Really?

TW: Yeah, who lives in Denver, and died in jail. And so, he's a real guy. And so, that's, you know, a song that is about a lot of things. But mostly, I think . . . the idea that a Matilda is a backpack, you know? So, you--- it's about going out on the--- being on the loose, out on the road, chasing your dream, and all the things you encounter in the process.

DD: Well, that's one of the ones we'll hear when we get to the concert portions of things. Tom, thanks a lot for your time.

TW: Yeah, yeah.

DD: We totally appreciate that. And congratulations to you and Kathleen on this work. It's just, I think it's just great to have it.

TW: I agree. Thanks a lot, man.

DD: Tom Waits. Coming up, a concert from the tour for Tom Waits' new *Orphans* album, where we hear that classic song Tom and I were talking about, that "Tom Traubert's Blues." This song has been called one of his finest. You'll hear it in a moment, here on the *World Cafe.*

DD: Tom Waits, our guest today on the *World Cafe.* Let's go to the stage for excerpts from his recent *Orphans* tour. We'll hear "Tom Traubert's Blues" after this version of "Tango Till They're Sore."

> Tom Waits recording: "Tango Till They're Sore"
>
> Tom Waits recording: "Tom Traubert's Blues"

DD: "Tom Traubert's Blues," live from Tom Waits. Got more performances coming up. Tom Waits is our guest today here on the *World Cafe.*

DD: Let's go back to the stage from the recent *Orphans* tour with Tom Waits and his band. This is "Murder in the Red Barn."

Tom Waits recording: "Murder in the Red Barn"

Tom Waits recording: "Trampled Rose"

DD: Finishing up our set of music from Tom Waits, recorded over this past summer on the tour, this is "Bottom of the World." Tom Waits, here on the *World Cafe.*

> Tom Waits recording: "Bottom of the World"

ELTON JOHN

THIS ONE IS WORTH A BIT OF BACKGROUND. This is the first time I have had to fly to another country to do an interview. But hey, it was Elton John, so fly to Toronto I did to meet him in a suite at the hotel. Through hushed hallways, ushered into the room, not one but two attractive helpers offering beverages, and in comes Sir Elton.

Now I was prepared for anything, but actually he was attired in kind of a low-key tracksuit and relatively subdued glasses, but yes, he had an enormous diamond-studded wristwatch and rings on his left hand. He was all business in the interview, and as you can tell, extremely focused and open.

Wherever Elton's career has taken us of late, we all have a fondness for his glory days of the 70s.

David Dye: This is the *World Cafe.* Elton John is one of the most visible, successful, and prolific songwriters of our time. He has sold over 250 million albums. A remarkable performer, he has dazzled us live for the last three decades. And when you look at his string of albums he produced in the 70s, you realize how deeply embedded the songs that he and Bernie Taupin wrote are in our psyche, beginning with "Your Song" on the first album in 1970. Elton John's new album, *The Captain and the Kid,* picks up the story of Elton and his lyricist Bernie Taupin that began on his massive hit album, *Captain Fantastic and the Brown Dirt Cowboy,* in 1975. I asked Elton about how the original idea of doing an autobiographical record with the original *Captain Fantastic* album came about.

Elton John: I don't know what the original idea was for *Captain Fantastic.* It must have come from Bernie. Umm, but I know it's so long ago now. It was thirty-one years ago. I actually don't really remember the actual reason why we did it. I just know that when we did do it, it was written out and recorded in running order, which helped a lot. Because, you know, one of the hardest things to do . . . to an album [is to] put all the tracks in some sort of semblance in which they fit together. This album was a result of my ex-manager saying, "You know, you were always talking about how you became these two people, how Elton became Captain Fantastic and Bernie became the Dirt Brown Cowboy and lived their dreams. Why didn't you write the follow-up album?" 'Cause the first album basically goes from 1967, when Bernie and I first met, to 1970, before we came across to America for the Troubadour Club. And so it was an album that was really dealing with the start of a great friendship and relationship, but with a lot of disappointment and rejection. And this current album goes right up to the present day and deals with having to deal with success, excess, stress, and getting a balance in your life, and all the things that go with becoming incredibly successful very quickly.

DD: Were you at all prepared for what happened when success finally came to you? It was funny, there was a song about New York City in here, but Los Angeles really was where it all started.

EJ: Yeah, Los Angeles was, you know, was the first place we played in America. It was the Troubadour Club, September, 1970. Actually I didn't really want to come at that particular time. I always wanted to come to America, but I thought we were getting our--- as a band we were learning our craft in England and getting a good reputation. And I--- even on the *Elton John* album, [as it] was being released in America, I thought maybe it wasn't particularly the right time. How wrong can you be? And so everything that happened to us at the Troubadour Club was a complete surprise, and a surprise to the audience, because with the *Elton John* album, they thought because of the album graphics and the artwork . . . and the content of the music, that there was going to be a serious performer that met them on stage. And, of course, I was not a serious performer. I was, but I mean, I came out in hot pants and flying boots and I had a three-piece band and we completely rocked the house down. And we did, you know, much more rock and roll versions of the songs like "Sixty Years On," "The King Must Die," stuff like that. And so I think it was a surprise for both the artist and audience. I wasn't remotely prepared for what was going to happen so quickly. I mean, it was, you know, I wouldn't say it was a fluke, but we were . . . certainly in the right place at the right time. I mean, Robert Hillburn gave us the review at the *Los Angeles Times* which spread across the country. And then we went to San Francisco and played the Troubadour then and the Playboy Club in New York City. But from then on it was just, you know, gung ho. "Your Song" came out and it was a hit. And we never really ever looked back. It was a case of being in the right place at the right time, and then just making sure that you just enjoyed it. And then the next five years of our lives was just completely adrenalin, instinct, and the best five years you could possibly have.

DD: So, let's begin with the way the album begins--- back in 1970. This is "Postcards from Richard Nixon." This is a live version of the song from Elton John and the Band.

> Elton John and the Band recording: "Postcards from Richard Nixon"

DD: That's "Postcards from Richard Nixon." That's where we pick up the story with the Captain and the Kid, and the story that we left off with back in 1975 with *Captain Fantastic and the Brown Dirt Cowboy*. And I'm talking with Elton John. Elton, people may not know that when you first met Bernie Taupin, for the first six months you two wrote together having never met.

EJ: That's correct. It was, you know, an odd arrangement, to say the least. And it's kind of carried on that way. We never write together in the same room. But, no, he lived in Lincolnshire, and, you know, he sent the lyrics down by post or to Ray Williams at Liberty Records, and he gave them to me. And I was just experimenting, and I really enjoyed the fact that I was writing to lyrics. I knew that I wasn't a good lyric writer. People even now say, you know, "Why don't you write your own lyrics? You're very verbose, you're, you know, you speak very well." But, you know, there's an art to writing lyrics. I write melodies. I'm not a very good lyric writer and I've, you know, given that over to Mr. Taupin, and it was strange, yeah.

DD: What did you find out about him from his lyrics before you met him? Did you think you knew him?

EJ: Oh, I just thought he was this incredibly romantic, incredibly mature--- I mean, when you consider that "Your Song," I've always--- it's always continued to amaze, never continued to amaze me that "Your Song," which is the most, I think, beautiful lyric, although he thinks it's very naïve, was written by a nineteen-year-old; a teenager. It's astonishing. And his . . . things on *Tumbleweed Connection,* and *Elton John.* Yeah, some of the lyrics were kind of influenced by contemporaries of the time, but he was so far ahead of his game as far as--- he had an incredible knowledge and love of Americana. And that shaped not only our songs, but it definitely shaped the music in our songs.

DD: Did you worry at all about his reaction to your melodies at first?

EJ: Yeah, of course. I mean, I had no idea what he expected. I mean--- but you know, we clicked immediately we met. We were two lost souls and we bonded immediately. We became like two brothers, even though he had two brothers of his own. He became the brother in my life that I never had. He became my best friend and we shared everything. We went to cinema together. We went to shows together. We were inseparable. We, you know--- he taught me about certain types of music. I taught him about others. It was an incredible kind of--- all the time that we spent together we really, really enjoyed it. Apart from the fact, and as I say, in the early days we were getting knocked back some of the time. We had to write some lyrics and songs for other people, which we weren't very good at. We've never been good at that.

DD: Elton John is our guest today and we're talking about *The Captain and the Kid,* the new album that continues tracing the relationship between Elton and Bernie Taupin over the years. Now, for this new album, what kind of, what kind of conversations did you have before Bernie went off and wrote? Because he, he's picked certain highlights along the way. And did you all agree on what those were?

EJ: I never ask him what he is going to write. It's always been the surprise factor. I never say, "Listen, you should write something like this." I would never dare. He's always, you know, gone away and surprised me. And that element of surprise is something that keeps our relationship fresh and exciting. I mean, I still haven't lost the pleasure of writing a melody to one of his lyrics and seeing his face when he really loves what I've done. That hasn't changed from "Your Song" up to the present day. So I just, you know, I thought, "Good luck. You know you're going to have to . . ." I didn't want it to be a double album, and nor did he. And I, you know, he just picked little very important parts of our life. I mean, the second track on the album is called "Just Like Noah's Ark," and it tells about when we first came to America--- very successful--- we were being followed around by every manager, everybody wanting a piece of the pie. And we, because we were inseparable, we were kind of like a human shield to these people. Because even then, even though we were inexperienced and somewhat naïve, we could see that these people weren't exactly the best people on the planet. But he pinpointed so many things: the drugs, the fact that, you know, we were getting on each other's nerves, because he traveled with us as a member of the band, really. And he wasn't a member of the band, but you know, we were everywhere together. And "Tinderbox" is a song that really explains on how, you know, we were--- we could do no wrong. And all of a sudden a wind of change blew across our sails and we were in each other's pockets. And . . . we needed a break from each other. And there's a great misconception that when we did stop writing with each other for a while that we'd broken up. We actually . . . never did break up. We never put a statement out to that fact. But because we--- our names appeared on different records with other writers, people assumed that naturally . . . we'd fallen out with each other. That was not the case. We just gave each other the artistic freedom to write with other people and that saved our relationship. Because I think if we would've said to each other, "You can't write with someone else," that would have been the end. And although it was a difficult period, because I think we [were] both a teeny bit jealous of each other, we had to, which is natural because we were so close to each other, we had to let each other go in order for us to come back together again. We'd been through so much. We'd been--- you know, we produced so much product in five years, it was only natural that that was going to happen, and I think we both knew it would happen.

DD: Well this is "Tinderbox." This is "Tinderbox" from the new *The Captain and the Kid* from Elton John.

Elton John recording: "Tinderbox"

DD: Now, that song, "Tinderbox," is followed up by "And the House Fell Down," and--- which is a song about, in your eyes, things kind of collapsing--- yeah, collapsing from having five number one albums in a row.

EJ: More of a personal collapse, this song. It's about, you know, the drug taking, the paranoia that goes along with drug taking. Bernie, I think, thought I was going to write a ballad. There's no way that you could write a ballad. It's got to be very tongue in cheek, because the lyrics are pretty straight on. It's a bit like we wrote a song, I think on *Honky Chateau,* called, "I Think I'm Going to Kill Myself," which was a tongue-in-cheek suicide, teenage suicide song. And so this is the way I approached this one was as well. But it's, you know, it tells a story. I'd be staying up until three days, three nights. Every little sound I'd get paranoid. The leaf blower--- I couldn't sleep with the curtains open. I didn't know what time of day it was. And both of us had that kind of thing going on in our lives, which thank God we came through, but it, you know, it went on a little too long.

DD: And this is "And the House Fell Down."

> Elton John recording: "And the House Fell Down"

DD: The subjects that that song addresses were not totally unusual for the--- certainly the time--- and not unusual at all for what you do for a living. Why do you think that performers are so susceptible?

EJ: I think it's these ridiculous hours that we keep. We don't lead a normal life as far as going to bed. The traveling, the eating, everything is completely alien to what everyone else does. From my point of view, I'd never seen a drug or touched a drug until a long time into my career. I didn't even know my band[mates] were doing it. I mean, I was very naïve, and I just thought, you know, I don't smoke, so I'll--- maybe I'll try the cocaine. And that was the worst thing I could have ever done because I had an instant liking for it. And I'm an excessive person. I can't have one of anything. So initially, it was--- it made me very happy and it made me kind of get--- filled me with confidence because I was very shy. But it's the sort of drug that's very insidious. I'd give up for a long time, then I'd come back and the more that you stayed away from it, the more you wanted it. And when you came back and did it again, it got worse and worse. And eventually, I always say the drug opened me up because it made me verbose--- it closed me down because I ended up . . . living, sitting in my bedroom for two weeks on my own. I cannot really recommend that drug at all. It's a horrible drug, and as I say, I didn't know how to get out of the situation once I was in it. It's fairly easy, you just say, "Can I--- somebody help me please." But I couldn't. I didn't have that humility in me to do that.

DD: It's interesting, way before that, back in the 70s, I had the chance to be--- I was, you know, in a room with you, and you were being interviewed. And I was struck by your confidence at that point. You were very, very assured of yourself. And I believe it was after the second album had come out. And I was really impressed by that, and by your intelligence in the situation. I'd been around a lot of people and they didn't always have that confidence, a lot of people doing what you're doing.

EJ: Well, I was musically confident.

DD: Yeah.

EJ: Incredibly confident about my music, and the way I've handled myself on stage. Except, you know, there are two personas. There's one on stage, and one that, you know, the Elton John persona, and then offstage. Finding the balance between having that all-out success on stage and . . . everything to do with a career, and then you leave your personal thing behind. And there was no balance in my life. And as confident as I was, and I was confident of everything that I did, because I had adrenalin going for me. And I was young and, you know, when you're young you have no fear. And I wasn't thinking about a personal life. I wasn't thinking about anything at all except my career. And in the end that catches up with you. That led to me taking the drugs and then of course drugs completely lead you to a false illusion and a ridiculous mindset. Anything that was out of whack before gets completely heightened by the use of drugs. And that was the worst thing I could have ever done.

DD: Coincidence that you got sober and fell in love?

EJ: Yeah, I mean, I--- to be honest with you--- I didn't really grow up until I got sober. How can you? I mean you can't take drugs, and you can't drink and have that kind of lifestyle where you are so up one minute and down the next. You're not a stable person. Thank God I kept working when I was--- as a musician I toured and I made records. I didn't sit there just taking drugs. I wanted to work because I love music so much. But, you know, you can't, honestly, and no one can say to me that you can be a sensible, humble and decent person if you're taking as many drugs and drinking as much as I did from time to time. There's no way you can do that. And when I got sober in 1990, it was to me the best thing I'd ever done in my life, because I certainly learned how to live again. You know, I had to deal with my phobias and my shyness and find out what made me drink and take drugs in the first place. A lot of things that I needed to check out, I had to do it, and I had to work really hard at it. And I enjoyed every single minute of it, because it meant that I woke up every morning in a happy place and . . . it's been going on now for sixteen years and it's--- I just wish I had of done it sooner. But, you know, you can't regret that. At least I did it. But I wasted a lot, a lot of my life by doing that. I wouldn't recommend it. Young people are going to do it anyway. Young musicians, because I think it is the thing to do. But if you have a kind of personality that is an addictive personality, then I think it's a really dangerous position to put yourself in.

DD: A song on here that's called "Blues

Never Fade Away," which is kind of a survivor's guilt song in a way. It's talking about a lot of people who are gone.

EJ: Yeah, it says I put myself at risk--- at sexual risk, you know, in the days when AIDS came in. I had my Pre-AIDS thing in the 70s with Studio 54 and everything was great. And suddenly this dark, horrible disease descended upon us. And yes, I survived that. And it's also about people who are taken from us too soon. The first verse deals with a friend of ours. Bernie and I had a friend, a restaurateur [that lived] in Los Angeles who died of AIDS. The second is a friend of Bernie's who had an aneurysm at twenty-one and died on the floor of a Hollywood arcade. And the third one is Gianni Versace. He was shot outside his home. And it's a question of saying, "Why are these people taken from us so soon?" I mean, I've had two people--- friends of mine--- two of my close friends shot outside their doorstep in America. I've had countless people taken from me early because of AIDS. But a lot of things--- everybody--- I sing that song and say to that audience, "There's not one person here that cannot have had this happen to them." And you ask yourself, "Why them? Why them?" And this is kind--- yes, a guilt survivor song--- and it's like asking the question, "So right, we're playing this Russian Roulette game?" And some of us get to survive it and some of us don't.

DD: And there are so many other people--- you've alluded to John Lennon, but then there's Ryan White. There's so many other people in your life.

EJ: Princess Diana. I mean, it's just, you know, it's--- you know, you see someone like Ryan White. Ryan White was a huge catalyst, as people know, in getting me sober. I mean, it was just six months after he died that I kind of finally got myself together, because that whole experience of being with him for the last week of his life, along with his family in Indianapolis, was quite an eye opener for me, and quite a sad indictment of how my life was. So, you know, though, that's "Blues Never Fade Away."

> Elton John recording: "Blues Never Fade Away"

DD: Elton John and Bernie Taupin's work on *The Captain and the Kid*, and that's "Blues Never Fade Away." And we're going to get a chance to talk to Elton about many aspects of his life. Your success has been over decades. It's highly unusual.

EJ: It's because I think I'm still basically a fan at heart. I love trying new things. I'm not afraid to try new things. People still have a go at me in concerts, saying, "Thank God he's doing this instead of sickly stuff from *The Lion King*." Well, *The Lion King* was a different project. It wasn't anything to do with an Elton John album. It was written for a purpose, and the purpose it was written for was extremely successful. But you have to, you know--- people want you to stay in one pocket all the time, and if you venture outside of that pocket, sometimes you get knocked. But you've got to try or you're not going to improve musically, and then you're not going to have the chance to work with many more important and talented people. I still go and buy my records every Tuesday. I still love to go into a CD store, although I say one day it's going to be obsolete. I mean, Tower Records, in Sunset Boulevard, I've been buying my records from there for thirty-seven years, and it's closing. And it's like, I think I've spent more money in that store--- I guarantee you I've spent more money in that store than any other person. And to me, it's the saddest day. I went in there last week when I was in Los Angeles and it was a really sad day. I mean, they say that one day there won't be any CDs, and people will just download music onto their phone. It will be a criminal day if that ever happened. I mean, I just--- I like to have the object. It's like going in--- you know, for me buying a CD is like going to an artist's exhibition. You go in and look at every picture on the wall and see what you think of the exhibition. You don't just say, "Oh, I've seen one picture and it's a great exhibition," because then the next eleven could be awful photographs or awful paintings. So for me, it's about listening to the whole thing as a whole. And that's what, you know, satellite radio gives us a chance to do, and maintain that . . . quality control when you can actually go and listen to stuff that you normally wouldn't hear. We live in a sound byte mentality. We live in a ring tone mentality and environment. And I can't stand it. I'm older--- I hate it. I like to investigate an artist's talent from start to finish. So, that's kept me fresh--- liking younger bands, mixing with younger bands.

DD: Well, let's talk about the talents you end up giving thanks to on the album, because since this--- almost every one of these people has had a new record.

EJ: Yeah.

DD: And Scissor Sisters. Of course you're involved with *Ta Dah*.

EJ: Yeah, I helped write the first single, "I Don't Feel Like Dancing," which is an enormous record in Britain. They can't seem to crack it over here. I don't think their record company really knows what to do with them. But they're an enormous act all overseas. They broke in Britain first, as did Rufus Wainwright, whom I also thank. It seems we have a much better--- you know, there is more of a change for a Ray LaMontagne or a Rufus Wainwright to have success in Britain because Radio One plays newer artists. It doesn't play the same records time and time and again, like most formulated radio programs do on the normal radio networks. I find that really depressing. I think everything is so categorized and lumped in together, instead of being able to hear great music of a different kind next to each other. It's all of the same sort of music. And that wasn't the case when I first came to America, with the advent of FM radio. It was like, incredibly exciting.

DD: So, that leads me to the question about, you've been talking about working with Pharrell, doing a hip-hop record.

EJ: I don't know if that's going to happen now because I've left my record label--- by mutual consent, I think. I really don't want to go into that at the moment because, you know, it's a bit of a sore subject with me. We know what we are going to do as far as the next record goes. But we won't be recording it for quite a while until the situation gets sorted out--- which record label I'm on, which record company I'm with. It's a bit of a mess at the moment. I was very disappointed with the way the record came out. There was never a store poster. There was never any promotion in the stores. And I think, basically, the record company thinking I was going to do a hip-hop record, which has tremendous commercial possibilities, just thought they might just put this one out and say, "We'll just put this one out and . . ." I think that's the case, and I'm very--- and I met with the record company. I had lunch with them at my house in France. All the heads of the record company, and I didn't get that impression. I mean, I'm not under no illusion that I'm not going to put a record out and sell millions and millions of copies because those days are gone. But, you know, I just wanted a little effort, and to go into a record shop--- we've been all over Canada, and we've been all over America, and not one store that we've been in has had a poster. I don't think they spent a penny on in-store--- you can't do that. You have to let people know that the record's out. People--- we've had incredible reviews for this album--- but people don't read reviews. I mean, people in the music business do, you know, but . . . people have got their busy lives. They haven't got time to scan things. They might go into a CD store to buy a Justin Timberlake record or something. If they see a poster by someone else, they'll think, "Oh, that's out. I might buy that." It's like when you go to the cinema, you go--- you can't get in to see the film you've been to see, so you go see another movie. It's been incredibly disappointing and I feel slightly betrayed. But I'm not going to cry in my milk about it. It's--- I produced a really, I think, incredible piece of work that is the best that I can do at this particular time in my life. It's an honest piece of work. And all I wanted them to do was to promote it to the best of their abilities, and that hasn't happened. So, we parted companies.

DD: Let's finish up with a live version of "The Bridge" which comes at an obviously central point in the album. What's this one about?

EJ: Well, "The Bridge" is basically about our songwriting. Like you know, you think you've written the perfect song, and you're always in touch or in search of the perfect song. Ironically enough, early on in my career, "Your Song" was my first hit. And that is damn near a perfect song as we've ever written. And we've had to follow that up ever since. I mean, many an artist probably would have fallen by the wayside. Because that is, you know, lyrically, probably a faultless song. So, every time that you've written a great song, you think you've come to a point where you think you are unassailable, something happens. And you have to cross that bridge and you have to have the--- it's like us knowing that our record sales were going to fall off and that we would--- we knew that was coming. What we were going to do? Sulk? But it also applies to any walk of life. I mean, we all have crises in our lives which are really bad. Forget selling records, that's nothing. People have illnesses and loss and--- we've gotten so many letters from people saying, "You're right, you know, I haven't made that leap of faith yet, but I must do it. I'm stuck in a rut. I've got to make"--- Your instinct tells you when you should do something, but sometimes it's very difficult. You know, it's all right for me to say, you know, "This is a song that's easy for me. I am a very rich man, you know." But wealth doesn't come into it. It's about having the courage to not have a drink anymore, to not--- it's--- you must, you know--- those decisions . . . you must make. Otherwise you are going to get left behind.

2006

PAUL SIMON

THIS WAS THE SECOND TIME I HAD INTERVIEWED PAUL SIMON. And I was not looking forward to it. Frankly, that had everything to do with the first time we had talked.

For really important artists whose time is tight, the World Cafe will do extraordinary things, like fly to Boston in the middle of winter for a half-hour interview in a drafty backstage dressing room. That's exactly what I did in 2000 when Paul released the *You're the One* album.

I got my interview, but Paul was not in good spirits, or else he was playing with me. He gave long, overly thought-out answers that seemed almost purposefully uninteresting; this in light of the fact that as soon as the tape was turned off he regaled me with stories about rehearsing with Dylan at Simon's apartment in New York, and did hilarious impressions of Dylan trying to find his harmonica during the duet portion of their concert tour the past summer–all off the record.

This time, when *Surprise* came out, things went much better as we huddled at the kitchen table on a tour bus and Paul spoke softly about his creative process over the years. It was a free-ranging talk, and he even answered my question about the high points of his amazing musical life by reviewing his whole career with a clear eye to the successes and failures.

David Dye: The focus on the new album, all the conversation has been about your collaboration with Brian Eno and the songs and the sound of the album, but it seems to me that you've always been collaborating in one way or another, whether it's specific players, specific rhythm schemes. How is this different in kind of jump-starting your creative energy, or is it? I don't know exactly how it came about.

Paul Simon: I find it very helpful to engage in the collaborative process. It helps me to write songs, and the way that it helps is, I can start with a premise, like a rhythm premise, you know, like *You're the One.* That album is based on three different drummers and the rhythms that they make up. *Graceland* was based on South African sounds and rhythms, and that process of collaboration, it stimulates me to write. And it allows me to write songs that are different from sitting in a room with a guitar and making up songs, which is the way that I did it all through Simon and Garfunkel and most of the 70s, where I wrote a lot of good songs that way. I really did, but I felt at a certain point that I had kind of gone through my natural instincts about what melody and subject matter, you know--- [I] could be sitting with a guitar, and I needed things to be more complicated for me to have more interesting solutions. So that's why these collaborations are important to me.

DD: And one of the things you mentioned in there is instead of starting, obviously, with your song, and looking for what kind of framework to put it in, you kind of start with a framework.

PS: Well, I think if I do another one, another album--- I don't know that I will--- but if I do, I think I'll go back to sitting in the room with the guitar, just because I've been doing it this way for about twenty years now, so I understand about rhythm. I understand a lot about it, and I understand about doing the process in this way, which people used to say was doing it backwards, but now I think I could take the backwards and turn it around and make that backwards and do the old forwards way of, you know, sitting and writing simpler songs.

DD: I was thinking about one of the most famous riffs that a song came out of, and I'm wondering if it did come out that way. And I was thinking of the Steve Gadd riff that begins "50 Ways." Did it begin with that riff, or was that added after you'd written it?

PS: No, that was after I wrote it. I wrote the song on some primitive little drum machine and I came in and I sang the song, and everybody liked it, and Steve said, "I play this little practice rhythm on a pad on my drum." And so that famous [sings drum intro to "50 Ways to Leave Your Lover"]--- Steve, you know, who's probably the great drummer of my generation--- he was in the army, in the drum corps. And he learned all those marches and all that kind of--- so that's where that came from. And it was a practice thing that he used and he immediately saw it as connected to the song that I wrote and that's how it came about.

DD: I read a Brian Eno interview where he talked about the two of you at one point when you started working together, that at one point you were kind of sitting and looking at each other, and he sent you out shopping so that he could work on something so that you could react to it when you came back. And I thought that was kind of cute and kind of creative of him to figure something out to kind of jump-start things. Did you do things like that with him in how you worked together?

PS: Yes. First of all, this was my working pattern with Brian: we would get together every three, four, five months for five days at a time, and we did that on four different occasions, so all together we spent twenty days together over the course of like two years. So for the first couple of days we had to find how we would, you know, be together in the studio; two people who had been in studios for a long, long time, and were comfortable doing things their own way. Part of what Brian did that was really helpful to me was, he would bring a different soundscape to the track, because he has in his electronica all these, you know, virtual sound landscapes that are very beautiful or very arresting and interesting--- something--- so one of the things that he'll do is take the beginnings of a track and put it through some kind of filter and change the sound and maybe even change what the feel of the rhythm is. Since the songs were in a very early stage of composition that would often . . . stimulate me to change or clarify my thinking. Sometimes he would take what I did and add some space to it off of the electronica, and when that happened, when he wanted to do that, if it took a long time to do, he felt--- like, if he had an idea and he knew it was going to take him forty-five minutes to get through it, he'd say, "I'd like to do this idea, but I just don't want to make you sit through this forty-five minutes of ugliness until I get to the part where it's beautiful. So, I don't know what to do." And I'd say, "Look, it doesn't bother me at all to sit through the process, and it doesn't bother me at all to leave." So I think in the beginning he sort of felt awkward about saying, "Would you mind leaving so I can be alone to think?" So he sent me out once and he said, "Why don't you buy a Mother's Day present?" And I said, "Yeah, okay, fine," but what he wanted was time to himself, which was completely understandable. Because what I wanted from Brian was for him to indulge his obsession for sound and go wherever it was most interesting for him and most fun for him, so that the collaboration was one that was something that he'd look forward to as opposed to, "Oh God, here comes five days with Paul Simon, I'm going to be stressed out." And I think that's really my version of Brian's story of why I left the studio.

DD: That makes a lot of sense. When this

album came out, and it's interesting to talk to you now that it's been out for a while, I thought it was really refreshing that a songwriter of your stature--- I heard you say in a couple of interviews how you had no idea how the marketplace was going to view this album. You had no idea whether it was going to be relevant or how people were going to react to it, or if anybody was looking for a new statement from you. And I thought that was really refreshing and I wanted to compliment you on having that self-awareness, or awareness of the marketplace, I guess, is really what it is. Is that tough, to realize how the pop music business works nowadays?

PS: Well, it's not tough to realize how it works. I understand it more clearly now than I did when I approached the marketplace with *Surprise* and I would say--- if I had to describe the marketplace--- I would say that more predictable is a better--- is an asset in the marketplace, than unpredictable or, what--- experimental is the wrong word---

DD: Something that changes expectations, perhaps? I don't know.

PS: Yeah. I don't think--- that's not automatically considered a plus in the marketplace, whereas I, as an artist, think of it as a requirement, that I'm supposed to rethink the premises that I've built my music on each time and edit them and make the changes that are appropriate to my changing aesthetic. And so that's what I try to do, but what I found with this record, with the marketplace, is that the more typical songs were more easily absorbed, and the songs that were very interesting to me because I changed the form of writing songs, you know--- I've really never done anything in my life except write songs since I'm thirteen. I mean, I've been in--- that's all I've done to make a living since I started recording when I was fifteen, so I really know about writing songs. In order to write a really fresh song, I have to find some way to get around what I intuit as a very predictable structure. But the marketplace likes a predictable structure because it's familiar and it's singable. And so a song like "Father and Daughter," which is a conventional structure of verse-chorus form, and the subject matter is a very easily understood subject matter, you know, it is simple words on an emotional subject, a father's love for his daughter. So people--- I would say that's the song that people responded to most from this album.

DD: There's a lot of family on this album. There's babies, there's kids, there's aging, it's all--- was it difficult to figure out what to write about, or were those just the things that came to fore?

PS: In the beginning, and part of the reason that there was such a space between my previous album, *You're the One,* and this--- in the beginning, where 9/11 also occurred, I really didn't know what to say. I really thought, I better just be quiet and think for a while, because I just had no idea what was the function of art in this completely changed world and how was I going to deal with things that I was thinking. And finally after a while I said, "Well look, I really do not want to write an album where the premise is how angry I am about certain things," because--- well, first of all, it just doesn't seem to be what my art is about. I mean, I think there's a strain of melancholy that runs through some of my work, but it's not, for the most part, premised on anger. So I said, "I do not want to write about how angry I am. I don't want to write about politics," because everybody's polarized. They've got their opinion already and to me it's like, hearing about the politics in the context of popular music is just silly, you know. It's just the wrong context to have some sort of serious discussion, for the most part. Of course there are great political songs, but for the most part it's like, I don't want to hear about it. I know which side I'm on. So politics is out. Then there's no real reason in this time where we've lost all our privacy for me to cede any more information that violates my privacy, so why should I tell you, or anyone, about the deep privacy of my life? I'm willing to say, and really mean it, how much I love my daughter, and other aspects, but for the most part I'm not going to tell you about anything else. I'm guarding my privacy as dearly as I can. So those three areas were out of bounds, and then I said, and I really do not want to write a falsely optimistic thing where I say, you know, "But things are going to be great, and God'll look out for us," and I said, "I would dearly love to write something that had some optimism and compassion in it, but not if I don't believe it." So those areas are what I'm not going to do. Anything else is okay. So what the album is is anything else.

DD: Looking back . . . there have been so many things that have happened, and it's just been an unbelievable career. I was wondering what, at this point, feels like the most gratifying success of that. I mean, is it Tom and Jerry getting a single on the radio, or is it Simon & Garfunkel starting, or is it having your solo career? That was a shift and you didn't know how that was going to work.

PS: Well, all of those things that you mentioned, they were really exciting. When I was sixteen and I had a song played on the radio, that's all I wanted. So I said, "If I could just get a song on the radio, that's the end of my ambition." So that happened, and we were thrilled about that. Simon & Garfunkel becoming, you know, a worldwide phenomenon, really, for the period from 1968–1970, which was from *The Graduate* to *Bridge over Troubled Water*, I think. You know, only the Beatles were more of a force, so that was an extraordinary period and I learned a lot about fame in that period because we were intensely famous all over the world. So that was a good thing to experience--- that was a great thing to experience. It was extraordinary. Then when I left Simon & Garfunkel I was apprehensive whether I would be able to have a solo career, so by the time I won a Grammy for Album of the Year, that was an extraordinary occurrence, and then after that I said, "Well, maybe I should try to do some bigger things." So, I went and tried to write a movie, and I did. And I wrote a movie and made a movie that's not very good called *One Trick Pony.* And, you know, after that I was a little bit--- I didn't know what to do. I was a little bit at sea, and made an album that a lot of my fans call their favorite album, which is *Hearts and Bones.* After *Hearts and Bones* I said to myself, "I don't--- it's too frustrating for me to write a song and go into the studio and make a record and know that the record is not as good as the song, not as good as the little demo that I made." And that's when I said that I really wanted all the tracks to be what I wanted them to be, and I would figure out, because of my experience with writing many songs, how to write a song over a track. It wasn't the first time that I did that. I did it with "Cecilia," which was just a little rhythm track. I did it with "Mother and Child Reunion," where I cut the track first. I did it with "El Condo Pasa," which was a preexisting track, so I mean I had some experience with that, but that was the first time that I made a whole album that way. And of course *Graceland,* I guess, in a certain sense, *Graceland* would be maybe a peak, I don't know. It was in the sense that I had an enormous education in rhythm and in recordmaking that came from working with African musicians. So that was fabulous, and then the political discussions and debates and arguments and counterarguments that ensued taught me a lot about being attacked and defending yourself and made me think more clearly about the wisdom of a cultural boycott. And I arrived at the conclusion that a cultural boycott is a bad idea. Better off to have the ideas flow into a country that is oppressed and to have freedom emerge from the freedom of ideas than to keep [the] outside world out. Anyway, so *Graceland* had many great experiences in my life that I wouldn't have ever anticipated would have happened. And then the time that I played in Central Park by myself. So I guess those are the peaks, but I must say that the last two albums for me, artistically, were very satisfying experiences. They were not probably what would be described as the peak of my career because they weren't hits, you know, but I may be well past the point where I'm going to have hits anymore, so that's not going to be the definition of what "satisfying" is or--- well, you know.

DD: Well, you made it really clear that what you're looking for now is something a little different, too. This is one more question, which would be--- you're such a songwriter's songwriter, and I hear you analyze how songs move and how they work--- do you get enjoyment out of listening to other people's songs, or do you end up picking them apart and seeing, ah, this is doing this, or are there songwriters that you admire?

PS: Well, I'm not in a big phase of listening to music, and it's been going on for a couple of years now. I don't know why it is, but occasionally I will hear some piece of music and then I become enraptured when I love it. I'm so grateful that I fall in love with something, and it could be a piano piece, it doesn't necessarily--- in fact, it's unlikely that it will be a piece of popular music, but I hear popular music that I think is really interesting and good because Edie and I have three, you know, young children who are big music listeners and players too. And Edie is a big music fan. She listens to a lot, so I hear a lot of music. But actually, when I'm driving in my car, I listen to sports radio.

DD: You're right in your demographic.

PS: [chuckles] Yeah, I guess I am.

DD: Thank you, Paul, so much, for talking with us.

PS: Thank you for having me.

DD: It's a real treat. Paul Simon, our guest on the *World Cafe.*

2006

GEORGE MARTIN

THIS INTERVIEW SPEAKS FOR ITSELF. George Martin is the fifth Beatle. He was in the studio working on all the albums with them. In fact, his arrangements helped make some of their most famous compositions shine.

The thing you would never know about the circumstances of this interview is that George, who was sitting in Abbey Road studio, did not answer my spoken questions live. We refer to it in the interview, but George Martin, who was 80 at the time of this interview, has been progressively losing his hearing. He blames it on too much exposure to loud music in concentrated doses in the 60s, and he calls it "God's joke." It doesn't totally hamper his studio work as the loss is concentrated in one sonic area, but it does make telephone conversation near impossible. I was asked to write all my questions out and when I asked one, a "translator" with him would point to the question and off he'd go. You really can't tell, and what great stories he has to tell.

David Dye: *Love* is the new Beatles album, or least it's the new remix of the Beatles masterminded by George Martin, their original producer, and his son, Giles. They've created new works using nothing but the sounds the Beatles put in tracks in the 60s. Here's an example of the *Love* album. This [is a] version of "While My Guitar Gently Weeps."

> The Beatles recording: "While My Guitar Gently Weeps"

DD: "While My Guitar Gently Weeps," from *Love*, the new Beatles production commissioned by Cirque du Soleil and realized by our guests today, Sir George Martin, the original Beatles producer, and his son, Giles. Martin signed the Fab Four to Paralophone Records in 1962 and produced them throughout their recordings. Sir George turns eighty-one this January. Believe me, he had some tales to tell. And I started out asking him how he got involved with the *Love* project.

George Martin: When I was approached, first of all, with this show with Cirque du Soleil . . . I knew what had been going on, but I wasn't sure it had actually reached maturity. And Neil Aspinall of Apple came to me and said, "Would you like to do the music for this show? Because what we would like for you to do is to construct around about an hour and a half of continuous music from the Beatle recordings and not use any live sounds, not use any orchestra, but just create the soundtrack from the tapes that you've worked on for so many years with the Beatles way back in the 60s." And they--- he said, "We give you absolute license to do with those tapes whatever you fancy doing." And, it was really an offer I couldn't refuse. I mean it was such a trip to go on, to be given that freedom to just do what you thought was right for an exciting new show. So, that's what we did.

DD: Did you immediately involve your son, Giles?

GM: Yeah. My first thought, in fact, was that I really can't do this by myself. I need somebody to help me on this. And my immediate thought was my son, Giles, who is excellent in so many ways. He's a very good producer, a very good musician, and he has some--- two things that I don't have. First of all, [he's] got a marvelous pair of ears. And secondly, he's got a very deep understanding of modern technology and what you can do with digital sound, which I've got a grasp of, but not as good as he has. And he actually can manipulate all the sounds. So, he became my co-producer and engineer, really.

DD: Did you end up working with, at any time, the Beatles' tapes? Or what were your original source materials?

GM: Yes, we did work with all of the original Beatles tapes. They'd been stored for years and years here at Abbey Road, down in the cellars in a special vault. And I must say that they've been well looked after. The tapes were in good condition, but the first thing we did was to transfer everything into hard disc digital. And surprisingly, this hadn't been done. I mean, all of the Beatle recordings were still in the analog original state that they were: four tracks, two tracks, eight tracks, on tape, of course. So we were working from the original sounds, and I think what we did was to not change them, but we actually made them more presentable, or more--- I think the sound has been enhanced by modern technology.

The Beatles recording: "Here Comes the Sun"

DD: People know a lot, a *lot* about the Beatles, but maybe not about you, Sir George. And where did your interest in music begin?

GM: Well, I've, I've always been interested in music from a child. We had a piano in our house and I really cannot remember a time when I couldn't make a bit of music on that little piano. You know, from the age of five onwards, I just taught myself and found out about music myself. I played around with different chords and got terribly excited when I found a new chord. By the time I was fifteen, I was running a band. But you didn't think about making that a career in those days. I never thought I'd be doing that when I was a grown man. It was just good fun to do, you know, and earned a little bit of money on the side when you're a teenager. I was flying with the navy during the war and when I came out, I hadn't really gotten anything to do. And there was a very well known professor of music that I'd met in my travels and he was enormously encouraging and he said, "You really must take up music because you've got it." And I said, "Well, I'm too old now." By this time I was twenty-one. I said, you know, "I can't go back to school." He said, "Yes you can." And he said, "You, being an ex-serviceman, you can get a government grant to study for three years. And you can come work at our college," which was the Guildhall in London, which is what I did. And I was signed on as a student of composition, orchestration, conducting, and I took up the oboe as a second instrument, which I was able to earn a living at when I emerged. So that was basically how it all got started.

DD: Now, how did you make the transition from there to working in the music business at the engineering end of it?

GM: Well, the kind of fairy godfather who turned me into a musician at the Guildhall also led me into the direction of recording, because one of his mates was the senior producer at EMI for opera. And one of his mates was the guy who ran Paralophone Records, and he was looking for an assistant who could do some classical recording for him. And, fortunately, it was the kind of music that I liked because it was music of the Baroque period, of Beethoven, and before him, Bach and Buxtehude, and all those kinds of people. And I had a great group called the London Baroque Ensemble, which I took charge of and I enjoyed it. But, in no time at all, I was asked to do lots of other things as well.

DD: Now, what was the recording equipment like when you started out? Was it all one-track or two-track? Was it all about mic-placement and things like that then?

GM: Well, EMI Abbey Road in 1950, which is when I joined, was much the same as it looks today, but the equipment was completely different. For a start, we didn't even record on tape. I mean, far less digital. We recorded on, on direct disc of wax discs. So, they were cut on a lathe in real time as the music was played, so that all the music was divided into little sections. If you had a ten-inch record, you would try not to make it last more than two and three quarters to three minutes long. And if it was a twelve-inch record, you had about four and a quarter minutes to play with. But the trouble was, the longer you made your recording, the quieter it became, because you had to put the grooves closer together on the record. It was pretty primitive stuff. And I think this can be driven home by the fact that the lathe that we worked on, [that] the engineer worked on, wasn't driven by electricity, because electricity was so unstable that if you'd relied upon that, you would have ended up with a record with a lot of wear on it. So, it was driven by the most constant source of power known to man, and that is gravity. And before each take, the engineer would wind a heavy weight to the ceiling and then when he wanted the turntable to go around he flipped the switch and the weight would start falling and 78 rpm, dead steady as a rock, came out. And that was how I first met the recording world. Now, there were tape machines in existence at that time, but their signal-to-noise ratio was so horrendous that we didn't use them to begin with. And, gradually, as they got better we did [use them]. But it was still mono, and stereo was still to be--- still to turn up in our domain, anyway. And in fact, stereo originally was used just for classical records, so all pop records were mono.

DD: Now, when you moved over to the pop end of things at Paralophone, and originally began working with the Beatles' people regularly, people may not know they used this but they used session musicians during the recordings rather than using the actual bands. Why, why was that?

GM: Well, we did use session musicians for--- obviously for singers--- but we also used actual bands, as you put it, if they were an existing band. So that, I mean--- in America you had Glenn Miller, and you had Woody Herman, and those kinds of people. And they obviously recorded. They didn't use session musicians. Similarly here, we would have, amongst a jazz band, we would have Humphrey Lyttelton and Freddy Randall, and Joe Daniels, and so on. But for pop records, it was generally solo singers like Shirley Bassey, who's still with us, Matt Monroe, all sorts of good singers like that. And they didn't have a band. So, we had to provide the accompaniment for them, which is where the session singers came in, and which is where a good arranger came in to score for the session singers. And we still do that today with singers. We still provide them with session musicians.

DD: And--- but you didn't do that with the Beatles. Why? Why did you figure that they were different?

GM: Well, the Beatles were a good band,

except that after the first time I heard them, I took Brian on one side and said, "Look, I like what I am hearing, and I like the boys, but I don't think they've got enough consistency in their drumming and their drive. I think it's a bit dull. I think we would do with a better drummer. So, next time they come along, I shall provide you with the session drummer, a guy called Andy White I booked, and he will be much better than this guy," who was Pete Best. And I said, "You needn't tell the world, you know. Everybody can think he's Pete Best and that's fine." And he said, "Okay, then." But when they did turn up, they turned up with a fellow with a long nose called Ringo Starr. And I didn't know him from Adam. But I learned later that he was a pretty hot drummer with Rory Storm and the Hurricanes. But I, I'd already booked Andy White, and they said, "But we've got our drummer." And I said, "I don't know what he's like. I mean, your last one wasn't very good. Why should this one be any better?" So I wouldn't let him play and he didn't like that at all, and he's never let me forget it afterwards, either. Obviously, when I found out how good he was, he became my regular part of the recording band. But on that first session, it was Andy White playing drums for most of it. I think Ringo played tambourine a little bit.

The Beatles recording: "Love Me Do"

DD: Now, as you got to know them, did you work with them differently than you would with, with other musicians?

GM: The first thing I had to do with the Beatles was to find out what to do with their sound, you know, because they were something I hadn't heard before. I mean, mostly the groups that you got . . . in the studio--- like Cliff Richard was a solo singer with a backing band. Like Billy Joe Kramer and the Dakotas, and Gerry and the Pacemakers. They had a band for which the singer was probably a part, but he was the leader. But here you had a group of characters where three of them were singing, sometimes simultaneously, and there was no clear leader. I mean, it was a toss-up really between John and Paul, and I was still trying to work it out. And I was--- on that initial meeting, I was saying to myself, "Who am I going to make the star here? Who's going to be the one who steps up in the limelight?" And it wasn't until I got home that it suddenly hit between the eyes and [I] said to myself, "What are you on about? Why don't you take them as they are? Just record them as a whole group."

DD: Now, there are a number of times when you stepped in to arrange something or have something played for a Beatles composition and there are a number of those. And I am wondering what . . . your favorite musical contribution to their work was?

GM: Yeah, well, obviously the most famous one is the quasi-harpsichord solo in "In My Life." But, there are lots of others buried in the . . . music of the Beatles that people don't know about. I mean, for example, the middle part of "Michelle." That's mine.

The Beatles recording: "Michelle"

GM: We've "In My Life." The boys had gone out to dinner and left this--- we always left gaps for the solos and I wasn't quite sure--- nobody knew what they were going to put in "In My Life." So, I thought I'd try something. And while they were away, I got onto the keyboard and I, I wrote this little two-part invention Bach kind of thing. I wasn't good enough to play it up to speed with both hands together. So, to get it right, I lowered the pitch of the original recording by half. But it enabled me to play the complete thing, both left and right hands, and at that speed. And it had a further advantage: when it was played back it sounded quite brilliant. The way the playing was, I thought it was really clever. But the sound also changed because the piano--- each piano note became half the length it would have been otherwise. So, it sounded quite brittle and everyone thought it was a harpsichord.

The Beatles recording: "In My Life"

GM: It's a nice piece of music and everybody liked it. The Beatles loved it, which is great.

DD: Now you, you were the fly on the wall. You were the one who was there and [saw] all the creativity that went into the Beatles' recordings. Could you describe the atmosphere in the studio during the making of *Sgt. Pepper's*?

GM: Well, of course, *Sgt. Pepper* lasted quite a few months. And, I mean, we started out in November 1966 right through to April '67. Not all--- we weren't working all the time. But we were concentrating on what the whole thing was going to be. And to begin with, to describe the atmosphere, it was a sense of freedom to begin with, because for years the Beatles had been on their golden treadmill. For four years they'd been touring the world, locked in hotel rooms, eating hotel food, not seeing much of their families. And it was a boring existence. I mean, they were enormously popular, enormously successful, earning many, many dollars. But, at the same time, they weren't getting any happier. And they were having really unhappy experiences. In Germany, they were threatened with death. They had all sorts of weirdos coming out of the woodworks. When they went to the Philippines, due to a misunderstanding, there was a huge row. They were chucked out of the country. And, of course, there was the--- all that business with John shooting his mouth off about them being more popular than Jesus. Which I, I knew what his intention was, because he was speaking the truth. But it didn't go down too well in the Bible Belt. All their records started being burned and all that kind of stuff. And they turned to Brian and they said, "We've had enough of this. We don't want to do this anymore. We're not--- in fact, we're not going to perform again."

And this shook Brian because it was his main source of income. And he--- then they said, "Well, no, we're going to work in the studio with George without any time restrictions." Which for me was great, because up 'til then, I had been allocated a little day here and another evening or afternoon there, and it was hard getting really great stuff out of them, and in such a short time. Now, suddenly in November '66, we were able to go into the studio and work until we decided not to. And the first thing we started out on was "Strawberry Fields Forever," which is of course one of the great icons of all time, as far as I'm concerned. A wonderful song and that was the beginning of *Sgt. Pepper.*

The Beatles recording: "Strawberry Fields"

DD: Now, *Rolling Stone* magazine has touted that as the best album of all time. Do you remember the reception when it first came out?

GM: Yeah, well, the reception in England was pretty good. I mean, most young people thought it was a fantastic record. Some old folk thought it was outrageous. Some people thought it was inspiring young people to go the wrong way and start taking drugs. I mean, the BBC, for example, banned the playing of "A Day in the Life," saying it was anarchic and shouldn't be played. So, it was never aired on the British Broadcasting Corporation, which I thought was a bit stupid. They played it since, of course.

The Beatles recording: "A Day in the Life"

GM: To begin with, I was a little bit scared that we were pushing our frontiers too rapidly and maybe people wouldn't catch up with us. But I was wrong, because when the record came out, everyone *was* with us. And it was great. And all we had to do then was worry about what we were going to do next.

DD: "All You Need Is Love" kind of became the hippie anthem in the Summer of Love that you hear in the States. What did you first think when you . . . heard that song?

GM: "All You Need Is Love" is still a damn good song. And when you think about the way it started, Brian came to me and said, "You know, we've been selected as being the band that should represent Great Britain in a worldwide hookup between all the countries in the world, on television, and it'd be live. Are you up for it?" And I said, "Well, fine, absolutely, but what are we going to do?" "Well, either John, or Paul, or both of them would write a special song." Well, John came up with "All You Need Is Love," and it was a great anthem. I mean, it was a great message anyway, because it still--- it's my motto--- my family motto now. And when I had my, my crest done, after I got knighted--- and I think it's such an apt one. And, it's become everybody's thought, anybody who thinks a lot about humanity that it is true that all you need is love, and if you spread love around a bit, love is all you need. And that was the--- it was a simple song. And when we did it live here in the number 1 studio where I am sitting now with an invited audience--- but an audience worldwide of 200,000 million going out live, it was a wonderful occasion. I booked a band and I'd done the arrangement for the backing. I'd taken a bit of a precaution by pre-recording the rhythm, just to make sure we didn't break down in the middle of it, but most of it was live. And I thought the song was great and the broadcast was good. I still think it was great. And it ends up on the *Love* record, which just has come out.

The Beatles recording: "All You Need Is Love"

DD: Now, working on the *Love* record, working in the studio as you've gotten older, a lot of engineers and producers, particularly musicians who play live a lot, suffer hearing loss. Has that been a problem for you, and is it work related?

GM: Yeah, well, working in the studio hasn't been more difficult for me as I've gotten older because, you know, you get experienced and things come more easily. And if you're a good musician, you can put that to good use. And I've had the--- I've been so lucky to work with so many good people in my life. Not the least of which are the rank-and-file musicians over here in England. They're--- they're really great people. But of course, I've had--- I do suffer from hearing loss. A lot of musicians do. A lot of famous people have, have hearing problems. But you see, in the 60s nobody warned us about this. It's like in the 30s, nobody told you you shouldn't smoke because you'll get cancer. And in the 60s, nobody said, "If you listen to loud sounds for too long, you're going to get deaf." And they didn't tell you, either, that there was a delayed effect. And so I preach the gospel wherever I go. All my recording engineers are under pain of death not to use excessive sounds. And I always tell young people if they go to a disco or something like that where they--- or a rock concert--- if the noise is really obscenely high, then they should limit themselves, ration themselves. And if for one hour of subjected heavy music, they should get out and listen to silence for ten minutes, and that will help. That will stop them [from] getting deaf. Because it's not just these loud sounds that deafen you. It's the duration of the loud sounds that does it. And I was listening--- I was in the control room listening to loud sounds for eighteen hours a day. And I'm afraid that's why I have now got bad hearing. And I don't like it, and [there is] nothing I can do about it. I do wear hearing aids, but it's not the same. I've just come to the conclusion in my advanced state of life that God has a sense of humor. And he decided to take away the one thing that he made me so good at: music.

DD: Sir George Martin, our guest today . . . on the *World Cafe*. And you've accomplished so much in your life that this is really a difficult question. But, from your life so far, what would you want to be remembered for?

GM: Oh, gosh. I don't really want to be remembered at all, except [by] my family. And I hope I am remembered by them with love. I guess I'm, you know, I've had more than my share of fame and adulation. And I do appreciate it. I think the people, my fans, have been absolutely wonderful. But after I'm gone, I don't want them to think anymore about it all. That's it. There's somebody else they'll latch onto, which'll be great. So I won't care about it because I won't be around. So, I don't mind.

DD: Sir George Martin, our guest today. Thank you so much for talking with us.

GM: Thank you very much, and it's been nice talking to you.

DD: Again, thanks to Sir George Martin for spending time with us. That new production of the Beatles' music, *Love,* is available now. And if you're looking for it, you'll find it at our *World Cafe* CD store at our website, which is www.worldcafe.npr.org.